Mark Blake

NINE
EIGHT
BOOKS

Us and Them

Us and Them

The Authorised Story of Hipgnosis

Mark Blake

NINE
EIGHT
BOOKS

NINE
EIGHT
BOOKS

NEB 013

First published in the UK in 2023 by Nine Eight Books
An imprint of Bonnier Books UK
4th Floor, Victoria House, Bloomsbury Square, London, WC1B 4DA
Owned by Bonnier Books, Sveavägen 56, Stockholm, Sweden

 @nineeightbooks

 @nineeightbooks

Hardback ISBN: 978-1-7887-0567-7
Limited ISBN: 978-1-7887-0900-2
eBook ISBN: 978-1-7887-0570-7

A CIP catalogue record for this book is available from the British Library.

Publishing director: Pete Selby
Senior editor: Melissa Bond

Cover design by Lora Findlay
Typeset by IDSUK (Data Connection) Ltd
Printed and bound in Great Britain by Clays Ltd, Elcograf S.p.A

1 3 5 7 9 10 8 6 4 2

Nine Eight Books is an imprint of Bonnier Books UK
www.bonnierbooks.co.uk

'When you bought a long-playing vinyl record, you studied the sleeve, you read the lyrics, you looked at the pictures and you went, "Wow!"'

– Roger Waters, 2022

'Michelangelo was commissioned by the Doges, Stubbs by the landed gentry, and Hipgnosis by the reprobates of rock 'n' roll.'

– Storm Thorgerson, 1982

Contents

Foreword

I recently worked with Anton Corbijn, the director of the Joy Division biopic, *Control*, and *The American* starring George Clooney. Anton was making *Squaring the Circle*, a documentary about Hipgnosis, with myself as the film's narrator. It was a strange experience to be on the other side of the lens and under the scrutiny of someone for whom I had the greatest respect.

The stars must have been aligned, because at the same time, author Mark Blake approached me to write a biographical book around the three partners in Hipgnosis: Storm Thorgerson, Peter Christopherson and myself. Mark wanted to tell the story of 'the three musketeers' prior to Hipgnosis, during our years making album sleeves and music videos together, our acrimonious breakup in the mid-'80s, and our later lives and work.

What piqued my curiosity was why this close-knit and hugely successful rock 'n' roll design team fell apart quite so suddenly and dramatically. Mark wanted to explore what enticed the likes of Pink Floyd, Led Zeppelin, Paul McCartney, Genesis, Peter Gabriel, Yes and 10cc to Hipgnosis, but also the personal bonds and creative glue that bound Storm Thorgerson and myself together, but ultimately forced us apart.

Like many successful creative partnerships, cracks often appear the bigger they become. Lennon and McCartney, Simon and Garfunkel, and Noel and Liam Gallagher are prime examples – and Hipgnosis was no different. *Us and Them* captures the important milestones, the personality differences, and the peaks and troughs of what was essentially a platonic love affair.

I loved Storm and he loved me, but we imploded one day and didn't speak to each other for twelve years. It was wonderful to have such freedom, yet agony to be so detached. We had relied on one another for so long.

This is a roller coaster of a book, bringing the story back to life and explaining what it was like to live through the vinyl heyday, and a time in the music business when nobody ever said no.

Aubrey 'Po' Powell, August 2022

Introduction

I first met Storm Thorgerson and Aubrey 'Po' Powell in the summer of 2006. I was writing a biography of Pink Floyd and wanted to interview them about growing up with three of the band. Storm and Po were a familiar Greek chorus in several books and documentaries: Storm seemed prickly but super smart, and Po came across as a bit roguish and a skilled raconteur.

I sent several emails to Storm, one of which he replied to with a brief answer: 'Too busy.' But Po answered immediately and agreed to talk. I met him in an editing suite in London's West End, where he was working on stage films for the Who and eating sushi for lunch. He talked for two hours' straight, long after the last mouthful of sashimi, and delivered well-polished anecdotes about a 'discombobulated' Syd Barrett and the time he'd set a man on fire for the cover of *Wish You Were Here*. He wasn't afraid to gild the lily, but neither was I.

At the end, Po asked if I'd spoken to Storm. I told him he was ignoring me, so Po rang him up. 'There's a journalist here you need to speak to,' he said. 'Doing a book about the Floyd . . .'

I could hear Storm's voice buzzing, wasp-like, on the other end of the line. Po told me to call him tomorrow. I did, but when he finally answered, Storm sounded noncommittal. Nevertheless, I prised a time and date out of him. 'Tuesday, two o'clock, Black & Blue,' he barked, before hanging up.

I had to Google 'Black & Blue' to discover it was the restaurant beneath his studio in Haverstock Hill, NW3. Of course, he cancelled on me. Twice. By the time it was rearranged, I'd been asked to write a magazine article about Hipgnosis. I extended my offer to include lunch, naively assuming I could nail both assignments by the time we had coffee.

Storm told me to call him as soon as I arrived at the restaurant. Of course it went to voicemail. Finally, he picked up. 'Hello, dear,' he whispered. 'Turn to your right, roll up your left trouser leg, raise your right arm and recite the lyrics to "Atom Heart Mother" . . . Then I will come down.' He giggled and hung up.

Storm appeared forty-five minutes later with his emollient design partner, Peter Curzon, rambled at great length about Hipgnosis and ate several chips off my plate. He walked with a cane after suffering a stroke in 2003 and told me he was usually only allowed healthy food. By the time the coffee arrived, Storm had told me precisely nothing about growing up with Pink Floyd. 'I don't know if I want to talk to you for this book,' he huffed, hauling himself up, before Peter opened the restaurant door and the pair disappeared upstairs again.

Several weeks and emails passed before Storm relented. He rambled at great length again; this time about Pink Floyd, but his body language told me he didn't want to be here, talking about any of this stuff.

I was surprised then when he called me after the book was published in 2007, asking if I would work with him on some projects for the band. It was never easy. Dates were arranged and then re-arranged. Or I'd show up to find Storm in conversation with Floyd drummer Nick Mason and dismissively waving me away. I soon became acquainted with most of the shops and benches on Storm's stretch of Haverstock Hill and wondered why I put up with his shit.

Things improved once I tuned into Storm's chaotic wavelength. He could be spectacularly brusque and charming, sometimes in the space of one sentence. He was also great fun and his eyes twinkled the moment you disagreed with him. I learned to accept that nothing would happen when it was meant to, but it would eventually.

A mutual friend later told me Storm had been diagnosed with cancer and I didn't hear from him again for almost a year. Then he rang and asked if I would be interviewed on camera for a documentary he was making about Syd Barrett. I told Storm that anything I knew about Barrett came from interviewing him and his friends, but he was adamant he wanted someone to talk about Pink Floyd's history. I wasn't going to refuse.

I arrived at the restaurant and, unusually, Storm was waiting. He'd just had another round of chemotherapy and looked terribly frail. His mouth worked fine, though. 'I can't pay you for this interview,' he said, briskly. 'But I'll give you a print. What's your favourite Pink Floyd cover?'

I told him it was *Animals*, partly because I knew this would annoy him, as the pig over Battersea Power Station wasn't his idea. Storm snorted derisively and sent one of his staff back to the studio. He returned with *Wish You Were Here*: 'Much better,' said Storm.

We went to his house in West Hampstead where I drank my bodyweight in tea while waiting for Storm to interview me. He was amused by the role reversal, even more so when he discovered he had a lump of snot hanging from his nostril.

'Did you know I had a bogey?' he asked, accusingly.

'Yes,' I replied. 'It gave me something to focus on.'

'Thank you for doing this,' he said, finally. It was the only time I remember Storm thanking me. I had a feeling I wouldn't see him again and, sadly, I didn't.

In 2016, my mobile phone rang and Po's name flashed up. We hadn't spoken in a decade. Following Storm's death, Po had taken over as Pink Floyd's creative director and was putting together what would become *Their Mortal Remains: The Pink Floyd Exhibition* at the Victoria and Albert Museum. Would I write about the albums for the official book? And could I write some of the text to go on the walls?

Po was like the anti-Storm. I'd arrive for a meeting at the V&A at an appointed time, be whisked into some antechamber behind the eighteenth-century baroque collection and be back out on Cromwell Road an hour later.

After the exhibition, Po and I continued to talk: for magazine articles and other books (his and mine). He was an endless source of anecdotes and information and appeared to know everybody ('Here's his number, tell him I gave it to you . . .'). But I also learned how Hipgnosis worked. Storm's maddening, brilliant artistry was enabled by Po's practical nous and Olympic gold medal-standard hustling. Had you removed one or the other, the whole thing would have collapsed.

Storm was the rough and Po was the smooth. So smooth I fell into one of his traps in the run-up to *Their Mortal Remains*. I'd been commissioned to interview Floyd's Roger Waters for a magazine cover story. Po got wind of this and the night before asked would I mind terribly if they filmed the interview as they needed some soundbites for the exhibition. It was an expertly delivered fait accompli because he knew I couldn't say no.

I arrived at London's May Fair Hotel to find sound and camera crews, Po and his smiling producer, Fiz Oliver, already in situ. The room was booby trapped with tripods and cables and you were in the way, wherever you stood. No music journalist wants their interviewing technique scrutinised by others. 'Can you ask Rog these questions as well?' said Po, stuffing a sheet of paper in my hand, two minutes before showtime.

Hipgnosis wouldn't go away, though. I was asked to write other magazine articles which touched on them, and their story was always hovering in the back of my mind. One weekend, I took a load of old LPs out of one cupboard and stashed them in another. The sleeves were faded and smelt of the '70s and '80s. I didn't own a record player any more, but I couldn't bring myself to get rid of them. As I carried a pile downstairs, I watched Led Zeppelin's *In Through the Out Door* ricochet off the banister. Was it a sign?

In spring 2020, the UK went into lockdown and I sat in my garden, as magazines closed and work projects were put on hold. Then the phone rang: it was Po.

We talked about the pandemic and mutual acquaintances and how much we missed seeing friends, before he got to the point: 'So,' he said, with that slightly conspiratorial air I'd grown to recognise. 'Have you ever thought of writing a book about Hipgnosis . . .?'

Mark Blake, August 2022

Cast of Main Characters

Dan Abbott: designer, illustrator, StormStudios. Seen on the cover of: Pink Floyd, *Echoes*

Barbie Antonis: Storm Thorgerson's wife

Bruce Atkins: photographer, studio assistant. Seen on: Wishbone Ash, *Argus*

Roger 'Syd' Barrett: Pink Floyd's ex-guitarist, vocalist (died 2006)

Howard Bartrop: photographer, Bad Company, Pink Floyd, 10cc, Wings

Marcus Bradbury: studio assistant, designer, illustrator

Rosemary Breen: Syd Barrett's sister

Rob Brimson: photographer, Genesis, Pink Floyd, Al Stewart, UFO, Wishbone Ash, Yes. Seen on: Yes, *Tormato*

Gai Caron: former fashion model, Aubrey Powell's ex-wife. Seen on: Flash, *Flash*; 10cc, *How Dare You!*

Peter Christopherson: Hipgnosis partner, musician, film-maker (died 2010). Seen on: Genesis, *The Lamb Lies Down on Broadway*;

the Alan Parsons Project, *I Robot*; Brand X, *Moroccan Roll*; Bad Company, *Desolation Angels*

Lindsay Corner: ex-Hipgnosis cover model. Seen on: Audience, *The House on the Hill*; 10cc, *How Dare You!*

Peter Curzon: designer, co-founder of StormStudios

Andrew Ellis: designer, photographer, founder of Eyetoeye Digital

Richard Evans: designer, now thewho.com website master. Seen on: 10cc, *How Dare You!*, Genesis, *The Lamb Lies Down on Broadway*, Brand X, *Unorthodox Behaviour*

Jill Furmanovsky: music photographer

Peter Gabriel: musician, songwriter, defaced Hipgnosis cover star

David Gale: Cambridge friend, author, playwright

David Gilmour: Pink Floyd guitarist, vocalist, Storm's childhood friend

Kevin Godley: 10cc ex-drummer, vocalist, one half of Godley & Creme

Graham Gouldman: 10cc vocalist, guitarist

Peter Grant: Led Zeppelin manager, Hipgnosis patron (died 1995)

Alex Henderson: photographer, Barry Gibb, Led Zeppelin, Roger Waters

Libby January: Storm's ex-partner, mother of his son, Bill (died 2019)

Richard Manning: former airbrush artist/retoucher

Nick Mason: Pink Floyd drummer, occasional sleeve designer (handwrote the lyrics inside *Animals*)

Phil Mogg: UFO vocalist

Iain 'Emo' Moore: Cambridge friend. Seen on: Edgar Broughton Band, *Edgar Broughton Band*; Toe Fat, *Toe Fat*; AC/DC, *Dirty Deeds Done Dirt Cheap*; Pink Floyd, *A Nice Pair*

Fiz Oliver: film producer

Jimmy Page: Led Zeppelin founder, guitarist

Gala Pinion: Hipgnosis cover model. Seen on: 10cc, *How Dare You!*; AC/DC, *Dirty Deeds Done Dirt Cheap*

Robert Plant: Led Zeppelin vocalist

Andy Powell: Wishbone Ash guitarist

Aubrey 'Po' Powell: Hipgnosis co-founder, photographer, film-maker, Pink Floyd's creative director

Matthew Scurfield: Cambridge friend, actor. Seen on: String Driven Thing, *String Driven Thing*

Nick Sedgwick: Cambridge friend, author, Roger Waters' golf partner (died 2011)

Paula Stainton: Pink Floyd exhibition producer/curator

Storm Thorgerson: Hipgnosis co-founder, designer, film-maker, 'Pink Floyd's art department' (died 2013)

Vanji Thorgerson: Storm's mother

Lana Topham: film producer. Seen on: Scorpions, *Animal Magnetism*

Rupert Truman: photographer, StormStudios

Cosey Fanni Tutti: musician, author, seen on: UFO, *Force It*

Roger Waters: ex-Pink Floyd bassist, songwriter, Storm's childhood friend

Richard 'Rick' Wright: Pink Floyd, keyboard player (died 2008)

SIDE 1

Chapter 1

'Hard, sir, very hard, sir . . .'

*A young Storm Thorgerson struggles with authority,
bath-time, Pink Floyd's kitchen appliance and
has an epiphany courtesy of Federico Fellini.*

'Storm always had a big mouth.'

– David Gilmour

★

Roger Waters vividly remembers the first time he met Storm Elvin Thorgerson. It was in the 1950s, Storm was around ten years old and had been billeted at the future Pink Floyd songwriter's home in Cambridge. 'It was the first morning after Storm arrived and I heard him on the landing,' says Waters, his voice tinged with the barely suppressed ire heard on many Pink Floyd albums. 'He woke me up by banging loudly on my mother's bedroom door . . .'

'Storm by name, Storm by nature' would become a familiar mantra, but it wasn't always so. Throughout her pregnancy, Storm claimed his mother, Vanji, referred to her unborn child as 'Geraldine'. Storm gestated in what he later called 'the dark side of the womb', unaware his parents were expecting a girl. He arrived in the world on 28 February 1944.

'Vanji' was Anna Evangeline Collier, born in 1918 into a family of decorated army officers and former Queen's Counsels. Her oldest brother, William, inherited their father's peerage and became the fourth Baron of Monkswell, but her family had progressive ideas about education.

As a small boy, Storm attended Scottish educator A. S. Neill's Summerhill Free School. Neill and his wife, Lilly Ada Neustatter, had opened Summerhill in 1923, in Lyme Regis, Dorset, to educate children struggling in the traditional school system. Summerhill championed greater personal freedom; lessons were voluntary and the pupils decided any punishment for anti-social behaviour at weekly meetings. Summerhill's philosophy was 'To be on the side of the child'. 'And if you want to know why I'm mad, there you are,' Storm later declared.

It was all Storm's maternal grandmother's fault. Lily Grant Duff was a poet and novelist and 'the freest parent there has ever been,' according to Vanji. Lily was fascinated by Summerhill's progressive approach. During the 1926 General Strike, she hitchhiked from London to Lyme Regis; arriving in style, having cadged a lift in a Rolls-Royce. Soon after, she left her first husband and moved her daughter and three sons to Dorset. They were Summerhill's first day pupils and the first not to have been branded delinquent at their previous schools.

The Neills made quite an impression. Lillian was a suffragette who'd served time in Holloway prison for smashing a post office window. A. S. Neill is remembered roaming the school grounds in a bright amber overcoat and corduroy trousers and, shockingly, without a tie.

As a member of the Men's Dress Reform Party, a movement in interwar Britain, Neill championed their drive for greater personal expression, a healthy diet and an open attitude towards sex and nudity. Later, Lily insisted her offspring didn't, in her words, 'gad about', but brought their sexual partners home. Neill's ideas enthralled many left-wing intellectuals but infuriated fellow headteachers, who considered them terribly bohemian and even subversive.

His insistence on pupil power also backfired. One Bonfire Night, Storm's Uncle Johnnie and his accomplices threw potatoes loaded with bangers into the fire. The subsequent explosion terrified the staff and kids and disrupted the party. Neill was furious, but at the weekly meeting, his attempt to punish the culprits was vetoed by a group of children, primed by Johnnie to vote against him. Neill was hoisted by his own petard.

Vanji Collier was a talented artist and shared her mother's liberal attitude. 'Vanji was magnetic and very dynamic,' says Storm's widow, Barbie Antonis. 'She was also a social creature who loved people and dancing.'

After the outbreak of the Second World War, Vanji enlisted in the Women's Land Army and met Elvin Thorgerson, a student of modern languages and soon-to-be lieutenant in the Royal Signal Corps. Elvin's father, Einar, was Norwegian and his mother, Mary, was British, and he'd grown up in the northern English town of Gateshead, Tyne and Wear.

Twenty-two-year-old Vanji wed nineteen-year-old Elvin in London's St Pancras in July 1940. The couple were already living together in nearby Mecklenburgh Street, Bloomsbury, but two months later, hundreds of Messerschmitts swept across the English Channel and began bombing the capital. The Thorgersons moved some 15 miles north of London to the small town of Potters Bar in Hertfordshire. 'I was a war baby,' said Storm, like so many of the musicians he'd later design sleeves for.

The Hipgnosis story is signposted with moments of serendipity and coincidence. Storm's future design partner, Aubrey 'Po' Powell's family briefly lived on the adjacent road to the Thorgersons. Years later, the pair returned to their childhood home to photograph a cow in a field for the cover of Pink Floyd's *Atom Heart Mother* LP.

Vanji enrolled Storm as a boarder at Summerhill's new school in Leiston, Suffolk, when he was four and a half. He remained there for almost five years. Jonathan Croall's 1983 biography, *Neill of Summerhill: The Permanent Rebel*, includes two anecdotes about Pink Floyd's future artist-in-residence. In one, Storm and his friends convinced Neill's daughter and future Summerhill head, Zoe, that the cottage in which she was sleeping was going to be burgled and set on fire.

In another, Summerhill's house mother was attempting to wash Storm but he refused to comply. 'I stamped my foot and said, "For Christ's sake, get into that bath!"' she recalled. 'Storm can't have been more than four and he just looked up and said, "You stamp once more at me and I'm going to bring you up at the Saturday meeting."'

More than a decade later, photography student Denis Waugh met Storm when they were both studying at the Royal College of Art in London. 'I was doing a project on Summerhill and found out that Storm had been a student there,' Waugh recalls. 'Storm and I used to talk about it a lot because he was intrigued that I had chosen this project. I visited the school several times and noticed there was a confidence and bravado that many of the pupils seemed to have.' However, it also had its drawbacks. 'Vanji was a good mother,' says Barbie Antonis, 'but during the school holidays, Storm sometimes spent time with his grandmother, Lilly, at her home near Aldeburgh in Suffolk. His gran figured large in his life. I know there was one stretch where he didn't see Vanji for a whole year.

'Storm couldn't understand emotionally how Vanji could have sent him away at four and a half years old, but his take on it was that she must have had a reason. Presumably that she and Elvin were getting on so badly it was better not to be subjected to what was going on at home.'

Despite his precocity, Storm was frustrated by Summerhill's casual approach to learning. 'The education was of your choosing,' he recalled, 'and in the long run, not good for me psychologically.'

'He hated it,' confirms Barbie. 'He could climb a tree and play sports, but he wasn't learning. So the story he constructed was that he was nine years old and couldn't read and write properly. He used this as his rationale to tell Vanji he had to get out.'

Vanji withdrew him from Summerhill and Storm joined his parents in their new hometown. Cambridge runs through the Hipgnosis story as assuredly as the River Cam through the East Anglian town. Academia dominated Cambridge and by association, Storm's life and work. Its world-famous university attracted students from around the world. Some of Storm's childhood friends, including Pink Floyd's Syd Barrett and David Gilmour, were the offspring of Cambridge University professors and lecturers.

'Our gang were all incredibly precocious and grew up in academic surroundings,' said Storm's teenage friend, the future film-maker Anthony Stern. 'The town itself impinged on our young lives.'

Cambridge's elegant architecture was also broken up by pockets of rural splendour, as if nature was surreptitiously breaching the walls. The River Cam, its lawns and meadows and the surrounding rugged fenland counterpointed the university's turrets and spires. 'It was an amazing and beautiful place to grow up in,' said Storm. However, nine-year-old Storm's first day at Cambridge's Brunswick Junior School was disturbing: 'I ran home sobbing because it was so strange and alien that we had to do classes,' he recalled. 'French was the worst because I didn't even know what French was.'

Vanji was good friends with a local schoolteacher, Mary Waters. The pair bonded over a shared interest in politics and remained friends long after their sons fell out in the late '70s. Mary was a member of the Communist Party. 'Vanji was in the same milieu and had her interests and affiliations,' suggests Barbie. 'But it wasn't ardent politics with a capital P.'

Mary had been widowed in 1944, after her husband, Lieutenant Eric Fletcher Waters, was killed in combat in Italy. Roger never knew his father, but remembers his mother steering him towards politics and social issues from an early age.

'She used to take my brother, John, and I to the Quaker Meeting House in Cambridge,' recalls Waters. 'The British China Friendship Association met there and we'd watch black-and-white films of Chinese blokes fighting the Japanese imperialist invaders.'

Waters later attended one of the early Aldermaston Marches against nuclear weapons, and chaired the Cambridge youth wing of CND. His family home at 42 Rock Road was a safe space for Labour Party members, *Morning Star* fundraisers and, for a time, provided a foster home for the young Storm Thorgerson.

'Storm turned up on our doorstep, presumably because his mum and dad were busy doing something else,' says Waters. 'Elvin was still around because he played cricket with Storm – he used to bowl at him. Not having a father myself, I was envious. But both parents had a laissez-faire attitude to their offspring, otherwise they wouldn't have put him in a boarding school and then left him with us.'

Waters can't recall how long Storm lived with his family, only their first morning together. He listened, astonished, as their house guest banged on his mother's bedroom door, demanding her attention. 'My mum said, "Who is this?" He said, "It's Storm." "What do you want?" "It's seven o'clock in the morning and I want my breakfast." "Then go down downstairs and put the kettle on."'

Waters heard Storm's feet pattering down the stairs. "Then, thirty seconds later, I heard his little feet coming back up again and then, "Bang! Bang! Bang!" . . . "What *is* it?" Followed by Storm's exasperated little voice: "How do you put a kettle on?"'

★

However lacking Storm's education and life skills might have been, in 1955 he passed his 11-plus examination, guaranteeing entry into the coveted grammar-school system. Either he could read and write a little better than he'd let on. Or 'his big brain meant he caught up very quickly,' says Waters.

'Storm must have had some serious coaching before the 11-plus,' maintains Waters, 'because after he stopped living with us, the next time we met up was at "The County".'

'The County' was the Cambridgeshire High School for Boys on Hills Road. It modelled itself on an English public school, with corporal punishment and compulsory membership of the Combined Cadet Force. The whiff of Victorian England prevailed, as masters in chalk-dusty gowns prowled the corridors or recited Latin conjunctions to bored pupils.

The headmaster, Arthur William Eagling, was nicknamed 'Crippen' after the infamous Victorian murderer and later inspired the tyrannical schoolteacher in Pink Floyd's *The Wall*. Many of Eagling's staff had served in the military and been brutalised by two world wars. Come the mid-'50s, men who'd survived the trenches of Ypres or the jungles of Burma now faced a new foe: 'Four hundred hormonally deranged lads,' said Storm.

These also included Storm and Roger Waters' friend, Roger 'Syd' Barrett. The school punishment book records them being caned for various misdemeanours, including truancy, fighting and, in Waters' case, throwing water at other pupils. But Storm received the most beatings. 'Which hardly surprises me as he was so truculent,' says Pink Floyd's drummer, Nick Mason.

'I don't know why Storm didn't like Summerhill,' ventures Waters. 'The kids had a school council and could vote on things. This was anathema to me and it sounded highly attractive compared to the Nazi hell-hole we both ended up in.'

Waters claimed to have been 'a complete twat at almost everything,' but he and Storm were both A-stream students. Storm learned quickly, had a thirst for knowledge and, like Waters, was a formidable sportsman. Both played rugby, cricket and football for the County.

A photograph of the 1960 rugby First XV shows Storm flashing a superior grin, but a head shorter and half as wide as most of his team-mates. 'Storm was quite small and not physically endowed,' says Waters. 'But he was a great rugby player.'

In his 2011 book, *After Summerhill*, author Hussein Lucas suggested that a key feature of many ex-Summerhillians was a 'virtual absence of fear: fear of failure, fear of authority, fear of life'. Storm exhibited this trait but with variable consequences.

During one rugby match Storm tackled a hulking youth twice his size. Waters witnessed the clash: 'His name was Scott and he was an American import visiting us for reasons known only to the Pentagon. Scott was built like a 35-year-old man, but Storm just hurled himself at this guy's huge calves and hams. His bravery and technique enabled him to bring down what amounted to a fucking elephant.'

The County's PE master Mr Thomas, a diminutive Welshman inevitably nicknamed 'Taffy', was so impressed that he boomed in his rolling Welsh valleys lilt: 'There you are! That's how it's done! The smallest man on the field tackles the biggest!'

However, Storm's refusal to accept authority later led to a showdown with the same master. One lunchtime, Storm, Waters and two other boys were playing badminton doubles in the school gymnasium. 'Taffy Thomas came in and told us to stop as he needed to set up the vaulting horses for the next lesson,' recalls Waters.

Storm asked if they could finish their game first, but Thomas told them to stop immediately. 'Storm walked up to him, so they were almost eye to eye, and repeated, "Sir, I don't think you heard me. We're in the middle of a game." *Whack!* Taffy hit him with the flat of his hand on the side of the head. Storm didn't move. He looked steadily into Taffy's eyes and said, "Hard, sir."'

Thomas struck him again. 'Storm's cheek was going red and tears were welling up, but he still didn't move. Instead, he said, "*Very* hard, sir." Taffy realised if he punched a kid there'd be problems, so he walked away. We stopped playing, but Storm had bested him. That was Storm's shtick for the rest of his life – besting people.'

The playwright and author David Gale first encountered Storm when they were thirteen years old. Gale's home on Luard Road was close to the County and one day he heard a foghorn-like voice blaring from behind some shrubbery. 'And it was Storm, who was with Syd Barrett, randomly whacking golf balls around the playing field,' he recalls. The volume of Storm's voice was compounded by its nasal twang, which he claimed was the result of toppling, hooter-first, onto a raspberry cane.

Gale attended the County's rivals, the Perse School for Boys. This inter-school rift dated back to 1900, when the Perse tried to veto the County opening, complaining its lower fees gave them an unfair advantage. The County's pupils called the Perse boys 'pigs'. The Perse in turn dismissed them as 'oiks' or the saltier 'County cunts'.

The divide between oiks and pigs was less rigidly observed by the river, though. The Cam exerted a magnetic pull on the town's young people. One of its most picturesque stretches, 'The Backs', was flanked by the King's College and Chapel buildings. At Silver Street Bridge, students and tourists could hire flat-bottomed punts from future Pink Floyd roadie, Alan Styles (of 'Alan's Psychedelic Breakfast' fame), and head downstream to Grantchester Meadows, the verdant grasslands which later inspired a Floyd song.

During the summer holidays, the banks teemed with adolescents from all over Cambridge. Everybody peacocking and promenading or reclining on the grass; everybody watching each other and wanting to be seen.

'My group used to be down by the Mill Pond, next to the weir and Anchor and the Mill pubs,' recalls David Gale. 'Storm hung out with his pals near the footbridge and the men's bathing sheds at Sheep's Green. There was a mix of boys and girls from different schools and gradually the groups started to intermingle, which is when I found out more about Storm.'

Perse pupil David Gilmour also encountered the young Storm. Gilmour had a 4-mile cycle ride from the Perse to his family home in Grantchester Meadows: 'And there was a shortcut over the Cam and a small millstream known as the Cut,' he says. 'Next to the men's swimming area was a narrow verge of grass with a fence alongside it. I began noticing people gathering, including Storm, and I just muscled my way in and started listening.'

Gilmour was thirteen and Storm was fifteen. 'Two years makes a difference at that age. Storm was the leader and the loud one. Very bright and knowledgeable and very sure of himself.' In 1994, Gilmour and lyricist Polly Samson revisited those days and 'the Causeway' and 'The Cut' in Pink Floyd's song 'High Hopes'.

'Comedians say they make people laugh to make themselves feel more confident,' suggests Gilmour. 'Storm used his voice, his wit and his intelligence to hide his insecurities. I never discussed Summerhill with him, so I'm not sure how much impact it had. I think Storm would have come out the way he did, regardless.'

'Looking at pictures of Storm as a little child, you can see he already has a character,' says Barbie Antonis. 'I think what Summerhill did was facilitate that character, but it wasn't very hot on discipline.'

Storm repeatedly challenged his teachers and elders. It wasn't malicious disobedience, but after Summerhill, he questioned everybody. Once, when David Gale's mother reprimanded her son in front of him, Storm responded with, 'Mrs Gale, I *really* think you should consider bringing up your son differently.' He was banned from the Gale house with immediate effect.

'Storm picked up being disobedient in Summerhill, but then took advantage of the structured learning at the County,' believes Gale. 'But he never understood why the County teachers wouldn't let him do what he wanted, like the ones at Summerhill. This made him a naughty boy. Which then confused the staff because he was so academically sharp and good at sport.'

Today, Gale remembers his old friend as 'warm-hearted, insightful, funny and bounteous', but also driven by 'a burning dysfunction'. 'I think it was alleviated by the good side of his schooling and the great side of his mum,' he says. 'Though I'm not sure these could ever compensate for the remoteness of his early schooling and his parents divorcing.'

Elvin Thorgerson left the family home for good and married second wife, Margaret Evans, in 1965. 'Elvin was having an affair,' says Barbie, 'and Storm thought he'd behaved very badly.' Father and son stayed in touch, but the family dynamic shifted for ever. 'The stress of my parents' separation faded away once my hormones started kicking in,' insisted Storm. 'The ages of fifteen to nineteen were one long period of pleasure.'

Vanji now taught art and pottery at the Ely High School for Girls, just north of Cambridge. 'Vanji was very arty and creative and had grey hair all tied up in a bun,' recalls ex-pupil and former Hipgnosis model Gala Pinion. 'Vanji got terribly cross with me once, though, when I made a clay bear and forgot to put it in the kiln – "Oh what a *silly* girl you are . . ."'

'Vanji was our best teacher,' says former student Sandie Blickem. 'Not because of what she taught us, but because she talked to us like adults when we were only fourteen and that was unusual. She also used to talk to us about Storm. We all knew who he was.'

Storm now had his mother's undivided attention at their Victorian middle-terrace at 19 Earl Street. Vanji rented out the spare rooms to lodgers and turned a small conservatory into a pottery studio. Meanwhile, Storm's adolescence dovetailed with a cultural sea change. Blues, jazz, rock 'n' roll, poetry, French New Wave cinema and American Beat literature signposted a way out of the post-war gloom and encouraged his transformation into an apprentice beatnik. The university and those designated spots along the River Cam were natural conduits, but ideas were also shared, knowledge and experience exchanged in the El Patio coffee bar, the Criterion pub and other fuelling stations around town.

Soon, many were aspiring to become what Norman Mailer called, in his 1957 essay, 'The White Negro': 'We became this excited, excitable core of people who were very enamoured of the Beat Generation,' says David Gale. 'Even though we were all still living at home with our parents.' Their bible was *On the Road*, Jack Kerouac's tale of American beatnik life. 'Kerouac originally wrote it in the late 1940s, but we read it as if it had all been written yesterday.'

Kerouac's heroes, Sal Paradise and Dean Moriarty, were on a quest for the elusive 'truth'. This involved having sex, taking drugs, listening to bebop jazz and hopping freight trains around post-war America. It sounded like Utopia after the daily grind of the Combined Cadet Force and A. W. Eagling's swishing cane.

'It was the Beats' style and philosophy,' explained Storm. 'Their laconic humour, political consciousness, drug habits, admiration for jazz, laid-back appearance and firm stand against the establishment.'

'Beat was a sensibility rather than a uniform ideology,' offered David Gale. 'It was incredibly exciting to grow up in. It seemed to unify art and personal behaviour into a marvellous, luminous, rebellious project that made everything mean something . . . even if you couldn't say what the hell that was.'

Kerouac opened the door to other writers. Storm and his peers all read poet Allen Ginsberg's 'Howl!' (with its telling line 'I saw the best minds of my generation destroyed by madness'), William Burroughs' non-linear novel *The Naked Lunch*, French existential-ist Albert Camus' *The Outsider* and J. D. Salinger's *The Catcher in the Rye*, whose teenage hero, Holden Caulfield, was as questioning as Storm.

As the 1960s gathered momentum, the soundtrack evolved. Bluesmen Lightnin' Hopkins and Leadbelly, soul giant Ray Charles and jazz saxophonist John Coltrane were interspersed with rock 'n' rollers Eddie Cochran and Bo Diddley. The one constant was the ever-present hiss of the Gaggia machines at the Kenya and El Patio coffee bars.

'The idea of growing up normally was not on the cards,' said Anthony Stern, 'so we would spend a lot of time doing things that were anti-social and likely to annoy one's parents. That's how a fascination with the blues and under-privileged black music took hold in our group.'

'Let's face it, there's a lot of rubbish written about the '60s,' suggested Storm. 'Revolutionary new philosophies, oodles of free love, terrific music and loads of sex and drugs . . . blah, blah, blah. But in my unblinkered view, it was a truly fantastic time. By now, we had a very big peer group. A gang of twenty people, of which there were another twenty more on the fringes.'

This gang included several County, Perse and state school pupils, townies, undergraduates and foreign exchange students such as Pablo Picasso's son, Claude. 'And a lot of girls, most of whom ended up with Syd Barrett,' said Storm. Many of them with spidery eyelashes and poker-straight fringes, and invariably called "Sue", "Lindsay" or "Jenny".'

All these young people later witnessed Storm's earliest endeavours. David Gilmour and Roger Waters would enlist him to design their album covers, while others would appear on Hipgnosis's album sleeves, their youth for ever preserved against the passage of time.

In 1961, David Gilmour's father, Doug, a senior lecturer in Zoology and Genetics, became a visiting professor at New York University. Fifteen-year-old David stayed behind and lived with family friends. The following year, his parents returned from the States bearing a copy of Bob Dylan's self-titled first LP for their son's sixteenth birthday.

Bob Dylan, the transplanted Greenwich Village folkie with the romantic tales of boho life, impressed them all. 'Dylan was about breaking new ground, stretching limits and altering perceptions,' said Storm.

What Dylan shared with the other musicians and writers was his drug use. Artists had been using stimulants to try to sharpen their creativity since the beginning of time and Jack Kerouac supposedly wrote *On the Road* on a steady diet of marijuana and amphetamines.

There was snobbery and resentment in Cambridge between 'town' (those who didn't attend the university) and 'gown' (those who did). Drunken fights sometimes broke out at the annual Bonfire Night party but social barriers dissolved when it came to marijuana and amphetamines.

Suppliers included entrepreneurial undergraduates and roughneck bikers from the Fen villages; teenage boys who'd purloined their mothers' diet pills and American GIs stationed at RAF Mildenhall and Lakenheath. One of Storm's acquaintances acquired a copy of *MIMS*, the medical profession's prescription journal, which listed hundreds of pharmaceuticals and their side effects. The business was often conducted in 'The Cri's spit-and-sawdust corridor, while the likes of Johnny Kidd & the Pirates' 'Shakin' All Over' boomed out of an overdriven jukebox.

'I think Cambridge was quite advanced for drug use,' suggests David Gale. 'Considering how close it was to London, certain avant-garde ideas would get there sooner than to other villages in East Anglia.'

Jack Kerouac based many of *On the Road*'s characters on real-life beatniks, including William Burroughs. Perhaps inspired by this roman à clef, Storm's friend, Nick Sedgwick, later wrote an autobiographical novel, *Light Blue with Bulges*, about growing up in '60s Cambridge. Its opening line summated their feelings perfectly: 'I was seventeen, I'd just left school and I thought I was going to live for ever.'

Sedgwick's first-person lead character strove to be as hip as his hero, Andy, with his baby-blue Vespa scooter. In real life, Andy was based on the future film-maker Nigel Lesmoir-Gordon. Gordon had been expelled from Oundle public school and breezed into Cambridge with his divorced mother in 1958, becoming an older-brother figure in Storm's set.

Gordon's credibility rose immeasurably after landing a job making espressos at El Patio and, like a devout Catholic invited to kiss the papal ring, visiting the Beat Hotel in Paris to meet William Burroughs. In 1976, Gordon helped Hipgnosis fly Pink Floyd's pig over Battersea Power Station.

'We were all children of the Second World War,' explained Gordon. 'We were all born into this strait-jacketed society, trying to put itself back together again after so much death and destruction. We were all looking for something different, something new.'

Soon everybody was trying to emulate their idols in Levi's, black polo-neck sweaters and, later, to guarantee instant credibility, a black leather jacket: 'But with proper lapels and a vent up the back,' cautioned Sedgwick.

Mothers gawped as their sons lay submerged in the bath, shrinking their precious Levi's to fit. ('For God's sake, don't tell your father.') Others did their shrinking al fresco, floating in the Cam, so everybody could see how hip they were striding out of the water, denim dripping.

Despite being Storm and Co's junior, Syd Barrett usually outstyled them all. The puckish, smiling Syd sauntered around in perfectly fitting jeans and, regardless of the weather, Ray-Ban sunglasses. Even Nigel Gordon was impressed: 'Syd was younger but already seemed way ahead of us,' he said. 'Effortlessly cool.'

Meanwhile, Roger Waters was far out on the periphery of Storm's social set. 'But I aspired to notions of beatnik cool,' he said. Waters acquired a leather jacket and a Norton motorcycle, on which he tooled around Cambridge, sometimes with Syd Barrett precariously riding pillion. 'Imagine how different the future might have been had we crashed?' he asked.

Waters, like Storm, delighted in challenging the County's staff. After being chastised by the school gardener, he exacted his revenge with a Dadaist art prank. He and his friends took a step-ladder to the orchard and ate as many apples as they could stomach from the gardener's favourite tree, but left the teeth-marked cores attached to its branches.

Waters' final act of rebellion was to hand in his Compulsory Cadet Force uniform and refuse to attend further training sessions. He claimed to be a conscientious objector and was dishonourably discharged. His actions sent shockwaves through the County.

The next stage for Cambridge's junior beatniks then was to hit the open road. Waters was the first to go. 'Roger and I went to Paris together when we were sixteen,' recalls his friend, ex-County pupil and philosopher Andrew 'Willa' Rawlinson. 'Two years later, we took his mum's Austin and drove to Istanbul.'

In 1961, Rawlinson joined Waters and three Cambridge under-graduates for an expedition to Baghdad in a converted ambulance nicknamed 'Brutus', but its engine blew up in Beirut, as none of them had thought to put any water in the radiator. The five went their separate ways, with Waters hitchhiking back to England.

His first ride out of Beirut was in a taxi. Waters was penniless, but its Arab passengers allowed him to travel for free. He arrived back in Cambridge, full of tales, which he later turned into a song called 'Leaving Beirut'.

Storm followed as soon as he was old enough or even a little before. He travelled to the Left Bank in Paris and, aged seventeen, hitchhiked through Europe to Morocco and back again on his own. En route, he purportedly lost his virginity to 'a very large Italian woman', later telling his friends it was 'a terrifying experience'.

It was certainly a relief. Storm had spent some time attempting to woo Roger Waters' next-door neighbour, Judy Trim: 'Roger, Willa and I were all chasing Judy,' he said. 'But Roger got the girl and eventually ended up marrying her.'

After reading about the American Beats' 'happenings', Nigel Gordon threw in his lot with William Pryor, an aspiring local poet and the great-great-grandson of Charles Darwin. The pair decided to stage their own 'happening', involving poetry, be-pop jazz and elements of performance art.

Pryor and Gordon made their debut at the Cambridge Guild-hall in spring 1963. One piece involved Nigel reciting verse over a melee of squawking saxophones. 'There was a shout of "Rubbish!",' recalled Pryor. '[Nigel] managed to finish the piece. The audience applauded, but people were booing as well.' The performance was heckled by a bunch of undergraduates, one of whom, Peter Jenner, would later co-manage Pink Floyd.

Andrew Rawlinson joined the pair for more happenings in Cambridge's Round Church and other venues. During one, a bicycle was dismantled on stage as a piece of performance art. And there was more poetry. 'I'm afraid we all tried to emulate our heroes,' admits David Gale. 'This led to the production of some quite mediocre verse.'

Sometimes, the group's creativity expressed itself in random acts of mischief. Storm's friend, Russell Page, diligently painted every window of Impington Village College's prefab classroom with red paint. Staff and teachers returned the following morning to find a set of seemingly blood-stained glass windows.

One night, Storm, Nigel Gordon and David Gale broke into the men's bathing sheds for no other reason than it was there and they could. 'Like Everest, it had to be conquered,' suggested Gordon. When a policeman let them off with a caution, a disappointed Nigel complained that 'It would never have happened to Jack Kerouac.'

Later, Storm would stake his insubordination further, as if daring the world to challenge him. He and David Gale both acquired sturdy, tank-like second-hand cars. Gale had a Daimler, Storm a 1940s Studebaker. The pair would gleefully ram each other's vehicles, knowing they were solid enough to withstand the impact.

On one occasion, Storm piloted his Studebaker down Regent Street in central Cambridge, pausing to smash an egg on the roof of a stationary police car. While others might have enjoyed this little victory, Storm drove back around and did it again, and then again after that.

'Was he a thoughtless vandal, a socialist revolutionary or a budding live artist?' posited Gale in his eulogy to Storm in 2013. 'Yes to all of the above.'

★

For all the showboating and rebellion, some of Storm's peers still took a conventional artistic route. After leaving the County, Roger Waters moved to London in the summer of 1962 to study architecture at Regent Street Polytechnic. Waters brought his guitar (ominously inscribed with the words 'I Believe to My Soul') and was soon playing in a group, originally known as the Sigma 6, with fellow students, keyboard player Rick Wright and drummer Nick Mason.

Syd Barrett now painted, wrote poetry and played the guitar. He made his musical debut in March 1963, with a local group, Geoff Mott & the Mottoes, at a CND fundraiser at the Quaker Friends Meeting House.

Two months later, while studying at the Cambridgeshire School of Art, Barrett and Anthony Stern staged a joint exhibition at the Lion and Lamb pub in Milton. 'It wasn't a resounding success,' admitted Stern. 'Syd's paintings were much better than my rather feeble attempts at psychotic surrealism.'

The following year, Barrett took up his place at Camberwell Art College in south London. Within months, he was playing in Waters' group and fumbling through Slim Harpo's '(I'm a) King Bee' in the backrooms of pubs and at college balls. After Barrett arrived, Waters switched to playing bass and encouraged his friend to sing and write songs. He'd already composed several, including 'Let's Roll Another One' later recorded by Pink Floyd as 'Candy and a Currant Bun'.

'Syd played his songs at parties,' recalled Storm. 'His efforts were nice enough but showed little indication of the greatness to come. But it's amazing what you don't notice because it's sat right next to you.'

Similarly, David Gilmour was a gifted guitar player who began performing in groups when he was fifteen. The latest, Jokers Wild, would become a fixture at the Dorothy and Victoria Ballrooms, playing Everly Brothers', Beach Boys' and Four Seasons' hits. 'We were a five-piece and everyone had to be able to sing,' Gilmour recalls. 'We pulled it off and had an extremely successful run for a couple of years.'

'Syd had an attractive voice but David had a good voice,' said Storm in 2006. 'I never saw virtue in comparison, but I have fond memories of Jokers Wild. I can still hear David now singing those Four Seasons' songs.'

However, Storm didn't write poetry or songs and didn't play guitar or sing. 'There was,' David Gilmour points out, 'no one more tone-deaf.' But Storm was fascinated by the visual world.

'I remember Storm buying these big art books and studying them together when we were still at school,' recalls David Gale. '"Woooh! Look at *that*!" Storm never described himself as a visual artist and he couldn't draw or paint, but this was the beginning of his interest in the visual world.'

'I wanted to be a painter,' said Storm. 'But unfortunately, my hand wouldn't do what my brain told it. But my mother encouraged my interest. Van Gogh, Picasso, René Magritte . . . *especially* René Magritte.'

Magritte would inspire Storm off and on for the next fifty years. The faceless, bowler-hatted businessman on Pink Floyd's

US AND THEM

Wish You Were Here album cover was a direct descendent of his 1946 painting, *The Son of Man.*

Storm realised that many of these images acquired greater resonance under the influence of marijuana. 'Smoking dope made you see depths in the pictures,' recalls Gale. 'In the same way, it made you listen more closely to John Coltrane's music or Rimbaud's poetry.' Record buyers, both stoned and compos mentis, would later pore over Hipgnosis's record sleeves in the same way.

With his art books and big brain, Storm became a sort of self-appointed cultural weather-vane. It could be intimidating. 'I was frightened of him,' said William Pryor. 'It was his biting wit and indomitable self-assurance and his cutting certainty of opinion. He knew so much.'

Number 19 Earl Street's front door alone stood out from its neighbours. Storm's friend, art student David Henderson, had painted it with a large '1' and a '9', but in such a way the numbers were only obvious from a particular angle: 'Full size and all the way up,' remembers David Gilmour. 'Most unusual for a front door in Cambridge at that time.'

Inside, Storm's bedroom was part-schoolboy refuge, part-beatnik salon. A huge Toulouse-Lautrec poster, liberated during his trip to Paris, dominated one wall. On another, he'd invited his friends to scrawl graffiti ('Who blew their minds in flying saucers to cool the tea?' . . . 'Surely God has saved the queen by now'). Another space was given over to a montage of images scissored out of comics and magazines; Syd Barrett's charcoal sketch of a pair of army boots and, later, David Henderson's half-finished painting of fairies and toadstools.

Storm would orchestrate the conversations, usually lying on the bed, and with an LP spinning on his Grundig record player. To heighten the experience, he later acquired a zoopraxiscope:

24

a cylinder in which a disc of still images, including a galloping horse, turned at such speed they became a moving picture. His guests were invited to peer into it as the music played.

The Swinging Sixties hadn't started swinging, but Storm and his friends smoked dope freely. 'Lots of all-night conversations and stuff went on at Vanji's house and she didn't seem to mind,' says Gilmour.

The party came to a temporary halt in the summer of 1963. Having completed their time at the County and the Perse, many of Storm's friends moved on to colleges and universities. Anthony Stern, William Pryor and David Gale went up to Cambridge, while Storm signed up to study English and philosophy at Leicester University – 'Philosophy? Storm?' says Roger Waters. 'What a waste of fucking time.'

To celebrate the transition, the group holidayed on the Balearic island of Ibiza. They drank wine, smoked grass and swam in the sea off Cassa Bela, and took a ferry to the sparsely populated island of Formentera.

'At the time I was aware we were going our separate ways and I was worried about losing my friends,' said Storm. 'But there was a wonderful ratio of boys to girls at Leicester University – three girls to every two boys and half of those boys were engineering students and rather spotty, so out of the running anyway.'

The bonds didn't break. Instead, the following summer, Storm, David Gale and William Pryor took a trip to Greece in Storm's latest vehicle, a cumbersome 1950s-era Humber Hawk. 'By the time we reached Zagreb only one of the doors would open and the engine sounded utterly miserable,' said Pryor. The party made it to Athens before the car sputtered to a halt.

In Greece, Pryor tried heroin for the first time, leading to years of addiction, recounted in his memoir, *Survival of the Coolest*.

'I suppose in any group of young people there were always going to be a certain amount of casualties,' admitted Storm. 'Half of us were semi-crazy anyway, and if not semi-crazy had serious emotional defects and our own problems to bear.'

While studying at Leicester, Storm was kept abreast of events at home by David Gale. In one letter, Gale told him about his latest discovery: Iain 'Emo' Moore.

Emo had grown up in a large, unruly family on a council estate in north Cambridge. He'd left Chesterton Secondary Modern at fourteen, unable to fully read and write, and missing two front teeth. What he lacked in education and incisors, he made up for with charisma and bawdy wit.

'David Gale told Storm about me, so I was summoned to Earl Street for an audience,' recalls Emo. 'Storm's attitude was, "Who are you? What are you about? Who do you believe in? Where are you going?"' Instead of trying to ingratiate himself, Emo spent the next two hours silently mimicking his host. 'Eventually, Storm started laughing and I was accepted into the youth club.'

Emo's role was the modern equivalent of a cap-and-bells-wearing jester at the court of some Elizabethan monarch. His new posh school pals lived vicariously through him. It was Emo who pedalled a pushbike into the Cam while wearing a top hat and was thrown out of Woolworth's for exposing his testicles in a passport photo booth. And it was Emo whom Storm later hung upside down naked at Smithfield Market for an Edgar Broughton Band album cover.

Storm and Emo made an odd couple. Emo had spent his life fighting for attention among several siblings: 'And Storm and his mother had a whole house to themselves, which was such a novelty to me.'

Vanji was unlike Emo's other friends' parents. 'She was cool,' he says. 'She had this wonderful smile and giggle, and long black-grey hair. There was this Bohemian middle-class set in Cambridgeshire, and they all seemed to be potters, painters or sculptors. I presumed Vanji would have been part of that scene from the 1930s.'

'Cambridge was full of all these brilliant, strange creative types,' suggested Anthony Stern. 'William Pryor's grandmother, the painter Gwen Raverat, used to get wheeled out onto the common with her easel on the other side of the mill water. She'd be there for hours – almost as part of the scenery – and then collected at the end of the day. There was licensed eccentricity in Cambridge.'

So much so that the spectacle of biophysicist and DNA pioneer Francis Crick zigzagging his bicycle down Trinity Lane with little regard for passing pedestrians became part of the scenery: 'Cambridge was full of eccentric men on bicycles, who looked a little out of time,' confirms David Gale. 'Syd's father, Dr Max Barrett, was one of them.'

'I don't know any world other than the one I grew up in,' cautions David Gilmour. 'All these people had some connection with academia and learning and were a very bright group. But there's a lot of noise made about that Cambridge thing – and maybe it is overplayed a bit.'

There was a pattern emerging within the group, though: of fathers who were either physically or emotionally absent. Elvin Thorgerson was now living in Penzance with his new wife; Roger Waters' father had died on the battlefield when his son was an infant; Dr Max Barrett had passed away when Syd was fifteen and Nigel Lesmoir-Gordon's father had left his family for another woman during the war. David Gilmour's parents were together, but overseas and would soon emigrate to New York.

The party at 19 Earl Street resumed whenever Storm was home from university. Members of his surrogate family crowded into the bedroom, listening to *The Freewheelin' Bob Dylan* and discussing drugs, art, sex and movies.

'And Vanji rarely said a word,' recalls Emo. 'When we were stoned and hungry, we'd go down to the kitchen and eat breakfast cereal. Storm told us we couldn't make toast. Presumably, the smell disturbed his mum's sleep or the sound of the toast popping woke her up.'

Emo regularly slept over in a downstairs spare bedroom, although the two ex-Summerhillians' casual approach to nudity surprised him: 'Sometimes when I had a bath, Storm and Vanji would come in and talk to me, as if it was the most natural thing in the world. After the first couple of times, I became used to it.'

Concerned by Emo's illiteracy, Storm sent him to Andrew Rawlinson's schoolteacher mother for lessons. Mrs Rawlinson prescribed Steinbeck's *Of Mice and Men* and Dostoevsky's *The Idiot*. 'An extreme introduction,' Emo concedes. 'But it was what I needed as I wasn't educated. I'd only gone into school to get fed, for the lunches. Storm was the opposite. I'd never met anyone as hungry for knowledge as him.'

Learning to read opened another door. Storm's bedroom was filled with science fiction paperbacks, their illustrated covers a brilliant collage of monolithic spaceships and alien citadels. Everybody worked their way through novels by Theodore Sturgeon, Arthur C. Clarke, Robert A. Heinlein, 'because you could lose yourself in another world,' says Emo.

Storm's passion also extended to the Marvel comics *Strange Tales* and *Spider-Man*. He and his friends were entranced by these fantasy characters, decades before they were spun off into a Hollywood movie franchise.

'That first summer together, in 1964, we all sat around, reading the comics out loud to each other,' recalls Emo. 'Storm loved Spider-Man because it appealed to the kid in him. But Doctor Strange, the Silver Surfer and the Ancient One appealed to the thinker, the intellectual. Marvel was better than the English comics we'd grown up on, like *Eagle, Lion* and *Dandy*. They were more adventurous and had a mystical, spiritual side.'

For many, the books and comics were a natural progression. 'Kerouac, Ginsberg and Burroughs,' said Andrew Rawlinson. 'Add Ornette Coleman, Snooks Eaglin, Rauschenberg, Cage and the first Marvel comics, and you can see what we were all swimming in.'

The sleeve for Pink Floyd's *A Saucerful of Secrets* later incorporated elements of Marvel. The children spirited away by extra-terrestrials in Arthur C. Clarke's *Childhood's End* were reinterpreted on Led Zeppelin's *Houses of the Holy* and a gurning Emo was photographed surrounded by comics for Floyd's *A Nice Pair*.

Emo came with a sidekick, a wild-haired, piratical-looking boy from the Fens named Ian 'Pip' Carter. The pair were often spotted wobbling around Cambridge on scooters or tumbling out of a house at 27 Clarendon Street, popular with students and drop-outs. Before too long, they were joined by a younger local teenager, Matthew Scurfield. Matthew and his half-brother, John 'Ponji' Robinson, would become close friends with Storm. While Ponji was academically gifted, Matthew struggled.

'I failed dismally at everything,' he says, 'and ended up at the Criterion and Mill Pond, peddling pills I'd taken from my aunt Alice's medicine cabinet. By following Pip and Emo around, I met Storm. It was inspiring to be in Storm's company because he wasn't held back about anything. He was the first so-called intellectual to take me seriously and seemed to enjoy my company.'

Pip and Emo did a roaring trade in amphetamines down by the Mill Pond, but they broadened their palette after discovering the hallucinogenic effects of Morning Glory. These flower seeds could be acquired legally but contained tryptamine, a naturally occurring chemical related to the one found in the hallucinogenic, LSD.

Packets of Morning Glory seeds were often liberated from a florist's shop on Newmarket Street. They were then ingested on toast, smothered with jam or peanut butter to mask the wretched taste. 'You took 250 seeds, or 500 if you wanted the full experience, and you had to endure the stomach cramps first,' explains Emo. 'But after that, you'd start to see fairies.'

Storm and most of his peers progressed from Morning Glory to LSD in early summer 1965. Lysergic Acid Diethylamide was created in a Swiss laboratory just before the Second World War. The chemist Albert Hoffmann was synthesising a compound from the fungi ergotamine as a treatment for respiratory issues. The resultant drug, LSD-25, was deemed unsuitable and sat on a shelf for almost five years until Hoffmann decided to test it again. He accidentally absorbed the compound through his skin and experienced the first-ever acid trip.

The CIA thought they'd found the perfect truth serum and began testing LSD on military personnel, often without their knowledge. Some psychiatrists and doctors began prescribing it as a treatment for alcoholism and mental illness. One, Dr Humphry Osmond (who coined the phrase 'psychedelic', from the Greek for 'mind-manifesting'), also explored LSD as a way to increase human consciousness and creativity.

For several years, LSD remained an open secret within the medical profession and among an elite group of creative types. In 1954, the British philosopher Aldous Huxley described his psychedelic experience ('It was without question the most extraordinary and significant experience this side of the Beatific Vision') in *The Doors of Perception*, which quickly became required reading among Storm and his friends.

In 1961, Harvard lecturer Timothy Leary was introduced to LSD by Michael Hollingshead, an old Etonian scientist working in New York. Soon after, Leary transformed from a mainstream academic into an outspoken LSD advocate and was fired from the university.

Similarly inspired, Hollingshead returned to London in 1965 with a mayonnaise jar containing enough for 5,000 trips. He established the World Psychedelic Centre at his flat in Pont Street, Belgravia. Hollingshead administered curious pop stars and thrill-seeking aristocrats with LSD, recited from the ancient meditation manual, *The Tibetan Book of the Dead*, and spun records by chanting Buddhist monks and Indian sitar player Ravi Shankar.

In the States, the Vietnam War had polarised the nation and widened the generational divide. Ginsberg, fellow poet Lawrence Ferlinghetti and other Beat writers were soon espousing LSD as an alternative to war and suffering. Meanwhile, an alternative scene was growing in the Haight-Ashbury district of San Francisco, where its cheap rents attracted authors, musicians, street theatre performers and self-styled anarchists.

Word filtered back to Cambridge of their favourite writers' endorsement of LSD, of Haight-Ashbury and of 'Kool-Aid Acid Tests'. These were initiated by *One Flew over the Cuckoo's Nest* author Ken Kesey and his fellow LSD enthusiasts, the Merry Pranksters. They threw parties with music, light shows, dancers and Kool-Aid orange drinks spiked with acid. It was a primitive version of the mixed-media events in which Pink Floyd would participate later and of rave culture in the 1980s and '90s.

Nigel Gordon took his first LSD trip through one of Hollingshead's contacts in spring 1965 but found it deeply disturbing. 'Because I couldn't let go,' he said. 'Instead of seeing the beauty of the infinite nature of consciousness, I saw lizards, dragons and people looking demonic.' He took it a second time, 'And it was a divine experience as I was able to let go and fall into it.'

LSD was usually ingested on a piece of blotting paper containing 500 microdots or the same amount split across two sugar cubes. Storm and his friends approached the drug with great curiosity. They'd read their LSD users' manuals: *The Doors of Perception*, Timothy Leary and Ralph Metzer's *The Psychedelic Experience* and Alan Watts' *The Joyous Cosmology*. 'So we all wanted to see what this wonder drug was about,' says David Gale.

Some took trips outside the city, in the Gog Magog Hills, where they watched the distant chimney on Addenbrooke's Hospital change shape and colour. As a boy, Anthony Stern and his schoolfriends were taken by their headmaster up into the eaves of the King's College Chapel: 'Where we were allowed to crawl over the medieval gallery, these little kids, hundreds of feet up in the air and nobody seemed to care.' Now Stern spent hours seeing imaginary planets in the same vaulted ceiling.

Storm was often asked if Hipgnosis's covers reflected his drug experience. He'd rarely give a straight answer, but the drug stimulated his fascination with the visual world and taught him to think sideways: 'Imagine swimming underwater with goggles medically sutured into the eyeballs and seeing everything as though perpetually looking through a microscope,' he later wrote in *Classic Album Covers of the '60s*. 'Above all, colours became abnormally powerful, so vivid and bright they would mesmerise and entertain for hours on end.'

During a picnic at Grantchester Meadows, the young hedonists staged their Kool-Aid Acid Test, swigging from a bottle of LSD-laced orangeade before swimming in the Cam. 'Rain started to spatter on the river surface,' Storm recalled. 'The river bottom was made of soft mud and we began to sink. Broken twigs floated down the surface towards us and we feared they might be crocodiles. And then we laughed out loud, laughing at the way we were terrifying ourselves.'

No two people shared the same experience. Storm embraced the drug but had reservations. 'Taking acid was exhausting,' he said. 'It was like going away to see relatives. When you came down from the effects of the drug it was similar to returning from your visit.'

At opposite ends of the spectrum were Nigel Gordon, who became evangelical about LSD, and David Gale, who found it terrifying. However, when Gale's parents went to Australia for several months that summer, his friends descended on his house in Luard Road.

One afternoon, Storm, Syd Barrett and others ingested a dose of LSD on sugar cubes at Gale's house. Partway through his trip, Barrett was found in the back garden, transfixed by a plum, an orange and a matchbox: 'They seemed to provide profound and endless fascination,' recalled Storm.

Barrett's reverie was only broken when somebody squashed the fruit underfoot. In 1974, Hipgnosis photographed the same objects for the cover of a Barrett solo collection but it would be ten more years after that before Storm revealed their provenance to the outside world.

'Cambridge between 1963 and 1967 was insane,' suggests Emo. 'Not for us, because it was all we knew, but anyone from the outside looking in would have thought, "Christ! What *are* these people?"'

'It wasn't happening in a bubble,' cautions David Gale. 'We were tentatively surfing a wave gathering throughout the '60s. But we did think we were in tune with it all and ahead of everybody. It took me a long time to realise the '60s only happened in towns and cities. This was quite clearly the case if you walked into a village and said, "Hi, man!"'

★

One day in summer 1964, Anthony Stern's father wandered into his dining room to find Nick Sedgwick lying on the table wearing just his underpants. Stern's family house was the location for Storm Thorgerson's latest short film, *The Meal*. As Storm couldn't draw or paint, he'd decided to make movies instead and his passion for film matched his passion for art.

When Storm broke his arm and couldn't join his friends in Ibiza, he spent much of his time at the Rex and Victoria Cinemas. 'Day after day, we saw *The Forbidden Planet*, *The Fiend Who Walked the West*, anything science-fiction,' recalls Emo. 'And anything with Burt Lancaster. Storm was obsessed with Burt Lancaster, but I have no idea why.'

After going up to St John's College, David Gale became president of the Film Society. Storm, Emo, 'Ponji' Robinson and Matthew Scurfield wangled invites and underwent a crash course in European New Wave cinema and more.

Storm soaked it all up: Michelangelo Antonioni's *L'Avventura*, Jean-Luc Godard's *Breathless*, François Truffaut's *Jules et Jim*, right back to Luis Buñuel and Salvador Dalí's *Un Chien Andalou*, with its infamous eyeball-slicing scene. 'It seemed that a new Nouvelle Vague film, or something European with a similar spirit, was being released every week,' says Gale.

'We saw everything coming out in the early '60s,' adds Scurfield. 'I think we all wanted to be film-makers, but Storm was really on the case with cinematography and knew about the history of film from the beginning.'

One weekend, Emo joined Storm in Leicester. The pair took LSD before visiting the local cinema for a screening of *Elmer Gantry*, a film about an evangelical travelling salesman, played by Burt Lancaster. 'It was horrendous,' says Emo. 'Watching a movie about God while on acid, but Storm wouldn't leave.'

Instead, Storm wallowed in the sensory overload. Later, he took a 250-mg dose of LSD and watched Federico Fellini's surreal comedy-drama *8½*, about a film director struggling with writer's block. Its opening three minutes showed a panic-stricken motorist expiring in the middle of a traffic jam. The only sounds heard were his frantic gasps and his fingertips squeaking against the car windows as he struggles to breathe. Surrounding drivers and passengers watched the scene with eerie detachment. Later, a man hovered a hundred feet above the sea, attached to a kite before plunging into the water.

These few minutes alone contained motifs Storm would twist, subvert and revisit in his art. The ocean, the stationary car, the airborne figures and the characters with thousand-yard stares would all reappear in one form or another with Hipgnosis. '*8½* made me want to become a film-maker,' Storm said. But it would take time. Storm acquired a 16-mm Arriflex cine camera and enlisted his mother as an unpaid actress – 'I think Vanji was in a few of his early films,' recalls Emo. 'I remember once dragging her across a field with a rope around her neck while I had a bag over my head.'

Storm's first proper film, *The Breadwinner*, was 'a stoned romp', according to Nick Sedgwick, and was shot around Earl Street.

The Meal followed soon after and involved a cocktail party where one of the guests was stripped, prepared for the oven and then 'eaten' by his friends. For all its humour and absence of blood, the film had an uneasy edge. Like René Magritte, it was all about 'the juxtaposition, the contrariness of reality,' said Storm.

'*The Meal* was a surreal fantasy, a bit like Buñuel's *The Phantom of Liberty* some years later,' recalled Stern. 'At one point Nick Sedgwick's semi-naked body was lying on my parents' dining table, which raised a lot of disapproving tut-tuts and "For God's sake, Anthony, what are you doing?" from my father.'

There was a motive behind these movies other than stoned entertainment, though. Storm Thorgerson wanted to go to London, just like his friends in Pink Floyd. But he wanted to make films instead of music. He was about to embark on the biggest trip of his life.

Chapter 2

'Where's my whisky? Bring me my whisky!'

In which Aubrey 'Po' Powell gets kicked out of school, discovers 19 Earl Street and joins the rock 'n' roll circus, via a giant jelly.

'I refuse to take any of this seriously.'

– Roger Waters

★

So what am I going to do now? he thought. It was July 1963 and sixteen-year-old Aubrey Powell, known to his friends forever as 'Po', was standing outside the gates of King's School in Ely. He'd just been expelled. 'The headmaster told me, "I don't care what you do, just get out of here."'

Po had been boarding at King's School since the age of eight. His parents were living in Tehran, he was an only child and didn't have any other immediate family. All he had were the clothes on his back, a few possessions, including a guitar, and £50 his father had deposited with the school in the case of emergency.

Po telephoned a friend, who collected him in his mother's car, and drove the 13 miles south into Cambridge and straight to 27 Clarendon Street: the first stop for any apprentice beatnik about to start living on their wits. The landlord was outside when Po arrived and offered him a sparsely furnished room for £2 a week. 'It was all coincidental, all serendipity,' he says.

Po's next call was to his friend, Norman 'Nod' Brown. When he wasn't selling dope, Nod's current job was waiting tables at the university. The following evening Po was being paid to ferry plates into the King's College dining hall while braying under-graduates clicked their fingers at him and demanded more port.

'In the space of twenty-four hours I'd been expelled from school, found somewhere to live and acquired a miserable job,' he says. 'And I was in heaven. This was an adventure.'

Aubrey Lloyd Powell's adventure started on 23 September 1946, in the Sussex seaside town of West Worthing. Po spent most of his early childhood living overseas. In the early 1950s, his father, RAF Wing Commander Harley Powell, flew his wife, Sybil, and Po to join him at his new posting in Egypt.

The country's reformist prime minister Gamal Abdel Nasser had recently led a revolution against the monarchy. The British were vulnerable, too. The Powells were living in the compound at RAF Abyed, near the Suez Canal, when a nearby village was torched.

'I was six years old, and it was my formative memory of fear,' Po recalls. 'It was late at night, there were gunshots, explosions, fire engines and military police. We were evacuated to Cyprus forty-eight hours later and then back to England.'

The family settled in Potters Bar. But the Wing Commander was soon stationed in Beirut, before moving to Tehran in 1961: 'My father spoke Arabic, Farsi and French. The Cold War was in full swing and he was helping build radar sites on the Caspian Sea to keep the Russians out.'

With both his parents in the Middle East, eight-year-old Po was sent away to board at King's School, a distinguished seat of learning which claimed Edward the Confessor among its earliest alumni. Po shared a dormitory with many of the same boys for the next eight years. In an adjacent bed was his friend, Alan Yentob, the future creative director of the BBC.

'My formative years at King's School were happy,' he insists. 'I could draw and I could paint, but I was not remotely interested in any lessons other than art.'

Nicholas Wadey, the school's art master, spotted Po's potential and took him and Yentob to art exhibitions in London. 'It was quite illegal taking us out of school, but Nick Wadey turned us on to surrealism and alternative ways of painting.'

Teacher and pupils pondered Mark Rothko's abstracts or Francis Bacon's grotesques one month and Georgia O'Keeffe's labial flowers the next. 'There was a lot of inventive art coming out of America then – Jasper Johns, Jackson Pollock, Robert Rauschenberg. The influences of the period stayed with me through the Hipgnosis years.'

Po also discovered the same authors which so entranced Storm. 'Kerouac, Ginsberg, Ferlinghetti,' he recalls. 'Alan Yentob and I sucked all that up. Part of my mid-teens was spent following the beatnik movement, wearing matelot T-shirts, a French beret and a "Ban the Bomb" badge.'

Po first encountered Storm Thorgerson when the County's rugby XV thrashed the King's School's equivalent one afternoon.

'Storm was incredibly bullish,' he recalls, 'but the boys all had tea together afterwards.'

There were parallels between Po's and Storm's childhoods. Neither had siblings, both were separated from one or both parents and became wilfully independent. 'There was no email or mobile phones and long-distance phone calls were out of the question,' stresses Po. 'Emotional contact was brief.'

Every school holiday, Po flew to Tehran and stood in the arrivals hall, with a placard around his neck, waiting for someone from the airbase to collect him. When he turned thirteen, his parents deemed him old enough to attend cocktail parties at the British Embassy: 'They gave me a linen suit, taught me how to smoke Sobranie cigarettes and told me I was allowed two whiskies a night – with one finger of whiskey and two fingers of water. I was encouraged to act older than my years.'

When he wasn't fighting the Cold War, Wing Commander Powell played piano and ukulele. Showbusiness was in his blood. Po's grandfather, Felix Powell, had been a composer and performer in the Edwardian variety era. Harley was born backstage at a theatre and named after the Powells' song-and-dance troupe, the Harlequinaders.

In 1915, Felix and his brother, George, composed the morale-boosting anthem, 'Pack Up Your Troubles in Your Old Kit Bag and Smile, Smile, Smile'. The song became so popular during the First World War it was even recorded in German, but the brothers felt uncomfortable about composing a piece of music many soldiers listened to before marching to their deaths. George was excused from military service on health grounds, but Felix served as a staff sergeant in the British Welsh army, where the blood and guts of battle left their mark: 'He came back a changed man,' says Po.

After the war, Felix Powell ran an estate agency in Peacehaven, Sussex, and continued writing songs, but finding another hit proved impossible. In 1937, he launched a comic operetta, later titled *Primrose Time*, which he planned to take to London's West End. But investment stalled with the outbreak of the Second World War. Felix borrowed money from his estate agency and a notorious loan shark, but was unable to pay it back.

On the night of 10 February 1942, he dressed in his Peacehaven Home Guard uniform and took his army-issue rifle to the nearby Lureland Hall. Felix walked onto the empty stage and shot himself in the chest. His suicide note read, 'I can't write any more.'

'Nobody talked about it in the family,' says Po. 'Only years later after my father died was I able to piece the whole story together from my mother.' The royalties for 'Pack Up Your Troubles . . .' were eventually passed on to Po.

Po's summers in Tehran and upbringing gave him a certain precocity. Back at King's School, he found more exciting things to do than study. Instead, he styled his hair in a sweeping DA, like George Chakiris in *West Side Story*, and spent his school-term money on Elvis, Eddie Cochran and Gene Vincent singles from Miller's music shop.

Wing Commander Powell taught Po some chords on the ukulele before he progressed to Spanish guitar. A Fender Stratocaster, like Buddy Holly's, was too expensive so Po spent £12 intended to last a term on a Hofner Club 40. He and his school friends formed a group, the Darktown Strutters, and played church halls and scout huts around Ely.

Performing gave Po and his friends a certain glamour, not least with pupils from the Ely High School for Girls. 'We used to go to Ely Cathedral for art classes but really to find out where the King's School boys were,' says Gala Pinion. 'Po and his friends would have been at the cathedral or long-distance running past our school and we'd be out on the netball court looking for them.'

'There used to be two pubs just off the market square in Ely,' recalls Vanji's former pupil Sandie Blickem. 'There was a loft in one of the buildings and boys and girls would congregate there, listening to music and chatting. Po was one of those boys.'

A teacher wrote to Po's parents, complaining his musical obsession was distracting him from his studies. Po's guitar was confiscated and his schoolwork and behaviour nosedived. During a trip to the ADC theatre to watch Shakespeare for an end-of-term exam, Po slipped away to the Criterion instead. It was his third misdemeanour in as many weeks: 'I was reported to the headmaster, who gave me six of the best and told me to leave immediately.'

After eight years of dormitory life, Po relished his independence. His new lodgings were a nexus for all sorts of bohemian characters and activity. 'Peter Cook's sister, Sarah, lived in the basement,' he recalls. 'Pip and Emo were in and out all the time . . .'

Po's parents finally discovered their son's expulsion three months later. 'They came up to Cambridge and were shocked – "What on earth do you think you are doing?" I said, "Look, I have a room, I have a job, I have a life . . ." Sybil insisted on sending Po to a psychiatrist. 'But the psychiatrist said to my parents, "Your son is on a path of his own. Let him go."'

Po's lodgings were barely a minute's walk from 19 Earl Street. It was inevitable he and Storm would find each other. 'We were in the Copper Kettle coffee bar and Nod said, "There are these guys you should meet,"' says Po. 'A couple of weeks later, I saw these hip-looking dudes with tight-fitting jeans and the longest hair walking down Earl Street and Nod said, "*Those* are the guys I was telling you about."'

Po was soon invited to number 19. On his first visit, he walked into Storm's bedroom to be greeted by the sweet tang of pot and ripples of laughter. Storm's entire entourage seemed to be present: Nod, Pip, Emo, David Gale, Nigel Gordon, Nick Sedgwick and Storm's girlfriend, Libby January, all draped over chairs or lounging on the floor among the Marvel comics and over-flowing ashtrays. Joints were passed around and the conversation flowed. But the fun suddenly stopped when the police knocked on the door at 5 p.m. It was rumoured on the hipsters' grapevine that the local constabulary had the addresses of all suspected dope-smokers.

Storm's panicked guests bounded down the stairs and raced out the back door and over the wall, shedding any contraband en route. A stony-faced copper propped open the letterbox with his fingers and watched this emergency exit. Po and Libby remained – 'And Storm looked at me as if to say, "Are you *mad*?"'

Libby January eventually opened the front door. Three uniformed officers and a plain-clothes detective piled into the narrow hallway, their suspicious eyes flashing back and forth. Libby smiled sweetly and offered them cups of tea.

Libby, Storm and Po watched as the officers scoured the house looking for incriminating evidence. Incredibly, they came back empty-handed. The disgruntled detective issued a warning before leaving, after which three of them burst out laughing.

'By staying behind, I'd passed a test,' suggests Po. 'After that, I seemed to spend every other day with Storm and his friends. Although I was a young whippersnapper, I'd read my *On the Road* and I was a Bob Dylan fan.'

'I had the feeling there was a movement afoot, but I didn't know what it was,' Po admits. 'I just knew I wanted to be involved with these people. But it could be intimidating. I'd failed my O

levels and been kicked out of school before I could take them
again. This crowd were smart beyond belief. Storm and Dave
Gale's banter was like Heidegger meets Ginsberg, so I had to try
to keep up.'

Po didn't know where this new association would lead, only
that it was an alternative to the life his parents had mapped
out for him – 'My father had high hopes that I would become
a pilot, so this was the beginning of a serious rift between us.'
However, with those parents 3,500 miles away, Po had more
freedom than many of his older peers. He ditched the waiter's
job and became a bus conductor. One future Pink Floyd roadie,
two Led Zeppelin road managers and a world-famous guitarist
also worked on the Cambridge buses. Po lasted three months –
'And then I got my girlfriend pregnant.'

It was summer 1965 and the mother-to-be was Ely girl, Carolyn
Smith. 'Carolyn and Po were quite the star couple,' remembers
Gala Pinion. 'Carolyn was blonde, had pouty lips and flick-ups in
her hair, always slouching around school and looking cool.'

The Powells made another emergency dash back to Cambridge. 'They were devastated,' says Po, who was a few months
shy of his nineteenth birthday. 'But my father made us get married. It was a shotgun wedding. For a time Carolyn and I tried
to live together in a little two-up, two-down in Cambridge, but it
was never going to last.'

In the meantime, Po took a stall in the town's Market Square
with Nod Brown and his girlfriend, Kisia Kuberski. The trio
sold trinkets, ties and clocks decorated in the fashionable monochrome op-art style. 'We borrowed the idea from I Was Lord
Kitchener's Valet [a Swinging London clothing boutique], but
every designer from Mary Quant to the Carnaby Street mod
shops had their own version of it.'

The boutique attracted a certain clientele. Syd Barrett, up from London for the art-school holidays, was drawn to these chic time-pieces and colourful ties like a magpie. Po and Syd became friends.

Like 19 Earl Street, Syd's bedroom at 183 Hills Road seemed to be exempt from parental interference. He could throw paint around the walls and play music long into the night and his wid-owed mother, Winifred, didn't object. Colour and sound were hugely important to Barrett.

The fourth of five children, Syd was especially close to his young-est sister, Rosemary Breen. 'Roger always had an original head,' said Rosemary (who never refers to her late brother as 'Syd'). 'But when he talked about how he felt, he would call it a colour.' Rose-mary believes he experienced synaesthesia, in which he could 'see' sounds and 'hear' colours – 'It didn't have a label when we were children. But sound was colour and colour was sound to him.'

Both Storm and Po wiled away evenings at Barrett's house, listening to records and watching Syd pick his way around the abstract canvases filling the room, 'often barefoot and with a cigarette smouldering between his fingertips,' recalls Po.

'Syd was a highly creative, artistic chap. At that time, I didn't see any evidence of the problems he'd have later, but he was also a secretive character.' All his friends commented on it. One min-ute, Barrett was there, in the Criterion or the Dorothy Ballroom, and the next it was as if he'd vaporised into thin air.

★

Nigel Lesmoir-Gordon married his girlfriend, Jenny, in March 1965. According to William Pryor, Jenny looked a vision in a short, futurist Courrèges suit, but 'the groom stole the show, with his Chelsea boots, long coiffured hair and flounced shirt.'

Gordon was now attending the London School of Film Technique and the happy couple were soon living together at 101 Cromwell Road, a Regency terrace opposite the west London Air Terminal in Kensington. There was a rotating cast of individuals in and out of the building, including trainee pop artist Duggie Fields and a penniless-student Roger Waters. Exiled hipsters and American draft dodgers could also tumble off a plane at Heathrow into a coach and be deposited right outside 101.

'There were seven rooms with nine or ten people living in them,' recalled Duggie Fields. 'But one could come home at night and find another twenty or thirty people lying around, none of whom lived there.'

Nigel Gordon kept phials of LSD in the fridge, which he sold for a pound a trip. 'George Harrison was a good customer,' he recalled. While folk-pixie Donovan later sang 'come loon soon, down Cromwell Road, man' in his song, 'Sunny South Kensington'.

One of Hipgnosis's entourage, the future music photographer Mick Rock also spent time at 101. Rock had befriended Syd Barrett while studying Modern Classics at Cambridge University. 'I came down for the summer holidays and slept in the hall at 101,' he said. 'That Cambridge crowd and Nigel especially were way ahead of their time – dropping sploshes of acid on blotting paper with an eyedropper. Plonk! Bingo! You were off to another dimension.'

Nigel and Jenny's residency plunged them straight into London's burgeoning counterculture. There was a scene developing around Cromwell Road; the alternative bookshop Better Books on Charing Cross Road; the Indica Gallery (where Japanese avant-garde artist Yoko Ono staged her first UK exhibition) and the London Free School in Notting Hill, an adult education/

drop-in centre frequented by beardy Beat poets and teenage girls from nearby Holland Park School.

In June 1965, the Gordons and their familiars attended the International Poetry Incarnation at the Royal Albert Hall. They watched Allen Ginsberg, William Burroughs and their British counterparts such as Michael Horowitz and Pete Brown reciting their verse to an audience comprised of every Nigel and Jenny from every town and city in Britain.

At the centre of all this was John 'Hoppy' Hopkins, a Cambridge physics graduate now working as a freelance photographer. Some in Cambridge also used his bespoke postal service, purchasing dope brought in Ladbroke Grove's West Indian cafés and then despatched in film canisters or hollowed-out books. Hoppy knew everybody and delighted in making connections. His contacts ranged from black-power activists to actress Vanessa Redgrave and included the Gordons, Syd Barrett and Pink Floyd's soon-to-be first managers, Peter Jenner and Andrew King.

After completing his degree at St John's College, David Gale took what's now called 'a gap year' in London. He found a job at Better Books, flogging copies of Ferlinghetti's *A Coney Island of the Mind* to other student beatniks, and moved into a grotty tenement flat in Tottenham Street with Syd Barrett, ex-County pupil Seamus O'Connell and Seamus's mother, Ella.

'Ella O'Connell was this very bohemian woman, who read palms and tarot cards,' Gale recalls. Ella even challenged Vanji Thorgerson for liberal parenting, gifting Syd Barrett with a first edition of occultist Aleister Crowley's *Moonchild* and introducing him to the ancient Chinese book of wisdom, *The I Ching*. These titles were added to the growing list of sci-fi novels, Marvel comics and art-house films firing up the collective imagination. On trips home, the Cambridge set became aware of how out of kilter they were with the mainstream. It was 'us and them' and sometimes even 'us *versus* them'.

In October, Great Shelford's premier estate agent Douglas January threw a twenty-first birthday party for his twin daughters, Libby and Rosie. Storm Thorgerson was still in a relationship with Libby, the eldest of the twins by five minutes. 'And Douglas positively loathed him,' recalls Po. 'Because he wanted his daughter to go out with a nice lawyer or stockbroker. But Libby was very smart and loved Storm's intellect and humour.'

Three hundred guests attended the soirée held in a marquee at the family's country home, Trinity House (whose French windows and manicured lawn would later appear on Pink Floyd's *Ummagumma*). Jokers Wild and Pink Floyd were both hired to perform, with Syd Barrett and David Gilmour blissfully unaware of how their musical lives would intersect. In between sets, a young American folk singer, Paul Simon, performed some of his own songs, including his soon-to-be hit, 'The Sound of Silence', and drifted among the guests, strumming a guitar and taking requests.

Floyd played a rickety version of Chuck Berry's 'Motorvatin'' and Joker's Wild delivered their slick Beach Boys' hits, while Libby and Storm twirled around the dancefloor. At one end of the marquee were young men in suits and ties with side partings and good prospects. At the other were Storm's coterie, with their Rolling Stones' haircuts, Levi jeans and pre-rolled joints. When Paul Simon started singing Woody Guthrie's 'Cocaine Blues', they all joined in.

'There was an obvious divide,' recalls Po. 'You could tell from Douglas January's body language that he did not approve of our lot.' It was around this time Douglas made Storm an offer:

'He said to him, "I'd rather you didn't go out with my daughter, so what do you want? What will it take?" Storm turned on his heel and walked out. I think Lib was with him and it caused a rift in the family.'

'It's all true,' says Barbie Antonis. 'Libby's father tried to pay him to get out of Libby's life. Libby and Rosie's dad was very rich so he could afford to pull out the chequebook.'

There was also another divide at the party: between those young people who were going to spend their lives in Cambridge and those who weren't. Po was about to become a father, but his loyalties were torn. In January 1966, Carolyn gave birth to their daughter, Sarah – 'Whom I love to bits,' he says. 'But I was too young to settle down.'

Po found it impossible to give up his social life and moved out of the family home. There was always someone, usually Storm, Emo or Syd Barrett to see, and mischief to be had. There was also more reasons than ever to visit London.

Barrett had started a relationship with Po's friend, another ex-Ely High School girl, Lindsay Corner. 'I'd known Syd for years as there was a family connection,' says Lindsay. 'His father was a mycologist and mine was a botanist. I have the loveliest memories of our early days together in Cambridge, punting on the Cam and drinking in the Criterion. But then gradually everyone started moving away.'

After signing up for a modelling course at the Lucie Clayton Charm Academy, Lindsay joined Barrett at 2 Earlham Street, a four-storey Dickensian house in London's Cambridge Circus. 'It had a bright purple front door and a winkle stall outside,' remembers Lindsay. Most days, the fishmongers stared at the "long-haireds" in and out of the building and wondered if they'd fought two world wars for this.

Earlham Street became another safe house for the Cambridge set. David Gale, Seamus O'Connell, 'Ponji' Robinson, Matthew Scurfield and Syd Barrett's ex-girlfriend Jenny Spires would all pass through. Also resident was Syd and Storm's friend John Whiteley, a former Buckingham Palace guardsman who later worked with Hipgnosis: 'I was also the handyman at Better Books,' Whiteley told me. 'The only one among those intellectuals who could change a lightbulb.'

Pink Floyd's lighting engineer, Peter Wynne-Willson, was similarly skilled and moved into Earlham Street with his future wife, Susie Gawler-Wright, nicknamed 'the psychedelic debutante' after appearing on the cover of the underground newspaper, *International Times*.

The floor of their flat was covered with a spaghetti junction of cables, projectors, ink slides and cellophane for Floyd's light show. Wynne-Willson also customised a pair of welder's goggles with glass prisms in the place of conventional lenses, nicknamed 'cosmonocles'. When worn outside, they turned London's West End into a kaleidoscopic neverland.

Barrett took the top room, with a bedroll in one corner and his guitar in another. Here, he wrote songs tracing a line between Cambridge's eccentric bicycling dons and the capital's counterculture; between the books he was reading, the art he was painting, the women he was sleeping with and the drugs he was taking. Floyd's blues covers were now being usurped by Syd's non-blues; songs that often dodged pop convention and spun off at bizarre tangents.

'I don't know what went on at Earlham Street and who took what,' says Lindsay. 'There weren't any hard drugs, as far as I'm aware, but Syd's early songs were extraordinary. Looking back, I wonder now if his mind was tipping even then or whether he was just being very inventive.'

Po often escaped to London and spent time with Barrett. They went to see Eric Clapton's new group Cream at the Marquee Club, smoked Lebanese hash and scoffed ice cream at the nearby Pollo café afterwards. Back at Earlham Street, he lay on the floor of Syd's eyrie, playing the Chinese board game Go or listening to his host picking out chords on an acoustic guitar: 'These were the beginnings of songs which would later end up on Pink Floyd's first album,' Po recalls.

The lasting souvenir of that year came courtesy of Nigel Gordon. One weekend in late spring, he arrived back in Cambridge with a cine camera borrowed from the film school. Gordon had scored LSD or magic mushrooms (the story varies with each telling) and headed to the disused quarry at Cherry Hinton with Barrett and some mutual friends.

The result was a short film later misleadingly titled *Syd's First Trip*. In 1994, David Gilmour bought the film rights to stop bootlegs from circulating. By then, Barrett had been in and out of psychiatric hospitals and had disappeared from public life but anyone with an internet connection can find the film today.

Syd's First Trip begins with its titular star clambering across the chalk pits. It was a familiar location, somewhere he used to ride his bike as a child and where his father would collect fungi. Two minutes later, Barrett is seen silently shouting at something off-camera before staring at the palms of his hands and placing mushrooms over his eyes, nose and mouth. It looks both staged and stagey but also feels voyeuristic.

The final scenes include hazy footage of Barrett's friends gathered around a bonfire. David Gale dashes forward to stop Nigel Gordon from standing too close to the flames; Russell Page appears wearing a pink shirt and Jenny Gordon, modelling a chic Mary Quant mac, strikes up a one-sided conversation with a log.

51

It's a silent film, but one online version includes an ambient soundtrack, presumably intended to sound like Pink Floyd. This music alone makes it seem eerier than it probably was. The actual soundtrack probably contained lucid conversation and laughter.

'I'm not even sure it was Syd's first trip or whether he was tripping,' says David Gale. 'It was just a group of young people mucking about.'

'It is an unselfconscious film,' insisted Nigel Gordon. 'It was not planned, it just happened.'

Whatever the motivation, *Syd's First Trip* would become an artefact. Summer 1966 would be the last summer Storm and Po spent in Cambridge – and the first time fractures within their social set began to appear.

★

In *The Pendulum Years: Britain and the Sixties*, historian Bernard Levin reflected on the popularity in that decade of Eastern gurus in the West: 'Teachers, prophets, sibyls, oracles, mystagogues, avatars, haruspices and mullahs roamed the land,' he wrote, 'gathering flocks about them, as easily as holy men in nineteenth-century Russia.'

The Cambridge contingent had also found a holy man. During an LSD trip at David Gale's house, Syd Barrett's school friend, Paul Charrier, experienced a moment of revelation. Charrier discovered a book, *Yoga and Bible – The Yoga of the Divine World*, which explored the teachings of an Indian mystic. Huzur Maharaj Charan Singh Ji espoused a strand of Sikkism, known as Radha Soami Satsang Beas (RSSB) and commonly called 'Sant Mat' (meaning the 'path of saints'). Charan Singh Ji was referred to as 'The Master' by his followers, who were known as 'Satsangi'.

Sant Mat was about finding the centre of all being, of 'God', through meditation, yoga and abstinence. But Paul Charrier, a noisy, mischievous young man and an enthusiastic drug user, would undergo a major transformation in the coming months.

Charrier found the Master's address in Beas, a small town in Punjab, borrowed the airfare from his girlfriend and flew to India in April 1966. He sent exuberant letters home and returned six weeks later, having been initiated by the Master. Charrier cut his long blond hair short, swore off all meat, alcohol and narcotics and found an office job with Cambridge Council – 'He even bought a suit off the peg at Burton's,' says David Gale.

Charrier was soon evangelising about Sant Mat and sent copies of his new set text, fellow satsangi Karpal Singh Ji's *Man, Know Thyself*, to his friends. In hindsight, the leap from LSD to religion wasn't so great: 'Takers of acid held a holistic and unifying attitude towards nature,' said Storm. 'Eastern religions and mythology, Buddhist and Hindu philosophies were cobbled together, diluted, reworked and then restated.' As importantly though, LSD hadn't delivered the wisdom and inner peace Timothy Leary and his disciples promised. Nobody had found 'God' and they were open to alternatives.

Charrier's conversion divided the group. Syd Barrett was so inspired by Paul's transformation, he showed up at 101 Cromwell Road and told Nigel Gordon he wasn't smoking dope any more. Gordon smiled benignly and handed him a joint.

Storm, Po and David Gale were less convinced. 'I've never had a spiritual experience in my life,' says Gale. 'And I sincerely hope I never do. But some very clever, thoughtful people we knew went down that route.'

In July, the Master held an audience at St Ermin's Hotel in St James's Park. Gale and Storm attended out of curiosity, but Syd Barrett wanted to be initiated: 'And the Master turned Syd down,' said Storm. 'He told him he wasn't ready and should complete his studies. To some extent, I think that was a problem but in hindsight, you think all sorts of things about people's fragile personalities. I thought the guru was very good. He talked about using the intellect and it felt very impressive listening to him talk. You could understand how one would feed off that energy.'

'I think Storm was in a dilemma,' suggests Gale. 'He toyed with the idea of a master but always bounced back and remained sceptical.'

Within months, though, others including Andrew 'Willa' Rawlinson and 'Ponji' Robinson, would take their first steps towards becoming Satsangi. Once again, they'd proved themselves a precocious lot. It would be almost two years before the Beatles made their trip to Rishikesh in the Himalayan foothills to meet Maharishi Mahesh Yogi and the Who's Pete Townshend discovered his guru, Meher Baba.

Not everyone in Pink Floyd was smitten by an Indian master or LSD. During the college holidays, Rick Wright, Roger Waters and his girlfriend Judy Trim joined the Gordons on the Greek island of Patmos. Nigel administered the two Floyds with their first dose of LSD. Waters stood motionless in front of a window for several hours, and Wright was later discovered, sunburned, in a foetal crouch. When a boat came chugging around the harbour, the tripping party were convinced it was a fire-breathing dragon.

The experience compounded Waters' ambivalence towards acid and psychedelia. 'What was *that* all about?' he said. 'Tune in, turn on . . . fuck off.' But Waters wanted to make a living out of music. He'd had a stint designing bank vaults for a West

End architect and loathed it. Hitching Pink Floyd to the passing psychedelic bandwagon made sense.

On their return from Greece, Floyd signed a management deal with the newly formed Blackhill Enterprises, comprised of enterprising vicars' sons Andrew King and Peter Jenner. India and the Master would have to wait, Syd Barrett was going to become a pop star.

Storm Thorgerson left Leicester University with a BA (Hons) in English in late spring 1966 and was accepted at London's Royal College of Art. 'The Breadwinner' and 'The Meal' had served their purpose, and Storm would now be studying for an MA in Film and Television. Serendipitously, David Gale and David Henderson had also been offered places at the RCA: 'It was the hardest college to get into and these three friends had managed it,' says Po. However, studying in London required money and Storm's mother Vanji earned a modest schoolteacher's salary.

At which point Storm received a letter from his bank. 'It turned out I had an anonymous benefactor,' he explained. 'Who had given me £1,000 to be spent on fun – on art, literature and films.' The money came with a caveat though: that Storm never tried to enquire as to who his mystery benefactor was – 'And he never did,' says Po. 'He never found out who gave him that money.'

With three of his friends about to move to London, Po was determined not to be left behind. Since becoming a father, he'd taken a job as a window-dresser at the Eaden Lilley department store in Sidney Street. It made use of his artistic talents, but was hardly challenging: 'I'd smoke a joint, wave to any friends walking by the window and then go to the pub for lunch.'

While draping a mannequin, Po found himself kneeling on a week-old copy of the *Daily Telegraph*. His eye was drawn to a personal ad, 'Wanted: An assistant to Scenic Designer in film and TV. Must have experience, be based in London, be prepared to travel and be over twenty-one'.

Po didn't have any experience and was only nineteen, but he applied anyway. The scenic designer Julian Pemberton invited him for an interview at his home in Kew Gardens. After which, Nod Brown told Po that the ADC Theatre's scenic designer happened to drink regularly in the Criterion. Po found his prey, plied him with beer and emerged a few hours later, his brain whirring with tales of crackling glaze and stencil graphics.

The next morning, Po drove his Morris 8 to London for the interview. Three weeks later, Pemberton chose him out of forty more qualified applicants. 'You'll find we're a fairly informal and relaxed lot . . .' wrote Pemberton in his job-offer letter. It was just as well – 'I didn't know jack shit,' Po says, 'but I'd taken a lot of speed before the interview, so every time Julian asked if I could do something, I said, "Yes! Yes! Of course!"'

Po started as a freelance scenic designer in late summer. Soon after, he, Storm and David Gale moved into Flat 1, Egerton Court. It was the perfect location: on the corner of Old Brompton Road opposite South Kensington tube station, within walking distance of the Royal College of Art and with the hip clothes shops Hung On You, Granny Takes a Trip and Dandie Fashions just a short Vespa ride away on the King's Road.

'Kensington & Chelsea was a good place to see the '60s come to fruition,' says Gale. 'Posh people lived there and could afford the frocks. But if you had a large enough flat and could put enough people in it, the rent was manageable.'

Egerton Court was a white stucco townhouse with faux marble fittings and had surrendered much of its charm after being carved up into self-contained apartments. Other students lived there, including their RCA contemporary, Roger Dean, who'd later draw dying planets and floating islands for Yes album covers.

Flat 1 was on the first floor near a grille-fronted elevator, whose every move was accompanied by an ominous clanking of gears. Roman Polanski had filmed some of his recent psychological drama *Repulsion* in Egerton's gloomy corridors and Flat 1 would become the scene of much real-life drama.

The apartment contained five bedrooms, a bathroom, a windowless lavatory and a cockroach-infested kitchen, all leading off a narrow hallway. Nigel Gordon had graduated from film school and was working as an assistant editor at Cammell, Hudson & Brownjohn, the film company responsible for the opening titles of the James Bond movie *Goldfinger*.

Nigel and Jenny had left Cromwell Road and took the prime double room at Egerton Court, draped the floor with Afghan rugs and invited their rock-star pals over for tea and a smoke. Fellow film school student 'Ponji' Robinson took the second-largest room and David Gale the smallest, with his bed on stilts to allow a desk below. Po's room was 'my safe haven', with his guitar and record player within easy reach of the bed.

This just left Storm's narrow, high-ceilinged chamber, to which he gave a unique makeover. 'I helped him paint the room,' says regular guest Emo. 'We did the walls bright orange and the floor-to-ceiling window in red gloss. I don't know how he could stand it.'

Polanski's film crew had also left some of their lights behind on the staircase at Egerton Court, which Storm scavenged and stashed in his room. 'Nineteen sixty-six in London was fantastic,' he said. 'We were all full of hormones and life and the physical centre of our universe was Egerton Court.' Without a communal area, Storm's flatmates gravitated to his carrot-coloured room, where he pronounced on books, movies and music, usually while puffing on a Gauloise.

'Storm was a very good critic,' says David Gale. 'You'd go to the movies with him and he'd always argue his position. He was astute at absorbing from visual art in general.'

Sometimes, Storm would continue arguing from the lavatory, espousing the merits of Jean-Gabriel Albicocco's *Le Grand Meaulnes*, with his trousers round his ankles. 'If you wanted a shit, you didn't go to Egerton Court,' cautions Emo. 'Because Storm would be in there for a hundred years – "Talk to me, Emo, talk to me . . ."'

There was plenty to discuss. As 1966 became 1967, the Beatles dominated the singles charts with 'Paperback Writer', 'Yellow Submarine' *and* 'Eleanor Rigby', the Beach Boys gave the world 'Good Vibrations' and Jimi Hendrix exploded onto the London club scene. On-screen, Antonioni's latest, *Blow-up*, showed the Yardbirds' Jeff Beck smashing his guitar and Jane Birkin flashing her pubic hair. Meanwhile, Pink Floyd were becoming the toast of the underground music scene.

One of Nigel Gordon's contacts had invited Floyd to perform at a series of 'happenings' at the Marquee club. The first, 'Spontaneous Underground', promised 'pop singers, hoods, Americans, homosexuals (because they make up 10 per cent of the population), twenty clowns, jazz musicians, one murderer, sculptors, politicians and some girls who defy description'.

Pink Floyd were soon performing at fundraisers for the London Free School, Oxfam and the anti-apartheid movement and appearing at mixed-media happenings, where, as Nick Mason explains, 'People painted their faces, did creative dance and bathed in jelly' – 'It was very much a Syd thing, though,' insists Mason. 'I don't think Roger, Rick or I were into any of that. It was Syd and his friends, his entourage.'

While most of Pink Floyd were using these gigs as a stepping stone, they were a welcome distraction for their friends. Po continued to bluff it out, designing sets for BBC shows, but he sometimes showed up late and still shivery from taking LSD – 'After a few months, Julian Pemberton fired me. He knew I was talented and could paint, but I didn't know how to do all the other stuff and I was turning up later and later.'

Casting around for anything to help pay the rent, Po accepted Peter Wynne-Willson's offer to drive Pink Floyd's light show. Po owned a mini-van and Floyd's lighting rig wouldn't fit in their regular transport. He recalls making his Floyd debut on 15 October 1966 at an 'All-Night Rave' in aid of Hoppy's latest venture, the *International Times* underground newspaper. For one night only, the Roundhouse in Chalk Farm, a half-derelict former gin distillery, littered with old horse-drawn carts, became a psychedelic fairy-tale palace.

Pop singer Marianne Faithfull showed up wearing a nun's habit which barely covered her bottom and a performance artist doused his naked body in paint and rolled around on a sheet of wallpaper. 'But in daylight,' admits Po, 'with these carts lying around, it looked like something out of *Steptoe and Son*.'

Nick Mason's jelly was a 6-foot-high art installation, which was destroyed when Floyd's roadie, Pip Carter, reversed his van into it. Later, the audience wondered whether the clods of gelatinous matter on the floor were real or the product of their fevered imaginations.

For the next few months, Po gunned his mini-van up and down the country and tried to find time to sleep. In 1967, Pink Floyd would end up playing around 200 dates: a non-stop blur of Mecca ballrooms and late-night roadside cafés. 'The itinerary was unbelievable,' says Po. 'Saturday at the Birdcage in Portsmouth, playing to eight mods who just wanted to hear Tamla Motown, and then driving to Manchester the day after to do a TV show with the Move.'

Two days before Christmas 1966, Floyd played the opening night at UFO, a new club co-founded by Hoppy and a young American record producer Joe Boyd. On Friday nights, UFO took over the womb-like basement of the Gala Berkeley cinema on Tottenham Court Road. There were poetry readings, psychedelic light shows, alternative pop music, a macrobiotic food stall and a German acid dealer named Manfred.

Most of Egerton Court trooped down to UFO. Floyd bleeped and honked through their improvised signature song, 'Interstellar Overdrive', while the club's patrons gyrated wildly and threw their hands in the air. 'All these amazing girls in floaty dresses, doing that uncoordinated hippy dancing,' says Po. 'All rather funny when you look back on it.'

Perched on a makeshift tower at the rear, Peter Wynne-Willson and his helpers loaded projectors with microscopic slides covered with paint, ink and bodily fluids and heated with a Butane torch. It was a ramshackle operation and the liquid was spilt and fingers burned, but the result was a galaxy of colours exploding across the backdrop, turning Syd Barrett into a multi-hued elf and Roger Waters into a towering green giant.

UFO quickly became a place to be seen, even if you were already famous. Before one Floyd performance, Paul McCartney sauntered backstage and handed Syd Barrett a joint. The Who's

Pete Townshend watched Floyd at UFO, while tripping on LSD, and was terrified Waters was going to eat him but he was smitten by Syd.

For Barrett, those first few months of 1967 were the relative calm before the storm but there were already signs something was amiss. Occasionally, the others asked Po if he'd take Barrett home. Syd was smoking more dope than ever, perhaps to alleviate the boredom of so much time on the road. On the drive back from Portsmouth, he spent two hours smoking, giggling and barely speaking – 'I found him a bit odd,' admits Po. 'He wasn't the same Syd I'd met a year or so before.'

Barrett wasn't the only band member going through changes: 'Roger Waters was becoming terribly demanding. Saying things like, "Where's this? . . . Where's that? . . ." It was quite interesting to see.'

Po spoke to Wynne-Willson about Waters' behaviour: 'Peter said, "Oh *man*, we're all supposed to be in this together . . ." Except, of course, we weren't all in this together, because Roger – God love him and good luck – was on a mission to become a pop star.'

On 29 April 1967, Pink Floyd made an appearance on the Dutch TV show *Fan Club* in a suburb of Amsterdam, then caught the ferry back to Harwich and drove to north London for another booking: 'The 14-Hour Technicolor Dream', an all-night happening in the grand hall at Alexandra Palace.

Floyd were the star turn above fellow counterculture poster-boys Soft Machine and the Crazy World of Arthur Brown. Further entertainment included the Tribe of the Ancient Mushroom dance troupe, a helter-skelter, a plastic igloo in which patrons could smoke banana skins (Ken Kesey's new buzz, apparently) and Yoko Ono having her clothes cut off with a pair of amplified scissors.

A BBC documentary camera crew prowled the room looking for soundbites. 'I think it's bloody mad myself,' declared one young lad in a suit, staring at the peacock parade around him. 'They ought to go to the looney bin.' Throughout the night, a neon flasher board projected ticker-tape messages – 'Vietnam is a bad trip' – around the hall, like scores at an American football game.

Pink Floyd weren't due on stage until dawn. By then, the cavernous space was strewn with bodies. Those still upright shared an identical spaced-out look or roamed the hall, looking for something, *anything*, to happen – 'I think we'd all been up for about thirty-six hours, some people were tripping and everybody was exhausted,' recalls Po.

The mood was already tense when Roger Waters started issuing orders. 'Roger said, "Where's my fucking whisky? Bring me my whisky, Po." "What whisky?" He said, "I always have a bottle by the side of the stage." I reminded him I was just there to drive the van and carry the lights. Then he said, 'Well, fucking go and find me a bottle of whisky then." At which point I said, "Goodbye", got in my van and left.'

Po arrived back at Egerton Court and went to bed. He woke up sometime on Sunday and lay there, gazing at the ceiling. Not for the first time, he thought, *So what am I going to do now?*

Chapter 3

'So I stuffed the money up the chimney . . .'

How a bank job, a court case, **Sgt Pepper's Lonely Hearts Club Band** *and the 1968 Paris Student Riots helped create Hipgnosis.*

'We were young, stupid . . . unfettered.'

– Storm Thorgerson

Carl Jung, Edgar Allen Poe, Aldous Huxley, Marilyn Monroe, Laurel and Hardy, William Burroughs . . .

The Beatles' *Sgt Pepper's Lonely Hearts Club Band* cover pictured Hollywood film stars alongside counterculture pin-ups. Peter Blake and his wife and fellow artist Jann Haworth had posed the group in front of life-size cutouts of their heroes. It was unlike any record sleeve before.

In May 1967, the residents of Flat 1, Egerton Court, gathered in Storm's room to listen to the album. They pondered the LSD-inspired whoosh and drag of 'Lucy in the Sky with Diamonds', the harps, sitars and tablas, and the final sustained forty-second chord of 'A Day in the Life' – and then studied the sleeve again: 'It was a piece of living sculpture,' says Po. 'So radically different to anything we had seen before.'

Peter Blake was a Royal College of Art graduate and a pioneer of British pop art. Blake's creation for the Beatles fired Storm's imagination, but he was still busy studying to become a film-maker. 'I was negotiating everything from love affairs to illicit deals to supposedly working at college,' he recalled.

The pursuit of pleasure continued without fear of conse-quences. Some obliging doctors could even be relied on to pre-scribe tincture of cannabis. One chemist's shop on London's Shaftesbury Avenue dispensed it three times a month. But the drugs didn't work for all.

At Christmas, everyone gathered in Nigel and Jenny's room for a festive dinner. Unbeknown to most, the turkey was laced with hashish, which had permeated all the trimmings. 'Halfway through the meal, I realised I had to lie down,' says Po, who staggered back to his room, where he remained for the rest of the day.

In his befuddled state, Po heard the sound of a dog howling. But there wasn't a dog at Egerton Court. It was one of his flat-mates in distress: 'I couldn't move, couldn't help. There was a lot of anger after that – "Why did you do this? Why was the food spiked without telling us?"'

There was also a new addition to the household. Matthew Scurfield now slept on his brother Ponji's floor and became Storm's protégé. 'I was three years or so younger,' he says, 'and

Storm read me *The Doors of Perception* and *Childhood's End* and introduced me very slowly to LSD.'

Scurfield was in awe of his worldly flatmates, not least Nigel and Jenny. Nigel floated around in a floral Granny Takes a Trip jacket, ushering his famous friends into the flat. 'There were times you'd see Mick Jagger and Marianne Faithfull going into their room. Storm took LSD as an experiment. Nigel took it in a spiritual, poetic way. But there was a lot of dissecting of the cosmos and the universe, especially with Storm.'

Matthew wanted to become an actor and would later appear in movies, theatre and TV productions, including *Raiders of the Lost Ark*. This made him an ideal candidate for Storm's college films. Storm had already shot one movie with Po driving around town dressed as a 1920s gangster, and Pip and Emo goofing around in the Cherry Hinton chalk pits for a silent movie. Its sequel, *The Mad Buggers*, was a scatological comedy starting Emo and Matthew, with some scenes filmed at Scurfield's Great Aunt Fanny's house, Gestingthorpe Hall in Essex.

Most of Egerton Court descended on Gestingthorpe for the weekend. 'Fanny, with her bohemian streak, welcomed us eagerly,' says Scurfield. But she remained blessedly unaware of some of the film's content. In one scene, her nephew appeared to consume mud and chicken shit. In another, Emo played a French artist painting Scurfield's life model reclining on a chaise-longue. It was like a homoerotic take on a Buster Keaton caper, with lots of nudity.

'If Storm could get your clothes off, he would,' says Emo. But he also pushed his actors too far, until they refused to go any further. Some comic simulated sex scenes meant Storm couldn't get all of the movie printed. Two reels of 16mm negatives remained in his fridge, moving from kitchen to kitchen into the next century.

Storm's desire to continually push the people around him was soon impacting his friendships. Then came the tipping point. In their ceaseless quest for truth, everybody at Egerton Court began having therapy.

David Gale was the first. The Scottish therapist R. D. Laing's 'anti-psychiatry' movement challenged conventional wisdom surrounding mental health. One of Pink Floyd's first Marquee dates had been a fundraiser for Laing's controversial project, Kingsley Hall in east London, where patients and therapists lived together as a social experiment.

'R. D. Laing was the Elvis Presley of psychotherapy,' says Gale. Like 'The King', though, he was powerfully charismatic but had his demons, later diagnosing himself with clinical depression and alcoholism. Laing believed psychosis wasn't a medical condition but the product of two warring personas. One was the supposedly 'sane' version of one's self, the other was the more 'authentic' or 'mad' self.

American acid-rockers the Doors' self-titled debut album had arrived in January 1967. Its opening song echoed Laing's philosophy with the Doors' lead singer Jim Morrison imploring the world to 'break on through to the other side'. Like a call to prayer, it rang out at Egerton Court, but its message was harder to put into practice.

The anti-psychiatrists had tapped into this new generation's desire to reconstitute reality. 'This entailed finding out just how mad you could sanely be,' explained Gale. 'You had to take acid. You had to break through, go mad, get out the other side and then really start living. But I couldn't seem to get there.'

Gale started seeing Laing's colleague, David Cooper, in Primrose Hill. It wasn't an auspicious start. At their initial meeting, Cooper greeted him naked with his leg in plaster, having recently toppled down a flight of stairs. His first question was to ask if Gale could buy him a bottle of whisky.

Storm, Po, Ponji and Matthew Scurfield also signed up with therapists; Storm with another of Laing's colleagues, Hugh Crawford, in Wimpole Street. Laing's books, *Knots* and *The Divided Self*, were soon being passed around Egerton Court like Kerouac's *On the Road* at Earl Street. A decade later, Storm distilled Laing's ideas into the artwork for 10cc's *Look Hear?*, which posed the question, 'Are you normal?'

That summer, David Gale and Matthew Scurfield saw Laing speak at the Dialectics of Liberation at Camden's Roundhouse. It was like a psychoanalysts' version of the 14 Hour Technicolor Dream happening at Alexandra Palace, where poets, black power activists and common- or garden-anarchists discussed social issues and the eternal quest for freedom. Some talked of turning on the world with LSD in the water supply, others disagreed. As one attendee later remarked, 'There was an awful lot of talking, spouting, stuff like that.'

One of the results of this self-analysis, though, was Storm being challenged by his newly enlightened flatmates: 'Seeing David Cooper enabled me to look at things in a more informed psychological way,' says Gale, 'and it dawned on us that Storm was acting weirdly. He wanted to be some sort of leader. We told him we no longer wished to participate in his films and suggested he look into his own behaviour, rather than manipulate ours.'

After being confronted, Storm retreated to lick his wounds – 'I was not in the best emotional state,' he admitted, but he tempered his behaviour, at least in the short term.

By now his friends in Pink Floyd were having hits. Floyd had signed to EMI Records at the beginning of 1967. To celebrate, they were photographed kicking their legs in the air like French can-can dancers outside EMI's West End office. It was what pop groups did, but Pink Floyd weren't like other pop group. They were signed after EMI's in-house producer Norman Smith visited UFO. Smith, who'd worked with the Beatles and was nicknamed 'Normal' by John Lennon, didn't profess to understand Pink Floyd's music but he believed they could sell records.

'Normal' Norman brought his new pupils into London's Abbey Road Studios and introduced them to the Beatles, who were making *Sgt Pepper*. Smith encouraged Pink Floyd to dial down the weirdness, the improvisation – 'The Floyd music of the time wasn't like Tom Jones or Vera Lynn,' said Storm. 'It was at the other end of the spectrum.'

Pink Floyd's debut single, 'Arnold Layne', tempered its droning Farfisa organ with a nursery-rhyme chorus. It reached the top twenty but was banned by the BBC, who objected to lyrics about a male pervert wearing stolen women's underwear – 'A true story,' said Waters. 'Bras and knickers belonging to our female lodgers were stolen from my mum's and Syd's mum's washing lines.'

A second baroque pop single, 'See Emily Play', arrived in June and became a top-five hit. The song distilled Barrett's childlike whimsy with echoes of Shakespeare's *Ophelia*. It all happened so fast, though. One moment Syd was a carefree art student, the next he was on *Top of the Pops*, sat cross-legged on a cushion, looking a bit vacant in his best Thea Porter silk shirt.

Syd and Lindsay Corner had found a new home at 101 Cromwell Road. Over the years, there have been tales of daily LSD trips and acid in the water at 101. The truth is submerged under decades of hearsay and bullshit but most of his old friends believe Barrett was taking a lot of LSD at this time and supplementing it with copious amounts of dope and his barbiturate-du-jour, Mandrax. It was a heady cocktail.

'Roger was always looking for the next thing,' recalls Rosemary Breen. 'And that applied to drugs. "Oh, if I take one of these and feel like this, what will I feel like when I take two?" Most people know when to stop, but he didn't.'

There was a general bad juju surrounding 101. 'It was this beautiful building with a wonderful sweeping staircase,' remembers Lindsay, 'but it became stairway to hell. Duggie Fields was lovely, Duggie was fine. But most of the people there seemed to be out of their heads. I went home to Cambridge for the weekend and locked my door before I left. When I came back, everyone had broken in as I was the only one with a TV set. There weren't any boundaries.'

Personal relationships splintered and two tenants woke up one day to discover their respective partners had become a couple overnight, like a psychedelic wife-swap. The new couple, Jock and Sue, briefly passed into Barrett folklore. In real life, Jock was the actor and male model Alistair Findlay, later seen in Hipgnosis's artwork for folk-rockers Audience's *The House on the Hill*, and Susan Kingsford was a *Vogue* model, glimpsed clutching a daffodil in the film of the 14 Hour Technicolor Dream.

Duggie Fields observed this romantic drama from a distance. 'Dear old Jock and Sue,' said Fields in 2007. 'Sue was very beautiful and wacky, and the last time I saw Jock he was advertising a whirlpool spa bath in one of the Sunday supplements.'

Pink Floyd's debut LP, *The Piper at the Gates of Dawn*, arrived in August. Glimpses of a shared Cambridge childhood emerged during a listening session at Egerton Court. It was all there: the Gog Magog Hills, Hilaire Belloc's *Cautionary Tales for Children*, the River Cam, Marvel Comics, *The I Ching*, even Syd Barrett's boyhood mode of transport in one song, 'Bike' – 'It was mysticism crossed with fairy tales and full of free association,' said Storm.

During their LSD trip two years earlier at David Gale's house, Emo remembers Barrett jumping up and down in the bathtub, shouting, 'No rules! No rules!' 'Syd had this thing about rules – his own life, his own world, his own environment,' says Emo. 'I think he believed once he made it with a group, he could just do as he pleased, but of course, it wasn't so. There were more rules.'

Some diehards at UFO were now grumbling about Pink Floyd's new pop-star status. In the parlance of the time, they'd 'sold out'. Even their previously loyal supporter Pete Townshend declared *The Piper at the Gates of Dawn* 'fucking awful'.

Roger Waters claimed to have no time for those wanting to bracket Pink Floyd with the musical avant-garde. He found Stockhausen and John Cage and their disregard for tonality a turn-off: 'Absolute bollocks,' he insisted. 'I always felt much more connected to the Rolling Stones, the Beatles and the Who than I did to any of that stuff.'

Nothing was going to stay the same, though. 'The Beatles and the Stones were like deities,' said UFO's co-founder Joe Boyd. 'But they were a threat to the order of society and there was the inevitable crackdown. The media took their cue from the authorities. Before it had been all mini-skirts and Swinging London, and by summer '67 it was all depravity, dope and addiction.'

UFO were kicked out of the basement of the Berkeley Cinema at the end of July. Pink Floyd played the final night. The police had pressured the landlord to close the club after LSD horror stories in the Sunday papers: 'Drug That Is Menacing Young Lives!' screamed the *News of the World*.

Mick Jagger and Keith Richards had already been the victims of a trophy bust. The same newspaper had tipped off the police about a gathering at Richards' country pile. Jagger was given three months for the possession of four amphetamine tablets and Richards a month for allowing illegal substances to be taken in his house. But the collusion and harsh sentences left a bad taste, even among some who loathed long-haired pop stars. *The Times* printed a questioning editorial under the head-line 'Who Breaks a Butterfly on a Wheel?' Jagger and Richards were released within a week, but their incarceration proved anyone was vulnerable.

Storm's friend Russell Page had been arrested in Knights-bridge the previous year. LSD wasn't illegal yet, but Page and his co-defendants were charged with possessing ergot (which was banned under the Poisons Act) and selling LSD-25 without a prescription. It was a landmark case, with Albert Hofmann summoned from Switzerland as a prosecution witness. Page was acquitted and disappeared back to Cambridge.

John 'Hoppy' Hopkins wasn't so fortunate. On the week *Sgt Pepper* was released, he began a six-month sentence for mari-juana possession. His imprisonment sounded the death knell for UFO. The club had found a new home at the Roundhouse but now disappeared for good in a cloud of incense. By then, the net was closing in. The police had arrived at Egerton Court and Po had been arrested.

The day after quitting as a Pink Floyd, roadie Po received an unexpected phone call from Julian Pemberton, offering him his old job back. Pemberton's business partner had died suddenly and he urgently needed an assistant set designer.

It was only a temporary position but Po threw himself into the work. 'Something in my head said, "Don't fuck this up." Work-ing again with Julian and watching Storm make films, I started wondering if I could become a photographer, even though I barely knew how to pick up a camera.'

For all Po's bravado, he was two years Storm's junior and frequently reminded that his education had stopped at sixteen – 'Storm called me "Pea Brain" and Dave Gale called Po "El Thicko,"' recalls Emo.

'I remember hypocritical discussions about whether we should kill the ants in the bath – whether this was cool or not,' admitted Gale. 'Yet we were quite happy to be appalling to each other on occasions.'

Storm became Po's mentor. One afternoon, he took him to Hyde Park for a photography lesson. Storm, the ever-present Gauloise dangling from his mouth, demonstrated how to use a 35mm Pentax camera and a Sekonic light meter: 'Of course, he was impatient,' remembers Po. '"No, no, no, Po. Not like this. Like *that*." But he taught me everything he knew.'

After a lecture on focus, composition and setting the aperture on the light meter, Storm suggested they find something to photograph. The pair wandered down to the Serpentine, where they spied a gold Maserati Ghibli. Ten minutes later, Po had shot thirty-five frames of the gleaming Italian sports car. They were the first serious photographs he'd taken.

The Royal College of Art's photographic school was near the main campus, just off Cromwell Road. Storm and Po marched into the studio, where the technicians presumed they were just another couple of photography students. Storm ushered Po into a darkroom hidden behind heavy drapes and lit by a single red bulb. Po watched as his friend retrieved the canister from the Pentax and performed what would become a familiar ritual: winding the film onto the sprockets, placing it in the developer, the washing, the drying . . . And then the Maserati slowly appeared as if by alchemy.

'It was an epiphany,' says Po. 'A blank piece of paper had turned into a picture. I was still working with Julian Pemberton at the time, but I'd found what I wanted to do. I had to do *this*, but I didn't know how to.' One drawback being the possibility he might be sent to jail: 'I had,' Po says, 'fallen in with a bad crowd.' Even worse than the crowd he was already in with.

Life for most at Egerton Court centred around college, Pink Floyd, therapists, girlfriends, drug dealers and the National Film Theatre. Saturday nights were sometimes spent at the newly opened Arts Lab, where alternative movies were screened and one might see John and Yoko wandering around. Except on Thursday nights, Po snubbed convention and went to the nearby pub: 'Where I'd drink beer, play darts and come home half-cut. Storm couldn't understand it – "Why are you drunk, man? It's very uncool. That's what old people do . . ."'

'At the time,' said Storm. 'We rarely spoke to anyone over the age of thirty.'

Po and some of his pub friends began stealing cars and selling them. Po was building sets for the BBC medical drama *Dr Finlay's Casebook* and one of his unwitting customers was the doctor's housekeeper, Janet. 'It was easy money,' he admits. 'Storm wouldn't have dreamed of doing something like that, but I was drawn to any kind of chaos and the late '60s in London were fucking lawless.'

The gang hot-wired cars, fled restaurants without paying and once turfed a sofa off the roof of a block of flats: 'We were bad eggs, hooligans, whatever you want to call it.'

Then they crossed the line. Barclays Bank launched its first credit card, Barclaycard, in June 1966. Po and five friends devised a cunning scam. They offered students £100 each to open a bank account. The students then gave the gang members the chequebooks and credit cards and waited forty-eight hours before reporting them stolen.

Meanwhile, the fraudsters acquired up to £200 each time by flashing the card and cashing a cheque. There wasn't any CCTV and bank tellers never asked for proof of identity. 'And there was something like twenty-seven banks between Marble Arch and the top of Edgware Road,' explains Po. 'If there were three of you in a car, you could do the lot in a day.'

In an apartment full of impoverished students, suddenly Po was dropping £750 in a night at the Cromwell Mint casino. He was also the only one of his flatmates to own a car, stolen or otherwise.

Then some of the gang started travelling further afield to hit up banks in Brighton and Birmingham. The police soon realised what was happening. Finally, one of their number, Harry Dodson, walked into Barclays Bank in Park Lane to cash a cheque: 'And the police jumped all over him,' says Po, 'dragged him down to West End Central and he served us all up.'

It was a while, though, before Po was apprehended. His girl-friend, Gabrielle Boumphrey, was a fashion model working under the name of Gai Caron: 'So I hid out at Gai's place, just going home to collect my clothes at night. The police had taken evidence from the other gang members' flats. So I stuffed the money up the chimney at Gai's.

'Of course, some detectives came looking for me at Egerton Court. Storm, understandably, was furious – "Look, man, we're smoking dope in here, we don't need the police coming round."'

Po eventually gave himself up. He was taken to Bow Street Magistrates Court and allowed one call to make bail: 'So I phoned the only person I knew who had any money, which was Peter Jenner. The alternative was three weeks on remand or begging my parents for the cash.'

Jenner presumed it was a drug bust until he arrived at Bow Street and discovered it was bank fraud and bail was set at £1,000. He turned around and went home. 'It was Syd Barrett who made Peter go back,' says Po. 'Syd was conscious of looking after other people. Oh, the irony . . . But Peter returned with the money, for which I am forever grateful.'

Po spent his twenty-first birthday, 23 September 1967, with his co-defendants in the dock at the Old Bailey. However, their parents had persuaded several respected individuals to speak up as character witnesses. 'It was the old boys' network,' Po admits. 'We had a bishop, a general and a captain of industry. They all stood up and said we were decent public schoolboys who'd made a terrible error of judgement.'

Nevertheless, the jury returned a guilty verdict and the judge imposed sentences of nine months each. Po's head span and his knees buckled: 'And then the judge said he'd suspend it for three years but if we did anything wrong during that time, we'd go to prison for nine months and three years on top.' It was a testament to the power of a 'good education' that the guilty boys went on to careers in journalism, local politics, the restaurant business and, aptly, second-hand car sales.

After the shock of his acquittal subsided, Po realised neither the police nor Barclays Bank had asked for the stolen money back. The stack of crumpled notes remained hidden in Gai Caron's flat. Four years later, Harry Dodson, the one who'd given them all up, appeared on the back of Audience's *The House on the Hill*, where his 'dead' body was shown being dragged through the hallway of a country house.

Po escaped prison, but his post-trial comedown had just begun. 'It was a culmination of the drugs and the court case,' he explains. 'I'd never had a bad trip, but LSD had seeped into my psyche and if I smoked a joint, I'd be right back there. I also developed some neuroses. I had a headache for three months, started obsessively washing my hands and imagined the buildings were collapsing around me whenever I walked down Oxford Street.'

'There was an upheaval at Egerton Court,' continues David Gale. 'As well as Po, this was a difficult period for Storm. He had to re-evaluate his behaviour, in a group of people with a novice understanding of R. D. Laing and his ideas.'

The cast of characters also changed. Ponji Robinson left and was soon en route to India. His room was taken by David Henderson, an art student who preferred painting to bank fraud and later played the lone drinker on the sleeve of Led Zeppelin's *In Through the Out Door*.

There was a new regular visitor, too. David Gilmour had spent most of the past year playing around Europe with his own group. Gilmour and his fellow musicians had performed at beach clubs in St Tropez and met Jimi Hendrix in Paris but by September 1967, they'd run out of gigs, food and money.

Gilmour was hospitalised with suspected malnutrition before the group scraped together enough francs for a ferry to Dover. His bandmates headed home to Cambridge: 'But I thought that would have been one defeatist stage too far,' says Gilmour. His parents had emigrated to New York and there wasn't a home to go back to. Gilmour moved to London instead. By day, he drove a van loaded with leather jackets and nude-look chiffon dresses for designer Ossie Clark's Quorum boutique. At night, he went to gigs or visited Egerton Court.

'I remember the rickety old iron lift and Nigel Gordon had the nicest room overlooking Dino's, the Italian restaurant,' says Gilmour. 'I was a bit lost and lonely in London so I spent a lot of time hanging out at that flat.'

Pink Floyd were already recording their second album, *A Saucerful of Secrets*, but Barrett's songwriting had slowed down and his live performances had become erratic. One apocryphal tale from their first American tour claims that before a date in Santa Monica, Barrett emptied Mandrax into his Brylcreemed hair and let the capsules dissolve under the stage lights. His bandmates don't remember this and it would have been considered a shocking waste of barbiturates.

Syd stories filtered back to Egerton Court, like stoned Chinese whispers. Was Barrett trying to break on through to the other side, as R. D. Laing and Jim Morrison suggested? 'Odd, colourful behaviour was taken as harmless eccentricity,' admitted Nigel Gordon. 'We did not recognise it for what it was.'

Gilmour saw Pink Floyd several times that winter, including at the Royal College of Art's Christmas ball. 'I'd only seen them before when they were doing Bo Diddley covers,' he said. 'Syd was now definitely a bit on the gone side. He'd passed his peak and was incapable really.'

'He had begun to travel his own pathway,' said Storm. 'To the extent of playing a different tune from the others on stage.'

Backstage at the RCA, Nick Mason mentioned to Gilmour the possibility of him joining the band. But no more was said for now.

If one event illustrates Barrett's frame of mind it was how he spent New Year's Eve, 1967. He joined the Gordons and other thrill-seekers on a trip to Wales. Nigel Gordon had the keys to a cottage in the Brecon Beacons and was writing a film script for Mick Jagger, but also had enough LSD to keep them all floating for days.

Barrett spent several hours holding onto an overhead beam while balancing his feet on a wine bottle. Later, he urinated and defecated on the doorstep – 'Even on acid, that wasn't a terribly sane thing to do,' understated Nigel.

Something had to change. David Gilmour finally received the call in January 1968. 'Nigel Gordon rang me on Pink Floyd's behalf,' he recalls, 'and said, "You better get down there and meet up with them. They want you to join."'

So began a curious few weeks where Gilmour and Barrett played together in Pink Floyd. Barrett often appeared disorientated and didn't seem to understand why Gilmour was there. There were still moments of clarity and fun, though, such as Barrett tap-dancing backstage at a gig in Weston-super-Mare. Then the lights went out again.

'At first, we had this idea we'd be a five-piece,' explains Nick Mason. 'David would do the heavy lifting and Syd would stay home and write songs. We wanted to preserve Syd in Pink Floyd in some way. But it didn't work.'

Storm's last project before his death was the Syd Barrett documentary, *Have You Got It Yet?*. Its title alluded to the time Barrett tried to teach his bandmates a new song. Whenever they reached the chorus, 'Have You Got It Yet?', he'd mischievously change the tune and they'd have to start again. The prank also showed Barrett's reluctance to repeat himself: 'He didn't want to keep anything because once it was done, it was done,' explains his sister Rosemary. 'It was the same with music. Why do the same thing twice? It always had to be original.'

In later life, Storm shared his own theory about Barrett: 'Syd was creatively spontaneous and would create/produce paintings, artworks and songs without much effort,' he suggested. 'But there was a potential downside: namely the absence of a work ethic. Syd had no idea how to "work at it". Instead, stuff just came to him.'

One day, on their way to a gig at Southampton University, Pink Floyd decided not to collect Syd. It was a bloodless coup. 'But it was upsetting,' says Gilmour. 'To be frank, no one tried hard enough to help him and like most ambitious young people we were too busy getting on with other things in life to dedicate the time to sort him out.'

Joe Boyd (who'd later produce records for Nick Drake and R.E.M.) summed up the dilemma many faced: 'The counterculture was meant to be exempt from capitalism. But how could it be?' he said. 'The scene was full of hustlers, schemers and dreamers. I know because I was one of them. Desires and competitive urgencies surged among us all.'

This included Storm and Po. It was spring 1968 and student protest was rife. On 17 March, anti-Vietnam War protestors marched on the American Embassy in London's Grosvenor Square. There were clashes with the police and Storm and Po narrowly escaped arrest. Passive observer Mick Jagger fled the melee but was inspired to write the Rolling Stones' 'Street Fighting Man' as a result.

More than 150 students and activists then occupied Paris University at Nanterre. Others at the neighbouring Sorbonne campus came out in support. A 20,000-strong protest march at the Sorbonne was later met with heavy police resistance and tear gas. Further student occupations and workers' strikes ensued across France.

In Britain, student sit-ins and strikes commenced at colleges including the London School of Economics, partly in protest of poor, outdated teaching methods: 'Young people were given a licence to criticise and try to change the way they were being educated,' explains David Gale.

The Royal College of Art's governing body was afraid of similar insurrection and closed its campus down. When it finally re-opened, Storm and Po embraced the administrative chaos and started attending photography school. Storm was, at least, an RCA student; Po wasn't. 'But nobody bothered to check my credentials,' he says, 'as everyone in authority was worried the students would stage a sit-in, so we were treated with kid gloves.'

Denis Waugh, an RCA photography student from the time, recalls the deception: 'We all assumed Po had come from some other department, like jewellery or filmmaking. We didn't realise until later he wasn't even a student. I just loved the bastard's audacity.'

Matthew Scurfield was now sleeping on Storm's floor and remembers a meeting in Ponji's old room with Storm, Po, David Henderson, David Gale and regular visitor Nick Sedgwick. 'This is my first memory of what became Hipgnosis,' he says. 'We had this romantic notion of an artistic collective, doing anything from painting and decorating to taking photographs and painting pictures. We were all going to contribute. But the rest of us fell away, it was Storm and Po who had the tenacious energy to move it forward.'

Henderson christened their collective 'Consciousness Incorporated'. 'A hideous name,' said Storm, 'but at the time we thought it was pretty cute.' But they weren't allowed by company law to present themselves as an incorporated company when they weren't.

The popular explanation for the name 'Hipgnosis' is that they discovered the word scrawled on Flat 1's front door. Po thinks Syd Barrett was the graffiti artist but Storm claimed it was the poet Adrian Haggard, one of the Better Books crowd and a friend of Nigel Gordon's. The word intrigued them. 'Hip' suggested 'now' and 'gnostic' came from 'gnosticism', a Greek word for an ancient religious belief system.

Hipgnosis's neighbour Roger Dean designed the company's first business cards – 'Because I can't draw for toffee,' admitted Storm.

One card read: 'Hipgnosis – photos, designs, artworks etc . . . far outs, groovies, weasels and stoats'.

'Don't ask me why,' says Po.

Their first job came via Victoria Walker, an aspiring children's author and David Henderson's girlfriend. Victoria had a contact at Mayflower Books who wanted to overhaul the company's staid image. Storm met Mayflower's publisher in a Chelsea bistro. After several glasses of wine, he was commissioned to shoot four paperback covers, for £40 each; enough to keep them all in cannabis tincture and therapy for the summer.

The titles were westerns, crime thrillers and what Storm called 'tawdry sex novels'. The pair hired fedoras and capes and used their friends as models. Emo, David Henderson and Harry Dodson were among those photographed dying dramatically in Richmond Park or brandishing guns on the roof at Egerton Court for *Sabres on the Sand* and *A Few Days in Madrid*. Meanwhile, female models flashed a hint of cleavage or bare buttocks for the covers of *Flower Power* and *Tiger Street*.

Elements of the counterculture had filtered into the mainstream so Storm and Po shot several using infra-red film and with coloured filters. These created tints and hues which distorted reality, just like an LSD trip: 'Like Stagecoach on acid,' offers Po.

Gala Pinion, down from Ely to visit Lindsay Corner, witnessed one shoot: 'I'm sure they were all on something, running about the place in curly wigs and velvet coats,' she recalls. 'I didn't know what was happening. I was still doing my O levels, so it was all a bit beyond me.'

Storm and Po printed the pictures in the photography school's darkroom. With four book covers complete, Storm then convinced Mayflower's publisher to commission more: 'Storm was a compulsive and single-minded hustler,' observed Nick Sedgwick, 'and a one-man bandwagon upon which others were tempted to jump.'

Everything happened quickly that spring. Storm insisted David Henderson was approached by Pink Floyd to paint the artwork for their second album, *A Saucerful of Secrets*. 'But Dave, for reasons best known to him, turned them down. I was listening at the door, jumped in and said I'd do it.'

'When I wasn't working on the album, I was often at Egerton Court,' says David Gilmour. 'I recall Storm saying, "Hey, can't you get Floyd to book us to do the album cover?" He was quite persistent, but I thought, "That's not such a bad idea." So I suggested it to the management and that's what swung it.'

The image on the cover of *The Piper at the Gates of Dawn* had been taken by fashion photographer Vic Singh and was refracted through a prism lens. 'That image was typical of the time,' says Po. 'The band in fancy shirts from Thea Porter or trousers from Hung On You, because that's how pop stars were meant to dress. But that wasn't Pink Floyd. When Storm and I saw what Peter Blake had done with *Sgt Pepper*, it changed our thinking overnight.'

This sea change had been a long time coming. Early shellac records came in plain brown or green paper sleeves. In 1939, Columbia Records' art director Alex Steinweiss presented songwriters Rodgers and Hart's latest collection with a cover showing a photograph of a theatre marquee. Sales boomed; Steinweiss had unwittingly invented the album cover. However, it took the arrival of the first vinyl microgroove long-player in 1948 for most record companies to raise their game. Andy Warhol and art director Reid Miles messed with the form and helped shape jazz label Blue Note's aesthetic through the 1950s and early '60s. They swapped traditional bland photography for sex and sepia tones on Sonny Clark's *Cool Struttin'* and a semi-abstract line drawing for Johnny Griffin's *The Congregation*.

Miles also infuriated his photographers by cropping the musicians' faces or rendering them unrecognisable. But Storm understood: 'Because there's nothing more boring than a photo of a band on a record cover.' Blue Note inspired designers at fellow jazz labels Verve and Bethlehem, who soon decorated their sleeves with distorted ink-line illustrations and X-rays of saxophones. Their audience was drawn to the perceived intelligence of the music, a mindset Hipgnosis exploited years later.

In the early '60s, though, rock 'n' roll record covers rarely went beyond photos of cheesily smiling groups. But just as the Beatles' music put down the marker for their contemporaries, so too did their artwork. Robert Freeman's portrait for 1963's *With the Beatles* showed the unsmiling mop-tops in stark monochrome, while David Bailey's later image for the Rolling Stones *No. 2* made a virtue of the group's surliness.

'But they were still simple photographs of four or five young men,' points out Po. 'Storm wanted to break away from the David Bailey-style pictures.'

After 1965, though, the Beatles' LSD experience informed their image as much as it did their music. On Boxing Day 1967, the BBC screened the band's new film, *Magical Mystery Tour*. Older viewers spluttered into their leftover turkey as the group embarked on a Merry Pranksters-style road trip and performed the curious-sounding 'I Am the Walrus'. This was no longer the cosy pop group of Richard Lester's *Help!*

LSD-inspired imagery was soon everywhere: in designers Hapshash and the Coloured Coat's billowing typography for the UFO club; in the garish colour explosions on Cream's *Disraeli Gears* and the lenticular image of the Rolling Stones wearing wizards' hats and cloaks on the front of their new LP, *Their Satanic Majesties Request*. But Hipgnosis weren't enamoured. 'We were in direct opposition to the album covers of the day,' said Storm. 'As these were mostly group shots or fantasy illustrations.'

More inspiring for them was the Doors' latest, *Strange Days*. The group's faces only appeared on a shop-front poster; the rest of the gatefold image was given over to a New York street circus scene, containing dwarves, a juggler and a circus strongman. William S. Harvey, Elektra Records' art director, wanted a picture redolent of Fellini's 1954 movie, *La Strada*. *Strange Days* looked like a Storm Thorgerson creation before Storm had properly started creating.

All this imagery was zooming around the ether when Hipgnosis designed *A Saucerful of Secrets*. It was a bold move for Pink Floyd to reject EMI's art department and employ a couple of unknowns. '*The Piper at the Gates of Dawn* had us as sort of psychedelic mop-tops,' says Nick Mason. 'A bit old-fashioned. So we'd decided to take control of our covers, the Beatles and *Sgt Pepper* proved to EMI that the artists knew better than the company did. So we took full advantage.'

Rick Wright and Nick Mason had only come to know the Hipgnosis duo in London. 'There was one slightly oddball character in Storm and one slightly more measured character in the shape of Po,' recalls Mason. 'And it stayed that way for the next fifty years.'

Just as many groups' first albums consisted of songs they'd been playing forever, Hipgnosis's debut corralled their influences into one piece of art. The pair spent hours chopping out images from Marvel comics, zodiacal charts and astronomy textbooks. There were six background pictures, including the seventeenth-century illustration Basilica Philosophica alongside Storm's beloved Doctor Strange from *Strange Tales No. 158*. The old and the new, the hip and the gnostic.

'All of us, including the Floyd, shared the same interests,' said Storm. 'Atmosphere, emotions, space, politics, the war, drugs, girls . . .'

It was a painstaking process, involving trial and error and the photography school's darkroom facilities. 'We hand-tinted it with coloured inks,' recalls Po. 'Spent hours doing it, with Storm overseeing, "No man, that's no fucking good, try green . . ."'

Friends helped, too. Earlham Street's psychedelic handyman John Whiteley created the cover's marbling effect; David Henderson suggested spelling out 'Pink Floyd' in Letraset letters and Matthew Scurfield took the prints to be developed in Baker Street.

Storm tried to banish the group's image from the cover, but EMI intervened. Po photographed Floyd using infra-red film on Hampstead Heath and Storm reproduced the picture as small as he could get away with. The pair hand-delivered the sleeve to Ron Dunston, the head of EMI's art department.

'There's me in my velvet flared trousers and beads hanging off my wrists saying, "Hey, man, here's the Floyd cover,"' recalls Powell. "I handed him this *thing* with scrappy Letraset letters on it and he looked at me like I didn't exist. It was at that moment Storm and I realised we would never work for the record companies, only for the artists.' Hipgnosis received £110 for the sleeve, the equivalent of £1,400 today.

With Syd Barrett gone, Pink Floyd had gradually given up trying to write hit singles. Their new music was as much a leap of faith as its artwork. These were songs inspired by Tang-dynasty Chinese verse and the time Pip Carter's father saw a flying saucer over the Fens, with a Salvation Army band playing on Barrett's swansong 'Jugband Blues'.

The whole package was timely. Shortly before *A Saucerful of Secrets'* release, Stanley Kubrick's sci-fi epic *2001: A Space Odyssey* arrived in cinemas. Pink Floyd had even pitched to record the soundtrack. 'But I don't think we'd have been right for it,' admits Mason. Storm splashed some of his anonymous benefactor's cash, hired a limousine and took eleven friends to see the film in London's West End – 'Emo pre-rolled some joints and we had flasks of tea laced with gin,' he recalled.

Others remember Storm watching the movie at least four times and once on LSD. There was a lot to watch: Kubrick and co-writer Arthur C. Clarke's story encompassed artificial intelligence and the birth of mankind. Almost a decade later, Hipgnosis presented a variation on *2001*'s mysterious black obelisk as a cover idea for Led Zeppelin.

A Saucerful of Secrets reached the top ten, proving Pink Floyd could survive without their mercurial ex-frontman. But Blackhill Enterprises had chosen to continue managing Syd Barrett instead of Pink Floyd: 'We backed the wrong horse,' admitted Peter Jenner. 'But at the time it required quite an adjustment to accept the Floyd were going to make it without Syd.'

Pink Floyd's booking agent, Bryan Morrison, took the band on instead. Morrison and his junior agents, Tony Howard and Steve O'Rourke, were a stark contrast to Jenner and Andrew King. In 1969, Steve O'Rourke became Pink Floyd's manager and would spend the next thirty-four years frequently butting heads with Storm, both emotionally and financially.

'Tony and Steve were very hard-nosed and great for the Floyd,' says Po. 'Bryan Morrison was this old-time Tin Pan Alley music guy, who was building up a song publishing empire. Bryan wore immaculate suits, lots of aftershave and always had a cigar on the go.'

The Bryan Morrison Agency's original office at 142 Charing Cross Road was above an all-day drinking club popular with record executives. There was a steady traffic of boozy A&R men and pop hopefuls up and down the stairs. Hipgnosis were soon working for Morrison's other acts: designing artwork for British bluesman Alexis Korner and rendering ex-Jeff Beck drummer Aynsley Dunbar's new group, Retaliation, unrecognisable on the cover of their self-titled debut album.

Morrison's pride and joy, though, were the Pretty Things. Once pitched as a filthier Rolling Stones, the Pretty Things had watched their rivals conquer the charts while their career stalled. The group became valued Hipgnosis clients and their oval-faced singer, Phil May (whom Storm nicknamed 'The Singing Avocado'), became a regular tennis partner. However, Po's first experience of them was fraught. 'They were,' he recalls, 'a bunch of fucking hooligans.' Hipgnosis had arranged a photo shoot in Hyde Park, near a horse trough filled with water: 'Just as I was about to press the shutter on the Nikon, Phil May tossed a huge stone into the trough, soaking me completely.

'It dented my confidence hugely,' he admits. 'But I realised the Pretty Things had been famous since 1964 and I was like a schoolboy, all bluff and bluster but no idea how to deal with rock 'n' roll bands.'

They learned as they went along: by photographing Pink Floyd holding junk-shop amulets in Kew Gardens and dressing them up as World War I aviators in the video for their next single, 'Point Me at the Sky' – 'I think our work encapsulates the spirit of uncertainty and experimentation at the time,' says Po.

'I don't think Pink Floyd knew any more than we did,' said Storm.

'It was incredible really,' remembers David Gale. 'When Storm first joined the RCA, he was a loud, distinctive presence in the corridors. But he gradually sloped off down the road to the photography department and spent all his time making album covers with Po.'

By now, though, poring over a developing tray in a darkroom was sometimes preferable to going home. There was trouble brewing at Egerton Court.

Chapter 4

'You just wanted a free trip to Timbuk-fucking-tu!'

A cow in **A Clockwork Orange,** *footballs in the Sahara Desert, the most disappointing album cover ever made and why Roger Waters and Storm Thorgerson stopped playing squash for ever.*

'Everything was beautiful, for a while.'

– Aubrey 'Po' Powell

★

Nigel and Jenny Gordon flew to Beas in Northern India in September 1968. Like many of their Cambridge peers, they wanted to follow the Master. The day before they left, Nigel asked Mick Jagger if he too was interested in a spiritual path – 'It's not for me, Nigel,' Jagger told him. 'I want to have fun.'

Soon after they arrived at the Dera Ashram, Nigel sent a letter to Storm and his flatmates. 'Love and hope to all ye questing spirits,' he wrote, alongside an ink drawing of a *Dark Side of the Moon*-style pyramid and the premonitory words, 'Remember that triangle, Storm.'

He wouldn't forget.

The Gordons spent three months working at the ashram before being initiated by Maharaj Charan Singh. Meanwhile, Syd Barrett and Lindsay Corner moved into their old room. Syd was recording a solo album but making slow progress. Blackhill Enterprises hoped that being among old friends might aid his creativity.

Barrett's problems hadn't diminished his stock among other musicians, either. Pete Townshend was appearing in his friend RCA student Richard Stanley's course-work film, *Lone Ranger*. Stanley enrolled Storm as an assistant cameraman and Matthew Scurfield to play Townshend's clownish younger brother.

Townshend invited them all to dinner and urged Matthew to bring Syd Barrett to the Who's upcoming gig at Essex University. 'And I think the whole point of the meal was to get Syd to come to the show,' says Scurfield.

Syd drove Matthew to the Who's concert and refused to stop at any red lights during the journey. Once they'd arrived, Barrett disappeared into the crowd. The Who played 'Arnold Layne', but he was nowhere to be found.

Rosemary Breen thinks her brother may have had undiagnosed Asperger's syndrome. 'We are all on the spectrum, but he was way over the other side,' she says. 'He would have been diagnosed nowadays. I also think it was dangerous when a brain like his got in touch with LSD, because there was already so much going on in there.'

Nobody was breaking through to the other side. Instead, the Doors' song 'The End' captured the prevailing mood at Flat 1. Huddled whispers in the kitchen and furious arguments between Barrett and his girlfriend had replaced verbal sparring and communal laughter. Everybody started locking their bedroom doors at night.

'Syd could be violent towards Lindsay,' says Po. 'I never saw it, but I heard things and once confronted him about it.' That evening, Barrett came lolloping down the hallway, stripped to the waist in ratty velvet trousers, like some fey skinny prize-fighter. Voices were raised and accusations made, but no punches were thrown.

'Poor old Syd was going a bit bonkers and that was his downfall,' says Lindsay. 'So much dope was smoked and I think that was why he became so ill. It triggered things in his mind and it was terribly sad to see him like that.'

Many stories about Egerton Court could have been scripted for a movie, like some variation on the feckless hippy comedy *Withnail and I*. One example was the writer and film-maker Jonathan Meades' revelation. In 1968, Meades was a drama student and a friend of Harry Dodson's. Twenty years later, he was interviewed for *Days in the Life*, Jonathan Green's oral history of London's counterculture.

Meades talked about visiting Egerton Court with Dodson and hearing a noise in the corridor: 'I said, "What's that?" One of [his flatmates] giggled and said, "That's Syd having a bad trip. We put him in the linen cupboard." And that seemed a terrible thing to do.'

'Even Harry was amazed,' said Meades, 'and he was pretty much up for anything.'

The News of the World then repeated Meades' story, which compounded the myth. Except there wasn't a linen cupboard at Egerton Court. Barrett had locked himself in the windowless lavatory and was having a panic attack. Po spent twenty minutes explaining how to undo the lock – 'And I made a flippant remark to Jonty Meades,' he admits, 'and was mortified when I later read it in a newspaper.'

Barrett's friends wanted to help him but didn't have the experience or knowledge. Peter Jenner was wary of traditional psychotherapy: 'Because I'd read Erving Goffman's *Asylums*,' he said. 'I knew you shouldn't go into one of those places because they'd give you a lobotomy or electric shock treatment. But R. D. Laing was different.'

'Oh, R. D. Laing,' says Lindsay. 'All those psychiatrists were as bad as each other. None of them could have helped him. They didn't have the medication back then.'

Roger Waters made the call to Laing and arranged an appointment for Syd. 'I drove him there myself,' Waters recalls, 'but he refused to get out of the car.' David Gale tried again some weeks later. Laing agreed to another appointment, but insisted Barrett had to attend voluntarily. Syd's flatmates only mentioned the meeting when the taxi was outside, but he refused to leave the flat. Po recalls them scrabbling around for cash to pay the driver off.

Waters eventually persuaded Barrett's eldest brother, Alan, to visit Syd in London. 'Which he did, against his wishes, I might add,' says Waters. 'Then Alan wrote to me later and said, "Oh, Roger [Syd] has had some problems, but he's fine now, so don't you worry any more, thank you, goodbye." And that was the end of it. But I know what Syd did, because I can see him now pulling the wool over his big brother's eyes and pretending to be normal.'

'We all tried to reach out to him,' said Storm. 'But you have to ask, "Are you in charge of yourself?" And the answer was no.

We all had issues. It wasn't easy for the young, untutored con-
federates. I loved him dearly, but I couldn't cope.'

David Gale also thinks they were constrained by 'our absurd
'60s coolness'. By 1968, 'it was all people in Afghan coats, cured
in goats' urine, down the Portobello Road market. I hated it –
"Far out, that's cool, you're beautiful, we're all beautiful . . ."'

'This was the end of the period of having fun,' says Po. 'Storm
and Dave Gale were deep thinkers and the reality of life was
kicking in: "What are we going to do now?" Storm looked at
Pink Floyd and didn't want to be left behind. But we were both
ambitious. After nearly going to prison and seeing what was
happening with Syd, I wanted to drag myself out of the mire.'

Egerton Court began to break up. Po was one of the first to
leave, taking his guitar and record player to nearby Gloucester
Road. He moved into a converted stable in Astwood Mews with
five women, including his new girlfriend, Angela.

Aspiring photographer Mick Rock found a billet at Egerton
Court and witnessed its death throes: 'Syd had become strange
with the people he'd grown up with,' said Rock. 'I knew some
weird stuff was going on, but he was fine with me. Storm was the
strongest personality and the most articulate. He used to hold
court on the khazi with the door wide open and I thought that
was stranger than anything Syd was doing.'

When Syd and Lindsay's relationship ended, Barrett joined
Duggie Fields in a seventh-floor flat in Wetherby Mansions, a
red-brick affair on Earl's Court Square. But there was still no
escaping old friends: their kitchen window overlooked David
Gilmour's in the block opposite and Hipgnosis were soon designing the artwork for Syd's solo album, *The Madcap Laughs*.

Making the record had been an arduous process. 'At some
point we all went down to Olympic Studios,' remembers Po.

'There was Syd, Nick Mason, David Gilmour, myself and some-body else, not Roger Waters, playing bass.'

Po brought his guitar and accompanied them on a never-ending version of Willie Dixon's 'Back Door Man'. It was like the musical version of artist M. C. Escher's staircase: 'For four hours, with Syd playing along, then dropping his plectrum . . . then playing again. It was to try to get him into a creative place.'

Back at Abbey Road, some of Barrett's new songs had such irregular rhythms, his musicians struggled to find their place. EMI were close to abandoning *The Madcap Laughs* when Syd asked David Gilmour to help.

'It was murder trying to get him to do anything,' Gilmour recalled. Barrett would swallow a Mandrax, lapse into a semi-conscious state and slide off his stool. 'You can practically hear him fall asleep on some of the takes. But I also felt there was a part of him that wasn't impaired. You'd have these anarchic changes in metre – things I would never be brave enough to do – but I loved it.'

Storm later said that songs such as 'Terrapin' and 'Octopus' 'were like catching glimpses of the old Syd'. The smiling boy strumming his guitar at parties in Cambridge was still there, but becoming harder to find.

Mick Rock began his journey as a photographer working with Storm on *The Madcap Laughs*. When the pair arrived at Wetherby Mansions, Syd had just painted the floor of his room with alter-nate orange and navy-blue stripes. He'd moved the furniture but hadn't swept the boards first and had started painting next to the door: 'So there were cigarette ends stuck to the floor and he'd painted himself into a corner, literally,' said Duggie Fields.

A giggling naked woman wandered into the room to see what was happening. Evelyn Joyce flitted around the London club scene and had recently appeared in a newsreel about the King's Road boutique Granny Takes a Trip. Evelyn's nickname was 'Iggy the Eskimo', but she was the daughter of an Indian mother and a British father.

Iggy was Jenny Spires' friend and had needed somewhere to stay. She moved into Wetherby Mansions and had a fleeting affair with Barrett. Iggy remembered jollying him along as Storm and Mick Rock took the photos – 'I put the kohl around his eyes and tousled up his hair,' she told me. '"Come on, Syd, give us a smile. Moody, moody, moody . . ."'

Iggy joined Syd for more photographs taken outside the building. In one sequence, the couple, all angular cheekbones and black-rimmed eyes, crouched down alongside Barrett's Pontiac Parisienne.

Po visited Wetherby Mansions later to take further pictures. Iggy had vanished and he arrived to find the curtains drawn and the air stale and heavy. Po photographed a topless Syd performing yoga poses. He was practising the Indian discipline for mind, body and spirit. But while the body was agile, the mind and spirit weren't: Syd didn't say a word to him.

Duggie Fields had graduated from Chelsea School of Art and spent most days preparing for his first exhibition. His flatmate rarely left his room: 'Syd's was a slow and subtle decline,' said Fields. 'While he lay in bed, he could imagine he was doing anything. But as soon as he got up, he limited his possibilities. The communal activity of being in the band was gone and he was marooned.'

'Syd always seemed distracted,' says Jonathan Meades, who met Barrett again at Wetherby Mansions. 'But you never knew how much of the weirdness was put on. It's like that thing Kingsley Amis said – that if you keep parodying a word and putting it in inverted commas, sooner or later you start using it without inverted commas.'

The Madcap Laughs wasn't released until March 1970, with a cover photograph of Syd crouching down on his newly painted floor. The back cover showed him with a naked Iggy posing in the foreground. Po's picture of Barrett performing yoga appeared as part of a collage inside the gatefold, next to a baby holding a pipette: a nod to Nigel Gordon's eyedropper of LSD.

In the meantime, Po's moonlighting at the photography school had ended abruptly. John Hedgecoe, the department's principal, realised he'd been hoodwinked: 'And I was told in no uncertain terms to vacate the premises,' says Po. 'They banned me from then on.'

Without access to the school's facilities, Hipgnosis bought a second-hand enlarger and print dryer and created a darkroom at Astwood Mews. 'Angela and I slept on a sofa in the front room,' explains Po. 'She worked at a shoe shop on the King's Road, and the other girls were secretaries and all went to bed at ten o'clock, which is when I took over the bathroom.'

Po swapped its plain lightbulb for a red one and washed the prints in the bath. Nouveau bluesmen Free's first publicity photographs, posing on the steps of the Royal College of Art, appeared overnight, on a washing line next to five pairs of drying bras and knickers.

'We worked like that for six months,' recalled Storm. 'In a bathroom which measured no more than 10 feet by 6. Impoverished, beset by terrible conditions, no capital and no idea of the future . . .'

Despite the psychological trauma of three years at Egerton Court, Storm had graduated from the Royal College of Art in the early summer of 1969. Director Roddy Bogawa's documentary,

Taken by Storm, included one of his subject's student films: an untitled animation beginning with a close-up of Storm's buttocks, which then parted and became a railway tunnel down which hurtled various comestibles and a photograph of Oscar Wilde.

After graduation, Storm went to France and Po to the Balearic Islands for several weeks' respite. Pink Floyd had just released their soundtrack to Iranian/Swiss-born film-maker Barbet Schroeder's *More* (1969), a tale of sexual and narcotic adventure set in Ibiza. One song, 'Cymbaline', even mentioned Storm's favourite Marvel Comics sorcerer, Doctor Strange.

Hipgnosis had been shown an early print of the film and suggested its title. 'We observed that the central character always wanted more,' said Storm. 'More thrills, more sex, more drugs.' Hipgnosis took a still from the movie showing two characters playing at the foot of a windmill and over-exposed it to give the image a lysergic tint.

On 21 July 1969, American astronaut Neil Armstrong became the first man to walk on the moon. The BBC covered this historic event with a live broadcast, featuring contributions from Dudley Moore and Judi Dench, and Pink Floyd performing a noodling instrumental in the studio.

Syd Barrett watched the moon landings with Susan Kingsford at Wetherby Mansions. 'I think we all thought it was a conspiracy by the Americans,' Susan told me. 'None of us believed it.' Once again, Barrett didn't utter a word all night.

A few days later, he caught a plane to Ibiza and made the two-hour ferry journey to Formentera. Po and Emo were in San Fernando Square when they spotted their friend squinting into the sun and wearing the same clothes he'd fled London in. Barrett was carrying two bags, one filled with dirty laundry, the other banknotes from a recently cashed royalty cheque.

Over the next few days, Syd's mood skittered between playful fun and sullen non-communication. He stayed out in the sun too long and stumbled along the beach in his satin shirt and Gohil boots, telling girls he was a pop star: 'Syd was like a younger brother who needed looking after,' remembered one friend.

One photograph from the trip shows Barrett performing the Urdhva Hastasana (Upward Salute) yoga pose behind a naked American woman, draped in a diaphanous red veil. Hipgnosis's artwork for Pink Floyd's *Wish You Were Here* later included a similar veil.

Storm was once asked if this picture was inspired by Barrett in Ibiza. 'Oh, don't be ridiculous,' he grumped. 'No, it was not.' But the 1970s would be all about the meaning in Hipgnosis's art. Whether it existed or not.

★

The women of Astwood Mews were unhappy. Most mornings, they woke to find photographic prints washing in the bathtub or drying alongside their underwear. Nobody wanted to perform their ablutions with the Pretty Things staring at them. When Po and Angela split up, Hipgnosis needed to find a studio.

Number 6 Denmark Street was on the fringes of London's Soho and in the middle of 'Tin Pan Alley'. Guitar shops and music publishers flanked the building, with Regent Sound Studios, where the Who and the Rolling Stones made records, two doors down: 'It was the sort of place you'd expect to find old dogs nosing through the dustbins on the pavement,' recalled Nick Sedgwick.

The studio was above Zeno's, a second-hand Greek bookshop, and leased by a male dance teacher. When Hipgnosis arrived for a viewing, the teacher's girlfriend appeared, clad only in a pink dressing gown, and began playing a grand piano in the middle of the room.

Po suspected a sexual angle to the couple's business. 'I don't know what the full story was there, but the teacher told us they had to leave quickly. The rent was something like thirty pounds a week and they wanted a deposit and two months upfront.'

Vanji Thorgerson loaned them £1,000, and Wing Commander Powell a more cautious £500. 'Vanji was supportive, being a creative soul herself,' suggests Po. 'I'd been in trouble with the law and had a child at eighteen, so my father worried I'd repeat my failings and fritter the money away, but my mother persuaded him.'

The couple vanished but left their piano behind. Po flogged it to Heal's furniture store and Hipgnosis spent the money on new cameras and flashlights, and paid their parents back. Though Storm took a while to reimburse Vanji: 'Deal with this, you naughty boy!' she wrote in a letter to her son.

Hipgnosis had found the studio before Storm graduated, but didn't start work there properly until after the summer holidays. They painted the walls black and hired Jokers Wild's old road manager to construct a makeshift darkroom. At the rear of the space was a bathroom, containing a Victorian roll-top bath and a porcelain sink for washing prints, which doubled as a urinal when too lazy to use the communal lavatory.

Po had resumed his relationship with Gai Caron, who helped decorate the space. 'Nothing compared to the grimness of Denmark Street,' says Gai. 'It was so filthy, I don't know how they could invite rock stars up there. They had pages of newspaper – not even cut-up bits of newspaper – hanging next to the loo because God forbid anyone would spend money on loo paper.'

So disgusting was the lavatory that Storm recommended their clients use the darkroom sink instead. A year later, Hank Marvin, the former Shadows' guitarist, now working with other ex-Shadows in Marvin, Welch & Farrar, became the first: 'To have him in our studio, pissing in our sink, was an event,' said Storm.

It wasn't easy, to begin with. Storm and Po arrived at the studio after one bank holiday weekend to find their downstairs neighbour, Mr Zeno, in distress: 'We'd employed an out-of-work chum to build a print-washer system in the bathroom,' said Storm. 'It was supposed to run overnight and drain away the water, but it became blocked and flooded Zeno's.'

'I walked in and saw all these rare first editions floating in the water,' says Po. 'It was one of the worst days of my life.'

Hipgnosis wasn't insured, but Zeno was. He claimed thousands of pounds for stock that had been languishing on the shelves for years and refurbished the whole shop – 'After that, he became our best friend,' says Po.

Insurance remained an issue, though. One Sunday, Storm joined Pink Floyd's football team for a game in Hyde Park. Po's Austin A40 was broken into during the match and all their cameras and lenses stolen. 'And we *still* weren't insured,' he admits, 'which set us back considerably in our plans for world domination.'

It was a lean time, surviving on scraps from the Bryan Morrison Agency table. Some of Morrison's acts were signed to Island Records, who needed a sleeve for their new compilation, *You Can All Join In*. Island boss Chris Blackwell proposed an 8 a.m. photo session with all the groups in Hyde Park. Po arrived to discover random members of Spooky Tooth and Traffic wandering around in various states of discombobulation: 'Most of them had been in the Speakeasy. Nobody had gone to bed and they all turned up looking like toe-rags.'

Hipgnosis cast its net wider to survive. For the next eighteen months, they took on outside work. When fashion designer Thea Porter needed someone to shoot her latest collection and couldn't afford David Bailey or Clive Arrowsmith, she called Po. It was his entrée into a world of couture and Mayfair cocktail parties.

Po was soon freelancing for the American trade journal, *Women's Wear Daily*, and shooting everything from minor celebrity weddings to drag artist Danny La Rue's birthday party: 'I hadn't a clue what I was doing,' he admits, 'but I learned how to deal with people.'

Meanwhile, Storm manned the scalpel and cow gum, producing artwork for the likes of keyboard-heavy rockers Argent. When the record company commissions dried up, they designed spin-off books for the TV cartoon series *Hattytown Tales* and fashion spreads for soft-porn magazine *Club International*; one image of a flasher in a gaberdine mac was later recycled for Pink Floyd.

It was Floyd that kept Hipgnosis afloat. Steve O'Rourke later negotiated a deal with EMI, giving the group unlimited studio time for a small drop in royalties. But this emphasis on albums increased the importance of the artwork.

Pink Floyd's latest work, *Ummagumma*, was released in November 1969. It was a Cambridge affair. The title was Emo's invented slang for sexual intercourse; the LP included a song called 'Grantchester Meadows' and Hipgnosis shot the cover at the Januarys' family home, Trinity House.

Storm always credited Libby with the idea to create a picture within a picture. *Mise en abyme* was a technique where an image contains a smaller version of itself, as seen in the seventeenth-century painter Velázquez's *Las Meninas*. Hipgnosis were familiar with a variation known as 'The Droste Effect', after a Dutch cocoa powder whose packaging showed a woman carrying a box of the same product on a tray.

Storm posed a barefoot David Gilmour in front of Trinity House's French windows, with the others on the lawn behind him – 'David was the most handsome, so it made sense putting him at the front,' he explained. A variation of the image, with Roger Waters on the stool, appeared in a picture on the wall. And so on, repeated infinitum – 'Like Aldous Huxley's idea of going through a door into another realm,' suggests Po.

Polystyrene letters borrowed from Eaden Lilly spelt out 'PINK FLOYD' on the floor below an original cast recording LP of *Gigi*. Floyd scholars later brushed tobacco strands off the *Ummagumma* sleeve and contemplated the meaning of Gigi. There wasn't any – they just needed something to fill the space.

Storm always grumbled that the photograph was poorly lit and the cutouts scrappy, but *Ummagumma* was the epitome of late-'60s Hipgnosis: 'It wouldn't have appeared any earlier,' he said. 'But it was still infused with psychedelic notions: bizarre, incongruous, surreal, romantic . . .'

The music had a similar quality and was split between four live recordings and five studio compositions. Pink Floyd with Syd Barrett often struggled outside London – their music wasn't aimed at the Top Rank ballroom crowd who'd been dancing to Geno Washington's Ram Jam Band the week before.

Ummagumma's live tracks were recorded at Manchester College of Commerce and Birmingham's Mother's club, part of an emerging circuit of university halls and pub backrooms, where patrons sat cross-legged on the floor, immersed in the music. This audience carried LPs under their arm as a way of advertising their impeccable taste. *Ummagumma*, with its *mise en abyme* artwork, was designed for this and became a top-five hit.

'Hipgnosis had a minimalist message,' suggests Humphrey Ocean, musician, artist and future Hipgnosis collaborator. 'They treated their audience intelligently. This was the period where the LP you carried under your arm said something about you. Record sleeves had replaced the Penguin book cover.'

'I didn't much like *Ummagumma*,' admitted Storm. 'But then I wasn't being paid to like it.' This was a transitional period for Pink Floyd. They couldn't write another 'See Emily Play' without Syd Barrett so they started to dabble in neo-classical concertos, film soundtracks and musique concrete.

Pink Floyd's live show had also become challengingly experimental. Hipgnosis had designed a poster for the group's gig at London's Royal Festival Hall in April. They performed two pieces, 'The Man' and 'The Journey', to represent an average day in the life. During the performance, the four stopped playing and began sawing wood and hammering nails on stage – 'They spent twenty minutes building a table,' recalls Po. 'It was incredibly avant-garde, but I started feeling embarrassed the longer it went on. I'm not entirely sure they felt comfortable either, especially David Gilmour.'

The guitarist was still finding his place in Pink Floyd and described this period as 'a lot of floundering around'. A description which also applies to Hipgnosis. For every *Ummagumma*, there was a corresponding misfire.

Honking blues-rockers Toe Fat's self-titled debut album showed Emo and his girlfriend, Cici, both naked and with their faces replaced by Storm's toe. The group's American label objected to the nudity and replaced the couple with a photograph of a lamb. *Toe Fat Two* appeared a few months later and resembled a pornographic fruits der mer. Hipgnosis talked up surrealist painter Man Ray's influence: 'But it's an awful cover,' admits Po.

Toe Fat demonstrated Hipgnosis's willingness to provoke record buyers. Their art wasn't whimsical or steeped in Victoriana, like many of their contemporaries. It was harder and more graphic. The sleeve for German art-rockers Birth Control's self-titled LP showed two condoms: one containing an eel, the other the contents of an egg. 'The women at the factory where the cover was printed nearly went on strike, refusing to handle it,' admitted Storm. They'd mistaken the yolk for semen. 'It also freaked people out when it made the shops so they didn't buy it.'

Toe Fat were signed to Rare Earth, a subsidiary of Motown in America. Many record companies now had bespoke imprints on which to release underground music. In summer 1969, EMI launched Harvest, a home for what music critics now called 'progressive rock'.

The film auteur Jean-Luc Godard was once asked whether a movie should have a beginning, a middle and an end. 'Yes,' he replied, 'but not necessarily in that order.' A lot of progressive rock followed this thinking and was given to classical virtuosity and jazz-style improvisation. The Moody Blues, Procol Harum and Deep Purple were also pushing the boundaries of conventional pop and making music with orchestras. *Ummagumma* had included Rick Wright's four-part piano concerto.

Ummagumma was Pink Floyd's first release on EMI's Harvest and its success helped bankroll their labelmates, Edgar Broughton Band, Quatermass, the Pretty Things and Syd Barrett. Blackhill Enterprises and the NEMS Agency (who'd recently acquired Bryan Morrison's roster) looked after many of these acts. With Hipgnosis as unofficial artists-in-residence, it was like one big dysfunctional family.

A design idea could be triggered by a lyric, a song title, the group's name or something entirely unrelated. Some clients gave

Hipgnosis complete freedom and others interfered. 'How far do we go to please?' said Storm. 'Early on, it was pretty confusing.'

'Later on, we had an operating principle – "We don't teach you guitar, don't teach us design,"' says Po. 'Storm saw it as his job to turn an audio event into a visual event. The medium wasn't important. In another life, he probably would have gone on to a career in film and I probably would have been a production designer for movies. But that's not what happened.'

Storm bought a film director's zeal to the work, though: 'He was very intense about the imagery and discussed things deeply. There had to be some intellectual or logical reason.'

Po remembers Storm pressing him to find the meaning in sci-fi rockers Quatermass's artwork, which showed pterodactyls flying between two high-rise buildings. '"No, no, no, Po, look again, what does it *mean*?" It was like the university education I'd never had.'

Storm sometimes arrived at work having dreamed up an idea overnight, a process he called 'plundering the goldmine' – 'He thrived on ambiguity and contradiction,' explains Po, 'on strange juxtapositions and visual puns, and making the real unreal.'

By now, though, Hipgnosis weren't the only designers challenging convention. Photographer David Montgomery shot a huddle of naked women for Jimi Hendrix's *Electric Ladyland*. Led Zeppelin's first album arrived with a stipple drawing of the 1937 Hindenburg airship disaster on the front. In the record shop rack beside it was King Crimson's *In the Court of the Crimson King*, with its post-psychedelic take on Edvard Munch's 'The Scream'. A year later, designer John Pasche's lascivious flapping tongue would define the Rolling Stones' brand.

In the United States, flowers, skeletons and ambigrams adorned the Grateful Dead's sleeves and German artist Mati

Klarwein's radical interpretation of Buddha, the Angel Gabriel and the Virgin Mary was used on Santana's latest, *Abraxas*.

After *Sgt Pepper*, the Beatles had headed in the opposite direction. Pop artist Richard Hamilton's sleeve for their 1968 self-titled LP was stark white and as utilitarian as its predecessor was vivid had been colourful.

'*The White Album* was the Beatles saying, "We can do anything we want and we're fed up seeing pictures of ourselves on the cover,"' suggests Po. 'But I thought it was a bit boring. Hipgnosis always had a narrative. What was the Beatles' narrative? It didn't say much about the Beatles.'

Yet its influence was apparent when Hipgnosis proposed a cow for Pink Floyd's next album sleeve. The group had requested something minimalist for the cover but there weren't many lyrics to bounce ideas off. The first side contained one instrumental suite of music, the second side finished with 'Alan's Psychedelic Breakfast', in which roadie Alan Styles could be heard frying bacon and muttering in his broad East Anglian accent.

Stanley Kubrick later requested to use the side-long instrumental in his adaptation of Anthony Burgess's dystopian novel, *A Clockwork Orange*. Floyd vetoed the deal because Kubrick wanted to chop up the piece to fit the movie.

The suite and the album were both untitled until Waters saw the words 'Atom Heart Mother' in an *Evening Standard* newspaper story about a woman with a radioactive plutonium pacemaker. The phrase was so incongruous, it was perfect.

The idea for a cow on the sleeve originated with Hipgnosis's friend and occasional collaborator, the American conceptual artist John Blake. Hipgnosis had met Blake at the Royal College of Art and he often dropped by Denmark Street. Those who did so sometimes ended up as cover models and

Blake appeared, nine years later, on the front of Genesis's *And Then There Were Three*.

Hipgnosis already had two ideas for *Atom Heart Mother*: a woman passing through a doorway and a man diving into an empty swimming pool. Both exuded what Storm called 'low-key normality'. Blake took this thinking further and suggested a cow: 'And how more normal can you get than that?' said Storm.

Storm and Po were soon back in their old rural hometown, Potters Bar, searching for a cover star. They found Lulubelle III, grazing with a herd of Friesians in a farmer's field. Storm soon had the bit between his teeth: the artwork had to be about the cow and nothing but the cow. Pink Floyd's name and the title would be completely absent from the sleeve. Hipgnosis later compared this minimalism to Dadaist sculptor Marcel Duchamp's fountain and Andy Warhol's banana and tins of Campbell's soup. But it made Po uncomfortable at the time: 'I thought it was a step too far,' he says. 'I was more pragmatic than Storm and didn't think so laterally.'

Storm pushed on, undeterred. The finished cover showed Lulubelle III standing in a field of brilliantly green grass. Hipgnosis's one concession was artfully airbrushing some excrement from under her tail.

They presented the image to Pink Floyd at Abbey Road Studios. When the group started laughing, Po's fears were allayed. Floyd loved it, EMI less so – they considered the missing group name and LP title tantamount to commercial suicide but there wasn't much they could do.

'Historically, this was the period when artists were incredibly scathing about record companies,' says Nick Mason. 'The power had shifted to us. If anything went wrong, it was always the fault of "the suits" – blame them. I don't know what Steve O'Rourke had to go through, but we wanted the cow.'

Nevertheless, it was still company policy for the managing director of EMI's record division to sign off every cover. In summer 1970, the task fell to Leonard 'L. G.' Wood, a former World War II pilot and long-serving company man. Wood stared at *Atom Heart Mother*, looking in vain for a title. He turned it over, to find three more cows staring back at him – 'Ah, Friesians,' was all the bemused MD could muster.

'He was furious, apoplectic,' recalled Storm.

Despite the parent company's reservations, Floyd's American label paid for billboard images of the cow on Los Angeles' Sunset Strip and furnished record dealers with pink promotional udders. *Atom Heart Mother* was released in October 1970 and became Pink Floyd and Hipgnosis's first number-one album.

The following year, the LP appeared in a record shop scene in Kubrick's *A Clockwork Orange* – a rare moment of calm in a movie filled with ultra-violence: '*Atom Heart Mother* is art that's all about nothing,' says Po, 'but all about everything.'

Hipgnosis had now established a second headquarters away from Denmark Street. Storm and Libby January were living together in Haverstock Hill. Douglas January had resigned himself to his daughter's choice of partner though there would still be issues. That summer, Storm borrowed Douglas's prized Bentley without his permission, pranged it and was unable to pay for the repairs.

In the years ahead, Storm and Libby's flat at Hillfield Mansions would host many late-night brainstorming sessions. It was also close to the Globe Tennis Club. Elvin had taught his son to play and Storm continued in adult life as a respite from the day job – 'Storm had amazing hand-eye coordination,' recalls Roger Waters.

Lindsay Corner took the couple's spare room for a time after she and Syd split up. 'Both Storm and Libby were seeing therapists,' says Lindsay. 'Storm was complicated but fun, unbelievably messy and untidy. But he and Po were hard-working and wanted to achieve something. They had a focus, whereas others from that crowd just lay around and did nothing. By 1970, though, I'd met my future husband and was moving into a different world.'

Lindsay drifted in and out of the Hipgnosis story throughout the '70s. She played a 1930s femme fatale on the cover of Audience's *The House on the Hill*, the sixth telephonist from the left inside 10cc's *How Dare You?* and a Wild West gambler's moll on a Bad Company single.

After Lindsay disappeared, her friend, Gala Pinion appeared in Syd's life: 'I had the nicer years with Syd,' says Lindsay. 'Poor Gala had the worst of it.'

'Gala and Lindsay were best friends and I think that might have caused some upset at the time,' suggests Po. 'Syd could be a very charismatic and beautiful man, when he was well, and women gravitated towards that. Gala wanted to look after him, but he needed professional help.'

Eighteen-year-old Gala was working at the Chelsea Drugstore on King's Road and was introduced to Barrett after moving into Astwood Mews: 'Syd came to see Po and told me had a spare room so I moved into Wetherby Mansions,' she recalls. 'Which was the beginning of a whole other story . . .'

A second solo album, *Barrett*, was released in November 1970. Once again, the members of Pink Floyd had helped push it over the finish line. One of its offcuts, 'Let's Split', was supposedly written about Gala, who struggled with Syd's jealousy and mood swings. Then the couple moved back to Cambridge and sur-prised everybody by announcing their engagement: 'I was very young and naïve,' she says.

During a celebration dinner at the Barrett family home, Syd suddenly tipped a bowl of tomato soup over his fiancée and dashed off upstairs: 'And nobody said a word. They all behaved as if it was entirely normal.' He returned later, having chopped several inches off his hair. Still, nobody in the family spoke about what had happened.

The relationship couldn't survive and Gala moved back to London, where she worked as a fashion model and a stylist, occasionally with Hipgnosis: 'They were always late payers and Storm was grumpy when I asked for my money.'

While everyone else was moving forward with their lives, Barrett was inert. Mick Rock interviewed him for *Rolling Stone* in 1971: 'I'd love to get it together,' Syd told his friend. 'I wasn't always this introverted . . .'

'Syd made a definitive decision to withdraw from the world,' said Rock. 'He decided he didn't want to deal with the hype, the rock 'n' roll bullshit. He couldn't be bothered with it.'

Storm and Po, though, were negotiating this world as keenly as their old friend was rejecting it.

★

In winter 1970, Storm walked into 6 Denmark Street and said he wanted to go to the Sahara Desert to shoot an album cover. He had drifted off to sleep the previous night, listening to their client, the Nice's forthcoming LP, *Elegy*.

Hipgnosis had photographed a Tyneside bridge for the Nice's previous album. The group had since broken up and *Elegy* was a posthumous release, but its fugal progressive rock demanded something artistically ambitious: 'A desert scape, with rolling dunes stretching way into the distance,' suggested Storm, 'but with red footballs curving from view in an elegant line.'

The Nice's showboating keyboard player Keith Emerson was sold on the idea, but Hipgnosis had to convince the group's label. Charisma Records' chief, Tony Stratton-Smith, was an inveterate gambler and immediately on-side. His pragmatic label manager, Gail Colson, less so. Gail listened to the pitch and asked why Hipgnosis couldn't just shoot at Camber Sands in Sussex.

'We had to explain that Camber Sands wouldn't have the rolling dunes we required,' says Po. They hustled Charisma into saying yes. In December, Hipgnosis flew to Morocco, like a rock group going on tour for the first time.

There was something opportune about Storm's idea. The New York artist Robert Smithson had recently created three ambitious land sculptures. The latest, 'Spiral Jetty', was a 6,500-ton installation of mud and salt crystal on Utah's Great Lake. Storm wanted a piece of land art for *Elegy*, but nobody had attempted such a thing for an LP cover before.

Once in Morocco, Hipgnosis left their Marrakesh hotel in a hired Renault van. They had 120 deflated red and candy-striped coloured footballs, two bicycle pumps, camera cases, tripods and one household broom stuffed in the back. It was almost 220 miles to Zagora, the nearest town to their chosen location, the Merzouga dunes: 'A nightmare drive over the Atlas Mountains,' recalled Storm. 'Six thousand feet at night, fog, hairpin bends . . .'

The pair made it to their destination unscathed and checked into a hotel – 'Which is when we discovered our bicycle pumps were useless,' says Po. 'It took twenty minutes to inflate a single ball.'

Storm's schoolboy French came in useful when he persuaded a local garage proprietor to inflate the balls in exchange for a handful of dirham. Hipgnosis returned the following morning to discover he'd enlisted a group of Berber boys to do the job for him.

Now, though, the inflated balls wouldn't all fit in the Renault. Hipgnosis paid the exhausted Berbers with a football each, squeezed the rest into the van and drove 50 miles to the dunes. They spent most of the day looking for the right spot – 'We found a place that would do but we weren't entirely happy with it,' said Storm. 'We decided to give it another five minutes and over the next rise we found a spot with the same dune configurations we'd imagined in our mock-up drawing.'

They laid out their props in a curving line heading towards the horizon. After each ball was placed, Po swept their footprints away with the broom.

'The sun was going down and we had ten minutes to shoot the picture,' recalled Storm. 'But we *knew* we had it.' Elated, they returned to the van, where Po discovered his Ossie Clark leather jacket and the key to their hotel room were missing.

Back in Zagora, the hotel manager refused to let them into their room until they paid him $100 for the lost key. The pair were already down to their last few dirhams. Po tried to call the British Consulate, but the telephone lines weren't working. The following morning, two police officers escorted the pair to a jail on the outskirts of town. It was a warning: 'Find the money or disappear in the desert,' says Po.

The pair returned to the hotel ready to throw themselves at the mercy of the manager. Instead, they found an American photographer and his crew in town to shoot an ad campaign for BMW – they'd transported three pristine vehicles to the desert and were looking for the best dunes in which to photograph them. Hipgnosis introduced themselves and walked away with a loan of $200: enough to pay off the hotel manager and bribe their way out of Morocco.

By the time they reached Marrakesh, the only currency remaining was the footballs. Po's market-trader instincts kicked in and he sold most to a shop owner and gave the last three to a police officer. The cop then merrily directed traffic with a ball under each arm and another wedged between his legs.

Ultimately, *Elegy*'s sleeve (and the backstory) was more interesting than the music inside. 'That cover captured a moment of tranquillity and strangeness,' said Storm. 'It was also a turning point for Hipgnosis – proof we could take a big idea and turn it into reality.'

Their friends and other clients were amused. All *that* for an album cover? 'Can you believe it?' says Roger Waters. 'They went off to the desert and put footballs all over the place . . . for Genesis or whoever. I thought, "You just wanted a free trip to Timbuk-fucking-tu!" Or wherever the hell it was.'

'The art comes first, the money comes second,' was Storm's mantra. 'And he was right,' concurs Po. 'Except we didn't know how much money we should be charging.'

In 1971, Hipgnosis were receiving between £120 and £250 for most covers. Po married Gai Caron that summer. The cash purloined from Barclays Bank was used as a deposit on a small place in Wandsworth. 'But the mortgage was thirty-five pounds a month,' says Po. 'Hipgnosis weren't making much money, so I had no idea how I was going to pay it.'

While Storm always put the art before the money, Po was adamant they shouldn't ignore the latter. His partner's disinterest in financial matters frustrated him: 'Storm liked having money but didn't always want to talk about it,' says Po. 'After we started earning more than £3,000 a year, I insisted we do things properly – write everything down, keep receipts, hire an accountant. Storm didn't seem to care about that stuff.'

When Po registered Hipgnosis as a limited company, Storm refused to become a co-director. 'I don't know if it had something to do with his Communist upbringing,' he suggests.

'I don't know why,' says Barbie Antonis. 'It's not like Storm never signed contracts in his life. This is pure speculation, but maybe it was a political statement, maybe Storm would have seen being a company director as domineering and autocratic.'

Yet these were the same traits that drove Storm creatively, often infuriating record company staff, managers and musicians. It soon became part of Po's remit to make the placatory phone call or referee between Storm and an aggrieved artist. Storm's laissez-faire approach to timekeeping was another issue, both in his professional and personal life. So much so his tardiness prompted Roger Waters to take drastic action.

Neither LSD nor psychotherapy had impacted Storm's love of sport. He and Waters regularly played squash. 'At least once a week until I finally couldn't stand it anymore,' divulges Waters. 'Not the defeats – of which there were many – I just couldn't take the fact he was always late. You get forty-five minutes on a squash court, and then there's usually some fucker banging on the door going, "Come on, hurry up!" Storm was always at least five minutes late and sometimes more.'

On one occasion, Waters waited twelve minutes for Storm to arrive. Exasperated, he went back to the changing room and took off his kit. At which point Storm came rushing in. '"Come on, get changed, what are you doing?" I said, "I am sitting here, what are *you* doing?" "We're meant to be playing squash," said Storm. "No, we *were* playing squash. But I have since changed back into my street clothes and we are never playing squash again." We never played again.'

Despite their hand-to-mouth existence, Hipgnosis hired Mick Rock as an underpaid assistant. Rock, a beanpole-skinny yoga freak with Bob Dylan's hair, looked and acted the part: 'Mick would stand on his head in the corner of the studio,' says Po. 'Which broke the ice if Rory Gallagher or whoever came in for a meeting.'

Po's earnings as a freelance photographer were still plugging the gaps but blonde-haired, blue-eyed Gai was in demand as a fashion model and was signed to the Wilhelmina agency in the States. She'd been back and forth, working in New York for some time. Po joined her there in February 1971, with a plan to drum up business for Hipgnosis.

Their friend, Royal Shakespeare Company actor Terry Taplin, was appearing in *A Midsummer Night's Dream* on Broadway. Taplin and his girlfriend invited the couple to share their apartment on East 93rd Street. Gai started work immediately and Po attempted to sell himself to record company art departments.

It was a humbling experience. 'The classic line I heard was, "We've got ten thousand out-of-work photographers and designers in this city right now, why do we need another?" I wasn't used to this, as I thought I was the dog's bollocks from London.'

Director Peter Brook's *A Midsummer Night's Dream* was a daringly modern take on the Bard, featuring stilt walkers, trapeze artists and a young Ben Kingsley. Po approached Brook about making a film of the production, 'but he spotted my naivety and quickly passed.'

New York was fascinating to any former British schoolboy weaned on American culture but the novelty of seeing the Empire State Building or eating in Hamburger Heaven quickly paled. 'New York was rough in the early '70s,' says Po. 'The peace and love and Hare Krishna thing were over. There were muggings, hard drugs, people OD'ing, places you wouldn't dare go after dark . . .'

When Gai went on a week-long shoot in North Carolina, Po filled his days learning to ice skate in Central Park: each lap of the ice was another reminder of the jobs he wasn't getting.

Nevertheless, every touring British group played Manhattan's hippest venue, the Fillmore East. Po and Gai were soon hosting Sunday lunches for the likes of Tyrannosaurus Rex and Wishbone Ash. 'English fayre, roast beef, Yorkshire pudding, beer and joints,' says Po. 'To give them a taste of home and a change from the tour bus.'

One newly formed 'supergroup' gleefully discussed how many 'rubber johnnies' they should bring on their next US tour. But a trip with ex-Small Faces' singer Steve Marriott's new group, Humble Pie, reminded Po that a touring musician's life could be desperately dull. Humble Pie had sold out the Fillmore and Po accompanied them to their next gig. He was shocked when their chauffeur-driven limo pulled up outside a high-school gym in upstate New York.

'They were on the verge of making it, but there was no glamour. Then the next day they had to catch a train to Philadelphia and stay in some miserable Holiday Inn. Everyone was missing their families and running up hundreds of dollars on phone bills. I remember thinking, "I can go home. They can't." They had another 200 dates like this.'

It was a foretaste of the arena-rock circuit on which many Hipgnosis clients soon found themselves. Another night, another sports hall and another group of exhausted Brits crashed out in an anonymous dressing room.

Every few days, Po scraped together the money to phone Denmark Street: 'And Storm would say, "This is happening, that's happening . . ." And I'd think, "What the fuck am I doing here?"'

Po thought he'd caught a break when Motown Records' art department requested a photographer but when he reached their office downtown, the assignment had already gone. It was minus four degrees outside and snowing heavily. Po had spent his last few dollars: 'I had to beg the art director for ten bucks for a taxi. That was the most humiliating moment of my trip.' The couple flew home at Easter: 'And I could have kissed the ground when we got off the plane.' Po hadn't taken a single photograph during the trip.

Back in Britain, news of these enterprising designers had reached the BBC. Po's schoolfriend, Alan Yentob, was now directing the TV arts show, *Review*, and commissioned a feature on Hipgnosis. The programme was broadcast that summer. Storm and Po appeared in their ramshackle studio discussing their respective roles. Storm, in his dun-coloured sweater and corduroys, looked like a dishevelled young academic. Po, with his flowing locks and Hung On You threads, came across as the archetypal King's Road hipster: 'I tend to be more sentimental, romantic . . . slightly old-fashioned,' he purred. 'Storm tends towards the rather brutal and surreal.'

The BBC joined them for a cover shoot at London's Smithfield Market. The client, Edgar Broughton Band, played heavy political blues, popular with the Portobello Road Afghan coat crowd. The artwork needed to reflect their social angst.

Po had once made sets for a production of Theatre of Cruelty founder Antonin Artaud's play *Spurt of Blood*. This involved hanging cuts of meat from the theatre ceiling, which dripped plasma and tissue onto the audience below. Hipgnosis's idea for

Edgar Broughton Band's third album repurposed Artaud and involved shooting a naked Emo, suspended between animal carcasses in the market's meat locker. Hipgnosis acquired permission to shoot after hours, but hadn't mentioned the nudity.

Knowing they were contravening every food and hygiene rule, Hipgnosis moved fast. Emo's ankles were bound with leather straps and the BBC's film showed him flashing a toothless grin while hopping across the locker floor. Two white-jacketed porters then flipped Emo upside down and hung him from the hook, as he clenched his buttocks to hide his balls.

'I could only hang there for a minute and a half as it was so cold and the blood was rushing to my head. All these butchers were looking on in disbelief.' A senior porter finally intervened and declared, 'This *has* to stop!' But Hipgnosis already had the picture.

The final artwork was striking and grotesque. EMI was outraged, but Storm remained defiant: 'Whatever your feelings about meat or not eating it for religious or health reasons, it's a striking photograph,' he told the BBC. 'The vitriolic reaction has been a testament to how effective it is.'

'It's very difficult to tell whether what you are doing is art,' he said finally. 'Whether the picture is what you want or proscribed by something else. Maybe it doesn't matter. Who cares if it's art or not? There's a quarter of a million homes with a little piece of us in it. That's nice.'

The company finished 1971 on a low. 'Pink Floyd once said that *Atom Heart Mother* was a better cover than the music,' said Storm. 'But the Floyd's next album, *Meddle*, was much better than our cover.'

Meddle was released in October. Pink Floyd had found their focus, with David Gilmour's choirboy voice and unhurried blues guitar finally given free rein. The lyrics to its centrepiece, 'Echoes', explored real life and real emotions. The piece began with a sound resembling the asdic ping of a submarine sonar, which made Storm think of water.

The group were touring Japan when he spoke to Roger Waters about the artwork. 'It was a very poor telephone line from the Far East,' Storm recalled. 'The band said they fancied a picture of an ear underwater . . . Or I *thought* that's what they said.'

Hipgnosis hired a specialist photographer, Robert Downing, to shoot a female model's ear ('The prettiest ear we could find,' says Po) and a tray of water into which Hipgnosis dripped coloured inks. The two images were merged, but the final artwork was indistinct. Many wondered if they were looking at an artist's impression of a cosmic black hole rather than a human orifice.

'They dropped the ball,' admits Nick Mason. '*Meddle* is okay, but it's just okay. If you don't immediately know it's an ear underwater, then I rest my case.'

Mason now had some experience in making album covers himself. Earlier that year, he'd drawn a charmingly rococo illustration for the Floyd compilation, *Relics*: 'EMI had set the picture budget at £25,' he says. 'So we decided to do it ourselves.'

Storm never got over *Meddle*, though, and embraced the opportunity to tinker with the image on later CD reissues: 'We didn't like it and the band didn't like it,' he said. 'It was the most disappointing cover we ever made.'

Hipgnosis needed another hit.

Chapter 5

'There was a lot of Viking-ology going on . . .'

Starring Led Zeppelin, Elvis Presley, Roman Polanski's sword, 'Samantha Fox' and the Great Pyramid of Cheops.

'Hipgnosis were like good cop, bad cop.'

– Jimmy Page

One of the young Jimmy Page's favourite LPs was Buddy Holly & the Crickets' *The "Chirping" Crickets*. Page was thirteen when it was released in November 1957, trailed by the hits 'Oh Boy!', 'Not Fade Away' and 'That'll Be the Day' – 'Everyone who played the guitar was in love with that music,' he says.

Its appeal also extended beyond the songs. The cover showed Buddy Holly cradling a Fender Stratocaster; a guitar unlike any found in Britain and as exotic to the nation's post-war adolescents as the first banana at the court of James II.

'That guitar was like something from Outer Space,' says Page. 'It was a wonderful piece of physics and design. *The "Chirping" Crickets* wasn't Mantovani, was it? This felt like a record sleeve designed for younger people. It looked like the future.'

Jimmy Page had one foot in the '70s before the '60s were over. A precocious musical talent, he became a session musician while still in his teens, playing guitar on such hits as Petula Clark's 'Downtown' and Tom Jones' 'It's Not Unusual'. Page later joined the Yardbirds and appeared with them in Antonioni's *Blow-up*, grinning serenely as Jeff Beck demolished a guitar on-stage.

In 1968, Page formed Led Zeppelin, whose music was purpose-built for arenas and stadiums. The '70s had arrived early. Like Pink Floyd, Led Zeppelin spurned the singles market and even refused to appear on television. They communicated with their growing audience via live performances and album releases only.

Led Zeppelin's fourth LP was released in November 1971, without a title. Instead, the inside sleeve contained four enigmatic runes which inspired its soubriquet, 'The Four Symbols'. Page understood the importance of image and Hipgnosis were soon on his radar.

'You'd go into a record shop and think, "Now that's a good cover," turn it over and keep seeing the name Hipgnosis,' he recalls. 'But there was one album in particular and it had a Viking on the front.'

The lyrics to Led Zeppelin's 1970 anthem 'The Immigrant Song' were about Vikings and their lead vocalist, Robert Plant, even resembled a woolly haired Norseman. 'So there was a lot of Viking-ology going on,' admits Page. 'But this was different. I've never heard the album, but I looked at the cover and thought, "Now *that* is cool."'

The album was *Argus* by Wishbone Ash. It wasn't a Viking on the sleeve, but 'a warrior of indeterminate lineage,' claimed Storm. The image suited the group's blues, folk and progressive rock, built around twin lead guitarists, Andy Powell and Ted Turner.

Wishbone Ash were managed by Miles Copeland, a young Anglo-American whose father had worked for the CIA. Copeland, who had an independent spirit and admired the same in Hipgnosis, hired them to shoot the group's publicity photos and design their previous LP, *Pilgrimage*.

In meetings with Wishbone Ash, though, Storm always homed in on bespectacled, blond-haired founding member Andy Powell. 'Because I was the spokesperson and had an A level in art,' suggests Powell. 'We'd have these conversations, which were more like therapy sessions, in Hipgnosis's disgusting premises. "Where's the toilet?" "Use that." I bet even Jimmy Page pissed in that sink.

'We'd listen to the music – which half the time I don't think Storm gave two shits about – and brainstorm ideas. But Storm also focused on me because he thought I was the most buttoned-up member of the group and he liked to shock me.'

During one therapy session around the time of *Argus*, Storm became fixated on Wishbone Ash's lead guitarists. 'Storm said, "It's all very homo-erotic, isn't it, Andy? How you and Ted weave and bob with those guitars?" I said, "Er, yeah, I guess so, groups are like that – lads together, like a military unit or the boy scouts – and a lot of our audience are lads."'

Storm proposed a cover photograph of Andy and Ted Turner kissing each other: 'A full-on lip lock,' says Andy Powell. 'Nowadays, you probably wouldn't think anything of that, but back then . . . I said, "Er, no, Storm, I get where you're coming from but I think you're going over the threshold." Storm wasn't happy. "What is the *matter* with you people? You can't give vent to what you are putting out there." He used to love confronting me like that.'

Hipgnosis looked to the album title for inspiration instead. In Greek mythology, Argus Panoptes was an all-seeing guardian so they suggested a guardian pondering an unidentified flying object overheard. 'The guardian represents the old,' explained Storm, 'and the flying saucer represents the new.'

Storm also suggested the influence of Swiss author Erich von Däniken, whose books, spearheaded by 1968's best-seller, *Chariots of the Gods?*, posited the theory that visiting extraterrestrials educated ancient civilisations and helped build the pyramids. Hipgnosis knew its market and von Däniken's ideas tapped into the hippy culture's fascination with UFOs.

Encouraged by their recent trip to Morocco, Storm and Po persuaded Miles Copeland to bankroll a jaunt to Gorges du Verdon, a river canyon 2,000 feet up in the Provence-Alpes-Côte d'Azur region of Southern France. All they needed was someone to dress up as an argus.

It wouldn't be Mick Rock. He'd recently left Hipgnosis to work with David Bowie, after meeting the singer on the first night of his Ziggy Stardust tour. 'Storm and I both said, "David . . . what? Ziggy . . . who?"' admits Po.

Rock's pictures helped define Bowie's image in the '70s and his reputation as the archetypal, louche rock 'n' roll photographer. But now there was a gap in the corner of the studio where Mick used to practise yoga.

Hipgnosis already used a floating freelance workforce of illustrators and re-touchers to do the jobs they didn't know how to. Their new studio assistant was Bruce Atkins, who was studying editorial and fashion photography, but eager for hands-on experience: 'Bruce was a whizz-kid in the darkroom,' enthuses Po, 'and an absolute genius with a Victorian sepia tone.'

'You never knew what was going to happen at the beginning of each day,' says Bruce Atkins. 'Working with Hipgnosis was a high point of my career. Storm was one of the most talented people I have ever met. He was also indecipherable and unbelievably rude but the most important lesson he taught me was to think sideways – never take the straight road ahead.'

Atkins was astonished by the chaos he found at 6 Denmark Street and used his technical skills to help turn some of Storm's more opaque ideas into reality. He was soon preparing for the trip to Gorges du Verdon.

The argus was kitted out with a cloak, a helmet, a spear and a sword, courtesy of Bermans & Nathans costumiers in London's West End. The helmet had just appeared in director Ken Russell's religious horror, *The Devils*, and the sword in Roman Polanski's film, *Macbeth*.

Storm, Po, Bruce Atkins and Gai Caron set off with the cameras, clothes and weapons stashed in a Victorian trunk. 'As always, we were in a huge rush and completely disorganised,' says Atkins. 'But we bought a British Rail insurance ticket for the props and camera gear, which turned out to be a very good idea.'

The party continued their journey by rail from Paris to Marseille then, early the following morning, by rental car to Gorges du Verdon. Storm had talked up the valley's breathtaking splendour, but everybody found its dizzying vertical drop intimidating and heavy mist obscured the scenery: 'Quite frankly, we could have been in Yorkshire,' says Po.

Po later thought his wife dressed up as the cover model. Gai couldn't recall if she had but thought it unlikely. Had she done so, it might have been Storm's subversive way of challenging Wishbone Ash's masculinity.

It was Bruce Atkins who wore the outfit. 'Storm and Po argued the whole time,' he explains. 'The reason we didn't get the shot was that they couldn't agree on anything. As we were driving back to Marseille to catch our train, we found a location and stopped at a layby. I remember being told, "Look, just stick the bloody costume on and stand there with the spear . . ."'

Storm decided Roman Polanski's sword was 'too Arthurian' and it was left against a wall next to the hire car. They took the cover photograph on the side of a hill some 50 yards from the road. 'I can remember clearly trying to cover my trainers up under the bottom of the cloak,' admits Atkins, 'because the original shot was wider than the one used on the album.'

Po insists they returned to the car and discovered the sword was missing. Atkins disagrees. 'It was not stolen,' he says. 'We drove off and left it behind on the side of the road.'

'All I remember is getting to Paris and everyone asking, "Where's the sword? Have you seen the sword?"' adds Gai.

'Roman Polanski was absolutely furious and wanted to sue,' says Atkins. 'But we claimed against British Rail, said they'd lost it, so the insurance paid up.'

The finished picture didn't reflect this disorganisation. A flying saucer was stripped into the image and became visible when the gatefold sleeve was opened flat. There was a stillness and a mystery to this argus on a French hillside – and his trainers were hidden.

Argus arrived in April 1972, reached number three in the UK and remains Wishbone Ash's biggest seller. 'I love that album and that cover,' says Andy Powell. 'I always say, "The Beatles had Peter Blake, but we had Hipgnosis."'

Five years later, director George Lucas released his space-age blockbuster *Star Wars*. Powell thought there was something familiar about villainous Darth Vader's cloak and helmet. 'Hipgnosis's work triggered the imagination,' he suggests. 'It was that post-hippy fantasy era and I'm sure some directors who were film students in the early '70s were influenced by rock 'n' roll covers.'

Bruce Atkins is more emphatic: 'When I saw Darth Vader, I thought, "Now that looks like *Argus*."'

Almost thirty-five years after the event, Atkins read a music magazine article about *Argus* in which Storm and Po claimed not to know the identity of its cover star. 'So I wrote a long letter to the magazine, telling them it was me,' he says. 'I live in the mountains in North Wales, and some fans read my letter and worked out where I was.'

Within days of the letter's publication, car loads of Wishbone Ash devotees were arriving outside Atkins's cottage, waving ancient copies of *Argus*: 'I couldn't believe it, but I signed them all anyway.'

Po arrived at Denmark Street one day in September 1972 to find Storm had just received a telephone call from Jimmy Page, praising the cover of Wishbone Ash's latest and requesting ideas for Led Zeppelin's next record: 'We were flattered, thrilled and fairly scared,' admitted Storm.

Zeppelin's four albums so far had all been top-ten hits, with the last three reaching number one. America's post-Woodstock generation – kids too young for the mid-'60s English invasion – had embraced their elemental hard rock. Zeppelin's potential endorsement meant millions of new consumers, including other groups, opening a record sleeve and seeing the name Hipgnosis.

Hipgnosis had two ideas. One had shades of Erich von Däniken and Robert Smithson's land art and involved bulldozing Jimmy Page's rune, ZOSO, into the plains of Nazca in southern Peru. They took the second from Arthur C. Clarke's *Childhood's End*, where the earth's children are spirited away from Planet Earth by extraterrestrials to take the next evolutionary step.

'We wanted to photograph a naked nuclear family – mother, father and two children – being led to safety by an alien,' says Po, who proposed covering his models with body paint and shooting them clambering over the rocks of the Giant's Causeway. Towards some 'unseen magical power force,' added Storm.

The Giant's Causeway on the north coast of County Antrim, Northern Island, was a natural wonder of hexagonal-shaped basalt columns, running from the cliffs down into the North Channel strait. The name comes from a Gaelic myth in which Irish and Scottish giants built the causeway so they could cross the strait and fight each other to the death.

Po remembers being summoned to Led Zeppelin's management's office at 155 Oxford Street. All four band members were present. Robert Plant was effusive and friendly, and drummer John Bonham was nursing a hangover. Bass guitarist John Paul Jones, a softly spoken session musician who'd accidentally become a rock star, barely spoke, while Jimmy Page puffed away on a cigarette, waif-like and inscrutable, but not missing a word of what was being said.

Storm and Po delivered their pitches. 'We had these things sketched out on scraps of paper,' says Po. 'I think we even sat cross-legged on the floor. It was so amateur.'

Plant, whose lyrics touched on Celtic mythology and *The Lord of the Rings*, loved the idea of the Giant's Causeway. 'Hipgnosis were really switched-on and their glossary was incredible,' recalled Plant. 'They had very bright, sharp, iridescent ideas and great reference points, a huge number of places to go in the world of art and surrealist film and photography.' Equally, Page knew all about the plains of Nazca, where ancient Peruvians had etched over 800 geometrical lines and drawings of trees and animals into a vast expanse of river basin.

Led Zeppelin's manager, Peter Grant, oversaw the meeting from behind a large mahogany desk. Grant – or 'G' as he was nicknamed – was a heavyweight, 6-foot-3 former wrestler and doorman, who'd spent the '50s and early '60s chauffeuring Gene Vincent and bouncing drunks out of Soho nightclubs.

Grant was a generation older than his charges, but had grown a Zapata moustache and beard and cultivated his thinning hair down to his shoulders. He looked like he should be striding across the Giant's Causeway in search of rival ogres. 'Peter was intimidating,' says Po. 'He had this nasally south London accent and when he spoke, you listened.'

Grant told Hipgnosis they should decide which cover idea to pursue but to do so quickly. Zeppelin were about to tour Japan and needed the artwork when they returned. Storm and Po bowled out of 155 Oxford Street with Grant's warning ringing in their ears: 'Don't fuck up!'

Once they were back in the studio, Po realised they hadn't discussed money and called Grant immediately. G casually informed him there wasn't a budget for the cover and to contact Zeppelin's accountant for an advance – 'It costs what it costs,' he said.

'There was a degree of trust there that we'd never encountered before,' admits Po. 'That essence of feeling wanted and having the freedom to do what you wanted was just extraordinary.'

One of Peter Grant's former associates described his management style like so: 'You were either on the bus or under the bus.'

In Jimmy Page's version of the story, one of Hipgnosis was under the bus already.

Page believes only he, Storm and Peter Grant were present at that initial meeting in Oxford Street. 'But beforehand we'd sent Hipgnosis a tape of the new album,' he insists. 'So they could listen to it, be inspired, get a feel for things.'

Led Zeppelin's fifth album, *Houses of the Holy*, paired its heavy-metal *Sturm und Drang* with dreamy ballads, folk-rock, funk and even reggae. Page produced Zeppelin's music with scientific attention to nuance and detail. He expected Hipgnosis to take it seriously.

'Storm came in and showed us various cover ideas,' Page recalls. 'I wondered which had been rejected by other bands and which he'd done after actually listening to the album.'

Page's gimlet eye settled on one particular image. 'It was an electric green tennis court with a net and a racket. I said, "What's this?" Storm replied, "It's a racket . . . Get it . . . a racket?" I said, "Hang on . . . Just hang on . . ." Bear in mind I've given him a tape to listen to. "Are you saying our music's a racket?" And Storm says, "Yeah . . ." I went, "Oh, no, no, no, no . . ."'

Led Zeppelin's artwork to date had included burning airships and cryptic symbols with possibly devilish connotations. 'So we needed something interesting,' stresses Page. 'I presumed whatever Hipgnosis came up with was going to be great. Maybe I'm overly sensitive, and I'm taking it too personally, but we'd just made a really good album and now somebody had described it as a racket.'

'So that was my unfortunate meeting with Storm Thorgerson and my introduction to these people. But I knew there were two of them in Hipgnosis, so I said, "Right, get us the other guy." So Po comes in and he has the idea of going to the Giant's Causeway. And I thought, "Wow! Now that's cool."'

However, Po is certain Storm's faux-pas with the tennis racket happened a year later when pitching ideas for Led Zeppelin's *Physical Graffiti* album.

Despite Storm's bullishness, Hipgnosis's pioneer spirit still impressed him. 'I realised you weren't going to get these ideas coming from just anyone and they were going to cost money,' admits Page. 'I saw Hipgnosis as a movement and an art form but it was Po we dealt with from then on.'

'The double act was amazing,' recalled Robert Plant. 'The charming, amiable bonhomie of Aubrey and the belligerent "Do I have to deal with these scum musicians?" approach from Storm. It was marvellous and everything we deserved at the time.'

As adventurous as Hipgnosis were, a photo shoot at the Giant's Causeway was easier to organise than bulldozing the River Grande de Nazca. It was Po who made the trip, with photographer Alex Henderson as his assistant. Henderson had just helped Hipgnosis shoot a cover for the folk-rock group String Driven Thing. Their fancy-dressed models included Royal Shakespeare Company actress and future dame, Helen Mirren.

Emo was offered a job on *Houses of the Holy* but turned it down: 'I thought, "Northern Ireland, war, troubles" – and it was October.' Duggie Fields' old flatmate, Jules Laughton, was hired to play the extraterrestrial instead; Gai Caron as the family's mother, model Mark Sayer as the father and child models, seven-year-old Samantha Gates and her five-year-old brother, Stefan, as their offspring. The *Houses of the Holy* family were all blonde and the siblings reminded Storm of the identical telepathic children in John Wyndham's novel, *The Midwich Cuckoos*.

The group flew to Belfast in the first week of October 1972. Earlier that year, the British military had shot thirteen civilians dead during a protest march. The Irish Republican Army's bloody campaign for independence had since escalated. British accents aroused suspicion and the boss at McCausland Car Hire advised them all to stay out of the city. After the umpteenth military roadblock, Po wondered 'if maybe we should have gone to Peru instead'.

After checking into the Bayview Hotel in Portballintrae, Po and Alex Henderson scouted their location. The Giant's Causeway was spectacular but daunting. The forecast predicted torrential rain and nobody was braving these treacherous rocks under those conditions.

The following day started at 4 a.m. Jules Laughton's long dark hair had to be concealed under a punishingly tight bald skull cap. Hipgnosis's make-up artist, Tom Smith, also needed two hours to spray-paint his models gold and silver. Smith was a film industry veteran who later transformed Jack Nicholson into a psychopath for *The Shining* and Ben Kingsley into Mahatma Gandhi.

'It was a fucking nightmare,' says Alex Henderson. 'We had to lie everyone down on special sheets before we sprayed them and we couldn't put them in clothes or a dressing gown straight away because the paint had to dry. So they're lying there freezing cold in this moth-eaten hotel without central heating.'

Down on the Causeway, the sun hid behind grey clouds and the rain bounced off the hire car roofs. Inside the vehicles, adults sipped hot coffee while the children shivered under blankets. Po marched up and down, his sheepskin coat and flared jeans flapping in the gale, before calling the shoot off. By late morning, the children's mother, Jean Gates, was back at the hotel, sponging the paint off her kids – 'Jean was remarkably good-natured about the whole thing,' admits Po.

The bad weather endured for the next two days and the mood plummeted after the third failed attempt. Jean was concerned for her children's welfare and Tom Smith admitted he only had enough body paint left for one more session.

'Tom had been using coloured hairspray,' explains Henderson, 'because it washes off easily, the skin can breathe and you don't end up doing a *Goldfinger*.' Henderson drove Smith to the nearest chemist's, but there wasn't much demand for coloured hairspray in '70s County Antrim. Tom Smith was in his mid-forties, soberly dressed and didn't attract attention, unlike twenty-something Alex Henderson.

'I was young and pretty, with hair down to here and stood in the chemist's shop with this old bloke,' says Henderson. 'Tom put his bag down and suddenly we were surrounded by police officers with machine guns – "What's in the bag?" "Er . . . make-up."'

The Royal Ulster Constabulary officers eventually lowered their weapons. Desperate to salvage the shoot, somebody suggested using car spray paint instead. The duo headed for the nearest garage: 'We knew we couldn't put this paint on the kids, but we could try it out on Jules, but not tell him first,' admits Henderson.

The following day, the adult models took a glug of brandy and swallowed a Mandrax each. The euphoric blur took some of the sting out of clambering naked over a chilly rockface in October. But Po quickly realised their original idea of the alien leading the family to safety would not work: 'The scene looked more comical than dramatic.'

The plan was abandoned and he photographed Samantha and Stefan alone, using black-and-white film. Hipgnosis could duplicate the two children and the rocks and change the colour back at the studio. The picture was also closer to the climax of Arthur C. Clarke's novel, where the adults are left behind and the children spirited away. The eventual cover shoot took less than an hour.

For the inside gatefold picture, they chose Dunluce Castle, a Medieval ruin 5 miles from the Causeway. Its jagged battlements provided a striking backdrop for Jules, naked except for his bald skull cap, holding up Samantha like a sacrificial offering. The picture made it look easy, but Po had to help lift the child over his head.

Later, back at the hotel, Hipgnosis's alien made a grim discovery in the bath: 'Jules started shouting, "It won't fucking come off!"' Alex Henderson sheepishly confessed they'd used car spray instead of hairspray. Jules's natural colour was only restored after a generous application of Turps.

Hipgnosis returned to London with an image markedly different from the one they'd sold to Led Zeppelin. They replicated Samantha and Stefan and created a collage of eleven children climbing over the Giant's Causeway – the mother and father were left on the cutting-room floor.

Mark Sayer recalled the shoot twenty-five years later: 'Brandy, Mandrax, freezing rain, car paint,' he said. 'Turpentine, tepid baths, bad food, boredom, damp beds and misery. And then they didn't use me and shot it in black and white anyway.'

Both the inside and outside cover images were re-photographed and delivered to freelance artist Philip Crennell for hand tinting. After seeing a hand-tinted photo of the Himalayas in a Sunday newspaper, Hipgnosis started hiring different artists to colour their images. Armed with sable brushes and steady hands, they were the 1970s equivalent of today's Photoshop.

Crennell lived and worked from a dilapidated boat on the River Thames. Hipgnosis instructed him to turn the sky blazing red and the Giant's Causeway a brilliant turquoise and green. Crennell was busy renovating his vessel and took several weeks to finish the commission. Po's nerves jangled every time Peter Grant telephoned the office looking for his 'fucking cover'.

It was December before Po finally retrieved the artwork from Crennell's boat. Led Zeppelin had just played Birmingham Odeon and Grant and Jimmy Page were catching a train to London and expecting to see a cover. Po met them outside St Pancras station with the artwork stashed in the boot of his Mini Cooper.

To Po's horror, Grant told him they needed a lift to Victoria station. Jimmy Page slid effortlessly into the back as Grant folded his giant frame into the passenger seat. Peter's enormous knee dwarfed the lever, but Po managed to get the car into first gear and drive away.

It was the longest 4 miles of his life. Po listened to the pair analysing the previous night's performance, but neither of them mentioned *Houses of the Holy*. This was one of Grant's psychological tricks: making his subject wait for urgent feedback or information.

Once at Victoria, Grant unfolded himself from inside the Mini and asked to see the cover. The car boot flipped open, to reveal Hipgnosis's ethereal landscape and its luminescent inhabitants. Nobody spoke for a few seconds until Page finally cracked a smile. It was the sign Grant had been waiting for: 'Well done, Po,' he beamed.

'I thought it looked absolutely beautiful,' says Jimmy Page today.

A crowd of onlookers, who'd gathered around the rock star and his escort, broke into a round of applause. Grant and Page sauntered off to catch their train and Po breathed a sigh of relief, but the job wasn't over yet.

★

Storm and Po had created a game-changing piece of art, but nobody foresaw the impact it would have: 'We still staggered along week to week,' says Bruce Atkins, 'and there never seemed to be any money.'

Artistically, though, Hipgnosis were becoming more confident. Storm regularly contradicted his theory that there was nothing duller than a band photograph. But he justified it by giving Emerson Lake & Palmer's faces an art nouveau treatment on their new album *Trilogy* or covering soft-rockers Quiver's faces with spiders' webs.

There were still hits and misses. The folk-rock group Trees' LP, *On the Shore*, showed an inscrutable-looking girl in Victorian clothing throwing a glass of water in the grounds of a stately home. There was something of Frances Hodgson Burnett's *The Secret Garden* or Henry James' ghost stories about the image. Contrastingly, the Climax Blues Band's *Tightly Knit* showed a bald male model with a sock in his mouth – 'Probably a bit left of centre for a blues-rock band,' observes Po.

Bare bodies remained a reliable go-to. Gai Caron thinks it's her bottom on the Yes offshoot Flash's second album: 'But I'm not entirely sure.' ('It is,' confirms Po.) While Electric Light Orchestra's *ELO II* showed a semi-abstract image of a girl's open legs, a star constellation protecting her modesty.

Not everybody was a fan. When a burglar broke into the studio and failed to find the cameras, he ripped a print of country-rockers Cochise's bare-breasted album sleeve off the wall. The intruder tore the picture into tiny pieces and then defecated on the studio floor.

Hipgnosis's offering for Pink Floyd's soundtrack album, *Obscured By Clouds*, was a happy accident. Barbet Schroeder's latest movie, *La Vallée*, was about a French diplomat's wife discovering her sexual self in the jungles of Papua New Guinea. Storm and Po worked through a pile of 35-mm slides taken from the film. One was an outtake of its male lead, Mark Frechette, standing in a tree. When the projector's lens jammed, the image was thrown out of focus.

The tree's blurred foliage reminded them of the oil slide projections at UFO. But those hours Storm spent studying art books at Earl Street also hadn't been forgotten. Hipgnosis later compared the picture to French painter Georges Seurat's pointillist art, where patterns of tiny dots created an image.

'*Obscured by Clouds*,' ponders Nick Mason. 'Hipgnosis probably did drop the ball a little bit with that one.'

Pink Floyd were still exploring ideas outside mainstream rock 'n' roll and drawn towards the big screen. The soundtrack followed Floyd's earlier contributions to Antonioni's latest movie, *Zabriskie Point*. In October 1971, a young French director, Adrian Maben, also filmed the group performing in the ghostly ruins of the Roman amphitheatre at Pompeii for a documentary and concert movie – 'I suppose it seems silly now,' says David Gilmour, 'but we thought of films as one of our possible futures.'

Pink Floyd were also approached to score avant-garde choreographer Roland Petit's ballet version of Marcel Proust's multipart novel, *À la recherche du temps perdu* (*In Search of Lost Time*). This involved being asked to read all seven volumes of the source material – 'I thought, "Fuck this,"' said Roger Waters. 'It goes too slowly for me, I can't handle it.' Instead, Floyd later appeared with Roland Petit's dance company, Le Ballets de Marseille, playing their greatest non-hits, including 'Echoes' and 'Careful with That Axe, Eugene' – 'But the reality of these people prancing around in tights in front of us didn't feel like what we wanted to do long term,' admitted Gilmour.

As soon as *Obscured by Clouds* was released, Pink Floyd went back to working on their new studio record. 'I had a strong, compelling notion that we could make an album about feelings, the human condition and things that impinge upon us,' said Waters. 'I was twenty-nine and suddenly realised, "This was life. This was not a rehearsal. Life was happening now."'

His peer group understood. These were post-war boys who'd turned a teenage pastime into a career and were all approaching thirty. Po had wed again and Storm and Libby January now had a baby son, Bill. Everybody in Pink Floyd, apart from David Gilmour, was married and Mason and Wright had become fathers.

Roger Waters' study of the human condition was fundamental and far-reaching. It was about money, violence, religion, travel, mortality, the fear of madness, good and bad, light and shade . . . Pink Floyd began road-testing what would become *The Dark Side of the Moon* in January 1972 and a bootleg recorded at London's Rainbow Theatre was released almost a year before the finished album.

Syd Barrett attended one of the Rainbow shows in February: 'Lurking in the hall,' said an eyewitness. 'Looking taut and gaunt.' Barrett inhabited some of these new songs, like the ghost of Pink Floyd past. It was as if Waters couldn't shake off the remorse he felt over his friend's demise.

The songs 'Brain Damage' and 'Eclipse', especially, traced a straight line from '60s Cambridge to '70s London. Lyrics about a 'lunatic on the grass' alluded to Syd Barrett and every other Morning Glory tripper still trying to find their way back to normality.

'It was about the stretch of lawn between the Cam and King's College Chapel,' explained Waters. 'That was always the piece of grass more than any other piece of grass that I felt I was constrained to "keep off".

'There was a residue of Syd in all this. When you see that happening to someone you've been close friends with, it concentrates one's mind on how ephemeral one's mental capacities can be. There but for the grace of God go I.'

The Dark Side of the Moon's music was as direct as its lyrics, but augmented with gorgeous gospel-like backing vocals, chiming clocks, beating hearts and horror-movie screams. There were spoken-word vignettes between songs, where Floyd roadies and familiars discussed madness and violence and whether there was indeed a dark side of the moon ('As a matter of fact, it's all dark . . .'). It was like eavesdropping on a conversation.

The dynamic within the group had also shifted. David Gilmour was no longer the new boy and the album's clarity and focus were achieved by him and Waters fighting their respective corners. The pair tussled over the final mix and the Beatles' former studio assistant Chris Thomas was brought in to referee.

'I can remember having a fantastic run-through of the final album and we all turned round and went, "Fuck me, that's brilliant,"' says Gilmour. 'We knew *The Dark Side of the Moon* was going to be more successful than anything we'd ever done. And the album cover tied it all together.'

Months earlier, Storm and Po had taken the group to Belsize Park for a photo shoot. They'd turned up at Storm's tennis club, wearing worn-out jeans and T-shirts, with Gilmour sporting a tatty velvet jacket: 'Before that moment, Floyd were a enigmatic, mysterious band who hid on stage behind a light show,' says Po. 'They rarely gave interviews or had their picture taken.'

Feeling comfortable around old friends, though, Floyd laughed, joked, covered their faces and sucked in their cheeks like fashion models. 'They're the only photographs I've seen of Pink Floyd since the earliest days where they look like a happy-go-lucky band, enjoying each other's company,' stresses Po.

'They'd made a fantastic album and they were on the cusp of enormous success.'

In December, Hipgnosis received the album title and *The Dark Side of the Moon*'s lyrics before an invitation to Abbey Road to hear the music. Adrian Maben's film, *Pink Floyd: Live at Pompeii*, included his interview with the group. There was something gladiatorial about the encounter, with Waters blowing smoke rings at his interrogator and answering every question with another: 'What do you mean . . . *happy*?'

Storm and Po were familiar with this verbal hazing but Storm still bristled when Rick Wright told him he didn't want 'one of your surreal ideas' for their next album: 'He challenged me in an extremely annoying fashion, to design something graphic and not pictorial,' he said.

'Rick wanted something simpler,' recalls Po, 'and he suggested something like the artwork on a Black Magic box of chocolates.' There was much braying laughter, but Hipgnosis couldn't ignore the client.

'Storm and I invented many stories as to how we arrived at the design for *The Dark Side of the Moon*,' admits Po. Storm said it was inspired by Pink Floyd's light show and came from glimpsing a prismatic reflection in a shop's revolving glass door; Po claimed it was from a photo of a prism placed on a stack of sheet music. Like Coca-Cola refusing to divulge every ingredient in its secret recipe, Hipgnosis wanted to maintain some mystery.

In 2022, though, Po revealed they'd discovered the image in a 1963 physics textbook, *The How and Why Wonder Book of Light and Color*. It was one of many second-hand books lying around the studio or Storm and Libby's flat, waiting to be plundered for inspiration. There, under the heading 'How to Make a Rainbow', was a drawing of a triangular prism with a ray of white light passing through and emerging, in multiple colours, on the other side. It was the back and front cover design of *The Dark Side of the Moon* in embryonic form.

'Remember that triangle, Storm,' urged Nigel Lesmoir-Gordon in his letter from India in 1968. And here was the triangle four years later. 'It was all serendipity,' as Po would say.

Hipgnosis hired George Hardie, from the design group NTA Studios, to create a maquette of the prism. Hardie had drawn Led Zeppelin I's flaming airship while a student at the Royal College of Art, but hadn't considered it worthy of submission towards his course. It was the beginning of a long working relationship between Hardie and Hipgnosis: 'I didn't have a record player,' Hardie later divulged. 'But I was always interested in ideas – and Hipgnosis always had ideas.'

Storm and Po returned to Abbey Road in December, with several ideas, including a variation on Marvel's Silver Surfer: a hangover, perhaps, from the cosmic Pink Floyd of *A Saucerful of Secrets*. 'I don't know what we were thinking,' says Po. 'But at the time it seemed like a good idea.'

The four musicians filed into the control room of Studio 2. Cigarettes were lit and curtains of hair parted, as the group perused Hipgnosis's designs. It only took a few minutes. 'There was no argument about it,' says Roger Waters. 'They came in with a few mock-ups and we all pointed to the prism and went, "That one." George Hardie's prism was beautiful.'

This snap decision took the wind out of Storm's sails. He'd braced himself for a fight but none was forthcoming. 'I loved Storm's concepts,' insists Waters, 'but we made our decision without allowing him to bang on for an hour about his other ideas or his philosophical notions of what it all was or wasn't about.'

The final cover was Hardie's airbrushed illustration of the prism and spectrum, with indigo and violet merged to make them stand out against the black background. Waters suggested extending the spectrum into the inside gatefold, to become a graphic representation of the heartbeat on the opening track, 'Speak to Me'.

The sleeve was only part of the story, though. Hipgnosis wanted the package to also include posters and stickers relating to the prism. For this, Storm proposed photographing the Great Pyramid of Cheops. 'We said, "Yeah, but Storm, that will cost a fortune,"' recalls Waters, 'And he said, "Yeah . . . So?" Another free trip to Timbuk-fucking-tu.'

In January 1973, Po, Gai, Storm, Libby and one-year-old Bill arrived in Cairo. 'We were in the queue at BA to get on the plane and Storm, unafraid of anyone and never embarrassed, began to scamper up on and down all fours,' recalls Po. 'He was pretending to be a dog, which Bill, who was crawling at that stage, found very entertaining. But after fifteen minutes I could see the exasperation in Libby's face. There were problems between Storm and Libby on that trip.'

Their mission ground to a halt a couple of days later when Po was stricken by an explosive stomach bug: 'The Nile was coming out of my bum.' Within hours, the others were similarly afflicted, except for Storm.

'Egypt was not a great experience for Libby, left alone in a hotel to deal with a sick baby and having great difficulty explaining what she required from the hotel staff,' says Po. 'Gai tried to help but it was complicated. Storm dumped Libby at the hotel and went off to take photos.'

'I decided to go to the pyramids on my own,' recalled Storm. 'At two o'clock in the morning. I hired a taxi to take me out there, thinking I'd be fine. I put the camera on the tripod to take a long exposure. It was a wonderful, clear night, the moon was fantastic and then suddenly I saw these figures come walking across — soldiers, with guns. I thought, "This is it."'

The soldiers explained in broken English that Storm was in the middle of a firing range and would have been shot during daylight hours. Baksheesh changed hands and Storm was allowed to carry on taking pictures: 'Though I was scared shitless,' he admitted.

For years after, Hipgnosis's poster of the Great Pyramid would decorate bedroom walls and student digs around the world, its owners unaware of the domestic upheaval, military intervention and stomach bugs involved in acquiring the picture.

Storm and his family flew home, but Po had more business to attend to. Jimmy Page had heard about the trip and had despatched Po on a covert mission to the Egyptian Museum in Cairo, home to some of the world's oldest Pharaonic exhibits.

Page was a scholar of Aleister Crowley, the writer, artist and Elvis Presley of occultists. Crowley regarded himself as a prophet and magician and in 1904 founded Thelema, a spiritual philosophy which cherrypicked from Eastern mysticism, Egyptian mythology and the occult. After he died in 1947, Crowley attracted a new generation of disciples drawn to his libertarian credo, Page among them: 'I feel Aleister Crowley is a misunderstood genius of the twentieth century,' he told *Rolling Stone*. Page purchased Crowley's old ruin, Boleskine House, at Loch Ness and had his mission statement, 'Do What Thou Wilt, So Mote It Be . . .' etched into the run-off grooves of Led Zeppelin's third album.

The Egyptian Museum's exhibits included the Stele of Ankhef-en-Khonsu (also known as the Stele of Revealing), an artefact from 680BC, depicting the three principal Egyptian gods of Thelema. Crowley had tried to purchase the Stele but had been refused – Page now wanted Po to bid on his behalf.

'Egypt was on high alert at the time,' says Po. 'The Yom Kippur War with Israel started a few months later so there was a military presence everywhere in Cairo and paranoia ran deep. The museum was already surrounded by sandbags in case of an air attack. There were no tourists anywhere and most of the exhibits had been hidden away.'

The museum's director had never heard of Led Zeppelin, but agreed to show Po the Stele. The coveted relic was stashed away in the basement. Po glimpsed dust-covered treasures, by murky torchlight, as he and the director wound their way along gloomy corridors further and further down into the vaults.

Some years later, Po was reminded of Indiana Jones' archaeological treasure hunt in *Raiders of the Lost Ark*, but minus the snake pit: 'Finally, there was the Stele in this wooden case. Very, very spooky. I got chills just looking,' he says. 'Peter Grant had told me to bid as much as I could. I think I went up to $25,000 or something. But the museum had no intention of selling.' Instead, the director offered to make a plaster cast for Page, just as the museum had once done for Aleister Crowley – 'I told Peter he could have a replica for two grand. But who knows what happened after that?'

Nine years later, Page appeared, cradling a replica of the Stele, in Crowley aficionado Kenneth Anger's movie, *Lucifer Rising*. 'Frankly, Jimmy was more delighted that someone else had paid for my air ticket,' suggests Po. 'He thought it funny that it was Pink Floyd.'

'I think it's good that Storm did his things with Pink Floyd and Po worked with us,' says Page. 'Between them, Steve O'Rourke and Peter Grant also really knew how to deal with the record companies.'

This was borne out, two months later, when Grant sent Po to New York to oversee the printing of artwork for *Houses of the Holy*. This was not the era of email or file transfer, it was an analogue age when the artwork was photographically recorded, turned into film and transformed into an LP sleeve on a lithographic printing machine resembling something from a nineteenth-century cotton mill. There weren't any international courier systems and goods could be detained for months if a customs declaration form was mislabelled. *Houses of the Holy* was expected to be a huge seller and Atlantic couldn't afford any delay: 'Peter Grant was not someone to take chances,' says Po. 'So I was sent to hand deliver the art to Atlantic.'

Led Zeppelin paid for Po's first-class flight on Pan American Airways. It was his initiation into their world and the power they commanded. The group's sales had turned them into a multi-million-dollar entity. Within a year, Peter Grant would reshape the business model further, by demanding a 90/10 per cent split of ticket sales revenue in the group's favour. The industry standard was a 60/40 per cent split. Ten per cent of a Led Zeppelin concert was still a lot of money, but Grant's coup enraged promoters and booking agents who'd been stripped of their percentages and their power.

Zeppelin also licensed their music to Atlantic Records and had never signed directly to the label. This meant Atlantic's co-founder and president, Ahmet Ertegun, often had to answer to Peter Grant. On Po's last New York visit, he'd had to beg Motown's art director for a ten-dollar cab fare. Now he was briefing the man whose company had signed Otis Redding and Aretha Franklin.

Po delivered the artwork and impressed on Ertegun the importance of the colours. Ertegun assured him their printers would do his bidding but when the proofs came back, Samantha and Stefan had turned bright purple.

'I stopped the print run and had a massive argument with the record company,' says Po. 'I was convinced the printers hadn't given it 100 per cent. Being young and impetuous I decided to go home and even went to the airport.'

When he arrived, Po telephoned Grant's American lawyer, Stevens Weiss, to explain the situation. Weiss was Grant's consigliere, had previously brokered deals between mob-connected families and was on first-name terms with the Mafia's so-called accountant, Meyer Lansky. Po was told to go back to the city and await further instructions.

Peter Grant then informed Ertegun that Atlantic wouldn't be getting Led Zeppelin's new album until the artwork was completed to their satisfaction. The result of this conversation was both speedy and miraculous. Twenty-four hours later, Po collected a set of perfect prints.

Hipgnosis and Led Zeppelin learned something about each other on this trip. Storm and Po wouldn't accept second best and Page and Grant would support them in their pursuit of excellence even if that meant withholding an album: 'I was tenacious,' admits Po. 'I wanted the best for me and them, and the devil takes the high road.'

As Po was already in New York, Steve O'Rourke asked him to fly on to Los Angeles. Pink Floyd's US label, Capitol Records, was preparing to release *The Dark Side of the Moon* and was using the artwork in their promotional campaign. Suddenly, Po was the in-demand English designer jet-setting across America.

He boarded the 747 'Friday Night Special' from JKF to LAX airport. Every weekend, the first-class cabin became an airborne party bus for East Coasters wanting to spend the weekend in

California. Within minutes of take-off, Po was sipping Champagne and being offered cocaine: 'When I came back from the States that first time, I'd said to Storm, "I am never going there again." But now here I was and it was remarkably different.'

Po arrived at Continental Hyatt House (nicknamed 'The Riot House' after its reputation for indulging rock-star misbehaviour) and marvelled at his glamorous surroundings. Palm tree-lined Sunset Boulevard was a world away from the overflowing dustbins of Denmark Street.

A Midsummer Night's Dream was playing in LA and Po joined Terry Taplin and his friends in the Royal Shakespeare Company on an overnight trip to Las Vegas. The RSC had a complimentary table for Elvis Presley's performance at the Hilton Hotel. 'The first rock 'n' roll record I ever bought was "Heartbreak Hotel", and the first music film I saw was *GI Blues*,' says Po. 'My group at school played "Blue Suede Shoes" and "I'm Left, You're Right, She's Gone". This was the music I'd grown up on.'

The Elvis of the '50s was rather different from this one, with his heavier jowls and rhinestone-studded jumpsuit, but it didn't matter. It was almost ten years since Po had been thrown out of school, for spending too much time playing guitar; the concert was an adolescent dream come true: 'Elvis sang all the hits and was the perfect showman.'

Just over a month after the American trip came Hipgnosis's long-awaited number-one hit. *The Dark Side of the Moon* reached the UK top ten before topping the American charts. Roger Waters claimed that when he first played the album to his wife Judy she burst into tears: 'She was very moved by it,' he said. 'I thought, "That's a very good sign."'

David Gilmour was confident of a UK hit, but not necessarily elsewhere: 'I had a bet with Steve O'Rourke. We had never been anywhere near the top ten in the States and I bet *The Dark Side of the Moon* wouldn't go top ten and he bet it would, and he was very right and I was very wrong. But I knew when I took the bet I couldn't lose.'

Capitol had insisted on trailering the album with a US-only single, 'Money', which reached number thirteen. Pink Floyd's American audience changed almost overnight. By spring 1973, they were selling out ice-hockey arenas instead of university gymnasiums and Andy Warhol was on the guest list for their date at New York's Radio City Music Hall.

'Massive droves of people started to turn up,' recalls Gilmour, 'and there was an immediate difference between the slightly more reverential audiences we were used to and the new ones who just wanted to hear the hit single and have a party.'

'Money', Roger Waters' stinging critique of financial gluttony, would come back and bite him later. *The Dark Side of the Moon* would sell in such vast quantities Pink Floyd would become part of the 'high-fidelity, first-class travelling set' lampooned in the song.

Waters wasn't the only one pondering the struggle between art and commerce. Neither Storm nor Po considered *The Dark Side of the Moon* their greatest work, but it would become their most famous. Storm later described the image as 'a blatant shop-front manoeuvre', knowing that multiple *Dark Side* sleeves would be plastered across record-shop windows, creating an endless spectrum to lure customers through the doors.

David Gale had recently co-founded a theatre company, Lumiere & Son, who'd also draw on Hipgnosis's services. Gale spotted a link between the cover and aspects of Sant Mat: 'Storm was aware of that,' he says. 'There are spiritual ideas, homilies and banalities in that elegant design. Rays, beams, colours and essences were so popular back then.'

Storm and Po both read American writer Carlos Castaneda's book, *A Separate Reality*, about a Yaqui Indian sorcerer, which included a scene where spiritual rays emerged from a character's torso. Rays were in vogue then and would soon re-appear in Hipgnosis's art for singer-songwriter Al Stewart and country-rock band Unicorn.

More than 50 million album sales later, *The Dark Side of the Moon* became a separate entity from the rest of the catalogue. It was a Pink Floyd album for people who don't always like Pink Floyd. Similarly, Hipgnosis's artwork was instantly recognisable to those who don't have a clue about their other works.

Storm and Po received £5,000 for the sleeve and, as the years passed, Storm started to believe they'd been underpaid. But in the spring of 1973, the company had a second hit to enjoy.

Houses of the Holy arrived four weeks after Pink Floyd's latest and swept to the top of the British and American charts. However, some Bible Belt states deemed its naked children offensive. Unusually, Led Zeppelin compromised and the album was re-packaged in certain territories with a wrap-around paper band displaying the group's name and the LP's title and covering the bare flesh – 'There was never anything smutty or seedy about it,' protests Page.

Hipgnosis hired NTA Studios' Bush Hollyhead to design the wrapper. Hollyhead's hand-drawn lettering was done on the fly but would become Led Zeppelin's official logo. The LP was nominated for Best Album Package at the 1974 Grammy Awards, but lost out to the orchestral version of the Who's rock musical, *Tommy*.

Decades later, Jimmy Page saw the cover-shoot outtakes, showing Mark Sayer on the Giant's Causeway. He found the flaxen-haired model's resemblance to Robert Plant off-putting.

Like many great rock 'n' roll partnerships, Page and Plant's was often fractious.

'If Po had said to me, "I am going to have an earth mother and an earth father, and the earth father is going to look suspiciously like Robert Plant," I would have given him the Storm Thorgerson treatment,' says Page. '"Hang on a minute, we're not having a clone of Robert Plant on the cover. What the hell are you talking about?"'

'I chose Mark because he was blond and had a good body and looked like he could be the boy and girl's father,' counters Po. 'It never once occurred to me that he looked like Robert Plant.'

During the 1980s a rumour circulated that the girl on the sleeve was the British glamour model Samantha Fox as a child. Fox had attended theatre school before appearing topless in the tabloids and becoming a household name. Even Jimmy Page wondered if the rumour was true: 'It could have been her, couldn't it?' he says.

The actual model, Samantha Gates, worked with Hipgnosis again and her brother, Stefan, made a BBC radio documentary about the cover shoot in 2010. Only then did he listen to *Houses of the Holy* for the first time: 'Before that, I found the cover enormously scary,' he said. 'It was very apocalyptic and the image followed me around like a cloud for years.'

In 1971, Storm told the BBC that Hipgnosis enjoyed knowing there was 'a quarter of a million homes with a little piece of us in them.' *The Dark Side of the Moon* and *Houses of the Holy* expanded that number – and some. But, like Waters and Gilmour or Page and Plant, the relationship in Hipgnosis had changed.

'After we did *Houses of the Holy* and I went to America on my own, it was different between Storm and I,' says Po. 'It was never going to be quite the same again.'

Chapter 6

'If he makes a move, hit him with that spanner!'

In which Hipgnosis get rejected by the Stones, seduced by a Beatle, hire a mysterious new recruit and experience the real dark side of the moon.

'I'm Sagittarius – half-man/half-horse – with a licence to shit in the street.'

– Keith Richards

Sometime in 1973, Hipgnosis almost drowned a member of Argent. The group had recently had a hit single, 'Hold Your Head Up', and were being photographed underwater for their new album, *In Deep*. Both titles tempted fate.

Po was shooting from a windowed corridor looking into Crystal Palace swimming pool when he noticed one of his subjects gasping for air. The musician was dragged out of the pool and driven home. He'd agreed to the shoot but hadn't told anyone he couldn't swim. *In Deep*'s gatefold sleeve later showed the four members of Argent in the pool, but with one looking like he'd never been underwater before in his life.

It wasn't the first time water had figured in one of Hipgnosis's concepts and caused problems. That same year, Po threw a bucket of water over Peter Frampton for the cover of his new album, *Somethin's Happening*. As willing to indulge Hipgnosis as he was, there were consequences. Frampton started complaining of a pain in his eardrum, at which point Po realised he'd forgotten to provide him with protective plugs – 'In hindsight, it wasn't such a good idea for a musician,' he admits.

Not every shoot went as well as those two. 'There were so many false starts,' says studio assistant/photographer Bruce Atkins. 'You'd set something up and it just didn't happen. It's one of the reasons I left.'

Atkins quit the company in the summer of 1973. One of the tipping points was an aborted photo shoot in Somerset: 'I think it was for the Edgar Broughton Band. But what I do know is we drove all the way there in Storm's Austin A40, with him talking non-stop. We arrived at this big house, but everybody was out of their heads and wouldn't move so we packed up the gear and went back to London. It was such a waste of time.'

Storm had taught Atkins to think laterally and he wanted to take that skill into a different medium: 'Storm impressed me so much. He'd think up an idea for an album cover, which had absolutely nothing to do with what we were talking about, but he'd convince the artist this was the solution. A year after I left, I worked on three feature films. None of that would have happened without Hipgnosis.'

In the meantime, freelance designer Richard Evans started work at the studio. Evans was a Nottingham School of Art graduate, who'd previously run a shoe-making business, Daisy Roots, in Knightsbridge. He and Po first met on the night of the first moon landing: 'This groovy couple arrived at the house,' remembers Evans. 'A guy with long hair wearing Oshkosh dungarees, with an English-rose model girlfriend. Hipgnosis had only made half-a-dozen covers at the time, but I knew who they were.'

Elton John, Marc Bolan and George Harrison were just some who wore Daisy Roots' platform shoes and boots, with Irish blues guitarist Rory Gallagher owning several pairs in emerald green. But the company wasn't making enough money and after their backer pulled out, Po offered Evans temporary work at Hipgnosis. His first commission was a poster for British bluesmen Stan Webb's Chicken Shack: 'It was never completed and remains a running joke between Po and I even today.'

The Dark Side of the Moon had just been released when Richard reported for duty. He cast his eyes over the horrific lavatory, the chipped black paintwork and ragged cardboard folders spewing out prints and transparencies and wondered how such elegant artwork had been created in such squalor.

Evans took a desk under one of the Georgian windows overlooking Denmark Street. His first task was laying out *A Nice Pair*, a re-package of Pink Floyd's first two LPs. This was an analogue age. Hipgnosis's collages were created on flat artwork and with every image painstakingly cut out with a scalpel. The back of the print was sanded down until it was as thin as Rizla cigarette paper before being glued to the master artwork – 'But I could only find a blunt scalpel and a ruler that had notches carved out of it,' says Evans, who smuggled in his own 'ammo box' of pristine tools the next day.

A Nice Pair's artwork showed historical Pink Floyd photographs spliced with bawdy or punning images. Evans was fastidious, so Storm suggested making deliberate mistakes, 'to suggest the designer had got bored while laying it out.' Pictures of the group were stained with ink and coffee or scrawled with graffiti ('Judy, Friday night . . .'). Storm appeared on the cover with the Pink Floyd football team and again on the reverse with Po, who was wearing a pair of bright red Daisy Roots.

'I loved the fact that we were making iconic artwork but putting humour into it,' says Evans. 'Po, Storm and I were extremely British in what we were doing, with the humour. Americans were making amazing album covers but nobody did covers like Hipgnosis.'

Later, Evans' hand appeared on Genesis's *The Lamb Lies Down on Broadway*; his eyes, peeking through Venetian blinds, on the debut album by Phil Collins' jazz-fusion side project, *Brand X*, and his head and shoulders inside 10cc's *How Dare You!*

Storm and Po both took photographs, sometimes working as a tag team: one directed the subject, while the other took the shot, before swapping. By now, though, Po took the majority of the images. His confidence had grown since *Houses of the Holy* and he regularly challenged Storm's thinking as he'd experienced, firsthand, the difficulty of turning his partner's grand ideas into reality.

'For Storm, the idea was everything,' he says. 'But I thought the style was important as well. I wanted us to combine the two. But the two areas we were both lacking in were lighting and the darkroom. Neither of us was good at lighting, nor wanted to spend our lives in the darkroom.'

That spring, Hipgnosis hired a new darkroom assistant. Peter Christopherson would later become a partner in the company while also performing with the art collective, COUM Transmissions, and the electronic group, Throbbing Gristle.

153

Christopherson was born on 27 February 1955, in Leeds, York-shire. His father, Derman, was a professor of mechanical engin-eering who later became the master of Cambridge University's Magdalene College and was awarded a knighthood. Peter was the youngest of several biological and adopted siblings. According to his former bandmate Cosey Fanni Tutti, 'His parents fostered many children, including one, Ann, whom they later adopted. Then his mum unexpectedly fell pregnant with him.'

Christopherson began boarding at Ackworth, a Quaker school in north Yorkshire, at the age of ten and credited it with giving him spiritual awareness: 'Learning the ability to sit quietly with one's thoughts for an hour or so is a great and wonder-ful gift.' Before joining Hipgnosis, he'd lived with Ann in New York, where he'd studied computer programming and video for a semester at the State University in Buffalo.

'All we knew about Peter is he had just been to America,' says Po. 'He was very wiry with dark hair and dark eyes, and I'm not sure he was even twenty. But he turned up with this amazing portfolio and we hired him on the spot.'

Storm and Po were impressed by Peter's collection of beauti-fully lit, unusually posed photographs of naked bodies. Some-thing was unsettling about the images, but it would be over a year before they discovered what that was. None of this mat-tered at the time, though. 'Peter instinctively knew what he was doing – how to light a subject, how to take a picture, how to process film and paper . . . After our first shoot with him, Storm and I looked at each other and thought, "Yes, great!"'

Christopherson was a generation younger, didn't share the same hippy aesthetic and brought a fresh eye to the work. In the coming years, he'd also make fleeting appearances on several Hipgnosis albums: running down a corridor on *The Lamb Lies*

Down on Broadway, screaming on UFO's *Strangers in the Night* and peering under the bonnet of a Cadillac on Bad Company's *Desolation Angels* (though he never learned to drive).

'Peter looked like an overgrown schoolboy, with his short hair and his Fairisle pullover, when he first arrived,' recalls Richard Evans. 'At first, he seemed to me to be completely naïve.'

How little they knew.

★

Like a group basking in the success of a hit record, Hipgnosis were suddenly in demand. In May that year, Marshall Chess, the president of Rolling Stones Records, requested a meeting. Hipgnosis had met Mick Jagger when he visited the Gordons at Egerton Court. Since then, the Stones had made a run of great gnarly rock 'n' roll albums – *Let It Bleed, Sticky Fingers, Exile on Main Street* – and currently drifted around the globe like gypsies in a tax-exile bubble.

Storm and Po were summoned to guitarist Keith Richards' Thames-side flat in Cheyne Walk and given an album title, *Goats Head Soup*. Within days, they'd dreamed up a concept: the Rolling Stones as mythical centaurs and satyrs in a woodland glade. 'Pre-Photoshop, that was some feat,' admits Po. But if any Stone lent himself to a pair of cloven hooves, it was Richards.

Hipgnosis explained that the group would be photographed wearing ballet tights; a blank canvas onto which the animal limbs could be grafted later. 'The Stones said, "Great, yeah, yeah, fine,"' remembers Po. 'They wanted this.'

Hipgnosis shot many musicians at Denmark Street but chose Bow Street Studios in Covent Garden for the Stones. They shipped in food, beer, a music system, ballet tights from Anello & Davide and a television set in case Jagger wanted to watch the cricket.

Alex Henderson worked at Bow Street and attended the shoot. Most of the Stones arrived after midday, but hours later, there was still no sign of Keith. 'Unfortunately, Richards didn't turn up until seven o'clock in the evening,' says Henderson. 'This didn't surprise me, as I'd seen him, out of his brain on Portobello Road, at 4 a.m.'

'Richards was in a foul mood when he arrived,' adds Po, 'and that set the others off, because they were pissed off he was late. So suddenly they were all in a bad mood.' Especially bass guitarist Bill Wyman, who'd been reluctant to dress up anyway and was now scowling in a pair of figure-hugging tights.

Sandwiches and beer couldn't lighten the mood. 'So we sent out for a bottle of Jack Daniel's and a gram of cocaine,' says Henderson. 'Once they arrived, Keith's mood changed. Suddenly, it's, "Yeah, man, this is a great idea," and he really got into wearing the tights."'

In the subsequent photos, Jagger and Richards resembled a pair of rock 'n' roll Nijinksys and even Bill Wyman cracked a smile. A maquette was created, showing the bare-chested Stones as centaurs, and Hipgnosis agreed to deliver the finished artwork in three weeks. Then, just before deadline, came an urgent call from Marshall Chess: the Stones had changed their minds and Hipgnosis should stop immediately.

Hipgnosis discovered David Bailey had photographed the group after them. Jagger was very taken with Bailey's shot of himself wearing a chiffon veil and wanted it for the cover instead. Apparently, it reminded him of Katharine Hepburn's character in *The African Queen*.

'We were upset and angry, and we didn't get paid,' grumbles Po. 'Very rarely did we do work on spec, but it was the Stones so we had no reason to think we wouldn't get the job. It was our biggest disappointment of the decade.'

Hipgnosis stuffed the negatives in an envelope, sealed it with Gaffer tape and threw it into a cupboard. It was the album cover that got away and the envelope remained unopened until after Storm's death.

Goats Head Soup was released that summer with a chiffon-draped Jagger on the sleeve. Alex Henderson was singularly unimpressed: 'That cover was shit,' he says.

'Marshall Chess was absolutely ruthless,' admits Po. 'He did not treat us well, but his attitude was, "Well, you know how it is." And he was right, we just had to suck it up.'

After being spurned by the Rolling Stones, 1973 was still the year Hipgnosis landed a Beatle. Storm was astonished when the same EMI executive who'd lambasted them for putting a cow on the cover of *Atom Heart Mother* asked them to work with Paul McCartney.

After the Beatles' split in 1970, McCartney made two solo albums before forming a new group, Wings, with his wife and keyboard player, Linda. Their third album, *Band on the Run*, was due for release in December and needed a cover.

The McCartneys already had an idea: Wings and a supporting cast of movie stars dressed as convicts and shot against a prison-style wall. They'd even booked a friend of Paul's from Liverpool, the esteemed fashion photographer Clive Arrowsmith, to take the pictures. But they needed Hipgnosis to round up their cover stars and direct the shoot.

'I agreed because of the groupie in me,' admitted Storm. 'I fancied riding in Paul's Roller and being in his kitchen, where it was rumoured there hung a real Magritte.'

The McCartneys' wish list included such Hollywood A-listers as Paul Newman, Rod Steiger and Robert Redford. 'Storm and I spoke to their agents,' says Po. 'But nobody was available at short notice or prepared to fly to England for an album cover, even for a Beatle. The only one we could get was James Coburn, who could not have been more accommodating.'

Coburn had wowed the teenage Storm and Po in *The Magnificent Seven*, but his fellow stars were all British and more readily available. Posed in between Coburn, Paul, Linda and Wings guitarist Denny Laine were the TV chat-show host Michael Parkinson, singer Kenny Lynch, Liberal MP and broadcaster Clement Freud, actor Christopher Lee and boxer John Conteh.

Footage of the shoot outside the stable house in Osterley Park showed Storm physically manhandling Parkinson: 'Michael, you're bringing up the rear with Kenny,' he said, looking and sounding like a film-director-in-waiting.

Band on the Run gave Hipgnosis another top-ten hit before the end of the year, but its sleeve was a McCartney creation: 'The pattern was repeated for the next seven years,' admits Po, 'with Paul asking us to submit ideas and then saying, "Ah, but I have one of my own . . ."'

Storm resented the loss of artistic control, but kept himself in check. This wasn't always the case. A year later, the folk singer Roy Harper railroaded Hipgnosis into using his naked body on the cover of his latest album, *Flashes from the Archives of Oblivion*. 'Front cover sleeve design from an idea by Roy Harper,' read the credit, after which the handwritten words, 'Yes, and it shows' mysteriously appeared.

★

Hipgnosis remained on safer ground with Led Zeppelin's manager Peter Grant, even if Storm never endeared himself to the big man. Richard Evans had acquired a book of Marx Brothers film scripts and Hipgnosis were amusing themselves one afternoon by reciting the lines. Storm picked up the studio's ringing telephone, squeezed his nose to sound more like nasally, wisecracking Groucho Marx and answered, 'Florida calling, Dr Hackenbush here.' Grant was on the other end and his naturally nasal tone outdid both Storm's and Groucho's: 'Less of the fucking jokes,' Grant whined. 'Get me Po.'

Po's entrepreneurial spirit was unbroken by the Stones' rejection. He'd now discovered that a total solar eclipse was due to take place on 30 June. It was predicted to last for over seven minutes and another of this duration wasn't expected until 2186. The optimum place to view it was the village of Chinguetti in northern Mauritania.

Po and Alex Henderson wanted to photograph it for a possible album cover. Knowing this was what Roger Waters might later call another 'free trip to Timbuk-fucking-tu', Po approached Grant, who agreed to buy the pictures on the understanding Led Zeppelin owned the rights.

Henderson had just sold a flat and says it was he who fronted the money, though: 'I knew the Beatles' photographer, Bob Freeman, and he wanted to do a film about the total eclipse. But Bob's backers crapped out. *The Dark Side of the Moon* had just been released, so I said to Po, "How do you fancy a trip to Mauritania?" But I don't remember Po approaching Peter Grant until after we came back.'

Like a new musician joining an established group, Henderson's presence ruffled feathers. 'Storm couldn't work me out. He'd say, "You seem to be Po's big mate and I need to know more about you." I think maybe he got a bit jealous and thought I was a threat to Hipgnosis, which I wasn't. The truth is, Storm intimidated me.'

Hipgnosis had three weeks in which to organise the expedition. Po wanted to create a piece of land art by planting seven 8-foot-long silver rods in the sand dunes and photographing them during the eclipse. A plumber friend suggested using chrome-plated showerhead tubes as they were lightweight but sturdy enough to survive the journey.

Flights were booked, but the world's astronomers were flocking to Mauritania and the country had run out of hire cars. 'We managed to get a long wheelbase Land Rover from an army base in Dakar, but don't ask how,' says Po. As a further precaution, they purchased a John, Bell & Croyden medical kit containing snake-bite and scorpion serum: 'I remember wishing Po would get bitten,' admits Henderson, 'so I could whack him up with some of this stuff.'

Five days before the eclipse, the duo boarded a flight to Las Palmas in the Canary Islands, the nearest stop-off point before Mauritania. As they landed, they saw the prototype *Concorde 001* idling on the runway. The plane had observation bubbles in its fuselage from which to watch the path of the eclipse. Flying at twice the speed of sound, it could keep pace with the eclipse shadow crossing the globe.

There would be no Concorde for Hipgnosis, though. Instead, they boarded a dilapidated four-engine prop plane to the Mauritanian capital of Nouakchott: 'This thing barely struggled across the sky,' recalls Po.

Their hotel in Nouakchott was the Park, but the letter 'P' had become detached from the sign outside and hung despondently over the entrance. Bedouin locals and their camels watched in wonder as Po and Alex dragged their excess baggage and 8-foot shower tubes into the hotel lobby.

The following day, Abdullah, their nineteen-year-old Tuareg guide, was waiting with the Land Rover. After loading up with enough water for seven days, they set off on the 325-mile trip across the Sahara.

Hipgnosis weren't the only ones making this pilgrimage, nor were they the most ill-prepared. For every professional scientist from the Smithsonian Institute, there were several amateur stargazers wandering around the Sahara, sunburnt and lost.

'We picked up two itinerant Dutch hitchhikers and a sweet-shop owner called Pam from the north of England,' remembers Po. 'Pam was besotted with *The Sky at Night*'s astronomer, Patrick Moore, and had followed him to Africa. She was carrying a round of sandwiches in a Tupperware box and one bottle of water to last ten days. If we hadn't arrived, she would have died. I believe she eventually met Patrick and was so starstruck, she couldn't speak.'

After three days of travelling, they realised they wouldn't reach Chinguetti in time. Instead, they set up camp 140 miles shy of their intended destination in the dunes near Akjoujt.

They'd dropped the Dutch hitchhikers, but picked up an American MIT student named Larry Frank. 'Larry was moonlighting for the Boston Globe,' explains Po. 'He'd hitched a ride with some Arabs, but been thrown off their truck in the middle of the desert when they realised he was Jewish. Larry was in a bad way when we found him.'

The travellers set up camp in the dunes and spent the night before the eclipse cooking frankfurters on a Primus Stove and listening to *The Dark Side of the Moon* on a small tape recorder. Abdullah, confused by the strange music and their constant chatter, made his bed some distance away.

At 5.30 the following morning, Po and Alex started positioning the rods and preparing the cameras. They wanted to capture the diamond ring effect, known as 'Baily's Beads', where spots of sunlight briefly appear at the beginning and end of a total solar eclipse. A strong wind had been blowing since they arrived in Mauritania and the sky was heavy with clouds. Then, an hour before the eclipse, everything cleared: 'The silence and sheer scale of the desert was breathtaking,' says Po. The light became translucent and grey as a dark shadow passed across the dunes and stars became visible as day briefly plunged into night.

'It was incredibly eerie,' says Henderson. 'Abdullah became spooked by it all and started praying. I just wanted to enjoy the eclipse, but we had to keep taking photos, for better or for worse.'

But it was difficult for them to capture the full effect of the rods and Baily's Beads in a seven-minute, four-second eclipse. 'It was a bad idea,' admits Henderson. 'The only way to do it would have been to strip the cover together in the studio – something Hipgnosis were very good at.' The final images were never going to usurp those for *The Dark Side of the Moon* or *Houses of the Holy*, but they needed to be sold if Henderson was to get his money back. In the meantime, they'd run out of cash and had to barter their expensive medical kit for two nights in a squalid hotel in Nouakchott.

The pair eventually managed to book a flight to Mauritania's second-largest city, Nouadhibou, from where they could catch another to Madrid and then on to Ibiza. 'We were both in need of a holiday after all this,' says Henderson. But when their plane was delayed, they spent the night on the airport floor, with camera cases chained to their wrists. 'I remember waking up in the darkness and thinking, "What the hell is that?" And a goat had wandered in and was licking my face.'

Once on board, they discovered they wouldn't be flying until one more passenger, a tribal chief, had arrived. Unwashed and undernourished, Po and Alex sat on the stationary DC3, as a fellow traveller's chickens fluttered up and down the aisle – *All this*, they must have been thinking, *for an album cover.*

Back in England, Peter Grant was delighted with the eclipse photographs but they were thrown into a drawer somewhere in Grant's country pile and forgotten about. The pictures never appeared on a Led Zeppelin album sleeve and have not been seen since.

'I don't remember ever seeing them,' says Jimmy Page. 'But I bet they were bloody expensive. Hipgnosis liked going to these exotic places which were very expensive. I imagine they had one of those airstream campervans and waited days to get the right shot. But none of this was stuff you could get from the photo library. Hipgnosis had style.'

A few weeks after the trip, a letter arrived at 6 Denmark Street, postmarked 'Washington DC', from the US Secretary of State, Henry Kissinger. Larry Frank, the *Boston Globe* reporter, was one of Kissinger's relatives. Despite being preoccupied with trying to end the Vietnam War, Kissinger wrote a letter to thank Hipgnosis for saving Frank's life.

Like the eclipse photographs, the letter was tossed into a drawer and never seen again. The studio telephone rang with another job offer and yesterday's adventures were forgotten.

On 5 May 1973, Led Zeppelin broke the Beatles' box-office record at Shea Stadium by performing to 56,800 at Florida's Tampa Stadium. They were now the biggest group in the world and Peter Grant's new residence, Horselunges Manor in Sussex, came with a moat, a drawbridge and at least one ghost. Grant, flush with more money than he'd ever dreamed of, looked for various byzantine projects on which to spend it.

Soon after his request to stage a Led Zeppelin concert at Waterloo station was refused, he threw his money behind a Zeppelin-branded racing car. Grant and John Bonham were both motor racing fans and the drummer had befriended driver Kaye Griffiths, who'd raced his Belgian-owned McLaren M8/ ED in several events, including the British Formula Libre. The sport was underfunded and Griffiths thought Zeppelin's endorsement would give him a financial boost.

Grant asked Hipgnosis to customise the McLaren with Led Zeppelin livery. Po nominated Richard Evans; a wise choice as Peter had spent the past year marching around the world in an enormous pair of Daisy Roots. Evans was introduced to Grant in Denmark Street: 'And this huge wardrobe-sized man gave me a big hug and told me, "Those are the best fucking boots I've ever worn in my life."'

The next time they met was at Po's flat, where Hipgnosis gained an insight into Grant's new lifestyle. By 1974, cocaine had long been the go-to drug for rock stars, managers, record company executives and ambitious sleeve designers. Grant's cocaine use had rocketed in tandem with his earnings and power.

Po's bijou apartment wasn't designed for a man of Peter's size. Even less so when he showed up with his emissary, Led Zeppelin's strapping tour manager Richard Cole: 'Grant and Colesy came thumping up the stairs of my little flat – wide load coming through – at about ten o'clock at night.'

Once settled, Grant reached into his jacket pocket and pulled out a big bag of Peruvian flake. After struggling to untie the knot, he scattered half of its contents over a plush Moroccan rug. Grant didn't seem to care: 'Get a fucking dustpan and brush, Po,' he said offhandedly. 'You can have that lot.'

Rather than chopping out lines, Grant scooped the powder into his nostrils from a silver spoon around his neck. For the next two hours, the bag and spoon were ceremoniously passed around as the room filled with a chorus of snorting, throat clearing and Grant's tireless spiel of conspiracy theories and gossip.

Evans had painted half-a-dozen beautiful designs, but it was midnight before Grant looked at any of them. Led Zeppelin eventually chose one with their name and an airship emblazoned across the car's nearside and offside, flanked by brilliant blue sky and white stars.

The Zeppelin McLaren made its debut at Silverstone race track in May 1974, but Kaye Griffiths lost control and the car span out. It was a metaphor of sorts. 'Like many things, Peter and Led Zeppelin soon lost interest,' says Po. 'The last I heard, the car was in California.'

With cocaine and power, though, came the increased threat of violence. Pink Floyd preferred simmering resentment to physical conflict. In contrast, Grant and Richard Cole were intimidating and unpredictable, and all of Led Zeppelin enjoyed the sense of invincibility this gave them. It would be a few more years before it backfired, but there were already warning signs.

In the same month Led Zeppelin's McLaren span out on the track, Po witnessed a bust-up between Grant and a rival band manager. It was 18 May 1974 and he was taking photographs at the Who's concert at Charlton Athletic Football Club in southeast London. Grant also managed blues singer Maggie Bell and a new group, meat-and-two-veg rockers Bad Company, and had talked them both onto the bill.

Like many outdoor shows at the time, the Charlton gig was a chaotic affair, with ticketless fans jumping barriers and the official 50,000 capacity swelled by at least another 20,000 more.

Grant added to the chaos by ensuring Bad Company arrived late as a ploy to get them moved up the bill to perform just before the headliners.

The Who's manager, Bill Curbishley, was not impressed, but nor was he a man to be trifled with. In the 1960s, Curbishley had served time for armed robbery, a crime for which he always protested his innocence. Po was in a backstage anteroom when he heard Grant, Richard Cole and Bad Company thundering down the corridor. He peered out of the doorway and saw that Cole was carrying a wrench: 'I remember hearing Peter say, "If he makes any kind of move, hit him with that spanner."'

Grant wrongly assumed Bad Company would be treated with the same reverence as Led Zeppelin and had under-estimated Curbishley. Bill calmly informed Grant that Bad Company wouldn't be playing today.

'Who the fuck do you think you are?' Grant roared.

'Close that door and we'll see who walks out of this fucking room,' Curbishley replied.

Grant shut up immediately. Bad Company's lead singer, Paul Rodgers, intervened and Curbishley allowed the group to play a shorter set.

'Bill was very clear with Peter – "Your band turned up late, you are to blame, you are responsible,"' recalls Po. 'Bill never raised his voice, but he had the upper hand and Peter backed down. There was a lot of violence and implied violence around Led Zeppelin, but some of the time it was all bluff and bluster.'

Bad Company's self-titled debut album was released the following month and was full of songs about sex, doomed romance and being an outlaw. On the sleeve, Hipgnosis inset the group's logo with fingerprints, as if they'd all been booked and thrown in jail. Grant hit the motherlode again when the album went to number one in America.

Po's admission that he was 'drawn to any kind of chaos' was compounded by his ongoing relationship with Led Zeppelin. He was at ease with the likes of 'G' and 'Colesy' in a way Storm Thorgerson clearly wasn't: 'Storm had this strong moral code and could be almost catholic about certain things. I respected that. He wasn't into that world in the way I was.'

There was another reason for Storm keeping his distance: his relationship with Libby January had ended. 'Libby was a lovely person and a free spirit and she'd had enough,' says Po. 'Storm was selfish. If he wanted to have a business meeting at the flat, he would. If he wanted to spend the afternoon playing tennis with Phil May, he would, regardless of what she wanted. So Libby thought, "I will do what I want."'

Libby started to spend evenings out in clubs, leaving Storm to look after their son. 'I remember a conversation with him – "She's started smoking dope, she's coming home at four in the morning . . ." This went on for something like six months.'

On occasion, Storm had to postpone meetings or bring Bill to the studio. Then, suddenly, Libby upped and left. She'd met somebody else and moved into her own flat. 'I was always pre-occupied with work,' admitted Storm, 'and Libby ran off with a neighbour.'

A tearful Storm phoned Po at the studio and they arranged to meet at a pub in Swiss Cottage. 'Storm walked in, dressed in a pinstripe suit,' he recalls. 'Normally he was the scruffiest dresser, but he'd gone to Carnaby Street and bought this suit, which he started to wear with dark glasses and old plimsolls. Then he had his hair cut short. I think it was a coping mechanism, a way of keeping himself together.'

Storm hired a solicitor and applied for custody of Bill; an unusual move for a father in the 1970s. 'It wasn't at all easy for Libby with Storm,' agrees Barbie Antonis. 'But Storm told her, "You are not taking Bill and if you fight it, I'll reveal the skeletons in the January family cupboard." He never needed to, because Libby backed down. He made sure she was still in Bill's life and it remained very congenial. Storm considered Bill his greatest achievement.'

'I had such admiration for Storm after that,' says Po. 'The way he looked after his son showed me a different side to him, someone who was very caring about people. But Storm was so affected by Libby leaving, I realised anyone who left him, for whatever reason, was going to be given short shrift.'

Gai Caron enjoyed seeing this gentler side: 'I was always nervous of Storm because he seemed to me so bright and intellectual and I worried he thought of me as Po's dumb model girlfriend.' Gai and Po's daughter, Charlotte, known as 'Charlie', was born that summer. 'And Storm and Libby came to visit me in hospital and he couldn't have been kinder. He was so sweet. He did have a soft heart underneath it all.'

Storm's change of circumstances had a profound effect on Hipgnosis. 'Po, Peter and I would be in the studio at ten o'clock in the morning,' says Richard Evans. 'But Storm wouldn't show up until twelve or one, but might not finish until two in the morning back at his flat.'

'Bill was Storm's priority,' explains Po. 'But Bill suffered, too. Storm might go home to cook dinner for him, but then there'd be meetings in the evenings. It was like a circus up there.' Any friend or colleague who crossed the threshold might suddenly become a childminder: '"Can you look after Bill? I have a meeting with the Hollies."'

Couriers were regularly given five pounds to wait outside the flat, while Storm signed off on some urgent piece of artwork. Just as at Egerton Court, he sometimes conducted his business from the lavatory.

'Two debt collectors from the gas or telephone company arrived at Hillfield Mansions,' remembers Po. 'Storm never paid his bills on time and always disputed them as a matter of course. These men were let in and Storm began to engage them in conversation while sitting on the loo. They were so shocked, they could hardly speak and beat a hasty retreat. It was funny but one could sympathise. I think Storm enjoyed the confrontation.'

There were also weekly brainstorming sessions lasting most of the night. 'Everyone was encouraged to attend – designers, photographers, Japanese groupies, knife-throwing drug dealers ... Hipgnosis was like an arthouse, a commune. Everyone could throw their tuppence in, even if Storm might tell them to piss off.'

The uncomfortable truth was that Storm's domestic situation also empowered Po: 'It gave me more opportunity to shoot things the way I wanted to,' he admits. 'But Storm was creatively productive and absolutely brilliant even if grief affected him strangely.'

Storm's driving often terrified his passengers: 'Talking non-stop, not looking at the road, doing 70 miles an hour round the back streets of Soho,' says Po. Storm now acquired a pair of roller skates, too. Richard Evans remembers repeatedly circling Centre Point in his Austin Mini, while Storm skated alongside, issuing instructions through the car's open window: 'Storm had some artwork under his arm and was on his way to EMI.'

Led Zeppelin's pulling power attracted several hard-rock groups to Hipgnosis, including Nazareth, the Scorpions and UFO, the last a north London group named after the psychedelic

club. UFO had recently signed to Chrysalis Records, who asked
Hipgnosis to design their next album, *Phenomenon*.

'The bass player, Pete Way, and I went to Haverstock Hill
on the tube,' recalls UFO's vocalist, Phil Mogg, 'and I distinctly
remember coming out of the station and seeing this bloke whizzing towards us on roller skates. We both said, "Fuck me! Look
at him" – and turned out it was Storm, come to meet us.'

Phenomenon showed a husband-and-wife couple faking a UFO
photograph, by tossing a car's hubcap into the air. Shot outside
a bungalow in suburban Cheam with the cover model, Mandy,
looking wonderfully guilty, it resembled a film still and told a
story. Initially, not everybody was sure the image worked.

'Storm showed me the cover and said, "What do you see?"'
remembers Emo. 'I saw it immediately – a hubcap in the air.
Storm turned to Po and said, "If Emo can see it, it works, and
Emo is thick." Not good for my self-confidence, but this is what
I had to deal with.'

Hipgnosis would create several eye-catching, lurid sleeves
for UFO: 'We struck gold,' says Mogg. 'If you flicked through
the rack in a record shop, our sleeves always stood out. I think
it's because they shot the images for real. One of them, *No
Heavy Petting*, had a girl with a monkey on her shoulder. Years
later, I met the model and she told me that monkey had shat
all over her.'

'Phil and Storm got on like a house of fire,' remembers Po.
'But you couldn't imagine two more different people than the
grumpy, intellectual Storm and the rock 'n' roller Phil Mogg.
Phil used to come swaggering into the studio in his spandex trousers – and my God, did he swagger – and say, "Come on, Storm,
man, show me something fantastic! I wanna be turned on."
Storm used to say, "For heaven's sake, dear, what are you doing

here?" "Storm, we need a thinking man's cover," Phil would reply, "We don't want any of your airbrushed crap."'

Among those who airbrushed UFO's sleeves and were routinely harangued by Storm was the freelance illustrator Richard Manning: 'I loved Storm, and I hated him, but ultimately, love won out,' says Manning.

After leaving school, Richard worked alongside Hipgnosis's original re-toucher, Terry Day. But Day eventually refused to work for Hipgnosis's paltry rates and Manning picked up the gig: 'I felt privileged to work for them, but I was also cheap and they couldn't afford anybody else.'

Manning brightened the bright red dice on Bad Company's *Straight Shooter* and airbrushed a wave onto the hull of a boat and flowers into a model's hair for the Pretty Things' *Silk Torpedo*. This image was in homage to calendar-girl artist Alberto Vargas and an example of Hipgnosis creating glamour in a most unglamorous environment. Hipgnosis's cover girl straddled a torpedo constructed out of polystyrene blocks in the middle of number six. But the finished article resembled a '40s pin-up painted onto the fuselage of a wartime bomber.

'I didn't always hold back with Storm,' says Manning. 'I sometimes told him to stick his work where the sun don't shine. I'd slam the phone down, but he'd always ring back an hour later, "Hello, dear, have you calmed down?" And we'd work it out. He was always right, too, so I never look at those covers today and think, "I should have done this," or "I should have done that."'

In between barking instructions at him, Storm also talked to Manning about his domestic situation. 'I became a shoulder to cry on and I think that cemented our friendship,' he says. 'Storm was going through the break-up, trying to be a dad and run a business. He'd have to bring Bill to the studio sometimes.'

Peter Gabriel, Genesis's lead singer, first met Storm that year and was surprised when he interrupted their meeting to pick up his son: 'I didn't meet many single men at that time who brought up kids and I think he did an amazing job,' said Gabriel.

Genesis were an art-rock group formed while most of them were still boarding at Charterhouse public school. Their sixth album, *The Lamb Lies Down on Broadway*, would be Gabriel's last before going solo and the beginning of his ten-year association with Hipgnosis.

Gabriel had a nagging feeling rock music was on the brink of change and didn't want to be left behind: 'This was 1974. It was pre-punk but we were beginning to get into the era of the big, fat supergroups,' he said, 'and I thought, "I don't want to go down with this *Titanic*."'

Despite Gabriel's fears, Genesis's latest was a dense concept album about a New York street kid's journey of spiritual self-discovery. The concept album had become a popular vehicle for music with a 'big idea'. *The Dark Side of the Moon* was an accessible example; *The Lamb Lies Down on Broadway* was a little less inviting.

Like Storm, Gabriel was fond of plundering the goldmine – 'I used to have incredibly scary, vivid dreams, and some of these inspired my work' – and an ardent film buff. *The Lamb Lies Down on Broadway* concept borrowed from *West Side Story and* Alejandro Jodorowsky's acid western *El Topo*.

For Storm, this was all grist to the mill. Hipgnosis's artwork presented scenes from the songs in a comic-book style with striking film-noir lighting. George Hardie illustrated the lyrics and a short story was reproduced across the inside gatefold.

When Gabriel's shocked mother, Edith, heard the album, she phoned him up to ask what it was all about. 'It's all repressed sex,' admitted Gabriel, forty years later. 'The Stones used to come right out and say, "I want to fuck you." Genesis could never do that, so we dressed it all up.'

Gabriel's fears about a musical *Titanic* weren't unfounded, but it would be another twelve months before Storm and Po became aware of the sea change. Until then the '*Titanics*' were keeping them afloat and they were making more money than ever.

One day, Storm suggested asking clients what they were prepared to pay for a cover, rather than setting their own fee. 'Storm said, "We need to change the psychology,"' recalls Po. 'Reluctantly, I agreed. So we tried it out when Sweet's manager rang up.'

Sweet were a glam-rock group who'd enjoyed a run of chart hits but wanted to be taken more seriously. Po nervously asked their handler, '"What do you want to pay?"' He replied, "I've seen some of those other covers, what did they pay?" I said, "That's irrelevant." I was persistent and he finally said, "Do you think you can do it for £800?" Storm and I rubbed our hands with glee.'

★

Storm was also considering work beyond Hipgnosis, but this wasn't easy. Following *The Dark Side of the Moon*'s success, he approached Pink Floyd about writing their biography. The group were noncommittal, but he pushed ahead regardless and asked Nick Sedgwick, now a schoolteacher and song lyricist, to collaborate: 'Storm admitted that his offer was entirely self-interested,' recalled Sedgwick, who was Roger Waters' close friend and regular golfing partner.

Storm sold the idea to Sedgwick of a band history with fly-on-the-wall coverage of their next tour. It would be a year-long project and Storm promised he'd be delegating his work with Hipgnosis for the duration. That summer, Nick took a sabbatical from his teaching job and joined Roger and Judy Waters at their villa in the Greek coastal town of Volos.

The trip revealed Waters' increasing cynicism about the music business and revealed the parlous state of his marriage. Storm wasn't the only one whose partner was going to leave him.

In his posthumously published book, *In the Pink (Not a Hunting Memoir)*, Sedgwick recalled Judy criticising Roger for being 'invulnerable and remote' and Waters worrying she was about to have an affair with their German neighbour. Whenever he grew bored of arguing or tired of zooming around the bay in his new speedboat, Waters tried to write songs.

'Scribbling on scraps of paper, a line or couplet,' wrote Sedgwick. 'Sometimes he'd pick up an acoustic guitar, and strum it for five minutes before stopping with a comment along the lines of, "Ah well, that's another ten thousand quid earned."'

By the time Sedgwick packed his bags, the villa had become 'an emotional frontline'. But after arriving back in England he was furious to discover Storm was still immersed in Hipgnosis.

Sedgwick suggested abandoning the history and turning the book into an eyewitness account of the upcoming tour. Storm agreed, delegated the writing to Nick and ensured the pair shadowed Pink Floyd's every waking moment on their winter UK tour. He also recruited twenty-year-old photographer Jill Furmanovsky. In 1972, Jill, a student at London's Central School of Art and Design, became the Rainbow Theatre's official photographer: 'I had more bravado than skills,' she admits. Jill photographed Pink Floyd at the Rainbow and the Brighton Dome, where she roamed backstage to take more pictures: 'This was unheard of, but maybe they let me in because I was so naïve.'

'She was cool':
a teenage Storm and his
mother, Vanji Thorgerson,
19 Earl Street, Cambridge.

A young Aubrey 'Po' Powell
before discovering rock 'n' roll.

The Beat Generation:
Roger Waters (*left, back
to camera*), David Gale
(*centre*) and Syd Barrett
(*fourth right*) at the
January sisters' twenty-
first birthday party, Great
Shelford, October 1965.

Above: Po at the *A Saucerful of Secrets* cover shoot, with (*from left*) David Gilmour, Matthew Scurfield, Judy Trim, Roger Waters, Rick Wright, Juliette Gale and future Pink Floyd touring guitarist Tim Renwick, Hampstead Heath, 1968.

Below: Hipgnosis's business card, drawn by future Yes sleeve artist, Roger Dean, 1968.

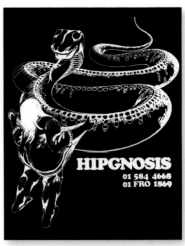

'Remember that triangle': Nigel Lesmoir-Gordon predicts the prism for *The Dark Side of the Moon* in a letter to Storm, September 1968.

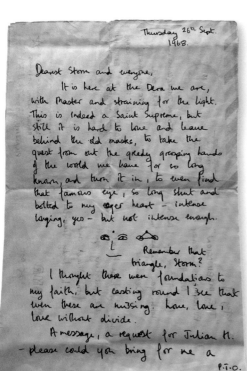

Pink Floyd preparing to demonstrate the Droste effect, photographed for *Ummagumma*, Trinity House, Great Shelford, 1969.

Desert storm: Po readying the dunes for the Nice's *Elegy* cover shoot, Merzouga, Morocco, December 1970.

The naked truth: Gai Caron, Jules Laughton and Mark Sayer on the *Houses of the Holy* cover shoot, Giant's Causeway, Northern Ireland, October 1972.

'Ticking away the moments that make up a dull day': Storm and Po pretending to be clocks, test shot, circa 1972.

Right: Po and Alex Henderson preparing to shoot the total eclipse in Akjoujt, Mauritania, for a Led Zeppelin album cover, June 1973.

Below: Where the magic happened, Hipgnosis's studio, 6 Denmark Street, London WC2, 1974.

Brothers in arms: Po and Storm in the courtyard of 6 Denmark Street, 1974.

Storm testing the water for Peter Frampton's *Somethin's Happening*.

Hipgnosis's designer Richard Evans modelling for Genesis's *The Lamb Lies Down on Broadway*, Brecon Beacons, Wales, 1974. Only his hand appeared in the finished artwork.

Artists in residence: Storm and Roger Dean in the studio, 1974.

Hollywood stuntmen Ronnie Rondell and Danny Rogers on the set of *Wish You Were Here*, Warner Bros backlot, Burbank, California, April 1975.

Ronnie Rondell goes up in flames at the cover shoot.

The boy wonder: Peter Christopherson, *Wish You Were Here* shoot, California, 1975.

Po and Linda McCartney on Wings' private jet, somewhere over America, May 1976.

Break on through to the other side: Hipgnosis's studio door, 6 Denmark Street.

Learning to fly: 'Algie' and the marksman on the set of *Animals*, Battersea Power Station, 4 December 1976.

Po wearing his Sex Pistols-baiting Pink Floyd sweatshirt,
6 Denmark Street, circa 1977.

And then there were three: Hipgnosis's new partner Peter Christopherson
with Po and Storm, 1977.

Photographers/assistants Rob Brimson and Richard Draper pondering the proofs for Rick Wright's *Wet Dream* cover, 6 Denmark Street, 1978.

'No two days at Hipgnosis were ever the same': (*from left*) Peter Christopherson, Wishbone Ash's manager John Sherry, Po and designer Marcus Bradbury, 1978.

Poster boys: illustrator Colin Elgie and designers Richard Draper and Marcus Bradbury, 1978.

Left: The sculpture of Assyrian goddess, Semiramis, shot for *Wings Greatest*, Rothorn mountain, Switzerland, October 1978.

Below: Po (battling a fear of heights) and his team, shooting the sculpture.

Storm, studio assistant Paul Maxon and Po road-testing the 'melting face' for Peter Gabriel's third album, 1980.

'I was up to no good': Po preparing for a swift getaway, 1980.

Below: Storm plays ping-pong on the set of Hipgnosis's rejected artwork for Queen's *Greatest Hits*, 1981.

Above: Storm and *Creepy* comic, test shot for Roger Taylor's *Fun in Space*, 1981.

High hopes: friends David Gilmour and Storm, circa 1984.

A masked Robert Plant (*left*) with Po and Peter Christopherson for the 'Heaven Knows' video, Zagora, Morocco, 1988.

Whole lotta love: Po and Robert Plant, Formentera, 1994.

Edgar Broughton Band, *Edgar Broughton Band*, 1971. 'I could only hang there for a minute and a half as the blood was rushing to my head.'

Wishbone Ash, *Argus*, 1972. 'I remember being told, "Look, just stick the bloody costume on and stand there with the spear..."'

UFO, *Force It*, 1975. 'We had to spend hours in the bathroom being doused with cold water.'

10cc, *How Dare You!*, 1976. 'The lady on the cover is a housewife whose businessman husband neglects her and is furious at being interrupted at work, again – "How dare you!"'

Steve O'Rourke bought the photos and brokered an introduction with Hipgnosis. Jill arrived at 6 Denmark Street and inwardly gasped. 'It was only recently Emo told me there was a toilet in the building,' she reveals. 'I only saw the sink everyone peed in.'

A year later, Storm asked her to cover the Floyd tour. 'Some time afterwards, I asked him why and Storm told me I had a good portfolio, but it was also because I had a pretty face and nice tits,' Jill recalls. 'I'm afraid this was the '70s, the sexist days.'

'Jill was very attractive and, to my shame, I was more interested in her chest than I was in her portfolio,' confessed Storm. Yet the pair remained friends for the rest of his life.

Hipgnosis had created an elaborate tour programme which borrowed from Marvel comics and *Mad* magazine. The four Floyds had a comic strip each, including 'Rog of the Rovers' and 'The Exploits of Dave Derring', which presented exaggerated or fictitious versions of their personalities. Sedgwick would soon get a close-up view of these four individuals and Pink Floyd's inner workings.

The tour began at Edinburgh's Usher Hall on 4 November. 'Everywhere was grey, sodden and, above all, cold,' recalled Sedgwick. 'A kind of gloom set in: a languorous melancholy, which seemed commensurate with the prevailing rhythm of the national psyche.'

The country was in recession and inflation was running high. Barely two weeks into the run, the IRA bombed two Birmingham pubs, killing twenty-one people. The group arrived in the city a few days after and had their luggage checked for explosives before being allowed into the hotel.

Pink Floyd were a tight-knit clique and outsiders were never entirely sure who was and wasn't persona non grata:

'Record-company people were barely tolerated and wives were just about allowed backstage,' Jill recalls.

Furmanovsky's photographs showed the access Hipgnosis enjoyed, though: Sedgwick watching Waters and Gilmour play backgammon; Po drinking beer in Floyd's dressing room and Storm engaged in some intellectual prize fight, nose to nose with Waters and surrounded by bottles of vino.

'Storm was always at the core of it,' recalls Jill. 'Fine wines and arguments.' However, the stoner's band of choice were also keen sportsmen. 'Which was incomprehensible to me at the time,' admits Jill, who thought there was something very un-cosmic about their games of squash or rushing back to the hotel to watch *Match of the Day*. One freezing morning, Jill was sum-moned to a desolate golf course to take photos of Waters and Sedgwick playing a round.

There was no respite either. 'I might go back to my room to relax for the night and Storm would ring up, "Quick! There's backgammon going on in room whatever. Bring your camera." Storm was a slave driver, but there was nothing he wouldn't do himself. You worked hard for him because he pushed himself so hard.' However, the group were in a creative slump after *The Dark Side of the Moon* and everybody, including the crew, was discontent. Floyd's gifted but outspoken lighting engineer, Arthur Max, fell out with them over money and left mid-way through the tour – 'A brilliant guy,' says Gilmour, 'but his eccentricities got the better of him.'

The Dark Side of the Moon drove the show, but there were tech-nical glitches to overcome. The projected images of animated clock faces and worker-ant commuters on the screen behind the stage were sometimes out of sync with the music. There was even a heckler at the Newcastle Odeon, shouting for T.Rex's

'Telegram Sam'. Roger Waters responded with a comically exaggerated yawn.

Rock writer Nick Kent wrote a withering critique of one of the Wembley Empire Pool shows in *New Musical Express*. Kent compared Pink Floyd to 'four navvies who've just finished their tea break' and said David Gilmour's 'hair looked filthy . . . with a spectacular festooning of split ends.'

Kent's review was greeted with fury backstage; Gilmour had another reason to feel aggrieved as he'd recently helped the writer with an *NME* profile of Syd Barrett. However, the gist of his review was that Pink Floyd appeared disengaged and bored on stage, and Waters agreed with him.

'He's talking about a general attitude we do display,' admitted Waters, backstage in Cardiff, 'and we display it because we're confused . . . Because we don't quite know what we're doing there any more . . . We do shamble out on stage and we don't have any connection with audiences.'

Sedgwick recorded several after-show post-mortems and discussions. 'It's all there and verifiable on a set of cassette recordings, which still exist,' says Waters. During one exchange, Rick Wright accused Waters of sounding like 'an old schoolmaster'. In another, Gilmour criticised Wright for his 'lack of enthusiasm' and told Nick Mason his drumming 'wasn't as good as it once was'.

After the Wembley shows, Storm and Po stayed in London to promote Cover Job, an exhibition of album artwork, which was running in the capital. The pair were interviewed on the BBC's flagship music show, *The Old Grey Whistle Test*, along with fellow exhibitor, Yes's sleeve artist, Roger Dean.

It was an awkward interview. Dean wore a sleeveless vest and greeted some of host 'Whispering' Bob Harris's earnest questions with a slight smirk. Po, with his beard, double denim and Wishbone Ash T-shirt, resembled a member of one of Hipgnosis's groups, while Storm, still in his post-breakup Sunday best, looked like a young maths teacher.

Pink Floyd's tour ended in Bristol on 14 December. Sedgwick then spent several months producing a first draft of his manuscript, copies of which were distributed between the four and Steve O'Rourke. The content was problematic and Sedgwick braced himself for the group's reaction. Waters and Mason cautiously approved the work, but Gilmour and Wright had serious doubts, which Storm translated as 'they were both quite angry'. In their view, Sedgwick's friendship with Waters had compromised the project but this most private of groups also preferred to keep their squabbles out of the public domain.

'Gilmour had a delayed explosion,' recalls Waters. 'Reading that manuscript was like lighting the blue touchpaper.'

'I felt aggrieved by it,' admits Gilmour. 'I don't think it portrayed us accurately and certainly not kindly and I probably did manage to get it canned.'

Storm and Sedgwick joined Floyd for further dates in the US, but Nick was now persona non grata with Steve O'Rourke and most of the group. In one excruciating episode, he recalled eating alone in the restaurant at the Seattle Hilton, with Gilmour, Wright and O'Rourke at a table behind him. 'All I could hear were the outbursts,' he wrote. 'My name plus expletives and wild attributions and accusations . . . The food turned rancid in my mouth.'

Sedgwick's closest ally in the group couldn't come to his rescue. That same night, Roger Waters called Judy from his hotel room only for another man to answer the phone. The couple separated soon after.

'The book idea was petering out by the time we went to America,' admitted Storm. 'I was busy, the band was busy, Roger was getting a divorce. There were also various indiscretions that might occur on foreign rather than domestic tours and that might have not gone down well, if reported. And we would have been very likely to have reported them.'

These indiscretions may have seemed raw to Storm in the light of his personal situation. 'One of the Floyd told me when I objected to infidelity to get the fuck off my moral high horse, because I had no idea of the difficulty in resisting temptation,' he wrote later. 'Being on tour can be heaven, but touring can turn good family men into liars and cheats.'

Pink Floyd refused to allow the book to be published and Sedgwick later admitted to experiencing withdrawal symptoms after being in their orbit for so long. He then spent three years working in Mexico and Peru, as if to purge himself of the experience. Like Hipgnosis's eclipse photos, his manuscript was thrown in a drawer and largely forgotten until the next century. Waters published *In the Pink: Not a Hunting Memoir* privately after Sedgwick's death in 2011.

By then, Waters and David Gilmour had torn each other apart in the press so many times, the story seemed positively tame. Sedgwick's account of Waters' marriage breaking down was more shocking than any backstage argument or Nick Kent's waspish comments about David Gilmour's hair.

In 1974, the ghost of Pink Floyd past hadn't been completely forgotten either. As his former bandmates breathed the rarefied air of wealthy rock stars, Syd Barrett hid from the outside world in his new flat in Chelsea Cloisters, less than a mile from Egerton Court.

Barrett had made a fleeting return to the stage two years earlier, performing in Cambridge as part of a trio called Stars. The group barely lasted a month. In August 1974, Peter Jenner and Bryan Morrison coaxed him back to Abbey Road Studios. 'I was hoping he'd emerge from the fog,' said Jenner. 'But he was still in the fog.' Nothing of any lasting merit came from these sessions.

EMI, desperate to glean some return on their investment, reissued his two solo LPs three months later. Hipgnosis's cover for *Syd Barrett* comprised of an old photograph of the composer, cross-legged on the floor at Wetherby Mansions. A matchbox, a plum and an orange appeared alongside his picture; an acid flashback to that summer's day in David Gale's garden.

The cover was a Plan B. Storm had spoken to Barrett on the telephone and he'd tentatively agreed to have a new photograph taken. Richard Evans accompanied him to Chelsea Cloisters. They knocked on the door and waited. And waited. 'Storm and I could hear him inside,' says Evans. 'But he wouldn't open up.'

'Part of me was angry,' said Storm. 'I thought, "Screw you, I'll be off." Here I was knocking on the door of someone I'd known since I was fourteen and he wouldn't let me in.'

Behind the door, Barrett sat in his womb-like apartment, with the curtains drawn and a TV set flickering away in the gloom; an image Pink Floyd would bring to life later in the song 'Nobody Home' from *The Wall*. Yet the more he stopped answering the door, the more the legend grew.

SIDE 2

Chapter 7

'Fortunately, Olivia Newton-John ignored the phlegm . . .'

Storm joins 'The Worst Band in the World'; Po sets a man on fire; Peter's secret life is revealed; 'The Titanic' springs a leak and a ghost appears at 6 Denmark Street.

'Depressed Miserable Tired Ill Sick Booed & Bored . . .'
— John Lydon's graffiti, 6 Denmark Street, circa 1976

★

First came the guttural growl and then a few seconds of silence. Then, like an oyster prised from a shell, it landed on the paving stone with a resounding *splat*. Po looked up from the camera towards the open window. Two whey-faced youths with unfashionably short hair glared back at him before spitting out another mouthful of mucus each.

Po was taking photographs of the British-Australian pop singer Olivia Newton-John in the courtyard behind 6 Denmark Street. Olivia would soon add 'film star' to her resumé after appearing in the musical *Grease* (1978). 'Fortunately, she ignored the phlegm,' says Po. 'But I couldn't.'

The guilty parties were John Lydon and Steve Jones, the nineteen-year-old vocalist and twenty-year-old guitarist in the Sex Pistols. The unknown group were renting a rehearsal space behind Hipgnosis's studio. They shared the same postcode, but the Sex Pistols were creatures from another planet. When Po challenged them, they told him to 'fuck off' – 'Storm and I didn't know what was going on,' he admits.

Peter Christopherson understood, though. In February '75, he'd hired two of his friends as cover models. The sleeve for UFO's *Force It* laboured the punning title and showed an androgynous couple about to have sex in a space filled with chrome shower heads and taps. The image was somewhere between a porn magazine spread and a bathroom fixtures catalogue.

The models were a real-life couple, Christine Newby and Neil Megson, aka 'Cosey Fanni Tutti' and 'Genesis P-Orridge', both members of COUM Transmissions, an art collective that formed in the pair's hometown of Hull and moved to east London in 1973. COUM Transmissions were a multi-media enterprise that explored music, film, poetry, publishing and theatre, and swapped letters and ideas with William Burroughs and other like-minded artists around the world. They knew their *On the Road* and *Naked Lunch* but were closer in spirit to the nascent Sex Pistols than Hipgnosis.

In COUM's world, everything was art and, their 1974 manifesto declared, 'There are NO boundaries in any form.' Cosey modelled for sex magazines; the money helped fund their cause and she considered the pictures her art. In March 1974, COUM staged 'The COUMing of Age' at London's Oval House Theatre: 'An odd collection of innocent, clichéd sexual fantasies and scenarios – but with twists,' explained Cosey.

COUM were already on Peter Christopherson's radar and he introduced himself before the show and asked if he could take photographs. 'There was something about the way he sidled up to us that day that made me nickname him "Sleazy",' says Cosey. 'It was a bit creepy but it also made me smile.'

'He was quite awkward,' recalled Genesis P-Orridge in his posthumous memoir, *Non-Binary*. 'Like a boy who has reached puberty and had a sudden growth spurt but hadn't quite figured out where to store his arms and feet when stationary.'

It was an eventful evening. Cosey appeared in a cage, wearing blood-stained latex tentacles; straddled a swing with a hole cut out of the seat, urinated over the audience and simulated sex with Genesis while dressed as dogs and daubed in Day-Glo paint.

Christopherson joined them the following month for the 'COUMing of Youth' at the Melkweg in Amsterdam. Genesis was chained naked to a cross and whipped by Cosey, while 'Sleazy' recited his public schoolboy fantasies from a chair at the side of the stage. 'The three of us together made for a volatile mix,' understated Cosey in her memoir, *Art Sex Music*. However, Christopherson's 'Sleazy' alter ego remained a mystery to his Hipgnosis workmates: 'We discovered Peter was gay, which we didn't care about,' says Po. 'We were liberal thinkers. But we had never heard of COUM Transmissions and knew nothing about what he was getting up to.

'After a few months, we realised Peter had a darker side. But that was because he came in after a weekend and said, "Oh,

I was in Reading on Saturday, re-creating injuries at a train crash." "You were doing *what*?"'

Christopherson was also a member of the Casualties Union, an organisation that staged accident re-enactments for the training of medical staff and emergency services. Christopherson sometimes played a casualty but more often used his make-up skills to turn actors into burns and crash victims. He also worked on a prototype of the London Dungeon, but claimed his reconstructions were considered too gruesome for a tourist attraction.

However, Christopherson also had an erotic interest in the subject: 'He would pick up boys at Playland, a classic game arcade out near Piccadilly, where the boy prostitutes hung out,' said Genesis P-Orridge. 'He would pay the boys to be in his photos and make it look like they'd been disembowelled and were trying to hold in their intestines.'

Christopherson regularly trawled Zwemmer's, the art bookshop on Charing Cross Road, and Watkins, the occult booksellers, in Cecil Court, looking for specialist titles. 'He came back once with a book of photos of horribly mutilated plane crash victims,' Po recalls. 'And then all these strange people with strange haircuts and clothes started showing up at the studio.'

'Oh, we were in and out of Denmark Street quite often,' says Cosey. 'The toilet was disgusting – "Do it quickly but don't sit down" – and the place itself was only a step up from the squat where Gen and I were living.

'This might sound horrible, but Sleazy viewed Storm and Po as old-school hippies and wanted to drag them into the here and now, with the two things they loved – film and photography. At that time, album covers were a great way to show off your skills and your view of the world and music. But Sleazy's other thing was to be subversive and think you wouldn't notice.'

Cosey remembers being driven to a half-renovated house somewhere in Fulham for the UFO shoot. She was used to being photographed half naked but she and Genesis had to spend hours in the bathroom, being doused with cold water: 'It wasn't pleasant, but it was interesting watching Sleazy work. He took a supportive role to Po, but you could see he always had something in mind to make the picture better.'

'Storm and I were conservative hippies,' admits Po, 'whereas Peter was plugged into an alternative scene and brought new ideas to Hipgnosis.'

Ambiguity and subversion were Sleazy's trademarks. Did the *Force It* cover show two women in a shower? Or a man and a woman? And, if so, was the woman forcing herself on the man?

Force It upset American record retailers and on the LP's US pressing, the couple were obscured by an airbrushed shower curtain. But Cosey's long dark hair also saw her mistaken for UFO's bass guitarist, Pete Way. 'We had loads of people asking us, "Oi, is that Pete in the bath?"' says Phil Mogg.

There was an emerging cultural divide, though. Just as Cosey and Genesis put their £30 modelling fee from *Force It* towards an overdue phone bill, Storm and Po flew first class to Los Angeles for a summit with Paul McCartney in March 1975.

It was Storm's first trip to America and the pair were booked into the Beverly Wilshire Hotel. 'I remember kissing the tarmac, I was so thrilled,' said Storm, who was delighted to spot Hollywood royalty Paul Newman on his balcony overlooking their hotel pool.

As assured as Storm might have appeared to the outside world, inside he was nervous. Po remembers him fretting over whether they should have brought more ideas to show McCartney. Po told him they should have: 'The trick with Storm was to agree with him, even if you disagreed. Then he would disagree with you and talk himself out of it.'

The next day a chauffeur-driven limousine arrived and took them to Wally Heider's Studio 3 in Hollywood. McCartney and Wings were mixing a new album, *Venus and Mars*. Hipgnosis listened to the music and made appreciative noises. Eventually, the group left, leaving only Paul and Linda. Po knew what was coming. 'So . . . Linda and I have an idea,' said McCartney, in the same sing-song voice they'd just heard on 'Listen to What the Man Said'.

McCartney wanted *Venus and Mars* illustrated by two different coloured pool balls on a baize table. Like neighbouring planets, perhaps? And he wanted Linda, a professional photographer, to take the picture, but with Hipgnosis overseeing.

'It was all too much for me,' said Storm, who told the McCartneys he didn't think it necessary for him to be present at the shoot. 'I'd been here before, realising an ordinary idea – the *Band on the Run* cover – for the wrong reasons.'

'Paul was a bit shocked by his attitude,' says Po, who assured the Beatle that it was a wonderful idea and Hipgnosis would be happy to assist. 'I don't know, but Storm just did not get along with Paul and Linda. He was too argumentative, too difficult. I don't ever remember Paul demeaning Storm's talent, but from then on, he didn't really like having him around.'

'He could be really crabby, old Storm,' said McCartney. '"Oh, I don't think that's any good." Well, we're having it Storm, so shut up.'

Serendipity saved the day. Jeff Smith, a friend of Nod Brown's and a Hollywood cameraman, was available for work. Po spent the following morning trying to persuade Storm to stay in LA. When he refused, Po hired Smith as his production manager after a brief conversation by the hotel pool. Smith was astonished to see Storm packing his bags and leapt at the chance to work with Paul McCartney.

Po and Smith both attended the cover shoot back at Wally Heider's. 'Linda was a good photographer, just not used to working with a larger format,' explains Po. He exchanged her usual 35mm Nikon for an in-plate camera of the kind used in advertising shoots. With the pool balls in place, all she had to do was click the shutter.

Hipgnosis had compromised on the image, but the McCartneys still needed a group shot for the inside sleeve. Paul wanted them photographed in an unusual landscape. The words 'ethereal' and 'otherworldly' were used and both were Hipgnosis's forté.

The following day, Po and his new production manager rented a Mercedes 270 convertible and spent ten hours scouting locations, north of Los Angeles, towards Death Valley. They found a spot in the foothills of the Sierra Nevada mountains and another nearby at the salt flats surrounding Owens Lake. Several Hollywood westerns had been filmed in this rugged terrain.

After checking into a motel in nearby Lone Pine, Po telephoned McCartney's manager, Brian Brolly, to tell him the news. He returned to the motel diner looking furious. Once again, McCartney had his own idea: he wanted Hipgnosis to photograph the group in Palm Springs and to meet them outside the Gene Autry Hotel, over 250 miles away, at six o'clock the following morning.

With just a service-station map to guide them, the pair spent six hours negotiating the desert backroads to Palm Springs in pitch-darkness. They arrived at the hotel on time, to find Wings' motorhome and a couple of limos in the parking lot.

All was not well. The RV's door swung open to reveal a distressed-looking Beatle and a ransacked living space. Wings' hot-headed young guitarist, Jimmy McCulloch, had drunk too much the night before and smashed up the furniture and fittings. Paul and Linda had locked themselves in a cabin at the rear of the vehicle until he calmed down.

McCartney told Po they were going to Los Angeles, not Palm Springs, and wouldn't be travelling in the motorhome or the limousines. Instead, Paul and Linda climbed into the back of Hipgnosis's Mercedes.

Jeff Smith's last job had been shooting a porn movie and now he was chauffeuring a Beatle. The McCartneys soon put him and Po at ease. Within minutes, a cloud of dope smoke was shrouding the rear passenger seat, as Paul regaled them with a leisurely stream of Fab Four anecdotes.

An hour later, the Mercedes broke the speed limit zooming through Riverside County and a wailing police siren interrupted McCartney's storytelling. Linda extinguished the joint she'd been smoking, but still had a bag of marijuana stashed under the seat. She had recently been busted in a car on Sunset Boulevard and couldn't afford another arrest. Damaging newspaper headlines flashed before Po's eyes as they pulled up by the side of the freeway.

The policeman sidled over, hand on his holster, and began lecturing Smith about the dangers of driving too fast. His famous passenger tried to remain inconspicuous as the cop wrote out a speeding ticket. Then the policeman glanced up and his eyes widened: 'Hey, is that John Lennon?'

'No, it's actually Paul McCartney,' Po replied, in his best English public-school accent.

The mood changed immediately. McCartney signed an autograph, the cop tore up the ticket and guided the Mercedes back onto the freeway. As soon as his car was out of sight, Linda sparked up another joint.

A few days later, Hipgnosis photographed Wings in the foot-hills of the Sierra Nevada mountains, as suggested. The night before Po flew home, McCartney threw a wrap party for the album. He was in the mood to celebrate as advance orders for *Venus and Mars* had already topped a million and a half.

The *Queen Mary*, a decommissioned ocean liner moored at Long Beach, became a floating Who's Who of the film and music industry. A drunk Dean Martin mingled with a starstruck Michael Jackson, while George Harrison pressed the flesh with Tony Curtis, Marvin Gaye, Mick Jagger, Led Zeppelin and Peter Grant.

It was an evening of alcohol and cocaine and endless con-versation. There was talk of Wings playing in the grounds of the stately home at Knebworth Park and of touring America. The next time McCartney performed in the States, Po would be sharing his private plane. From now on, Po would spend most of his life on planes and in exotic locations, until he eventually stopped going home at all.

Sadly, the enmity between Storm and McCartney lingered for-ever. Later, the McCartneys began throwing an annual Christmas party. 'Everybody got a personalised ceramic mug – "Love from Paul and Linda,"' recalls Richard Evans. 'I remember Po being invited, but not Storm, but Storm turning up anyway.'

'I told Storm I was going and he said, "How can you go with-out me?"' says Po. 'I said, "Easily, because I have been invited and you haven't, and they are a client." I turned up at the party and there's Storm behind me. Brian Brolly was stood there with a big bouncer and he said, "Storm, you're not invited." I went in anyway. I was direct with Storm. You couldn't afford not to be, or he would beat you into the ground.'

★

Hipgnosis's former photographers Rob Brimson and Howard Bartrop first met Storm Thorgerson when he was a visiting lecturer at Harrow Art School in 1974. Brimson had given up an engineering job to study photography, partly because of the celebrated British photojournalist Bill Brandt and partly because of Hipgnosis's art.

'*Ummagumma* in particular,' he says. 'So when Storm turned up to give a lecture, it was like the Queen dropping by. It was a spiky lecture and he upset most of the people. But I showed him some of my work and he agreed to give me a week's placement at Hipgnosis.'

Brimson arrived at the studio at 9.30 in the morning and sat on the steps until gone midday when somebody finally arrived. He stayed in touch with Storm after his week's placement and was eventually offered more work.

'I was there to load film, help with the lights, not mess up the processing and take photographs,' he explains. 'The job of the photographer was a technical exercise that required skill, but it wasn't an interpretative brief. On one occasion I rearranged a still life and was told, "You're not paid to think." It was harsh but a lesson I had to learn. I came to realise quickly what a brilliant man Storm was. He could charm and beguile and bully, but rock stars became malleable on a photographic session because he was just so intelligent.'

'Storm's lecture at the art school was abrasive,' recalls Howard Bartrop, who later photographed images for 10cc, Bad Company and Wings. 'But he saw something he liked in my work. The jobs weren't well paid, but Hipgnosis's images were so strong, they looked good in your portfolio when you went around the commercial agencies.'

Like everyone who worked at number six, Bartrop had to adjust to the studio dynamic and Hipgnosis's working methods.

'Peter Christopherson didn't like me,' he says. 'I think he saw me as a usurper. We were just on different wavelengths. Storm was the one I was closest to.'

So close that during a meeting at Hillfield Mansions, Storm insisted on continuing the conversation while using the lavatory. 'So I was in the adjacent room and he was still chatting away with the sounds of toiletry going on. I think he considered me a bit middle-class and wanted to shake me out of it.'

Brimson and Bartrop's arrival coincided with one of Hipgnosis's golden streaks. While Storm and Po had been in Los Angeles with a Beatle, Pink Floyd were in London trying to make their new album, *Wish You Were Here*. This arduous process had begun over a year earlier.

The Dark Side of the Moon had dragged the group into the mainstream, brought them great wealth and, for a previously cult band, a degree of fame. Everybody was living in bigger houses and driving more expensive cars. But Roger Waters struggled with his success: 'We'd reached the point we'd been aiming for since we were teenagers,' he says. 'We'd achieved everything we'd ever wanted to do. "Oh look! We're rich and famous." So what do we do next?'

To begin with, Pink Floyd revisited an idea they'd abandoned in 1970. They spent two months at Abbey Road Studios, creating sounds with aerosol spray cans, rubber bands, buckets of water and by running a finger around the edge of a wine glass filled with liquid. The project was nicknamed 'Household Objects' and Nick Mason thinks it was a delaying tactic, 'because we didn't know what else to do.'

The studio's engineers wondered which Floyd would be the first to crack. It was Rick Wright, who deemed the project 'insane'. Everybody else agreed and the idea was abandoned for ever. Nevertheless, the pressure to follow a huge hit intimidated them all.

'It was a tricky time and we all had to sit around and assess it – music and life,' agrees David Gilmour. 'But long before *Wish You Were Here*, I realised, "Right, I am a musician and I want to carry on being a musician."'

Before long, Floyd had two new songs. In 'You've Gotta Be Crazy', an ambitious businessman ponders his moral bankruptcy, while 'Raving and Drooling' reimagined human beings as bloodthirsty animals. Waters' defended his grim worldview years later: 'I suppose I have always appeared as a rather melancholy person, but I'm not,' he insisted. 'My situation is like the opposite of the comedian who when he's not performing is a miserable sod.'

The group left Abbey Road's household objects behind and started rehearsing this new material at Unit Studios in London's King's Cross. There was some self-flagellation involved. Unit was a windowless space, without a television set and only a Wimpy bar nearby.

'It was a shit-hole,' remarks Gilmour. 'Perhaps we took the point of view that if there was nothing else to distract us, the creativity would come and there was nothing else to do in this place but make music.'

Soon, Waters had written lyrics for another new song, 'Shine On You Crazy Diamond'. This was Pink Floyd making music about Pink Floyd. 'We always accepted the song was about Syd Barrett,' says Gilmour. 'With lyrics like "you crazy diamond", it couldn't be about anyone else.'

Floyd played all three songs during the winter 1974 tour. By the final lap, Waters was dedicating 'Shine On You Crazy Diamond' to 'Syd-nee Barrett'. But when they reconvened, at Abbey Road, in January the following year, progress was slow: 'Nobody was feeling terribly motivated,' admits Nick Mason.

'God! It was torture, torture, *torture!*' says Waters. The dispirited group began looking for other things to do, such as listlessly firing an air gun at a dartboard, or teasing Rick Wright, who was less resilient than the others and an easy target. 'We were a tough, cruel bunch,' admits Gilmour. 'Led by Captain Roger, who was the toughest and cruellest of the bunch.'

After six weeks of floundering, Waters proposed dumping 'You've Gotta Be Crazy' and 'Raving and Drooling'. He wanted to write new material and split 'Shine On You Crazy Diamond' into nine parts, turning it into a suite of music to bookend the album.

Floyd worked on three more compositions. Both 'Have a Cigar' (eventually recorded with guest vocals by strident folk singer and Hipgnosis client Roy Harper) and 'Welcome to the Machine' explored what Gilmour calls 'the negative aspects of the music industry'. The title track, 'Wish You Were Here', was a plea for happier times and especially pertinent considering Waters' domestic situation. 'I also think there's a bit of Syd in there,' says Gilmour.

Storm was shown the lyrics to 'Shine On You Crazy Diamond' during Floyd's West Coast tour. 'They seemed to be about an unfulfilled presence in general,' he said. 'A presence withheld . . . the way people pretend to be present when their minds are elsewhere. It eventually boiled down to a single theme – absence.

'An absence of Syd Barrett, an absence of wives – as some of the band were getting divorced – and, to some extent, an absence of commitment from the band themselves.'

'There were lots of conversations between me and Storm about what *Wish You Were Here* was about,' says Waters. 'I could talk to him about these things. Storm got it. Storm was interested.'

'I became very preoccupied with the number four,' revealed Storm, who'd always had a fascination with numerology. 'Four members of the group, four words in the album title and four elements to life – earth, air, fire and water – and four images for the package.'

Po suggested a faceless record company salesman in the desert to represent earth and a diver entering the water without making a splash. Storm proposed a red veil blowing in the wind to illustrate air, and two businessmen shaking hands, with one on fire. 'It was a big saying at the time,' says Po. '"Oh *m-a-a-n*, I've been burned", as in ripped off.'

Once again, Storm was stricken with nerves before pitching his ideas to Pink Floyd in the Abbey Road canteen. To his surprise, 'the tough, cruel bunch' gave him a round of applause.

Producing a cover package with four different images was a major undertaking. Storm returned to London, just as Po and Peter Christopherson flew to LA. Jeff Smith reprised his role as production manager and Po collected a sizeable wad of cash from Steve O'Rourke, before checking into the upscale Beverly Rodeo Hotel.

The three-week *Wish You Were Here* cover shoot was Hipgnosis's version of a stadium rock tour, complete with the same perks and pitfalls. Storm's brilliant concept was realised through a combination of bribery, charm, good fortune, quick thinking and what were euphemistically billed as 'medical supplies': 'There was a lot of cocaine around by this time,' Po divulges, 'and we were rather living the rock 'n' roll lifestyle.'

Their first task was shooting the two businessmen for the front cover. The Stunts Unlimited agency supplied Hollywood with men willing to throw themselves from moving vehicles and blazing buildings. Hipgnosis hired its co-founder Ronnie Rondell and stuntman Danny Rogers, both of whom had just worked on the hit movie, *The Towering Inferno*.

Rondell agreed to be set on fire but insisted on deciding when and how. Hipgnosis were summoned to a backlot at Warner Brothers studios in Burbank, where Rondell had brought his own fire-retardant wig and clothes and a safety team armed with fire blankets and fire extinguishers.

Po was determined to get his picture, whatever it took. Several spots on Rondell's wig and suit were soaked in a flammable napalm-like liquid. As soon as an assistant touched them with a lighted wand, Rondell burst into flame and the motor drive on Po's Hasselblad whirred into action.

Po took fifteen shots before a sudden gust of wind turned the flaming wig into a towering inferno. 'That's the funny thing about fire,' deadpanned Rondell. 'When it gets in your face, you're going to move, no matter what you are meant to be doing.'

Following Hipgnosis's edict that 'the art comes first', Po didn't stop shooting until his burning model staggered out of the frame and was smothered in foam and blankets. Rondell escaped with a scorched eyebrow and moustache, but the shoot was over: he was done.

Ronnie Rondell's career as a stunt man and coordinator continued into retirement in the 2000s. He appeared in the TV series *Charlie's Angels* and *Dynasty*, and in the movies *The Karate Kid*, *Lethal Weapon* and *The Matrix Reloaded*. 'But everybody ignores that and all anyone wants to talk to Ronnie about is fucking *Wish You Were Here*,' admits Po.

After photographing fire, Hipgnosis moved on to the next element. Pink Floyd's budget was no object and Po had chartered a plane and spent a day scouting locations across California. He decided on Mono Lake, on the edge of the Sierra Nevada. Meanwhile, Jeff Smith had hired a diver who could hold his breath underwater for ninety seconds, a prerequisite for this job.

'Storm and I wanted a natural action – a man diving into the water – but without any after effects, with the absence of ripples,' explains Po. 'So the diver had to hold his breath until the water was still again.'

Po and his team rowed out to a shallow bay, but found themselves at the mercy of the weather. A persistent breeze was creating ripples on the lake's surface. They waited until almost sunset before the wind suddenly dropped. The diver took his deepest breath before flipping upside down. He performed a perfect headstand while holding onto a yoga stool anchored below the waterline. Po fired off as many shots as he could manage before the sun dropped, the wind picked up and the moment passed.

In the final image, the diver's lower body mirrored the limestone rocks around the shoreline and his reflection on the water was so immaculate it's difficult to believe it was created without modern technology. It was worthy of an album cover but was relegated to the inside of the package.

There was a feeling of triumph as Hipgnosis loaded up their rented Cadillac and began the long drive back to LA. The conversation turned to how Peter Christopherson had come to work for Hipgnosis. Po asked if his portfolio of unusual body photos had been shot at art school: 'And Peter replied, "No, I worked in a mortuary and I used to rearrange the dead bodies at night and take photographs." Jeff and I nearly fell out of the car with shock.'

'Sleazy was strange like that,' says Cosey Fanni Tutti. 'Everything was compartmentalised. Those pictures he showed Storm and Po were real, but I don't believe he ever worked in a mortuary.'

Genesis P-Orridge had applied for a job in a morgue but was turned down because he was too slight and couldn't lift the corpses. Cosey believes Christopherson may have gained access to the facility through Genesis: 'But he probably didn't tell me because he knew I wouldn't approve. I didn't like the idea of invading someone's privacy like that.'

Po discovered more about his assistant's secret life when he returned to the Beverly Rodeo one night. 'There was a tremendous commotion – shouting and screaming – coming from Peter's room,' he recalls. 'So I burst in and found two big bikers trying to rape him. He'd invited them back, but things had gotten out of hand. They fled the scene, but Peter was terribly shaken, half-naked, with his shirt all torn. It wasn't the last time Peter ended up in trouble when working with us.'

To photograph the faceless salesman for the LP's back cover, Hipgnosis moved into the Holiday Inn in Blythe, a truck-stop town, a couple of hundred miles east of Los Angeles. It was a step down from the Beverly Rodeo, but Po wanted to shoot in a stretch of the Yuma Desert flanking Route 78.

The salesman would be photographed wearing a suit and bowler hat, but with his face, wrists and ankles removed later in the studio. However, their hired model was known for his Marlboro Man-style rugged looks and made an immediate impression on some of the Holiday Inn's guests.

The night before the early-morning shoot, the model and Jeff Smith found themselves attending a graduation party being held in the hotel. New acquaintances were made and both men were battling savage hangovers when Po summoned them from their beds at dawn.

Unfortunately, Hipgnosis's Cadillac wasn't designed for deserts and quickly became stuck in the sand. It was Dune Buggy Weekend and Route 78 was bumper-to-bumper with sand sport enthusiasts and their rugged vehicles. Mentioning Pink Floyd's name was enough for Po to persuade three drivers to transport them to their chosen stretch of sand. The only downside was answering questions about the famous band and the meaning behind *The Dark Side of the Moon*.

Po followed Storm's brief, but also photographed a second image: of their Marlboro Man model pretending to swim through the sand. 'I wanted it as a backup in case the other picture didn't work,' he explains. But the image would only be used in the promotion of *Wish You Were Here*.

The final piece of Storm's puzzle was created back in England. Hipgnosis's friend, the artist John Blake, had suggested a veil floating among some trees to signify air and absence. But it was Storm's idea to include a barely visible naked woman behind the muslin. Like the fragment of 'See Emily Play' performed by Rick Wright during the finale of 'Shine On You Crazy Diamond', this back-cover nude was so subtle many missed it completely.

Syd Barrett's presence suffused *Wish You Were Here*. There was something poetic about him showing up in the studio while they were finishing the record. Like the Japanese thriller *Rashomon*, where a crime is recalled by four contradictory eyewitnesses, everybody has a different version of this story. Some say Barrett came to the studio once, most likely on 5 June; others that he was there on several occasions.

Barrett also made an appearance at 6 Denmark Street beforehand. 'It was early afternoon and this strange-looking man shuffled in,' recalls Richard Evans. 'He had a shaven head, a pasty face and was wearing a mac that might have been trendy in the '60s.'

Evans initially thought it was Peter Gabriel, who was experimenting with his image since leaving Genesis. Then he looked closer. The visitor had shaved off his eyebrows, had a large barrel-shaped belly and was carrying a plastic shopping bag: 'To be honest, he reminded me of a character from *Monty Python*.'

'It was only when I looked into his eyes, I realised it was Syd,' insists Po.

'Syd told us he was looking for Storm,' says Evans. 'Po said he was at Abbey Road with Pink Floyd and offered to make him a cup of tea. Syd said "No" and shuffled off, looking a bit embarrassed. I wouldn't have known it was Syd Barrett, because I knew the good-looking Syd Barrett from the pictures on *A Nice Pair* and his album covers.'

After he'd left, Evans became aware of a chill in the air, as if a ghost had passed through the room: 'Maybe I imagined it, and it *was* the '70s,' he laughs, 'but Po noticed it, too.'

A few hours later, Storm burst into the studio and announced, 'You won't believe what just happened at Abbey Road?'

'No,' replied Evans, 'but let me guess . . .'

When Syd Barrett wandered into Abbey Road Studios later that afternoon, the group presumed he was a house engineer and ignored him. 'Then he came into the control room and someone said, "That's fucking Syd,"' says David Gilmour. 'I think it was me . . . Roger thinks it was him . . . and so on.'

Rick Wright remembered listening to a playback of 'Shine On You Crazy Diamond' when Barrett pulled a toothbrush out of his plastic bag, started brushing his teeth and asked, 'Right, when do I put the guitar on?' Nick Mason recalls being 'horrified by the physical change' and Roger Waters was 'in fucking tears'.

When pushed for his memories, Storm said his old friend 'looked terrible and was awkwardly asking the band if he could be of any help'. Nick Sedgwick was also present and remembered 'a bald, fat person in lace-less hush puppies and outsize trousers held up by a piece of string'.

Sedgwick sat next to Barrett when he listened to Floyd's new music and says he guzzled orange juice 'by the bucket load' and chewed mouthfuls of breath-freshening sweets. When Nick asked what he thought of the song, Syd replied, 'It's all . . . all a bit Mary Poppins.'

'I don't know what song we were working on when Syd was there,' insists Gilmour. 'We tried to engage Syd in conversation and then he wandered off down Abbey Road.'

Others, including Peter Jenner, swear they saw Barrett a couple of days later in the Abbey Road canteen. He supposedly told one of them that his weight gain was the result of 'having a large fridge' and 'eating a lot of pork chops'.

'I have heard people say he came for two or three days. I don't think that's true,' insists Gilmour. 'I also don't think he said any of the things people claim he said while he was in the studio. But people love to be involved with a moment and that's how these stories get about.'

Decades later, while creating artwork for a *Wish You Were Here* box set, Storm wondered why he hadn't suggested a picture of Barrett for the original package. But several ideas were abandoned before they arrived at the finished article.

One image was meant to depict the ultimate absence and showed a driver standing beside a Jaguar XK120 at the side of a deserted country road. A newspaper with the headline 'Pop Star Dies in Car Crash' fluttered in the foreground. Pink Floyd spent much of their working lives in transit and thought the image was tempting fate. Two years later, Hipgnosis used it on the cover of *Kitsch*, by the hard-rock group Heavy Metal Kids.

Wings never made it to Knebworth Park. Pink Floyd headlined the outdoor show, on 5 August 1975, instead. Hipgnosis designed a poster for the concert and, once again, the budget was fluid. Po and Alex Henderson flew to Italy, but after failing to find a suitable location in Pisa, Genoa, Florence and Milan, they caught a plane to Geneva and hired a limousine.

The finished image showed Henderson and his bicycle in the middle of a motorway near Lake Geneva, illustrated bike parts whizzing towards him like shrapnel. 'Po said I had to be the model, as it was cheaper than hiring one,' Henderson recalls.

Wish You Were Here was released in September. Its multi-dimensional artwork had cost an estimated £50,000, the equivalent of over £395,000 today. 'The cover was very beautiful and very clever and intellectually accomplished,' says Waters.

'It's an album about space and solitude,' said Gilmour. 'Storm produced something that was a visual mirror, reflecting the absence that pervaded both the music and the musicians at the time.'

The artwork was also filled with Storm's boyhood influences. 'Sleeve art is ridiculously plagiaristic,' offers David Gale. 'Utterly shameless. Dalí, Miró, Magritte . . . Hipgnosis mucked about with it all but nobody grumbled. An art tutor could spot a mile off where it was coming from, but there wasn't a great overlap between them and Pink Floyd's wider audience.'

Storm's coup d'état, though, was to wrap *Wish You Were Here* in opaque black plastic, rendering every image absent. An art tutor might have compared this to the environmental artists Christo and Jeanne-Claude draping a mountain in Colorado with 200 square feet of fabric. But Storm copied the idea from Roxy Music's *Country Life*. Roxy's cover models were too underdressed for American retailers, so the LP was covered in green shrink wrap.

Hipgnosis's decision prompted an urgent phone call from EMI to Steve O'Rourke. 'This was classic Storm – designing a great cover and then hiding it,' says Mason. 'But we too liked nothing better than baiting the record company, so we let them sort it out between them.'

Hipgnosis compromised. George Hardie had drawn a pair of mechanical hands for the vinyl record label. Hardie's robotic handshake was re-purposed in colour and turned into a sticker, with the group's name and album title plastered across the wrapper.

'Many record shop managers loathed the package,' claimed Storm, 'because they wanted to display the burning businessman in their window. But once the shrink wrap was removed, it couldn't be put back again.' None of this mattered in the long run. *Wish You Were Here* became Pink Floyd's first UK and US number-one hit. The group and their sleeve designers would never be quite so in sync again.

In the same month Hipgnosis's burning man arrived in record shops, Peter Christopherson photographed their new neighbours. The Sex Pistols' rehearsal space was a former rag-trade outbuilding in the courtyard behind Zeno's bookshop.

'The Pistols were charming in a funny way,' says Rob Brimson. 'They had to go through Zeno's, go into the yard, then climb over a wall and up a ladder to get into their rehearsal room. Then you'd hear this cacophony.'

The Sex Pistols' manager, Malcolm McLaren, and his fashion-designer partner, Vivienne Westwood, ran SEX, a King's Road boutique selling fetish wear and early punk fashions, though the term 'punk' wasn't in common use yet. Most of the Pistols were either employees, customers or shoplifters.

McLaren was a former art student who'd dabbled in radical politics and the avant-garde and envisaged the Sex Pistols as an art project. He saw them as usurping what Peter Gabriel had called 'the *Titanic* and the big fat supergroups'.

The war babies who'd formed rock 'n' roll bands in the early '60s were now in their thirties. The Stones were no longer angry young men and there was a remoteness to the likes of Led Zeppelin and Pink Floyd. This remoteness empowered Hipgnosis to create an image for them both, but there was also growing opposition.

Westwood and McLaren had recently designed a T-shirt bearing the slogan, 'You're Gonna Wake Up One Morning and Know What Side of the Bed You've Been Lying On'. Underneath were two lists of people: those they deemed acceptable and those they didn't. The second list included Mick Jagger, Yes, Rod Stewart and 'Whispering' Bob Harris from *The Old Grey Whistle Test*.

Christopherson was a SEX shop customer and his curiosity was piqued by the group's arrival: 'The Hipgnosis offices faced right onto our living quarters and they were always staring at us,' recalled Sex Pistols bass guitarist Glen Matlock. 'It got so bad we had to do the full old lady bit and put up net curtains. Then one day the main guy who'd been peeking at us asked if he could take some pictures.'

Christopherson photographed the Pistols behind the studio and at the local YMCA. The theme was 'wounded young boys': ex-reform school kid Steve Jones wore handcuffs and prison-issue pyjamas; John Lydon a straitjacket; Glen Matlock was styled as a male prostitute loitering in a public lavatory and drummer Paul Cook had his bare torso peppered with fake bullet holes. McLaren rejected the images as being too downbeat.

The Sex Pistols played their first live show in November at nearby Central Saint Martin's College of Art. McLaren invited Po to the show, but he turned it down: 'A decision I now regret,' he says.

With their DIY haircuts and SEX shop threads, the Pistols were visually arresting but so unprepared, they had to borrow equipment from the headline act, pub-rockers Bazooka Joe (featuring a pre-fame Adam Ant playing bass). The Pistols were messy and brutally loud. Lydon started kicking the speakers, a scuffle broke out and the plug was pulled. Steve Jones summed up the difference between the Sex Pistols and the headliners, but he could have been talking about the Pistols versus everybody else: 'We weren't being nice,' Jones said. 'That was the difference between us and them.'

'To begin with, the Sex Pistols were polite and we used to hold the door open for each other,' says Po. 'Then it changed after a few months and they became rude and aggressive – which was something Malcolm McLaren encouraged.'

The confrontation began with the spitting incident and was compounded when Po spotted Lydon, who'd adopted the stage name 'Johnny Rotten', wearing a Pink Floyd T-shirt with the words 'I Hate' scrawled above the logo. 'I said to Rotten, "Are you having a go at me?" And he said, "Yeah, you and all that other *shit* you listen to." There was a divide. Us, wearing flares and playing Crosby, Stills, Nash & Young upstairs, and the Sex Pistols doing what they were doing.'

In 2016, the group's former rehearsal space was given a Grade II listing and a preservation order was placed on the band's graffiti. The following year, *Their Mortal Remains: The Pink Floyd Exhibition* at London's Victoria and Albert Museum, exhibited a photograph of Lydon in his 'I Hate Pink Floyd' T-shirt.

Both ideas would have seemed inconceivable in the '70s, though. The old guard were keeping Hipgnosis in business and still selling lots of records. Seasoned folkie Al Stewart's *Year of the Cat* was released in the summer of 1976 and sold a million copies.

This meant a million homes also owned Hipgnosis's illustrator Colin Elgie's cover painting. Elgie also drew the fairy-tale characters on Genesis's latest top-five album, *A Trick of the Tail*.

Even the *older* old guard came to Hipgnosis, who designed sleeves for the reunited Shadows and the Hollies, two '60s groups re-launching their careers in the era of four-sided concept albums. There were new clients, too. *The Dark Side of the Moon*'s sound engineer, Alan Parsons, had formed a group, the Alan Parsons Project. Their debut album, *Tales of Mystery and Imagination*, revisited the works of American gothic horror writer, Edgar Allen Poe.

Over the next few years, Storm serviced the Alan Parsons Project with images of robots and mummified bodies; the escalator system at the Charles de Gaulle airport and the numerological value of pi. Their partnership thrived into the next century.

Storm found the same compatibility with 10cc, four Mancunian songwriters whose hits 'The Wall Street Shuffle' and 'Life Is a Minestrone' had a narrative quality and knowing humour. 10cc were deadly serious about their craft, but also self-deprecating. Their second album, 1974's *Sheet Music*, included a song titled 'The Worst Band in the World'.

Hipgnosis were surprised when 10cc's first manager, Jonathan King, commissioned them to design *Sheet Music*. In 1965, when King was studying at Cambridge, he'd recorded a hit single, 'Everyone's Gone to the Moon', and fancied himself as a pop star. Storm and Po, keen to divest him of this notion, spotted King reclining in a punt one afternoon and tipped him into the Cam.

'Storm and Po were the first rock star designers,' says 10cc's ex-drummer Kevin Godley. 'They understood that making good art can equal making good money. But Storm was like a design punk – the John Lydon of design. He didn't suffer fools gladly and if he thought you were a wanker, he'd tell you.'

Hipgnosis presented their ideas, mounted on the walls of 10cc's facility, Strawberry Studios in Stockport. 'We would walk around them like we were at an art gallery, looking for the one that jumped out,' says vocalist/guitarist Graham Gouldman. 'We always alighted on the same one. But Storm loved to tease us, asking what we thought they all meant.

'What Hipgnosis did was visually aligned with what we were doing. Some of our lyrics didn't make sense on the surface but they did on a subconscious level. I used to get asked, "Well, what does that mean?" And I'd often reply, "Well, what do you think it means?"'

10cc's third album, *The Original Soundtrack*, was music for a film that hadn't been made. Hipgnosis hired the musician and artist Humphrey Ocean to draw an illustration of film-editing equipment. A jumble of spools, lenses and screens was assembled in a Soho basement like a still-life. The group appeared on the final cover, but upside down, barely visible and as a reflection on a screen.

'10cc were saddled with this image as a pop band,' says Godley, 'but we never felt like a pop band. Hipgnosis's covers gave us an identity.'

For the follow-up, 1976's *How Dare You!*, Hipgnosis chose the theme of communication. The front and back covers deployed a split-screen effect, as seen in old movies when a couple were talking on the telephone: '10cc liked it because they had a song on the record called "Don't Hang Up",' said Storm. 'We chose characters and situations from the songs and added a sub-plot involving the couple that appears in every shot. The sad lady in the foreground on the cover is a gin-soaked housewife, wasting away in rich suburbia, while her smooth businessman husband neglects her. He is furious at being interrupted at work, again – "How dare you!"'

George Hardie's illustration of telephones connecting to the brain on the liner bags and the inside gatefold photo foresaw the ubiquity of the mobile phone. The gatefold party scene showed more than thirty models, including Richard Evans, Lindsay Corner, Gala Pinion, Jonathan Meades and Gai Caron, all speaking on telephones.

'It was about going to a crowded party and being unable to talk to anyone,' explained Storm. 'So better to be on the blower than face somebody directly.'

Storm art directed one half of the gathering and Po the other. 'It was absolute chaos,' recalls photographer Howard Bartrop, 'with both of them rushing backwards and forwards, and Storm shouting, "Take the bloody picture!"'

Godley, Gouldman and their bandmates, Lol Creme and Eric Stewart, were hidden, *Where's Wally?*-style, in the crowd. 'We liked that you had to look for us in that picture,' says Gouldman, 'because we never wanted to be on our covers.'

10cc were fond of puns and wordplay, and their intelligence sometimes tipped over into smart-arsery. In that regard, they were the ultimate Hipgnosis group. Storm always praised 10cc's music, while Po knew the hits but doesn't recall ever listening to one of their albums from start to finish. This was not unusual.

'We were still having meetings, two or three nights a week, in Storm's flat,' Po explains. 'Storm used to have whatever album we were designing playing in the background. He said it inspired him, but I found it an irritant. I rarely listened to the groups we worked with because it fogged my brain, I needed a break from them.

'I appreciated *The Dark Side of the Moon*,' he stresses, 'and I thought early Led Zeppelin was the dog's bollocks, but I never listened to, say, Wishbone Ash or Black Sabbath.'

Sometimes this was a positive. Hipgnosis designed the artwork for Black Sabbath's *Technical Ecstasy* and *Never Say Die!* albums without hearing a note. Sabbath's previous two sleeves had featured an unflattering band photograph and a painting of a dying man surrounded by winged demons. These were heavy-metal clichés writ large.

Technical Ecstasy showed a pair of robots, who looked like they'd been painted by Giorgio de Chirico, exchanging bodily fluids on an escalator. *Never Say Die!* came with airmen wearing fetishistic gas masks, like kamikaze pilots styled by Vivienne Westwood. Both covers were superior to some of the music inside.

Wishbone Ash's latest, *New England*, was released with a picture of bare-chested boys on its sleeve. This was far removed from how most blues-rock groups presented themselves. 'I liked that it was different,' says guitarist Andy Powell. 'It reminded me of a still from an old black-and-white movie – something from the 1940s.'

New England was another example of Peter Christopherson exploring his sexuality. One of the models was sharpening a stick as another looked on in anticipation: 'The implications are sinister,' suggests Po, 'and phallic.'

More so than Wishbone Ash realised. 'Sleazy's fantasies often involved castration and torture, sometimes of himself,' claimed Genesis P-Orridge, who recalled seeing a carpenter's vice in the kitchen of Christopherson's house. Peter told him he put his testicles in the vice's jaws and tightened them until the pain became unbearable. 'Why would you do that?' asked Genesis. 'I like it,' Christopherson replied.

Most of the album was recorded in Wishbone Ash's new home studio in rural Connecticut. Storm photographed the group wading through a swamp for the inside cover. 'He was being his usual provocative self,' remembers Powell. 'Later, we took Storm to a restaurant and he started throwing bread rolls around. He was behaving badly and more like a rock star than any of us.'

Hipgnosis could afford to behave like rock stars now. The creative freedom they'd fought for in the '60s was now a given. Record labels would fly Storm to Connecticut, to shoot the inside of a cover; Po to Miami to pitch ideas to Black Sabbath in the studio and would fund multiple photo shoots for the cover of one 10cc album.

'I don't know who paid,' admits Kevin Godley. 'The label or us? If it was the label, it still ended up being us. Like many labels at the time, the lunatics were running the asylum. I don't know if it helped us sell records, but it was always, "Get Storm and Po". We would have kicked up an almighty fuss if the record company said no.'

Even the companies printing the sleeves were wooing Hipgnosis. 'Sometime after *The Dark Side of the Moon*, AGI, who were printing millions of record covers, approached us with a deal,' says Po. 'They offered us ten cents on every album sold if we put the work their way. If you look at what that would have meant on, say, *Wish You Were Here*, it was potentially a huge amount of money.'

Storm turned the offer down. 'It was that weird morality of his. But he was right to do so because AGI was not the best company for Hipgnosis to use so it would have been a problem, especially if we also making money off a band's sales.'

Another offer was soon forthcoming, though, from Ellis Kern, the head of rival printers, Ivy Hill. 'Ellis said, "How would you like a couple of holidays a year on the company?"' says Po. 'Ivy Hill were better suited to Hipgnosis and always went the extra mile for us.'

Next thing, Storm and Bill took an all-expenses-paid railway trip from Chicago to Miami and Po started holidaying in the company's apartment in Palm Beach, Florida: 'This went on for about five years and it was Ivy Hill's way of rewarding us without paying us any money.'

Everybody was happy, except AGI, who eventually complained to the record labels that Hipgnosis were unfairly favouring one company. They reluctantly cancelled the arrangement.

'It was unlike Storm and I to be so honest,' admits Po. 'But we also worried that if the McCartneys or Led Zeppelins ever found out about this they'd have told us to fuck off and we'd be out of work.'

On the road with Bad Company in spring 1976, Po realised the line between photographer and rock star was becoming even more blurred. The group were touring their third album, *Run with the Pack*. The artwork commission had gone to Hipgnosis's rival, John Kosh. But Po was photographing the tour and flying with the group on their private jet.

After a show in Ludwigshafen, West Germany, everyone congregated in the hotel bar. Guitarist Mick Ralphs and drummer Simon Kirke started playing old rock 'n' roll numbers on the hotel piano as Po sat drinking with vocalist Paul Rodgers.

'I was tapping my fingers to the music,' he recalls. 'Paul told me to stop as it was annoying him, but I didn't.' Rodgers had boxed in his youth and now practised martial arts. When Po ignored his request again, Rodgers hit him: 'He clocked me, right in the face. Paul and I were laughing about this a few years ago when we met up again, but at the time I was so pissed off.'

Po had been drinking heavily and staggered back to his room with the beginnings of a black eye. 'I was so furious, I ripped down the curtains, smashed the TV and tore the sink off the wall,' he admits. 'And then I passed out on the bed.'

It was a coin-operated vibrating bed, which had developed a fault and didn't stop vibrating. A few hours later, Po regained consciousness to see his cowboy boots juddering up and down at the end of the mattress. His hangover was compounded by motion sickness and the realisation he'd done thousands of Deutschmarks worth of damage.

Po crept away early and caught the first plane back to London. Then he waited for Peter Grant's phone call. It was days before it arrived; Grant knew how to prolong the agony.

'Hello, Po,' Grant finally whispered down the line. 'Have you been a naughty boy?' Po confessed he had and offered to pay for the damages. 'I was also quite prepared for the possibility he'd fire us and we wouldn't work for him again.'

Grant listened to Po's apology. 'And then he said, "I'm gonna ask you one question, Po – and you have to answer it honestly, okay? Did you enjoy smashing up that hotel room?"

'I told him I loved every minute of it. Peter said, "Fine, we'll pay the damages, this one time, but don't ever fucking do that again." I never did. But I knew I'd crossed the line and was acting like a rock star.'

One day, back at number six, Rob Brimson was hanging prints and looking out of the darkroom window into the courtyard. The Sex Pistols were rehearsing with the windows open. 'I was still an unredeemed hippy with long hair and up until now I thought they'd sounded pretty terrible,' he says. 'But suddenly it changed. I think they were playing "Pretty Vacant", but whatever it was, it sounded pretty good. It was starting to gel.'

'Something was changing,' says Po, 'and I had a feeling Hipgnosis wasn't going to be a part of it.'

Chapter 8

'My problem was making sure we had a good pig . . .'

Hipgnosis versus sex, drugs, money and power.

'We were the last of the big spenders.'

– Sir Paul McCartney

On 4 August 1975, Robert Plant's hire car crashed into a tree on the Greek island of Rhodes. The singer and his family were on their way to see Phil May, who'd borrowed Roger Waters' villa for the summer. Plant's wife, Maureen, was driving when their Austin Mini span off the road. Maureen sustained multiple injuries, including a fractured skull, her husband broke an elbow and shattered his right leg, their daughter, Carmen, had a broken wrist and their son, Karac, had a fractured leg. A passing truck driver loaded the broken and bleeding family onto his flatbed and took them to the hospital.

214

Maureen was in a life-threatening condition, so Led Zeppelin manager Peter Grant arranged for a private surgeon and physician to travel to Rhodes. They insisted the couple were flown home, but the Greek authorities refused. An investigation into the crash was underway; Plant was a rock star and even though he wasn't driving, the police believed drugs or alcohol were involved somewhere.

Grant refused to wait and sent Richard Cole to Rhodes. Cole hired cars and a private ambulance, waited until nightfall and smuggled the injured parties, still attached to IV drips, into the waiting vehicles. Plant was cocooned in plaster from his hip down and wheeled on a trolley to a waiting private jet.

By the time the hospital realised what had happened, their patients were en route to Heathrow. Grant and Led Zeppelin were taking a year out as tax exiles, which limited how many days they could spend in Britain. Grant claimed he'd ordered the pilot to circle the English Channel until after midnight before landing. It was a good story regardless of its veracity.

Grant had tossed money at the problem, but he wasn't a miracle worker. Maureen's recovery was a long, arduous process. Back in London, doctors told Plant he wouldn't walk for six months and might never fully gain his mobility. Zeppelin's American tour was postponed as he pondered a future away from the group.

Suddenly, Led Zeppelin didn't seem so invincible. Yet the year had started so well. Their new album, *Physical Graffiti*, released in February, encompassed all Zeppelin life across four sides of vinyl. It was also the first release on their own label, Swan Song, and was a number-one hit in the UK and the US.

Hipgnosis had been passed over for the artwork, though. Po blamed this on Storm's faux pas with the tennis racket. Jimmy Page says it was because he had his own idea for the cover. *Physical*

Graffiti's sleeve showed a tenement building in New York's East Village, with windows die-cut to display the LP title on a paper insert and random photographs on the inside sleeve.

'I wanted something mechanical, as we'd had on *Led Zeppelin III*,' explains Page. The group's third album had a die-cut sleeve with a rotating cardboard wheel inside. 'With *Physical Graffiti*, everything inside the sleeve related to the windows. I was arguing with people about this because I knew what I wanted to do.'

Physical Graffiti was overseen by the American designer Peter Corriston, who'd later create art for the Rolling Stones. Page's handpicked images of Buzz Aldrin, Lee Harvey Oswald, King Kong, the Virgin Mary and Led Zeppelin in drag ('I think Robert made the best woman,' says Page) became visible in the windows when the paper insert was removed.

The rejection rankled with Hipgnosis, though, who'd already designed the Swan Song logo. Page had shown Po the nineteenth-century artist William Rimmer's painting *Evening (The Fall of Day)*, for inspiration. Freelance illustrator Joe Petagno was hired to recreate the work, though most Zeppelin watchers presumed his naked winged figure was Icarus, the mythological Greek who flew too close to the sun.

The image also bore a passing resemblance to Robert Plant. 'When we saw the Swan Song logo, some people thought it paid homage to Robert,' admits Page. 'But I didn't think so because I knew the painting. Hipgnosis also came up with marvellous Celtic-inspired calligraphy for that logo.'

Swan Song had launched in a blaze of publicity with parties in New York, Los Angeles and Chislehurst Caves in Kent. Grant and the label rented an office at 484 King's Road, a few doors down from McLaren and Westwood's SEX shop. Bad Company, Maggie Bell and the Pretty Things were all signed to Swan

Song but running a record company was a challenge, even without the boss's drug habit.

Led Zeppelin and their manager wielded great power within the industry but were compromised. Jimmy Page and Richard Cole were using heroin and Grant's cocaine use was clouding his judgement and decision-making. He was also surrounding himself with even more nefarious characters.

The latest was John 'Biffo' Bindon, who filled his time between acting roles in *Z-Cars* and *Love Thy Neighbour*, with protection racketeering, stints as a security guard and a rumoured affair with the Queen's sister, Princess Margaret. Grant employed Bindon for extra muscle on tour, but he was swift to anger and made most of Led Zeppelin feel uneasy.

Atlantic dutifully licensed Swan Song's artists; anything to keep their cash cow happy. But only Bad Company thrived. The rest languished in Zeppelin's shadow, buoyed up by the glamorous connection but neglected. Grant didn't know how to run a record company and Led Zeppelin were too preoccupied with their own careers to become A&R men.

On the lam from Her Majesty's Revenue & Customs, the band and its retinue spent most of the summer of 1975 in the Malibu Colony, a private beachside estate in California. Page sequestered himself in a rented villa and was rarely spotted during daylight hours, while a wheelchair-bound Plant gulped painkillers and tried to write lyrics. They eventually had the bones of a new album.

There was a sense of urgency to the work. 'You've got to take the mindset of the band into this,' explains Page. 'Robert had his accident, we didn't know if he could tour or what was going to happen in the future so we decided to make an album and throw absolutely everything at it – and fast.'

Led Zeppelin's seventh LP, *Presence*, was recorded in just eighteen days in Munich's Musicland Studios in November and December. The studio was in the basement of the Arabellahaus hotel, a utilitarian tower-block, known for its high suicide rate. Several cases were recorded of depressed Bavarians leaping to their deaths from the hotel roof.

When Led Zeppelin arrived, Plant was rattling with prescription pills and Page was self-medicating in other ways. Days passed without a note being played, before Jimmy's guitar rang out like a clarion call and everybody scrambled to the basement, Plant in a wheelchair steered by his faithful manservant.

Presence's opening song, 'Achilles Last Stand', sounded like the score to a biblical epic; something filled with plague and pestilence. 'I wanted to do something that had so much guitar orchestration, people would go, "Jesus Christ! What is this?"' explains Page. Like the rest of *Presence*, it had an overwhelming air of foreboding. 'It was a dark time in our lives,' adds Page, 'and I think we were channelling some of that stuff.'

Hipgnosis were delighted to be re-hired. At a late-night think-tank with Po and George Hardie, Storm suggested a black object, inspired by the monolith in *2001: A Space Odyssey*, but placed in everyday situations. Hardie turned a preliminary sketch into a cardboard and felt maquette. 'The object embodied an abstract power,' said Storm, 'like Led Zeppelin.'

It had been a prolific night as Hipgnosis also conjured up ideas for Al Stewart's *Year of the Cat* and Golden Earring's *To the Hilt*. However, Po dozed off during the brainstorming and was not au fait with the meaning behind the object. Storm wrote out a crib sheet before he presented it to the band. 'The object could be old or futuristic, but not unusual to the people in the pictures,' it read. 'Object has no perspective, no shadows . . . jet black, like a hole (wierd [sic]).'

Jimmy Page was still an avid Aleister Crowley scholar and had just investigated buying another of Crowley's old houses, the Abbey of Thelema, in Sicily. The sale never happened, but Page had now acquired Equinox, a west London bookshop specialising in esoterica. This knowledge was floating around Po's subconscious as he prepared for the pitch.

The night before his flight to Munich, Po experienced what he calls 'a waking dream': 'I saw this big building, all made of glass, with an atrium. Jimmy Page was standing there, smiling and said, "It's okay."' I woke up with a start, looked at my wife Gai, who had long curly hair, and thought she'd turned into a goat. It was so freaky, but there was absolutely no chemical enhancement involved.'

Po met Grant at Heathrow Airport. He was amused to see G wearing a fur hat, like a cross between a Cossack and the giant from *Jack and the Beanstalk*, but he couldn't shake off his uneasiness. It was early evening when the cab pulled up outside the Park Hilton in snowy Munich. Po peered up to see the same glass edifice from his dream.

Led Zeppelin arrived at Po's suite one at a time. Jimmy Page arrived first and went straight to the black object. Robert Plant did the same. Both ignored Hipgnosis's alternative designs. In one telling of the story, the singer turned over the maquette to see a list of other band names crossed out.

Plant often described Storm and Po 'as a couple of fucking chancers' and once compared working with them to buying a second-hand car in the back streets of Wolverhampton. 'You spent a lot of time and cheer and good intentions,' he said, 'and you may come out with a gem or you might come out with a right old banger.'

Genesis's ex-guitarist, Steve Hackett, is adamant they were also shown the black object: "And we all said no". Decades later, a maquette of the object was found with 'I Saw the Light' song-writer Todd Rundgren's phone number scrawled on its base. Hipgnosis later designed Rundgren's *Back to the Bars* album, but it's difficult to imagine the black object anywhere but *Presence*.

'Jimmy and Robert both saw the object and went, "That's it?"' says Po. 'John Paul Jones wanted to know the rationale behind it and John Bonham just went along with the others. Jimmy loved the black object because it was unsettling and subversive. When the meeting was over, I said to him, "Before I flew out, I had this weird dream . . .".

Page offered one of his crinkly-eyed, inscrutable smiles. 'He said, "I *know* . . . I was with you that night." I got chills. I thought, "Are you dabbling with my mind, Jimmy?" But I think he enjoyed playing games.'

Led Zeppelin's only criticism of the object was that its sides were too straight. 'It was my idea to put a twist in it,' Page says. 'Otherwise, I thought it was fantastic. It had a power, it had a presence.' Storm always told interviewers that Page named the album after the object.

Po flew home and the rest of Led Zeppelin soon followed. Page spent twenty-fours recording guitar overdubs with just his familiars and engineer Keith Harwood for company. The Rolling Stones had booked Musicland for their next LP, *Black and Blue*. 'I said to Mick Jagger, "Will you loan me two days of your studio time?",' says Page, 'and he did, which was bloody brilliant.'

Richard Cole recalled pleading with Page to finish so they could catch the last plane out of Munich. But neither a British Airways timetable nor a chemically enhanced state interfered with Page's work ethic. 'Jimmy was completely out there,' said Cole. 'Almost nodding off at the studio desk, but still functioning.

I watched him splice tape, do a perfect edit – Done! – Then we picked him up and carried him out of the studio.'

A softer-shaped object was created to appease Page. Peter Christopherson then suggested painting the object into nine photographs, most of which were sourced from back issues of *LIFE* magazine, to make it appear flat and two-dimensional. The object now resembled a black hole, mysteriously present on a golf course, in a suburban living room, in a doctor's surgery, outside Fort Knox . . .

When *National Geographic* refused to let Hipgnosis use their photograph of San Francisco's Fisherman's Wharf on the cover, they replaced it with one from the Earls Court Boat Show. Hipgnosis then collaged in a nuclear family gazing at the object on the table between them. Richard Manning was tasked with whitening the tablecloth and renovating the father's receding hairline.

The back-cover image was photographed at Westminster City School, but styled to resemble early-'60s America. A little girl watched as a matriarchal schoolmistress placed one hand on the object and another on a young boy's head. Was she transferring the power? Casting a spell? It was all very meta: the little girl was Samantha Gates, last seen crawling over the rocks on the *Houses of the Holy* album.

Peter Grant commissioned a hundred of Hipgnosis's plastic objects for promotion. He wanted to celebrate the album's release on 31 March, with photographs of the obelisk at world-famous landmarks, including the Taj Mahal and Buckingham Palace. This meant keeping the artwork under wraps until then.

Three weeks before its release, the black object appeared in the music press. Grant was convinced Hipgnosis had leaked it as a publicity stunt. Po protested their innocence, but his doorbell rang that night and he was confronted by Richard Cole and John Bindon, red-eyed, drunk and screaming abuse: 'They grabbed me and said, "You fucking cunt! Where are the fucking pictures?"'

Gai and Charlie hid in the bedroom, while Cole and Bindon upended drawers and threw open cupboards, looking for incriminating evidence. There was none. Po eventually telephoned Grant, who called off his dogs. 'Peter found out what happened,' Po says. 'Some silly boy in the PR department at Atlantic thought he was doing a good thing letting *Melody Maker* have the sleeve but Peter had to cancel the promotion. It was blown.'

It was a violent display of power and a precursor of more to come. *Presence* became a chart-topping hit, before sales levelled off. Audiences didn't love it the way they did Led Zeppelin's *I* to *IV*. Po thinks it's one of Hipgnosis's greatest works and Jimmy Page often names it as his favourite Zeppelin album. 'Hipgnosis were part of the creative process in all this,' Page stresses. 'The music's brilliant, the playing is brilliant, the singing's great and the artwork fits hand in glove with what's inside.'

'I *think* it's a masterpiece,' says Robert Plant. 'But I was so disturbed on that record. They're all songs from the wheelchair.'

★

Hipgnosis continued working with the McCartneys after *Venus and Mars*. The process was unchanged. They presented their ideas and then Paul and Linda suggested one of their own. Sometimes these were sketches on restaurant napkins or the backs of cigarette packets. When McCartney wanted the sleeve for *Wings at the Speed of Sound* to show the album's title up in lights, Hipgnosis hired a cinema frontage in Leicester Square. But it had to be Po, never Storm.

Richard Evans remembers Storm once ringing McCartney's office. 'But when they put him through, Storm said, "Hello Paul, it's John", and Paul slammed the phone down on him.' At the time, relations between McCartney and Lennon were tense.

McCartney was about to tour America for the first since the Beatles in 1966. Humphrey Ocean had drawn illustrations for *Wings at the Speed of Sound* and was invited on tour to sketch images from the road. Hipgnosis jumped on the commission and proposed a book of tour photographs with a twist. Every day at a certain hour, Po would take a picture, regardless of location. The McCartneys agreed, with the caveat they could veto the book's publication if they didn't like it.

McCartney had watched Led Zeppelin, the Who and the Stones deploy modern-day technology in arenas and stadiums. He was shocked when Zeppelin used lasers at their Earls Court shows in spring 1975: 'Because the only thing I knew about them was from the [James] Bond movie, where the baddie was about to slice Mr Bond with a laser.' Now it was the McCartneys turn to have lasers and a private plane, like Zeppelin's.

The Wings over America tour played to more than half a million people on thirty-one dates between May and June 1976. The touring party, including the McCartneys' three children, based themselves in New York, Chicago, Dallas and Los Angeles, and flew between them in a customised BAC One-Eleven jet, complete with a new-fangled video machine and a mini-discotheque. The obliging pilot even let his passengers have a turn at the controls.

Down below, 11.5 tons of kit was bussed between cities in three articulated lorries. Po had previously asked if he could paint 'Wings over America' on their roofs. Of course, said McCartney, 'whatever you want, whatever it costs . . .'

The McCartneys wanted to maintain some domestic normality, but being an ex-Beatle was anything but normal for Paul.
His office had received death threats and he now had a former
FBI agent as part of his security detail. There was a lot of whispering into walkie-talkies, as the McCartneys disembarked from
their flying charabanc and were hurried into limousines.

'This was way before John Lennon was shot but there was a
huge degree of caution,' remembers Po. 'People would find out
where we were staying and try to break into Paul and Linda's
hotel room. It was like Beatlemania all over again – the crowds
were enormous, the shows were selling out, but there was
still paranoia.'

Hipgnosis flew on the private plane. Po took a McCartney
family portrait and photographs of Linda horse riding. He captured the autograph hunters, the cavernous arenas, the security
guards and Ringo Starr besieged by admirers at the LA Forum.
Meanwhile, Humphrey Ocean perched on a chair at the side of
the stage and drew pictures. Then everybody piled into the limos
and was back on the jet, sipping drinks or smoking joints, before
the fans had left the venue.

After a few weeks, Hipgnosis found this luxurious environment stifling. For a change, Po and Humphrey travelled with the
crew and hired a Winnebago to drive themselves between dates.
The book, *Hands Across the Water: Wings Tour USA*, was published
two years later. Alongside pictures from the tour were time- and
date-stamped photographs from the road trip: the JFK memor-
ial and a rundown motel in Long Island; a stockyard foreman in
Kansas City and America's oldest woman in Atlanta, Georgia.

After a few weeks, niggling tensions surfaced within the touring party. When Jimmy McCulloch refused to play an encore
in Boston, McCartney had to be restrained from hitting him by

members of Wings' horn section. Drummer Joe English had a heroin habit, and downed bottles of cough syrup as a substitute, sometimes passing out for twelve hours at a stretch. A photo of the slumbering drummer appeared in *Hands Across the Water*.

Po was determined not to repeat the mistakes Nick Sedgwick made when he was writing about Pink Floyd on tour, but he discovered a line which should never be crossed. 'I was given complete freedom,' he says. 'But Paul wasn't always easy to be around. He had this laissez-faire persona – big, beautiful smile, thumbs held up – but he was still a Beatle and that brought its own issues. I also think he was a bit defensive about how people received his new music. He was out there playing "Magneto and Titanium Man" and some people just wanted to hear "I Saw Her Standing There".'

One afternoon, Po was invited to play cards with McCartney and his musicians. 'I'm not very good at cards, but we were playing poker, for a dollar a time, and I started winning,' he says.

Wings' Scouse sax player Howie Casey suggested a few hands of Liverpool rummy instead. 'And I happened to win at that as well, and I kept on winning, and Paul became very pissed off. He got up from the table, threw his cup down, walked to the end of the plane and didn't talk to me for a week.'

Po found the atmosphere so uncomfortable he eventually spoke to manager Brian Brolly. The following morning, McCartney sidled over to him, presumably flashed the big, beautiful smile and held his thumbs up: 'And immediately we were back to being buddies again.'

To celebrate the last night of the tour at the LA Forum, the McCartneys threw an extravagant party at silent movie star Harold Lloyd's former estate in Beverly Hills. Four hundred guests, including Po and Gai, Dustin Hoffman and Kirk Douglas, helped burn through the tour's $80,000 profits. Brian Brolly had cautioned his client about spending so much money, but McCartney did it anyway. 'Brolly's Folly' passed into folklore.

Theirs wasn't the only extravagance that summer. In November, the McCartneys attended the London premiere of Led Zeppelin's movie, *The Song Remains the Same*. Then on to an after-show party at Covent Garden's Floral Hall, so exclusive hardly anyone else had been invited. John Bonham and the Scottish comic Billy Connolly stood around, nursing drinks and looking awkward. Nobody wanted to discuss the film.

The Song Remains the Same had taken three years and two directors from conception to birth. It wove live footage from New York's Madison Square Garden around fantasy sequences, illustrating the band members' respective characters. 'The film was either an attempt to break new barriers,' says Jimmy Page, who appeared as a tarot-card hermit, 'or just *Spinal Tap*.'

Peter Grant played a gangster ordering a machine-gun hit on his rivals. It was a metaphor for Grant's war against anyone trying to get between him and his precious group, and was familiar to Hipgnosis. Most of Grant's associates were used to being summoned to Horselunges Manor at any hour, like a Mafia don mustering his *soldatos*. One evening, Po's presence was requested to discuss artwork for *The Song Remains the Same* soundtrack. He arrived at the manor to discover Grant and Richard Cole snuffling their way through great jagged rails of cocaine.

Grant's wife, Gloria, had run off with their farm manager and had filed for divorce. Peter acquired custody of his two children, Helen and Warren, but now lived a nocturnal existence, plotting revenge with whichever sidekick had the constitution to sit up all night with him.

Hipgnosis's cover suggestions were ignored. Before too long, Grant and Cole were convinced that Gloria's lover was lurking in the grounds and went charging around the estate, waving shot-guns. Po stood in the vestibule, half-heartedly brandishing a poker. After several gunshots, the pair reappeared and blithely informed him they'd shot the intruder. Probably. It was the drugs talking. But as Po drove home at dawn he wondered how long before Grant killed somebody, including himself.

Soon after, Peter was diagnosed with a heart condition. It was also his excuse to remove himself from negotiations with the film company. Instead, he despatched Po to Los Angeles to show Frank Wells, the President of Warner Bros, the proposed art-work, with an instruction not to accede to any of Wells' demands.

There were worse places to be than Los Angeles on Led Zeppelin's dollar. While Po was tooling down Sunset Boulevard in his hired Convertible, Storm was cooking Bill's tea at Hillfield Mansions. When Storm rang to tell him about their latest commission, the Australian rock group AC/DC's new LP, *Dirty Deeds Done Dirt Cheap*, Po photographed a sleazy West Hollywood motel for its cover. Back in Denmark Street, Emo and Gala Pinion were among the models collaged onto the picture with their eyes blacked out.

Po later spent weeks in New York's Plaza Hotel with a chauffeur on call, twenty-four-seven, finalising Led Zeppelin's artwork. When he needed backup against Warner's, he called Grant's mob-connected lawyer, Stevens Weiss. *The Song Remains the Same*'s posters and sleeve, showing George Hardie's art-deco-style illustration of Brixton's Scala Theatre, were delivered as a fait accompli.

Jimmy Page admits that everyone brought a bottle of brandy or 'whatever our respective tipple was' to the movie premieres. Nobody wanted to sit through the film sober. The live perfor-mances captured Zeppelin's spark and excitement, but had been filmed in 1973, while the fantasy sequences demonstrated that none of them were actors.

The Song Remains the Same was a wealthy rock star's indulgence, but clawed back $10 million at the box office within a year of release. Grant, who described it as 'the most expensive home movie' ever made, had long since lost track of how much it had cost.

The McCartneys' live album, *Wings over America*, was scheduled for a pre-Christmas release. Inspired by the artist Chuck Close's hyper-realism, Hipgnosis commissioned an airbrush painting of a plane's fuselage, complete with 2,000 rivets. 'I warned Storm this was a major job, but he was always reluctant to talk about money,' remembers freelance illustrator Richard Manning. 'I was charging £20 an hour and it took me fifty hours. In the end, I said, "Look, Storm, this going to cost you £1,000."

'He said, "A *thousand pounds*? That's more than a brain surgeon earns, dear." I said, "A brain surgeon can't do what I do." We then had a ridiculous argument about me moving to brain surgery and a brain surgeon working for Hipgnosis.' When the job was done, Storm paid for Manning to see an acupuncturist, as he was experiencing chronic pain in his neck and shoulder after painting all those rivets.

Wings over America earned Hipgnosis their fifth nomination for Best Album Packaging at the annual Grammy Awards. This followed *Presence*, *Wish You Were Here*, *Houses of the Holy* and *Flash*. Once again, though, they were passed over; this time for Linda Ronstadt's *Simple Dreams*, designed by rival British designer John Kosh.

Peter Christopherson's extracurricular activities were culturally light years from all this. The King's Road fashion entrepreneurs John Krivine and Steph Raynor had recruited him to design BOY London, the successor to their retro clothes store and early punk haunt, Acme Attractions.

Christopherson's BOY logo repurposed the eagle from the Nazi Party emblem, minus the swastika. Later, his window display for their new shop at 153 King's Road attracted a visit from the police. Christopherson had created a backstory to the work in which a youth burgled the shop, accidentally set it alight and burned to death. Fake charred flesh protruding from a boot, the remains of a hand and scorched remnants of a denim jacket were presented in glass display cases and were so lifelike, the police feared they were real.

BOY London's launch coincided with the end of COUM Transmissions: 'We got bored with everyone thinking what we were doing was art,' explained Cosey. 'So we decided to spoil it by doing whatever we were worst at, and we just did the music.'

The musical offshoot, Throbbing Gristle, were launched in October 1976, during COUM's final exhibition, 'Prostitution', at London's ICA Gallery. The exhibits included Cosey's pornographic model shoots and used tampons. Later, an audience of art buffs and London punks watched the group perform their 'songs from the death factory' about the Moors Murderers and the gas used in Nazi concentration camps.

'We wanted to deconstruct the notion of what music was in the twentieth century,' said Cosey. Christopherson had created a fake wound on Cosey's breast and smeared Genesis P-Orridge's face with stage blood. When the music ground to a halt, a stripper rolled around naked in the mess.

Prostitution had been funded by the Arts Council of Great Britain, prompting questions in the House of Commons. 'It's a sickening outrage,' the Conservative MP Sir Nicholas Fairbairn complained. 'Sadistic. Obscene. Evil. These people are the wreckers of civilisation. They want to advance decadence.'

Storm and Po were no strangers to nudity and casual sexism on album covers, but Throbbing Gristle challenged their liberal sensibilities. 'Storm and I were concerned about the effect they might have on the business,' admits Po. They came to an agreement: Christopherson could do as he pleased as long as his activities didn't adversely impact on Hipgnosis. 'Peter would say, "I won't be around for a week, I am touring Germany," and off he'd go,' says Po. 'Then he'd come back and pick up where we'd left off.'

Tabloid outrage was never in short supply and the press soon discovered another public enemy. On 1 December, the Sex Pistols appeared on the *Today* programme to promote their first single, 'Anarchy in the UK'. They'd recently signed to EMI and were given the slot after labelmates Queen cancelled at short notice.

The host, Bill Grundy, had been drinking and the group were easily provoked. Their teatime interview peaked with Steve Jones denouncing Grundy as a 'dirty fucker'. Disgusted viewers jammed the Thames Television switchboard and a 47-year-old Essex lorry driver kicked in his new colour television set in protest.

The Sex Pistols' TV appearance triggered more tabloid outrage than Prostitution at the ICA. 'Punk' suddenly become a catch-all term for these supposedly delinquent new groups, threatening the moral fabric of society. But while the Sex Pistols preached anarchy, their nemesis, Pink Floyd, sounded much angrier.

Day after day, during the broiling heatwave summer of 1976, Roger Waters drove past Battersea Power Station on his way home to Clapham. Pink Floyd were making a new album, *Animals*, in a studio in Islington. Their chilling songs about man's inhumanity contrasted sharply with the 37-degree heat and ABBA's 'Fernando' trilling out of transistor radios across Great Britain.

Waters felt drawn to Sir Giles Gilbert Scott and J. Theo Halliday's towering monument to coal-fired energy. 'Maybe it was the architect in me, but there was something menacing about the power station,' he says. 'But I also liked it as a symbol for the band. It reminded me of an upside-down table, with four phalluses, and there were four people in a band that had been turned upside down.'

Pink Floyd were recording *Animals* in their own newly built studio, Britannia Row. 'You've Gotta Be Crazy' and 'Raving and Drooling', originally written for *Wish You Were Here*, were re-titled 'Dogs' and 'Sheep' and incorporated into a new story. Waters' narrative borrowed from George Orwell's *Animal Farm* by re-imagining the human race as three sub-species, with the subservient sheep brutalised by authoritarian dogs and pigs.

There weren't many of *Wish You Were Here*'s softly rounded edges here. In its past incarnation 'Dogs' had so many words Gilmour insisted they were pared back so he could sing them properly. But he was still left with the chilling line, 'Just another sad old man, all alone and dying of cancer'. During 'Pigs (Three Different Ones)', Floyd denounced Mary Whitehouse, the out-spoken TV censorship campaigner, as a 'fucked-up old hag', which made Steve Jones's 'dirty fucker' sound positively tame.

There was something timely about the song 'Sheep', where the titular beasts rose against their captors. On 30 August that year, violence at the annual Notting Hill Carnival resulted in hundreds of injuries and multiple arrests and inspired the west London punk group the Clash's debut single, 'White Riot'.

Not that Pink Floyd cared. 'We weren't interested in punk,' says Nick Mason. 'But we were aware of it. There was a slight sense of what was happening at the time. Everybody was beginning to sneer at prog rock and the records were getting over-complicated.'

Along with its angry lyrics, *Animals* sounded more stripped-back than its predecessor. 'I think there was a feeling things needed to be a little more live and rawer,' says David Gilmour. '*Wish You Were Here* was a sumptuous album and we were moving towards a tougher sound.'

'We knew the music and lyrics were fuelled and characterised by anger,' said Storm. 'So was it an angry animal, or more like human behaviour of an animal nature? I can't say that I cared for it much myself because I found it too angry compared to *Wish You Were Here*.'

Storm's sideways thinking led to him presenting a photograph of three dead mallards nailed above the fireplace at number six. 'In England, the essence of bad taste is to put plaster ducks on the wall,' he explained. 'So I used real ducks, to suggest that people are animal-like in their artistic and moral decisions.' Floyd rejected the image and Storm eventually recycled it for a record label sampler, *Hey Drag City*, in 1994.

He also submitted an illustration showing a small boy, clutching a teddy bear in the doorway of his parents' bedroom, watching them have sex: 'Making love, caught in the act, appearing to be animals,' posited Storm. 'I thought it was brilliant, but the Floyd didn't like that one at all.'

'There were several ideas,' remembers Roger Waters. 'The kid looking at his parents fucking was the main one. Certainly the most shocking. I remember saying, "I don't like any of them," and Gilmour said, "Well, why don't you do better?" So I got in my car and drove over Battersea Bridge, looked up at the power station and thought, "Hang on a minute . . ."'

Pink Floyd had commissioned several stage props for a forth-coming American stadium tour, among them an inflatable pig, which would drift over the audience. Waters proposed photo-graphing a pig over Battersea Power Station. 'I suggested it to the other three guys and even Dave, a bit begrudgingly said, "Oh, that's a good idea."'

'I don't remember any of Storm's other ideas,' insists Gilmour. 'I just remember Roger saying he fancied doing the pig over Battersea Power Station. We were all happy to give it a go.'

For the first time since 1968, though, Hipgnosis's ideas had been passed over for one of Pink Floyd's. Storm was furious: 'I thought Roger's pig was a tad silly, not to mention low on mys-tery and meaning,' he grumbled.

Instead of Storm, Po met Waters to discuss the project over Sunday tea. After buttered muffins and a pot of Earl Grey, the pair drove to Battersea Power Station, where they wandered the grounds unchallenged, taking pictures for a couple of hours. Waters wanted the cover of *Animals* to show a pig incongruously floating between the power station's chimneys.

'We received permission from Battersea,' explains Po. 'The only thing they were worried about was the pig banging into one of the chimneys. I reassured them it was only a plastic pig.'

The pig, later nicknamed 'Algie', was a 40-foot-long, rub-berised cotton dirigible. It was designed by the inflatables com-pany, EventStructure, and created at Ballon Fabrik, where many First World War airships had been manufactured, in Augsburg, Germany.

'My problem was making sure we had a good pig,' said Event-Structure's Dutch designer Theo Botschuijver. 'The danger I noticed straight away was that it could look like a Walt Disney figure – too friendly, chubby – and Floyd wanted something more aggressive. The woman I was speaking to at Ballon Fabrik didn't like my pig. She wanted something jollier and I had trouble convincing her this was the pig the band wanted.'

The shoot was booked for 2 December. Storm and Po had hired eight photographers to be stationed at various locations, including the power station roof, a tower block opposite and the adjacent railway tracks. The police insisted Hipgnosis hire one of their marksmen in case the pig broke free.

Theo Botschuijver and representatives from Ballon Fabrik were also on site. 'The people from the factory were responsible for the execution but I began to doubt their professionalism,' Botschuijver told author Peter Watts. 'Their estimation of the amount of gas needed was wrong. We needed twice the amount of bottles.'

There wasn't enough helium to get the pig off the ground and by mid-afternoon, the shoot was called off. 'I was on the ninth floor of a block of flats,' recalls Howard Bartrop. 'I'd taken all my camera equipment downstairs when I noticed the sun had come out from underneath the lowest clouds.'

Hipgnosis later talked about the sky on the cover of *Animals* resembling J. M. W. Turner's stormy landscapes, 'The Fighting Temeraire' or 'The Slave Ship', perhaps. Bartrop dragged his equipment back to the ninth floor and fired off a single shot of the power station framed by this turbulent sky.

The next day, the photographers returned to their locations and waited for Algie to arrive. Film-maker Nigel Lesmoir-Gordon was also shooting the pig's maiden flight for a potential TV commercial. Gordon, his camera crew and Hipgnosis's stills photographer, Rob Brimson, had been allocated places in a Jet Ranger 206B helicopter. Its pilot, Marc Wolff, had flown combat missions over Vietnam and would later coordinate aerial stunts for several James Bond movies.

Algie arrived on the back of a truck, attached to a winch and flanked by enough helium tanks to keep him airborne for days. He inflated easily. Steve O'Rourke and Pink Floyd stood around, sipping coffee and waiting for the show to begin. At which point, Po realised he had forgotten to re-book the marksman.

'Predictably, in the rock 'n' roll way of things, the decision was made to take a chance and fly it anyway,' says Rob Brimson. 'The pig inched upwards as it filled with gas and was rubbing against the chimney, which was when the hawser snapped.'

'Somebody asked for the pig to get higher and the guy from Germany loosened the winch and it started to unwind,' recalled Botschuijver. 'He jerked the brake and I heard "*Ding!*" The ring broke. There should have been a ripcord you could pull to make the pig deflate, but it was just secured by this one metal ring.'

Botschuijver found the nearest telephone box and called his lawyer: 'This was the first time I had lost an inflatable so I made a statement that it was my design but the execution was German.'

Po was on Battersea Bridge when he realised something was amiss: 'The pig just took off. Gone! I drove down to where the group and the band were with this rising sense of panic. Roger Waters had a schoolboy look of glee on his face. But all of Floyd couldn't wait to piss off – "You sort this out, Po!" They jumped into their cars and drove away.'

'Of course we did,' confirms Nick Mason. 'That's one of the benefits of being higher up the food chain and I'm afraid Po was the human sacrifice. I do remember Pink Floyd's secretary watched the pig break free and said, "Oh my God, it hasn't got a carnet," because at that time, everything crossing a border had to have documents in triplicate.'

'We didn't have mobile phones, so we didn't know what had happened,' says Howard Bartrop, back in his ninth-floor eyrie.

'I felt so guilty as I hadn't got the shot. I came down from the tower block with great trepidation as I thought Storm was going to kill me.'

The police notified air traffic control and sent a helicopter pilot up to pursue the pig. In the meantime, Marc Wolff had given chase in his Jet Ranger. 'Air traffic controllers tend to be very dry,' says Wolff. 'So it was hilarious having to tell them an inflatable pink pig was rising into their airspace.'

'There was the very real possibility I could be charged with possession of an unidentified flying object,' says Po, who was escorted back to 6 Denmark Street by a policeman. 'Airline pilots at Heathrow were reporting seeing it at 30,000 feet. It was becoming a real danger and if it happened today, I'd be in prison.'

'It could have been cataclysmic,' admits Mason. 'We could have caused a major air disaster. Many years later, I met Captain David Voy, the police pilot sent to chase the pig. He told me he didn't have a hope in hell as the pig was climbing at a far greater rate than his helicopter.'

Radio and TV news bulletins urged the public to report any sightings. For the rest of the day, Hipgnosis's fielded crank callers and journalists wanting a quote. Fortunately, the pig had a safety valve. As the air pressure outside decreased, gas was expelled from the valve, causing the pig to descend.

In the early evening, farmer James Stewart of East Stour Farm in Kent rang Po to inform him that Algie had crash-landed in one of his fields and was terrifying his cows. Pink Floyd's road crew retrieved the deflated animal and brought it back to London.

'Everybody thought we'd let it go on purpose, as a publicity stunt, and I sometimes think we should have,' admitted Storm. 'Either way, it was the best publicity the Floyd could have had for any new album.'

The following morning, Algie flew again, with a marksman on standby. Rob Brimson was sent up in the Jet Ranger to photograph the pig directly above the power station. 'They'd taken the doors off the helicopter,' he recalled, 'and I had to sit on the edge with my feet on the skids and a harness connecting me so I didn't fall out.'

The noise of wind and the rotors was deafening. Through headphones, Marc Wolff instructed Brimson to tell him when he was ready to take the photo. As soon as Wolff received the signal, he tipped the helicopter over at a sharp angle and buzzed the chimneys as if he was back over Saigon.

'Suddenly I was hanging from the harness,' said Brimson. 'My cameras were all over the floor and sliding towards the doors. I managed to secure them against the lip. I took my pictures, shooting into the light and the cloud, low over the Thames.'

Nigel Lesmoir-Gordon's camera crew began filming just as Brimson started to feel nauseous. The power station's sulphurous smoke was now blowing into the open helicopter: 'I thought I would chuck up all over London. I was getting greener and greener until eventually we landed.'

The pig had flown without a hitch, but all the photographs from the third day were considered unusable. 'The sky was too blue,' explains Po. 'Whereas the pictures from the first day had those fantastic, doomy clouds.'

Howard Bartrop's last-minute photograph from day one was almost perfect, except it was missing a pig. 'So we took the pig from the third day and stripped it into the sky from the first day,' confessed Storm. Richard Manning then removed the deflated pig, lying like an enormous wrinkled condom, to the left of the power station.

'In hindsight, we could have just photographed the pig in a studio,' said Storm. 'It wouldn't have been as funny but it would have saved a lot of money.'

Waters wasn't the only Pink Floyd member to contribute to the artwork. Nick Mason transcribed Waters' lyrics on the inside sleeve; like a pupil ordered to write lines by a schoolmaster, perhaps.

Animals was released in January 1977. It was a hit, though not as big a hit as *The Dark Side of the Moon* or *Wish You Were Here*. Its sleeve art was an immediate talking point. 'Pig' was such a loaded word, suggesting 'Capitalist pig', 'fascist pig' or just 'pig', as painted on the door in blood during the Manson Family murders. Po had scrawled the word 'Animals' on a wall outside the power station. This picture appeared on the inside alongside photographs of scrap heaps and barbed wire; all evoked late-'70s Britain, with its striking workers and malcontent youths.

There was tension within Pink Floyd, too. Waters thought the four chimneys represented the group, but two of them were defunct since the power station began operating at half-capacity in 1975. *Animals* was solely credited to Waters, apart from 'Dogs', which was co-written with David Gilmour. This autonomy reinforced Waters' view of himself as Floyd's creative mastermind, an opinion not entirely shared by his bandmates.

Like Led Zeppelin's black object, Pink Floyd's pig would become better known than the music. After leaving the band in 1985, Waters fought a determined custody battle for his pig. So determined, his lawyers contacted Theo Botschuijver to confirm which band member had asked him to design it. Waters won the battle, but the redux Floyd circumvented the problem by creating a new pig with testicles – it was part of the brand and they couldn't afford to lose it.

'The pig wasn't such a silly idea after all,' conceded Storm, years later. 'It was psychologically stimulating and emotionally poignant.'

Peter Christopherson regaled his bandmates with stories about the cover shoot. One night, Cosey arrived for her shift stripping in a pub near Old Street: 'The DJ had a copy of *Animals* and was looking at the sleeve. I leaned over and said, "Oh, my friend did that cover." But he looked at me as if I was mad, didn't believe a word.'

In spring 1977, Christopherson was made a partner in Hipgnosis. 'We thought Peter would leave if we didn't and he was too good to lose,' admits Po. 'Storm and I were in total agreement about it.' Christopherson brought something else to the mix, too. He refereed his older partners, like Chris Thomas with Waters and Gilmour on *The Dark Side of the Moon*.

'Stormy' and 'Povis's relationship was increasingly volatile. Storm once scratched his thumbnail over a picture Po wanted to use and Po became so infuriated by his partner's demands, he once flung a Hasselblad across the studio.

'We loved and hated each other,' admits Po. 'Then ended up in this strange position where we would defer to Peter, the younger man. Peter would get caught in the middle and have to mediate but Storm and I always made up and the arguments often helped us get the best result for any given artwork.'

Christopherson also joined Greenback Films, which had just been launched by Storm, Po and Nigel Gordon, to explore new avenues in advertising and music video. Greenback would have a huge bearing on all their lives going forward.

Storm and Po now zoomed around the West End in matching Lancia Flavia Coupés and Hipgnosis had taken over the second floor at number six. The first floor remained as a photographic studio and darkroom, while the upstairs became a reception area and art room, devoid of home comforts, with employees and visiting rock stars alike perching on high wooden stools, and home to new secretary, Judy Reynolds.

There was also a change of personnel. 'I'd taught myself to use an airbrush by watching George Hardie,' says Richard Evans. 'So I left Denmark Street, because I wanted my own studio. But I still worked with Hipgnosis. It was always, "Hey, Rich, I've got another job for you . . ."'

New younger designers and assistants arrived; ones whose art tutors had shown them copies of *Elegy* and *Argus*. But they still faced the same challenges: finding a decent Chinagraph pencil and having Storm urinate in the darkroom sink while they were hanging up prints.

Several passed through 6 Denmark Street at this time. Names such as Richard Draper, Paul Maxon and Alwyn Clayden would be preserved in the small print on 10cc and Wishbone Ash covers, before they formed their own agencies or found alternative careers.

Clayden's friend, Marcus Bradbury, joined straight from Saint Martin's School of Art in 1977. 'Alwyn used to come back with all these stories about a guy called Storm,' says Bradbury. 'Then one day he said Storm urgently needed somebody who could draw.'

Bradbury met Po on a Friday afternoon and was sketching ideas for a new Genesis album by Monday. Storm described the scene in his head, impatient for Bradbury to turn it into a drawing. A year later, his sketch became reality on Genesis's *And Then There Were Three*. This job led to another until Bradbury found himself permanently employed. Sometimes he was sketching ideas, sometimes standing in as a test model and sometimes helping build a set: 'No two days at Hipgnosis were ever the same.'

At first, Bradbury didn't know how the three principals fitted together. 'A meeting with Storm were like talking to a scientist or a psychologist,' he says. 'He knew a lot about everything and was interested in everything, but also easily distracted. Po was a diplomat. Po could sell sand to the Arabs and managed to come in at nine in the morning after being up all night with Led Zeppelin.

'Then there was Peter, this highly intelligent guy who had amazing powers of concentration and understood technology. I remember he came back from the States with a hand-held computer football game and told me, "This is the future, Marcus." But we were old-school art guys, using pencils and paper, we didn't have a clue.'

Bradbury's junior status didn't preclude being summoned to meetings at Hillfield Mansions. 'The first one I went to, Storm was in the bath, dictating something to Judy, the secretary. I thought, "Am I in a Fellini film? What is this? It's *so* weird." But Storm didn't care.'

Storm had also found another musician to spar with. Hipgnosis had just designed Peter Gabriel's first, self-titled solo album: 'And there was nothing Peter liked better than arguing with Storm,' says Po.

Gabriel would arrive at 6 Denmark Street, ready to rebuff Storm's attempts to sell him whatever ideas other groups had rejected. 'I loved him to death,' said Gabriel. 'But he was provocatively difficult and enjoyed being so. He enjoyed winding you up and telling you that Led Zeppelin and Floyd had rejected this idea but it was good enough for you.'

However, Storm and Peter were artistic kindred spirits. 'I am old enough to remember flipping through records and not looking at the titles,' says Gabriel. 'I looked for pictures. I've always been better with pictures. Let's throw away the words. It always felt too commercial with branding. I wanted to throw away the name and the title, but of course, the record company hated that.'

Some of Gabriel's songs were inspired by Carlos Castaneda and Jean-Luc Godard. Like Storm, he also took a method approach to his craft. When Gabriel struggled to nail the perfect take on the song 'Modern Love', his engineer Gaffer-taped him under his armpits to a pillar in the studio, to coax out a better performance.

'I used to listen to meetings between Storm and Peter,' says Marcus Bradbury. 'They'd have these unbelievably in-depth conversations about everything you could imagine – farming, gardens, trees, Africa, Storm's mum.'

For Gabriel's self-titled album, he sat in the passenger seat of Storm's Lancia Flavia, half-obscured by the windscreen. 'At one point during the shoot, Peter had his eyes closed and was resting his head against the car door window,' remembers Rob Brimson. 'An old lady walked past and tapped on the window to see if he was okay.' Gabriel opened his eyes, forgetting that he was wearing mirrored contact lenses. 'And she nearly jumped out of her skin.'

The car had been waxed and hosed down with water beforehand, an idea inspired by Storm watching the raindrops on a taxi's bonnet as it sat in a traffic jam. Richard Manning then highlighted every drop on the Lancia to create a vivid, hyper-real image. Gabriel was just part of the picture; so much so the album was later nicknamed 'Car'.

Charisma Records were relieved then when the album and its first single, 'Solsbury Hill', became hits. Gabriel, who'd been to see the Sex Pistols at the 100 Club a few months earlier, was thrilled when his LP appeared in the window of BOY London. For the next single, 'Modern Love', Gabriel appeared naked on the disc label with a spindle hole covering his genitals.

Other Hipgnosis clients had either re-shaped themselves, like Genesis without Peter Gabriel, or split down the middle, like 10cc. Kevin Godley and Lol Creme left the group after *How*

Dare You! They'd invented a guitar device called 'The Gizmo' and wanted to make a triple-concept album featuring comedian Peter Cook. It was a drastic move after eight top-thirty hits.

'It was a tragedy we didn't stay together,' admits Graham Gouldman, who continued the group with Eric Stewart for 1977's *Deceptive Bends*. 'I was renting a house in London and driving to the studio in Dorking,' he recalls. 'Every day I kept seeing a road sign which read "Deceptive Bends". Not dangerous bends, just deceptive, which intrigued me.'

Storm took the phrase to its illogical conclusion and suggested a diver as a play on 'the bends', the nickname given to decompression sickness after surfacing too quickly in deep water. Hipgnosis's diver appeared on the cover, cradling a female model wearing an evening gown, as if she'd fallen overboard during a party at sea.

Gouldman wanted the actress Jessica Lange for the job, after seeing her as the damsel in distress in director Dino De Laurentiis's remake of *King Kong*: 'But we were told in no uncertain terms that Jessica was not available,' recalled Storm. 'Far too big a star.'

Unfortunately, the diver's wetsuit was so heavy, he could only hold the model for a short time. A metal frame was built on which to rest his arms and then airbrushed out of the picture. Two other divers, one played by Emo, appeared in the foreground.

'We shot it on the River Thames in Twickenham or Barnes,' recalls Emo. 'The diver's helmet must have weighed 50 pounds and in between takes I had to rest my head on the jetty. Another all-day shoot for just a fiver. Typical Storm – art for art's sake.'

Storm remained almost comically tight-fisted when it came to paying employees. But he was prepared to blow budgets in pursuit of Hipgnosis's big ideas. Those budgets were still high, with *Animals* costing less than *Wish You Were Here*, but still approximately £35,000.

There was also money sloshing around for groups further down the pecking order, such as Phil Collins' jazz-fusion side hustle, Brand X.

According to Collins, Storm considered Genesis, never mind Brand X, inferior to his other clients. 'Storm and Po found us a little difficult,' he said. 'We were always picky about what we wanted, but Hipgnosis had had a lot of success and always knew best. Genesis weren't quite as big as the Floyd or as important as other bands they were doing covers for, and I always felt we were a thorn in their side.'

Hipgnosis decided to shoot Brand X's latest, *Moroccan Roll*, in Tunisia rather than Morocco, because of the Berber town of Matmata, and a hotel in Hammamet, which had a swimming pool flanked by Saharan sand dunes. 'I figured we'd get two covers out of one trip,' says Po. *Moroccan Roll* showed Peter Christopherson dressed as a Panama-hatted tourist on the streets of Matmata and the swimming pool and dunes were used for Wishbone Ash's *Classic Ash*. Great artistic minds thought alike and the following year, Matmata's subterranean dwellings appeared in George Lucas's *Star Wars*.

Hipgnosis's trip wasn't without problems, though. 'A distressed Peter turned up at my hotel room, saying, "We've got to get out of here, a bunch of Arabs are trying to kill me,"' recalls Po. 'He'd tried to pick up a teenage boy on Hammamet Beach and now they were chasing him with sticks. It was ten o'clock at night and we had to find another hotel. I was furious.'

Back in London, Christopherson had snuck another subversive idea onto the sleeve of UFO's latest LP. *Lights Out* was shot inside Battersea Power Station – 'I suppose we should feel honoured,' says Phil Mogg. 'Pink Floyd got the outside, but we got the inside.'

Hipgnosis had recently photographed the sleeve for Hawkwind's latest, *Quark Strangeness and Charm*, in the same space. On arrival, Po and Rob Brimson discovered that the power station constantly vibrated, because of the generators. 'The whole building shook,' recalls Brimson. 'From the floor to the chimneys.' Taking a clear picture with a hand-held camera was impossible. Then Brimson remembered that a camera on a tripod would vibrate at the same rate as everything around it. A clear picture was achieved.

UFO's artwork depicted Mogg and guitarist Michael Schenker wearing green boiler suits in the station's vibrating turbine room. Mogg's suit was unzipped down past his navel, while a topless Schenker's was bunched around his waist. It suggested something sexual had either taken place or was about to.

'Homoerotic?' says Mogg. 'What do you mean? Yeah, I don't know what's going on there.' Richard Manning was also instructed to enhance an outline in the lead singer's suit: 'I was told to make the musician's member bigger.'

'Classic Peter,' says Po. 'Shooting a cover with a macho rock band and suggesting something sexual had taken place.'

Hipgnosis's newest client were the progressive rock group Yes, who'd split with artist Roger Dean before their next album, *Going for the One*. 'The singer Jon Anderson wanted a particular approach and I felt that it wouldn't work for me,' recalled Dean. 'So Yes went to Storm Thorgerson instead. But he didn't go with Jon's idea either.'

Instead, Hipgnosis photographed a naked man in what Storm called 'a da Vinci pose', superimposed in front of LA's Century Plaza Towers. The graphic lines emanating from his body were another nod to Carlos Castaneda's spiritual beams. But the nudity would prove problematic.

Rob Brimson joined Po at Mountain Studios in Montreux to present the work to Yes and take photographs for the inside sleeve: 'Po was flying in from somewhere else and I was amazed to discover I had a first-class ticket waiting at Heathrow.' Partway into the flight, the stewardess asked to check the ticket. 'Because somebody else in first class complained I shouldn't be there, presumably because of how I looked.'

Brimson then found he'd been booked into a five-star hotel, where Po told him to order whatever he fancied from the lunch menu ('He said, "I strongly recommend the bouillabaisse . . ."'). The penniless photographer was charmed by it all. 'Hipgnosis weren't paying for this, it was Yes,' he cautions. 'But Po didn't have to have me there and certainly didn't have to insist on a first-class ticket.'

Brimson was a Yes fan and listened as Po and their keyboard player and resident raconteur, Rick Wakeman, swapped war stories. Wakeman punctuated each scandalous anecdote with a comedy run of notes on the piano; one clandestine blow-job story was accompanied by the theme from *Captain Pugwash*. Behind the humour, though, Yes were struggling.

'I noticed they weren't working together as a group,' says Brimson. 'One of them would go in the studio for a couple of hours and then another after him. I think this was a crucial album for Yes. Punk had come along and if it didn't sell, they were going to be history.'

Going for the One's male nude also troubled their record company, Atlantic. 'They worried that the fans would think Yes had gone gay,' admits Po. 'But we stuck to our guns and the band backed us up.' However, a pair of trousers were painted onto the model's naked buttocks before the artwork could be shown on a billboard on Sunset Strip.

Hipgnosis's clients still had the power, but the artistic friction, the clashing egos and, for some, the drugs were taking the shine off it all. The same issues were slowly impinging on Hipgnosis. Po was now spending up to 200 days a year out of the country, on private jets or Concorde and living out of hotels: 'Flying off to see Paul McCartney in the Caribbean gives you this tremendous sense of doing well and loving every minute,' he says. 'Unfortunately, your personal life suffers. I was away all the time and behaving very badly and not paying attention to what was happening at home.'

Po had flown to Montreux via Germany. A year earlier, on tour with Bad Company, he visited Warum Nicht (Why Not), a Frankfurt nightclub, 'where there was more cocaine than you could shake a stick at'. Lounging in the VIP area with the band and several ice buckets filled with Champagne, Po noticed a couple of women dancing: 'And being the cocky little fucker I was, I called out, "Come on, girls, come over, we've got Dom Peérignon!"'

One of the women, Gabi Schneider, worked in the fashion industry: 'And Gabi and I starting seeing each other,' says Po. 'We fell in love and my marriage started to fall apart back in England.'

Po left Gai, and Gabi Schneider moved to London. She made her Hipgnosis debut in October 1977, wearing a swimsuit on the back of Wishbone Ash's *Front Page News*. The sleeve suggested a pastiche of the TV cop show, *Starsky & Hutch*, with blond Andy Powell and dark-haired guitarist Laurie Wisefield as the show's titular heroes.

There was a bigger story, though. *Front Page News* had been recorded at Miami's Criteria Studios and its cover photos showed palm trees, a nightclub, the sun-dappled ocean and Po's new canary-yellow Oldsmobile Cutlass Supreme. As well as a muscle car, Po had also purchased a house in Miami. He was now officially living the American Dream.

Chapter 9

'. . . I thought they'd all be blind when they woke up.'

In which Hipgnosis survive Paul McCartney's most dangerous assignment ever, sell their souls to the devil, create a shocking piece of art with bubblegum and upset their number-one fan.

'Dear Sirs, here is a list of my favourite Hipgnosis covers: *A Trick of the Tail*, *The Lamb Lies Down on Broadway*, *The Dark Side of the Moon*, *Wish You Were Here*, *Atom Heart Mother*, *Cunning Stunts*, *Going for the One* . . .'

– A fan letter, 5 August 1977

★

The Eagles recorded most of their hit album, *Hotel California*, at Miami's Criteria Studios in the summer of 1976. This cautionary tale of America's cultural decline was fuelled by cocaine.

So much cocaine that when Black Sabbath arrived at Criteria, they scraped mounds of it out of the mixing board. No strangers to the drug themselves, Ozzy Osbourne and his bandmates were surprised at how much was smeared on the desk and compacted, like white sand, between the faders.

This was Miami in the '70s, then. A sleepy town where retired folks in sun visors ambled from the front-porch recliner to the station wagon, but also a drug smuggler's paradise, where speed boats crammed with marijuana or Class-As tore up the waterway, the coastguard in hot pursuit.

Po discovered the joys of Florida after printer Ivy Hill loaned him their Palm Beach holiday apartment in 1976. The following year, he'd found a bungalow for sale with a boat dock and swimming pool, an hour's drive south on Miami's Golden Beach. 'I was getting run ragged at Hipgnosis,' he says. 'I was doing a lot of the business in the States and it made sense for me to be there part of the year. I also wanted to be somewhere warm, away from London.'

Miami offered prime locations for cover shoots, but its criminal underworld was also on Po's doorstep. His neighbours included a South American chemist, who'd gone missing under mysterious circumstances, and Meyer Lansky's granddaughter. Later, Po discovered his plumber had been arrested for murder.

'What happened is I had a lot of nefarious friends involved in the drugs business in Germany,' he explains. Many of these were associated with Frankfurt's Warum Nicht club. 'Some of those people introduced me to friends in Golden Beach, most of whom were also in the drugs trade and many of whom are now dead. But I became rather caught up in the excitement of it.'

Po was soon shopping in the chicest clothes stores, eating in the finest lobster restaurants and pulling up outside the hippest nightclubs in his Cutlass Supreme. 'I was,' he says, 'behaving like a dreadful cock.'

Before too long, he'd acquired a 30-foot Chris-Craft to keep in his boat dock, a less ostentatious vessel than the Colombian family's gold yacht moored opposite. When one of Po's friends threw a Christmas party, the harbour was crowded with boats, many with false bulkheads in which to hide drugs. Their owners were also generous with their cash. Po's young daughter, Charlie, was staying with him and worked behind the bar: 'When she went to bed at midnight, she said, "Dad, I can't believe it, I've made $600 in tips."'

'Po was with us a lot when we were in Miami,' recalls Wishbone Ash's Andy Powell. 'We were just leaving Criteria Studios when the Eagles came in to do *Hotel California*. Our producer, Bill Szymczyk, went straight to working with them and they moved into the house we'd been renting. We were doing a lot of the drugs in those days and Po came around for some of that – Po was always more rock 'n' roll than Storm.'

Living in Miami was ideal whenever any Hipgnosis groups were in town. Led Zeppelin were touring again, in a refurbished Boeing 720, nicknamed 'Caesar's Chariot', and with the Swan Song logo on its fuselage. Before their date at the Orange Bowl in Tampa, Florida, Po hopped aboard as easily as if he was back working the buses in Cambridge. He found a seat and tried to remain inconspicuous as chaos reigned around him.

John 'Biffo' Bindon's girlfriend was cartwheeling down the aisle in a mini-skirt, minus her underwear, and Richard Cole looked even more like Blackbeard the pirate after falling over in the King's Road and losing a tooth. Cole had also karate-kicked one of the porthole windows and left a crack in the first pane of glass.

Po couldn't hide for long and 'Biffo' soon found a seat beside him. Some months earlier, Bindon, Po and Steve O'Rourke had spent an evening at the Speakeasy in London's West End. O'Rourke had stashed a briefcase containing £4,000 in the boot of his Jaguar. Bindon knew about the money and disappeared early. When Po and O'Rourke left the club, they discovered the car had been broken into and the briefcase was missing.

'"Biffo" was obviously responsible,' says Po, 'but categorically denied it.' Bindon was still seething about the accusation and began discussing his plans for revenge on O'Rourke: 'So I'm sat there, with a guy telling me how he's going to murder Pink Floyd's manager.' Peter Grant realised what was happening and suggested Po sit with him and his children instead: 'Typical Peter, he always took care of me.'

The Orange Bowl show was abandoned after three songs. The awning over the stage was billowing with rainwater before the band arrived and the group quit as soon as another downpour began. Zeppelin's limousines and police outriders were heading for the airport before the 70,000-strong audience realised they'd gone. Back on Caesar's Chariot, Grant clutched a bag containing Zeppelin's fee in cash to his ample lap: 'I got the fucking money, Po,' he whispered, like a bank robber in a getaway car.

Back home, the Queen's Silver Jubilee celebrations were underway. At street parties across the nation, houses were draped with Union Jack bunting and trestle tables piled high with Double Diamond and sausage rolls. The Sex Pistols paid their own tribute with a hit single, 'God Save the Queen'. Its sleeve gave Hipgnosis their first glimpse of designer Jamie Reed's work. The words 'Sex Pistols' and 'God Save the Queen' were simply plastered in ransom letters across the monarch's face – it was a far cry from inflatable pigs and mysterious black objects.

Reed was a former Croydon School of Art student and only a year younger than Po, but the perception was everything at a time when Hipgnosis's clients were being dismissed as 'dinosaurs' and 'boring old farts'. 'Storm didn't like punk,' says Marcus Bradbury. 'But I think he was interested in some of it. The trouble was the punk artists didn't want to go to Hipgnosis. The word "old-fashioned" was getting used and that made Storm nervous.'

The Sex Pistols' first LP, *Never Mind the Bollocks, Here's the Sex Pistols*, arrived in October 1977. The group were absent from the cover, replaced by the provocative title, more ransom letters and a gaudy pink and yellow background. It was as effective a piece of branding as Pink Floyd's prism: 'We felt a wee bit paranoid,' Storm admitted.

'Jamie Reed fucked it for us,' confirms Po. 'Tearing up pieces of paper and sticking them on a plain background was not where Hipgnosis was at. *Wish You Were Here* cost fifty grand. Now record companies thought they could get a good cover for fifty quid. But of course, we carried on. We weren't ready to admit defeat.'

'We don't need Hipgnosis and we don't need nude tarts to sell records,' Colin Newman of Harvest's latest signings Wire told *Melody Maker*. 'We're not selling sex and drugs.'

A visit to any record shop revealed more of the cheap and cheerful competition. Two flagship punk groups, the Clash and the Damned, also released their debut albums that year. The Clash were shown posing in an alley behind their Camden rehearsal studio and the Damned appeared on *Damned Damned Damned* with their faces smeared with cream cakes after a food fight. Their production costs were low to non-existent.

The Damned now wanted to make what they called 'a psychedelic punk masterpiece' and approached Syd Barrett to produce their second album, *Music for Pleasure*. Barrett's publisher, Bryan Morrison, steered them towards Nick Mason instead.

Most days, the band dodged the ticket inspector at the tube station on their way to Britannia Row Studios. 'We'd say, "Fucking hell, Nick, I nearly got caught this morning,"' recalled the Damned's bass guitarist Captain Sensible, 'and all he could say was, "I came in my Ferrari." There just wasn't a meeting of minds.'

'I think I got rather more out of it than they did,' says Mason.

Storm complained about punk's 'lack of graphic qualities and ideas', but he shared its disregard for glamour. Hipgnosis's artwork for soft rockers Sad Café's latest, *Misplaced Ideals*, showed its cover model tearing a grotesque rubber mask off his face. In the TV soap *Coronation Street*, the local corner store was considering selling pop records, but shopkeeper 'Mavis Riley' was appalled when asked to display a poster of the LP cover in the window. In real life, *Misplaced Ideals* was reissued in an alternative sleeve.

Miles Copeland was managing the Bristolian punk group the Cortinas and asked Hipgnosis to design their single, 'Defiant Pose'. Storm gave them a teenage boy vomiting onto a kitchen floor.

The youth and his parents were shot in a typical 1970s kitchen in varying shades of beige. The mustard walls, tablecloth, cutlery and even the boy's tie corresponded with the colours of the vomit (in real-life oxtail soup). 'Defiant Pose' wasn't a hit but Storm always loved the sleeve, 'because it was succinct and revolting'.

XTC were another new group empowered by punk, but whose angular, brainy pop was gentler than the Sex Pistols. On arrival at number six, their frontman, Andy Partridge, became fascinated by a design he found discarded on the studio floor. It was a sheet of paper containing a typed explanation of the meaning and purpose of a record cover.

'This is a RECORD COVER . . .' it began. '. . . The DESIGN is to help sell the record . . . The more you read on, the more you're falling for this simple device of telling you exactly how a good commercial design works. They're TRICKS and this is the worst trick of all since it's describing the TRICK whilst trying to TRICK you and if you've read this far then you're TRICKED . . .'

'It was the office joke,' said Partridge. 'Hipgnosis admitted this joke had previously been refused by many major groups on the grounds of being too heavy, too blatant. This made us want it even more.'

'It was an idea I'd submitted to Pink Floyd some years previously, but they didn't like it,' confessed Storm. 'Then I showed it to 10cc, thinking they would, but not so.'

'Storm would have made a great chef,' suggests Nick Mason. 'If somebody didn't want his meal, he'd serve it to somebody else. Many ideas which Pink Floyd rejected can be seen on other people's albums.'

Hipgnosis's discarded office joke appeared on XTC's second LP, *Go 2*. However, thirty-eight lines of white type on a black background didn't have the visceral impact of Jamie Reed's ransom note. XTC's record company, Virgin, later blamed *Go 2*'s poor sales on its cover.

There were still times when Storm's sideways thinking surprised his workmates. During punk's year zero, Hipgnosis were commissioned by Styx, an American group whose satin-trousered pomp-rock was the antithesis of the Sex Pistols. Their album, *Pieces of Eight*, included the song 'Aku Aku' – also the title of explorer Thor Heyerdahl's best-selling book about the Polynesian islands.

From this, Storm imagined a group of American housewives attending a cocktail party on Easter Island. Hipgnosis shot four mature women wearing earrings modelled on the island's Moai statues and, unusually for the time, didn't shy away from showing a hint of grey hair and crow's feet. 'I didn't have a clue what Storm was thinking about this one,' admits Po. 'But what did I know? The band said, "Dude, we love it."'

That summer, Peter Gabriel re-appeared, scratching white stripes on the sleeve of his second album. Like Led Zeppelin's *Presence*, Gabriel's cover was what Storm called 'a 2D/3D conundrum' and created from pieces of paper and Tippex correcting fluid. But the idea had been languishing in Hipgnosis's 'rainy day drawer' or 'rejects box' as Gabriel calls it, for some time before the singer succumbed: 'Storm had used it on a poster for Lumiere & Son, but I still thought it was so powerful.'

Hipgnosis deployed the 2D/3D conundrum on UFO's latest, *Obsession*. Po was summoned to Los Angeles, where UFO were now living, and told they urgently needed a sleeve. 'Make them look bizarre,' said manager Wilf Wright. Hipgnosis recycled an idea they'd just used for the trade magazine, *Modern Purchasing*, in an article about how European markets were being flooded with Japanese ball bearings.

Po met UFO at the Animal Surgery department of the University of Los Angeles. Four of the five band members slicked back their long hair and wore ties and suits before being shot under the surgical lights. Ball bearings were later collaged over their eyes, noses and mouths, 'like metal fungi,' explained Storm.

Only guitarist Michael Schenker was spared. 'Michael was most perturbed,' says Phil Mogg. 'He asked, "Why do I have no balls?"' Storm suggested his bandmates had been afflicted by the ball bearings, but Schenker was immune. 'We knew it was going to be different from the teen idol picture we'd envisaged.

But we had no idea they'd come up with something so different. I thought it was absolutely knockout.'

By now, though, UFO were on that cycle of tour, album, tour, ad infinitum, which Po had first seen with Humble Pie in 1971. Hard drugs had also entered the equation and nobody in the group was taking any notice of the business. 'A hair of the dog had become *hairs* of the dog,' admits Mogg. 'I had a house in Laurel Canyon and came home one day to find the rental company taking the furniture away. The next day, another lot came for the car. I thought, "Hang on, where's all the money going?"'

UFO weren't unique. Many of their generation of post-*Sgt Pepper* rock groups were starting to burn out. When Po visited Black Sabbath to present ideas for *Never Say Die!*, the conversation turned into a slanging match as soon as Ozzy Osbourne arrived: 'I later discovered Ozzy was leaving the group or they'd just fired him.'

'Wishbone Ash didn't come up for air,' says Andy Powell. 'We were flogged mercilessly. It was always, "Another tour, another album, break Europe, break America . . ." We should have been like Pink Floyd and taken time off, and then we might have caught up with ourselves.'

The group's latest, *No Smoke Without Fire*, reunited them with *Argus*'s producer Derek Lawrence, in the hope they'd re-kindle the magic. The artwork showed studio assistant Richard Draper whispering into Peter Christopherson's ear, but obscured by illustrated cutouts and airbrushed squiggles: 'The band detested it, the manager hated it, the record company hated it,' recalled Storm. 'I liked it.'

Yes, however, made their disapproval known more dramatically. Their new album, *Yes Tor*, was named after the second-highest point in the Peak District. Rob Brimson was sent to photograph the tor for the front and back of the sleeve. Meanwhile,

Yes were photographed in Regent's Park for the back cover. Some of the group had fallen out with each other and all of them were wearing sunglasses and looking in opposite directions.

Po then shot Brimson holding a pair of divining rods in the studio: 'Quite often you'd be asked to pose for something, but you never knew if it was for a mock-up or the real thing, and I forgot all about it,' he says.

'The cover looked shit,' says Rick Wakeman. 'I was against us splitting with Roger Dean in the first place, because he was synonymous with Yes. But I remember walking into RAK Studios, where the *Yes Tor* cover was blown up big on an easel. That picture of the tor could have been a rock anywhere and all they'd done was turn it blue. I said, "How many thousands has this cost us?" They said, "Ooh, it's contemporary." I said, "No, it's horrible."'

Several members of Yes were vegetarian and their buffet lunch included a large salad. 'I'd had a few drinks,' admits Wakeman, 'and there was a tomato that had been in the salad bowl all day and was very soft. So I picked it up and threw it at the picture and there was this stunned silence.'

However, this act of vandalism was turned into art. The album's title was changed to *Tormato* and the sleeve was printed with pips and pulp smeared over both covers.

Over forty years later, Rob Brimson discovered he was on the front, holding the divining rods. 'I never knew it was me,' he insists. 'I presumed they'd hired a model and shot it again. Of course, I was never paid for this.'

Like many of the bands they worked for, Hipgnosis also fell back on familiar tropes. Cutouts similar to those used on *No Smoke Without Fire* were reprised for 10cc's *Greatest Hits*, among other sleeves. But Hipgnosis's watery artwork for the Strawbs's album, *Deadlines*, was as fraught as their earlier effort for Argent's *In Deep*.

Storm was fixated on the idea of a man trapped inside a telephone box full of water. The Strawbs were an ailing folk-rock group who hadn't had a hit since 1973's 'Part of the Union', and certainly didn't have the budget for such a high-production concept. But Storm was insistent and Hipgnosis built a reinforced steel and glass phone box in Po's back garden. There was something of Fellini's dying motorist in *8½* about the way the cover model pawed at the glass. Not without good reason, as he'd nearly drowned during the shoot.

Deadlines didn't sell, but Storm had turned his big idea into reality. 'One of the things Hippnosis did was we took it seriously,' he said. 'Album covers aren't serious, not compared to tsunamis and brain surgery, but if you're a band, I think it's comforting that the people doing your covers give a shit. We were extremely diligent and as ego-driven as the bands, but we weren't going to do a piece of work that was crap if we could possibly help it.'

10cc still refused to use anyone but Hipgnosis or consider any outside interference. 'Our relationship with the record company was, "Here is the record, put it out and sell it,"' says Graham Gouldman. 'We never had an A&R man come down and tell us what we should be doing. No one could tell us anything. So what are you going to tell Storm Thorgerson about art?'

The new album, *Bloody Tourists*, included the hit single 'Dreadlock Holiday', inspired by Gouldman and Eric Stewart's recent vacations in Barbados and Jamaica. Hipgnosis zeroed in on the idea of a tourist oblivious to the culture of whatever paradise island he was visiting. Storm showed 10cc a sketch of a man with a map blowing in his face to signify his cultural blindness.

Storm didn't mention it had been turned down by Genesis for *And Then There Were Three*. Genesis had become a trio after losing guitarist Steve Hackett and he thought the map signified a band looking for a new direction. But Genesis disagreed.

'Dreadlock Holiday' inspired a new angle for the picture. In June, Po, Gabi Schneider and Peter Christopherson flew to Barbados in search of the perfect beach on which to shoot their tourist but it poured with rain for several days and none of the locations were entirely suitable.

The flight home included a two-hour stopover in St Lucia. As the plane started to land, Po spied Vigie Beach, a location so idyllic it could have been created especially for them. Po retrieved their camera bags while Christopherson guarded the rest of their luggage. Po and his girlfriend then crossed the tarmac and climbed over the runway's perimeter fence towards the bay: 'Nobody seemed to notice or care,' he recalls.

Po photographed Gabi standing in the Caribbean and swishing her hair. He then set the timer on the Hasselblad and placed a plastic mask over his face onto which he'd glued a crumpled map. It was Po's first and final time as a front-cover model. The shoot had cost thousands of pounds in flights and hotels but took just fifteen minutes.

There was another narrative here besides the bumbling Brit abroad. It captured the universal experience, shared by most of the Hipgnosis stable, of a rock band on tour. 'You go to all these fantastic places but you don't see them,' says Gouldman. 'You see the plane, the hotel room, the car and the stage.'

Bloody Tourists also came with a new 10cc logo, designed by George Hardie and still used by Gouldman today. Other designers would soon experience the same as Bush Hollyhead after drawing Led Zeppelin's logo for *Houses of the Holy*. Namely, seeing their work preserved on LP sleeves, CD covers and merchandising for the next half-century and more.

Hipgnosis's branding for Wings, Bad Company and Genesis all had a shelf life beyond the albums they were originally commissioned for. NTA Studios' Geoff Halpin designed UFO's logo for *Obsession*. 'It was the usual thing,' Halpin recalled. 'Fifty quid and it had to be done in five minutes.' Within months, the logo was appearing on T-shirts and on the backs of denim jackets and is still used by the band today.

If Hipgnosis worried that a logo was too ornate, they canvassed members of the public for their opinion. Many an assistant stood on Denmark Street waving a sheet of paper at passers-by. Storm even succeeded in having a logo approved by EMI after their office cleaner told him she liked it.

Some of the stories behind the logos and sleeves had now become public. In 1977, Storm and Roger Dean compiled *The Album Cover Album Book*, an LP-shaped history of the genre. It was a hit and the following spring saw the publication of *Walk Away René: The Work of Hipgnosis*, Storm's version of the art books he'd pored over as a teenager, but with *Houses of the Holy* and *Deceptive Bends* replacing *Son of Man* and *Bedroom in Arles*.

Walk Away René was another hit and often attracted uninvited fans to number six. 'Fans who called in unannounced were usually treated harshly and I found myself doing a fair bit of counselling,' admits Rob Brimson. 'Some travelled from Europe to meet their heroes but were still chucked out by Storm. Po, though, being more pragmatic, saw free gofers.'

Letters now regularly arrived at Denmark Street from as far afield as Wisconsin and Tokyo. 'I feel my life would be fulfilled if I could design sleeves for the world's greatest ever rock band, Genesis,' read one. 'Please find enclosed a letter for Roger Waters,' read another. By this time, Waters was no longer a fan.

Walk Away René had included *Animals*, but Storm's text hadn't credited him for the idea.

'It drove Roger into a fury,' says David Gilmour. 'Roger can be a little unforgiving about things like that. They knew what he was like and I don't know how they made such an elementary mistake.'

'We didn't have a big falling-out,' insists Waters. 'I just said, "What the fuck is wrong with you? It had nothing to do with you! You fucking prick!" That was the end of it for me. I didn't sue them, I didn't demand a retraction. I thought the work Hipgnosis did for us was great. So why did they steal my little contribution?'

Pink Floyd went on hiatus for over a year after touring *Animals*, but Rick Wright's solo album, *Wet Dream*, arrived in September in an Hipgnosis sleeve. 'Rick didn't want anything bizarre,' Storm recalled, 'and we knew that he was fond of women, sailing and boozing.' The cover, with its swimming pool, cocktail, boat and topless Gabi Schneider, was like the anti-*Animals*.

The combination of Hipgnosis and water was again challenging. 'We had to put twenty-eight big sheets of Formica in the bottom of the pool to get the right shade of blue,' recalls Brimson. 'I had to shoot from above, using a high ladder and a high-powered flash, which, had it fallen into the water, would have electrocuted everyone. On reflection, we probably shouldn't have done this.'

It was Paul McCartney, though, who almost sent members of Hipgnosis to an early grave that year. *Wings Greatest* was about to be released, with the hits 'Live and Let Die', 'Jet' and 'Mull of Kintyre' illustrating McCartney's illustrious post-Beatles career.

Linda had just acquired a 2-foot-2-inch gold and ivory statue of the Assyrian goddess Semiramis at auction. Sculptor Demetre

Chiparus's deity was reimagined as a dancer with outstretched arms and a winged cape, and Linda wanted her on the cover of *Wings Greatest*, but posed on Mount Everest.

The highest mountain in the world was too much even for Hipgnosis, so Po suggested the Matterhorn in the Swiss Alps – it was more accessible and half as tall. McCartney agreed: 'But as I was leaving the meeting, Brian Brolly pointed out that Paul really wanted this to happen. Which was his way of saying, "Don't mess it up."'

McCartney was as dogged in his pursuit of an idea as Storm but the two still weren't speaking. 'Storm was a genius, stimulating, funny, erudite and interesting,' stresses Po. 'But after *Venus and Mars*, sadly, Paul didn't like to be in the same room as him after he was rude to Linda.'

Po put together a team, comprising the Australian still-life photographer Angus Forbes, his assistant Ian and Po's partner in hi-jinks, Alex Henderson, who was both a champion skier and comfortable with heights. Po had neglected to tell McCartney about his lifelong acrophobia. Whenever a commission involved tall buildings or high mountains, Po took a deep breath, a sedative and stayed away from the edges.

Hipgnosis decided to set up base camp in the village of Zermatt and persuaded the local helicopter company, Air Zermatt, to fly them, their vast selection of cameras and their five-and-a-half stone statue up to the Matterhorn. It took time for Po to convince the helicopter service that this was a legitimate request on behalf of *the* Paul McCartney. After which, they told Po the Matterhorn was too high at 14,691 feet for their helicopters to land. Air Zermatt agreed to fly them to the neighbouring mountain, the Brienzer Rothorn, which was 10,000 feet lower. 'We were also told in no uncertain terms that we had to employ their mountain guide,' says Po, 'and that they could abort the mission if they thought any of us were in serious danger.'

As gung-ho as the touring party were, the logistics of the expedition were daunting even before they left England. Insurance brokers spent hours photographing every detail of the statue before they'd sign off on the paperwork. Nobody told them Semiramis was taking a trip to the Alps.

The McCartney connection helped get their 5-foot-6-tall statue box through baggage control at Heathrow. But on landing in Geneva, Po discovered their documents weren't in order: 'I had to telephone our shipping agent and he had to pay a very large sum of money to his Swiss counterpart but it got us into the country.'

They were now hours behind schedule and discovered the boxed-up statue was too large to fit inside the helicopter. Po, Alex and Angus Forbes took the chopper, while their assistant, Ian, who'd stayed quiet about his fear of flying, accompanied Semiramis by road to Zermatt.

Hipgnosis's pilot, Berndt, and their guide, Victor, were in the business of human safety. Flying thrill-seeking photographers and a valuable piece of art around was not part of their job description. They were confused by the mission, but pragmatic. A reconnaissance flight to the Brienzer Rothorn brought home the difficulties they faced: firstly, too many people with too many cameras. Two helicopters were required and Semiramis was unpacked, swathed in a blanket like a newborn and given her own berth. However, the helicopter couldn't land on the Rothorn as it was simply too steep. Berndt suggested flying as close as he could so his passengers could jump down and pass the statue between them. Po experienced a rising sense of panic: 'But of course, I didn't say anything.'

Victor then brought his insider knowledge to bear and suggested an alternative: the flatter, more accessible Gorner Glacier. It offered a clear view of the Matterhorn and he could lower the statue onto the ground for them, leaving the surrounding snow untouched by human footprints. 'The statue wasn't that big,' explains Alex Henderson. 'But it was difficult to move around. We had to hold Victor by the scruff of his neck and his belt as he leaned out the helicopter and placed this thing in the snow.'

The choppers landed a few yards away on the glacier and Po, Henderson and Alex Forbes started shooting. After three hours of battling the bitter cold and their respective phobias, they realised the pictures weren't good enough: 'They didn't have that sense of being on top of the world,' said Henderson.

Plans were made to return at dawn the next day. This time, they'd be braving the Rothorn. Victor took the first flight and managed to place the statue in the snow but the others had to jump from the helicopter as it hovered at a 45-degree angle to the edge of the summit. 'It was a shock to the system,' says Po. 'But we'd come too far to stop now.'

Semiramis looked incongruous and surreal against the pure white snow. Victor watched, bemused, as his passengers took photographs; the still mountain air broken by the frantic whirr of loading film and the click of camera shutters. Then they flew back to Gorner Glacier to take more pictures. Victor, mindful of the ice floe's hidden crevasses, tied the group together and attached the rope to one of the helicopters.

'Victor and Berndt thought we were crazy,' says Po. The same thought crossed his mind later as they struggled to load their precious artefact back onto the helicopter. Not for the first time, Po wondered why they were risking their lives for an album cover. Back at the hotel, news of their adventures had spread through the village. Drinks were bought and stories told, and Po and Alex Henderson awoke the next morning in a strange house on the other side of Zermatt.

The mood on the flight home was muted as the agonising wait to discover whether the photographs were even usable had begun. Po dropped the film at the processing lab straight from Heathrow Airport. The next morning he peered through a loop at the transparencies and was relieved to discover McCartney had a front cover. Po took the images in person to the McCartneys' townhouse in St Johns Wood.

Paul and Linda gazed upon their Assyrian goddess framed by the whitest snow and the bluest sky. McCartney raised his eyebrows and flashed his pop-star smile. 'Very good, Po,' he said. 'But you could have just done this in a studio with a backdrop of a mountain.'

Everybody laughed, but McCartney's words rang uncomfortably true. *Wings Greatest* became a top-five hit in December 1978, but its exorbitant artwork had something of Nero fiddling while Rome burned. Britain had just entered what *The Sun* called 'The Winter of Discontent', with many public workers on strike and unemployment topping 1.5 million. There was a new mood afoot. The Sex Pistols had broken up following a disastrous American tour, but they'd left their mark on the record business: 'The labels realised you didn't have to spend a fortune on covers to have a hit and there was less money to splash around,' says Po.

New designers were following Jamie Reed's lead. Earlier that year, Manchester art student Malcolm Garrett helped design the Buzzcocks' debut single, 'Orgasm Addict', with pictures from an art magazine and an Argos catalogue. Fellow art student Peter Saville had designed stark modern branding for Factory Records and its flagship group, Joy Division.

Saville's heroes were the pioneering typographers Jan Tschic-old and Herbert Spencer. His strikingly simple artwork for Joy Division's debut album, *Unknown Pleasures*, repurposed a photo-graph of a pulsar's radio waves found in the *Cambridge Encyclopedia of Astronomy*. *Unknown Pleasures*' stark, scientific design suggested a *The Dark Side of The Moon* for the new decade. 'In hindsight, it was a natural progression,' admits Po. 'We were becoming the old men of that world.'

Closer to home, Peter Christopherson's graphics for Throbbing Gristle and their Industrial Records label were singular and dis-comfiting. Industrial's branding included a picture of Auschwitz, while 'Zyklon B Zombie', the B-side of their first single, was named after the cyanide gas used in German concentration camps.

'I told Peter I found it all pretty tasteless,' says Po. 'It looked like they were celebrating rather than condemning what had happened in Nazi Germany. He told me that wasn't his inten-tion and they wanted to draw attention to it, so these atrocities could never happen again.'

The group's most divisive figure, though, was Genesis P-Orridge. Cosey Fanni Tutti's memoir later revealed the couple's abusive relationship. To the rest of Hipgnosis, though, he was just Sleazy's unusual friend, who'd materialise in the studio with a great swathe of hair shaved from his forehead almost to the crown.

'I'd look at Genesis and he'd look at me, and we were like two alien species,' remembers Rob Brimson. 'I was still a bit of a hippy and he was off challenging sexual mores with Throbbing Gristle. But I found him inquisitive and engaging and had no idea he was such a manipulative person.'

'I was terribly suspicious of him,' says Po. 'I was never sure which side Genesis was on. How much of what he did was genu-ine art and how much was exploitation and showbusiness.'

Po attended three Throbbing Gristle performances, but never stayed until the end. He was reminded of the culture clash after driving to one in a bright blue Porsche: 'I left after half an hour because I couldn't stand it anymore and somebody had written "You cunt" on the Porsche in indelible ink. I thought, "Well, if you're going to see Throbbing Gristle in a car like that, somebody is going to do that."'

Walk Away René had attracted a readership beyond Hipgnosis's traditional fanbase. Advertising agencies had seen the book and wanted the company to help sell their products with the same flair they'd brought to Pink Floyd. 'It couldn't have come at a better time, because we needed a substantial cash flow,' says Po. 'But it meant we'd also sold out to the devil.'

This transaction took place the day Hipgnosis were commissioned to design a brochure for the Chrysler Sunbeam Talbot GLS. 'Probably one of the most uninspiring hatchbacks ever to grace the road,' says Po. 'More to the point, though, they would pay us a lot of money. We weren't naïve, but our reputation lay in the music business, so we were flattered someone in a business like that would seek us out.'

The Winter of Discontent hadn't reached the advertising agencies and the brochure led to further commissions but these were often fulfilled through gritted teeth. 'In the studio, we used to play the Valentine Brothers' song, "Money's Too Tight to Mention", over and over to remind ourselves why we were doing this,' says Po. 'Storm hated it because we had to put the product in the picture but I realised we'd get ten times the money we did for an album cover.'

'It was a difficult relationship,' says Rob Brimson, who photographed campaigns for Chrysler, Kronenbourg, Stella Artois and many others. 'A Hipgnosis album cover was never about selling the band. It was a tantalising mix of imagery and graphics to make you pick out that record from a pile of others. That's not what advertising does, though. The product is a tangible thing and not a fanciful idea of what it might be.

'The ad agencies wanted a bit of the Hipgnosis magic, but there was a lack of communication. Initially, Storm was under the impression he'd be involved in the creative process. He may have been at first, but that seemed to stop quickly as art directors came along with their sub-Hipgnosis concepts and expected Hipgnosis to shoot them.'

'A French agency once rang us and said, "We've designed six ads based directly on covers in your book, would you like to photograph them?"' said Storm. 'Then when they got round to commissioning us, they proceeded to tell us what to do. But the agency is trying to keep the peace with the client and, after a lot of aggravation, they probably wish they had never approached us in the first place.'

Storm treated the agencies the same way he did record companies. Ad managers would arrive at the studio only to be ignored while he fussed over some minor detail on Mike Rutherford from Genesis's solo album. 'Deadlines came, deadlines went,' says Brimson. 'Storm was never worried, which caused a lot of upset. It was actually horrible to watch because I felt sorry for the art directors, but I respected Storm's point of view, too. They were just a bad fit.'

Sometimes the meetings ended even sooner. One day, three executives in matching camel-hair coats arrived at the studio on behalf of Mercedes-Benz. They stared at the Brand X poster peeling off the wall and felt the soles of their shoes sticking to the spray glue-coated carpet. 'They told us they could never bring Mercedes to such a studio,' says Po, 'and I showed them the door. We had lost a prestigious client, but we were not about to change our colours.'

★

Hipgnosis lost Germany's biggest car company, but gained its biggest heavy-metal band. The Scorpions styled themselves after Led Zeppelin, but with shriller vocals and more histrionic guitar solos. The band wanted Hipgnosis to design their new album, *Lovedrive*, and vocalist Klaus Meine and drummer Herman Rarebell's cowboy boots were soon clattering up the stairs to Flat 20, Hillfield Mansions.

The pair squeezed onto the sofa in front of the gas fire and asked Storm how much he liked sex. 'I thought it was a trick question,' he recalled. 'Were they offering?' Storm had several girlfriends after Libby January but still lived alone with his young son. The group impressed upon him how much they liked sex, by mentioning pornography and the work of erotic art photographer Helmut Newton.

The Scorpions had a complex relationship with sex and art. The sleeve of their second album, 1975's *In Trance*, was shot by photographer Michael von Gimbut and showed a woman crouched over a Fender Stratocaster wearing an expression of faux ecstasy and with one breast exposed. Retailers insisted on a censored version.

For the Scorpions' next album *Virgin Killer*, von Gimbut photographed a naked ten-year-old girl, with a shattered-glass effect obscuring her genitalia. Understandably, the sleeve was rejected in several countries, including the UK, and concealed in black shrink-wrap in others.

Von Gimbut returned to shoot 1977's *Taken by Force*, which showed children playing with guns in a French military cemetery.

It was intended as an anti-war statement but was hastily replaced with a group picture following further complaints. After which, Scorpions approached Hipgnosis, hoping they might achieve a better balance.

'They wanted a cover with sex, women and strangeness,' recalled Storm, who thought of a well-heeled couple sitting in their limousine after a night at the opera. The 'strangeness' was that the woman's evening dress was open to reveal a breast, from which her companion was pulling dense strands of bubblegum.

Marcus Bradbury's original sketch showed the woman's flesh being stretched: 'But nobody could work out how to do that and there was no Photoshop, which is why we changed it to bub-blegum.' A wire apparatus was built to fit around their model's neck and over the nipple, to which the gum would be attached.

However, Hipgnosis's take on Helmut Newton lacked either his glamour or budget. *Lovedrive* was a night shoot in an under-ground car park reeking of petrol fumes; the models fixed their own hair and make-up, and everybody in the studio had chewed gum beforehand, which they regurgitated for use in the picture.

'It was like something from a film,' says Bradbury. 'I remem-ber being in a limousine in this subterranean place, fitting a wire apparatus under a woman's breast, while a guy sits next to me with his hand covered in bubblegum attached to the wire over her nipple. The apparatus was airbrushed out later.'

Lovedrive was released in January 1979 and was the Scorpi-ons' biggest hit yet. But its artwork was condemned as sexist by many, including Hipgnosis's friends. Storm claimed the picture's absurdity offset any chauvinism and that the female model's obvious disinterest in the act made it amusing. 'I seem to have lost my sense of humour,' said photographer Jill Furmanovsky at the time. 'This sleeve repulses me.'

'You have to put it in context,' says Po. 'In the '60s, a lot of the myth around sex was destroyed and we saw this as another slap in the face of our parents' generation. They were all walking around wearing a collar and tie, and we were walking around with our bollocks out. But we weren't motivated by demeaning women. Bubblegum coming off a breast is just a weird picture. It wouldn't have looked the same if it was coming off an ear. It was tense and uncomfortable, but not sexually motivated.'

The Scorpions' US record company refused it and put a picture of a scorpion on the sleeve instead. 'It was just sex and rock 'n' roll,' protested an oblivious Klaus Meine. In later years, though, Storm admitted that the image 'was a bit crude' and Po revealed that his daughters referred to *Lovedrive* as 'the tits and bubblegum picture'.

It wouldn't be the first or last time Hipgnosis's work was criticised for its portrayal of women. Storm always praised the hand-tinting on Montrose's 1976 album, *Jump On It*, but the combination of the title with a close-up of a bikini-clad crotch seemed a tad tasteless even then. Or, in the case of Humble Pie's *Thunderbox*, with its keyhole view of two naked women in a bath-room, naff and voyeuristic.

Hipgnosis justified these images by mentioning their sleeve for pub-rockers the Winkies, which showed four buff male bodies encased in figure-hugging shorts. But it was an argument they'd undermine with even crasser sleeves in the future.

Punk had now been succeeded by what music journalists christened 'new wave'. It was a convenient label applied to groups as diverse as the Jam, Blondie, the Boomtown Rats and Elvis Costello and the Attractions, all of whom shared punk's primitive energy but not all of its hard edges. None of these artists came to Hipgnosis, although the Attractions' drummer

Pete Thomas later breached the battlements at number six and married Judy Reynolds.

In spring 1979, the average record shop window displayed Elvis Costello's *Armed Forces* alongside Bad Company's latest, *Desolation Angels*. It was the old versus the new. One sleeve was shot in California's Death Valley and featured the Swedish Miss World contestant, Christel Johansson; the other showed a painting of elephants.

Running in tandem with the new wave were Hipgnosis's hard-rock acts striving to fill the void left by Led Zeppelin. The band hadn't played in Britain for four years and their 1977 American tour had ended in disaster soon after Po joined them in Florida. A violent altercation, involving a security guard at California's Oakland Coliseum, led to Peter Grant, John Bindon, Richard Cole and drummer John Bonham all being arrested.

A few days later, Robert Plant received a telephone call from home, telling him his five-year-old son, Karac, had died from a viral infection. The tour was cancelled and for the second time in as many years, Plant considered a life outside of Led Zeppelin.

The charges against Grant and the others were dropped, but John Bindon was later arrested for murder. It was as if there was a big black cloud over Led Zeppelin and its entourage, an awful sense of doom and foreboding. 'Aside from losing my boy, there was this whole hysteria that surrounded the mid- to late-'70s,' explained Plant. 'It was anything but conducive to normal family life.'

John Bonham, his closest friend in the band, was instrumental in Plant returning to the group, but the shifting musical landscape affected Zeppelin as much as it did their peers. It was a confused and confusing time. Plant and Jimmy Page experienced conflicting emotions when they went to see the Damned play London's punk haunt, the Roxy.

'I was aware there was a lot of nudging going on behind us,' recalls Page. 'When the Damned kicked off, you felt this wall of sound almost pressing down on you. It was magnificent.'

'There was a lot of dirge and crap around at that time,' says Plant, 'but the Damned had so much personality. They were like Vince Taylor and the Playboys and all those seminal rock 'n' roll groups, while we were getting written off as old monoliths.'

Led Zeppelin wanted their new album, *In Through the Out Door*, to harness the same energy. In November 1978, they shipped out to ABBA's Polar Studios in Stockholm. Page was delighted when ABBA's Björn Ulvaeus gave him a guitar and the group, minus Agnetha Fältskog, took him to a nightclub. 'I was rather hoping we'd get to meet Agnetha,' Page admits. 'But that wasn't part of the deal.'

Despite talk of new beginnings, when Po arrived to discuss the artwork he found a band split in two by recreational habits and the hours they kept. Plant and John Paul Jones worked during the day, while Page and Bonham often arrived after dark. Richard Cole's first task had been to find a heroin dealer near to the studio. His connection let them know when he was open for business by switching on the light in his living room: 'So I spent half my time in Stockholm looking out the fucking window,' Cole later confessed.

Nevertheless, Page wanted a piece of art which reflected the band's imaginary rejuvenated spirit. He talked about the blues and Po thought of a New Orleans barrelhouse. Page told him about a hip bar on the Caribbean island of Martinique that might work for a cover, but it had been given a makeover since. Then Po remembered the Old Absinthe House, a French Quarter juke joint he'd visited one Mardi Gras with the McCartneys. Among its features were business cards and other artefacts stuck to almost every inch of the walls.

Po flew to New Orleans and took pictures of the bar, which Humphrey Ocean used to create rough sketches. 'Jimmy and Peter loved it,' recalls Po. 'As always with Peter, there was never any mention of money. Zeppelin wanted something creative and different and it cost what it cost. There was nothing better than being told, "Just do it . . . oh, and take Concorde, stay at the Plaza . . ." Their support was unequivocal.'

Po's former BBC set-designer colleagues helped create a 360-degree version of the ultimate juke joint, with movable walls, so Hipgnosis could shoot from six different angles for six versions of the cover. 'Each one would depict a man in a white suit at a bar, taken from the perspective of one of the other people in the room,' Storm explained.

The walls and ceiling of Hipgnosis's set fluttered with business cards and every tumbler, bottle, beer mat and bar stool had been hand-picked by a professional prop artist. Storm's white-suited man, played by their Cambridge friend, David Henderson, sat at the bar, holding a burning business card. This was Storm indulging his film director fantasies; a movie scene, viewed from each of the bar's patrons, including the tattooed bartender and a woman leaning against the jukebox in the corner. 'The set was better than the album,' joked Jimmy Page.

The covers were tinted sepia, which added to the filmic quality and were given a single brushstroke of colour. 'It was like you were looking into the bar through a dusty window,' explained Storm, 'and the smear was where you'd wiped the pane with your sleeve to peer through.'

In later life, Storm was sometimes dismissive of his Hipgnosis work: 'Why do you want to live in the past, dear?' he'd ask. But he always held up *Wish You Were Here* and *In Through the Out Door* as evidence of its three principals working together and to their greatest strengths. 'Our personal lives were very different, with different strains and obligations,' Storm wrote in 2008. 'But the complementarity was particularly strong.'

The liner bag showed Humphrey Ocean's before-and-after illustrations of the lone drinker's glass, lighter, cigarette packet and smouldering ashtray. Jimmy Page suggested the pictures change colour when water was splashed on the bag; a simple gimmick used in children's colouring books. But consumers only discovered it by word of mouth or accident: 'If they knocked a glass of water or a beer on it,' says Page.

The final detail originated from Atlantic Records and Peter Grant. 'We got fed up with Peter and everyone at the record company telling us that it didn't matter what we put on the cover because a Led Zeppelin album would sell anyway,' admitted Storm.

Hipgnosis called their bluff and in another nod to *Wish You Were Here*, the six sleeves were disguised in an identical brown paper bag, showing just Zeppelin's name and the LP's title. 'But the paper bag also meant you didn't know which of the six covers you were getting,' points out Page. 'So you couldn't choose which one to buy. I liked that, because it kept the mystery.'

Po visited Horselunges Manor so Grant and Page could approve the artwork. They were joined by another Hipgnosis familiar, Bad Company's tour manager Clive Coulson. After everybody had admired the pictures, Grant suggested a toast to the Old Absinthe House and sent his Man Friday to the cellar for a bottle of the spirit.

Absinthe was banned in several countries due to its potent psychoactive qualities. Four glasses were poured, but Po left his untouched. 'The others all glugged theirs down,' he says. 'But I didn't want to be out of control. There were too many flakes in the music business and I didn't want to become another one.'

The conversation slowed and then stopped completely. 'Everybody's eyes closed and their heads dropped, one after another. All three were out for the count and Jimmy even had a cigarette between his fingers. I didn't know what to do. Dare I wake Peter Grant? Eventually, after God knows how long, they all came round and carried on talking as if it had never happened. The absinthe was from the 1850s or whenever and I thought they'd all be blind when they woke up.'

In *Through the Out Door* emerged from its brown paper bag in August 1979 and sold 1.7 million copies in a week. It was a mixed blessing for Hipgnosis as its success proved Grant's theory about the importance of the cover correct. It was a number-one hit on both sides of the Atlantic but reflected the schism within the group. There was retro rockabilly, samba, synthesisers and Godley and Creme's invention, the Gizmo, on one song, 'In the Evening', but *In Through the Out Door* didn't quite flow.

'It was a departure,' says Page. 'The thing about *In Through the Out Door* is that there's nothing like an "Achilles Last Stand" on there. It was another dimension.'

Hipgnosis's high-production artwork was also at odds with Led Zeppelin stripping away the hubris. The LP's release had been delayed because early runs of the paper bags weren't strong enough and kept tearing. Atlantic were furious about the delay and retailers loathed the bag. Really, neither party could re-invent themselves. 'Led Zeppelin were always preposterous,' said Storm. 'They were mega-huge, in terms of sales, their reputation, their behaviour patterns and their sound. We wanted to reflect that on our artwork, go way over the top.'

Page admired this quality, but Robert Plant had reservations: 'I didn't like the brown paper bag,' he said. 'And at first, I thought the six angles on the bar were a touch of insanity. But in the end, it worked a treat.' Later, when autograph hunters asked Plant to sign a pristine inside sleeve, he'd spit on the drawing, just to watch the colours emerge and the shock on their faces.

The album coincided with Led Zeppelin's first British dates since 1975. Grant booked two consecutive Saturdays in August at Knebworth Park but was rudely reminded of how long Zeppelin had been away. Ticket sales were sluggish and several new acts, including Dire Straits and Ian Dury and the Blockheads, turned down offers to support.

Zeppelin visited the stately home a month before so Po could photograph them for a souvenir programme. 'But Peter warned me the group hadn't spoken for months and the vibes weren't great,' he says. 'They all turned up separately. Robert was friendly enough, John Paul seemed like a complete outsider and Jimmy just chain-smoked cigarettes. Bonzo, though, looked awful. He'd been drinking and had put on weight, was scowling and belching, and had a bottle of Pepto-Bismol in his pocket.'

Po shot a few frames of the disgruntled musicians before a car swung into the grounds and parked a few feet behind him. The door opened and a young woman stepped out, switched on a portable radio and began to dance. Within seconds, she was removing her clothes in time to the music and John Bonham had stopped scowling.

'Of course, I denied all knowledge, but I needed something to break the ice,' admits Po, who shot a roll of film while his subjects laughed and applauded. 'I'd arranged this beforehand for a hundred pounds. As soon as the stripper finished, she put her clothes back on and drove off, without saying a word.'

The photo session ended when Robert Plant dropped his trousers in jest, evidence of which still floats around the internet today.

The group's bad mood reappeared when they saw the pictures: the sky was overcast and John Bonham thought he looked overweight. So Hipgnosis stripped in a brilliant blue Texan sky and airbrushed out Bonham's love handles.

Robert Plant had been persuaded by the others to play Knebworth. 'I was scared,' he says. 'Could we still do it? Could *I* still do it?' Both performances were ragged and seat-of-the-pants but also fleetingly brilliant. Zeppelin's rivals even turned up to watch. The Clash's Mick Jones and Topper Headon and ex-Sex Pistols Steve Jones and Paul Cook were spotted backstage, with their cropped hair and drainpipe jeans disrupting the standard uniform of soft perms and flares.

Led Zeppelin received £1 million for the two dates, plus a percentage from the hot dog stands, the beer stall and even the car park money, which Grant divvied up in secret with one other band member. Backstage, Richard Cole ferried bags stuffed with thousands of pounds from the promoter's office to the back of the band's limousines.

Grant had a sawn-off shotgun hidden in another holdall as he'd heard rumours they were going to be robbed by a gang from the East End. His cocaine paranoia was such that his aides didn't always know where reality ended and the fantasy began. But others within the organisation were now plotting to remove Grant as Led Zeppelin's manager.

'It was a very strange time,' remembers Po. 'It was all starting to fall apart in that camp. This was partly the result of Gloria leaving him. Peter was devastated by his wife leaving, but he was losing Led Zeppelin, too. *In Through the Out Door* was the last time Peter seemed fully engaged with what we were doing.'

Hipgnosis were paid well for the work, but none of this money filtered down to their assistants. 'They did make money but they spent a lot,' says Rob Brimson. 'Storm would spend money on an idea even if it meant losing some of their fee. They were generous in other ways. At Christmas, Po would throw a huge party and everyone was invited, and it was all very rock 'n' roll. But then you'd get asked to do a job for twenty quid.'

By the end of 1979, the situation had become a problem for Marcus Bradbury. 'When I started, they were paying me £70 a week. Then they told me they couldn't afford that and dropped it to £50,' he says. 'But they said, "If you want to stay, you will learn a lot" – and I did. But you had to do what they wanted and then they might let you submit an idea to a band.'

Godley & Creme's album, *Freeze Frame*, had just been released, with Richard Draper and Gabi Schneider's painted bodies on its sleeve. Bradbury's promotional poster idea was chosen by 10cc over Storm's: 'And Storm was extremely jealous about it. He came back from the meeting and said, "Yeah, you got it," but he was pissed off.'

Judy Reynolds eventually took Bradbury aside. 'She said, "Marcus, you need to ask for more money. Do you know how much those guys are making?" When she told me, I asked Storm for a pay rise, he said, "Oh yeah, yeah," but didn't do anything about it.'

Bradbury brooded for several weeks before finally losing his temper, in front of Phil Collins. 'Phil was having a meeting about a cover. But Storm was talking to him about how our American assistant, Paul Maxon, needed to get his visa sorted or he couldn't work. I don't know why, but something in the way he said it made me snap. I said, "Storm, you're a fucking arsehole!" and walked out.'

Collins, a year shy of becoming a pop star with 'In the Air Tonight', watched with the bemused air of someone whose working life was spent arguing with other musicians. A few minutes later, stood on Shaftesbury Avenue, Bradbury realised he needed his pay cheque if he was going to meet this month's rent: 'So I had to go back up the stairs, Phil Collins was still sat there and find Peter Christopherson. Peter's hands were shaking as he wrote the cheque because it was so awkward for him.'

Hipgnosis asked Bradbury to come back. They told him they were making films, opening an office in New York and there'd be more money. 'But I was stupid and I'd just had enough and wouldn't do it,' he admits. 'The thing is, Po was away and I wouldn't have walked out if he'd been there.'

Po was away a lot now. Storm's comment about their 'different strains and obligations' was pertinent. He'd learned to accept Po's independence as a photographer and a businessman, but was uncomfortable with aspects of his friend's current lifestyle.

'Let's put it this way, I was the only person at Hipgnosis wearing a Rolex,' says Po. 'Steve O'Rourke and Tony Howard were in Miami once and came over for a barbecue. Tony saw the pool and the speedboat and went, "Fucking hell, Po, you're living better than Pink Floyd." Gabi was working for Katharine Hamnett, so I told him she was earning the big bucks.'

Living on Miami's Intercoastal Waterway surrounded by drug barons, it was difficult for the lifestyle not to rub off. 'When you hang out with these people, things happen,' he says. 'Also, if you didn't do cocaine in the environment I worked in, you weren't part of the team. If you went to Peter Grant's house or a party at Steve O'Rourke's, you did coke.

'Storm took cocaine. He loved cocaine, but he could also be quite straight about it. He came out to Miami a few times to do shoots, but he didn't approve and could see I was on a slip-pery slope, hanging out with unsavoury people.' Once, as Po was driven back to his house on Golden Beach, he spotted a police car waiting outside, and urged the driver to keep going, not to stop. The cops were there for one of his neighbours, but he wasn't taking any chances.

One day at Hillfield Mansions, Storm offered Po some almost fatherly advice. 'Storm told me I needed to be careful as I'd been in trouble with the law before,' says Po. 'He said, "I don't want to lose you, you're my buddy, please don't go down that route." And he was absolutely right.'

Then one day an assistant picked up the phone at number six, to hear a heavily accented female voice asking if they'd accept a call from a "Mr Powell" at the Copacabana Hotel in Rio de Janeiro.

'The assistant said, "What the fuck are you doing in Rio de Janeiro, Po?" I said, "I'm just doing some business." He said, "But I only saw you a couple of days ago . . ." In those days, nobody went to South America for just a couple of days. I said, "Tell Storm not to worry and I'll be back in the office on Tuesday." I was up to no good.'

Chapter 10

'Do you know what this is? It's Aleister Crowley's fountain pen . . .'

Sheep and dogs return, Freddie Mercury says 'no', Spinal Tap become inspired, Led Zeppelin deflates and Paul McCartney delivers a goodbye kiss.

'As difficult as he was, I always thoroughly enjoyed my many arguments with Storm.'

– Peter Gabriel

★

Pink Floyd's *The Wall* began the night Roger Waters bled over the backseat of a limousine in Montreal. It was 6 July 1977 and he'd just scolded the audience at the Olympic Stadium for being unruly and throwing fireworks. Waters' anger peaked after he spotted one zealous fan scaling the wire in front of the stage and screaming for the old Floyd song, 'Careful with That Axe, Eugene'. Waters leaned over and spat in his face. 'Not very nice,' he says. 'What a terrible place to arrive at.'

Afterwards, Waters was fooling around backstage, tried to karate-kick Steve O'Rourke and cut his foot open. In the back of the limo after a visit to the emergency room, he announced that he loathed playing stadiums and wished he could build a wall between Pink Floyd and their audience. His fellow passengers included the record producer Bob Ezrin and his friend, a psychiatrist. Both men leaned forward and asked Waters to tell them more.

Pink Floyd's concept album, *The Wall*, co-produced by Bob Ezrin, arrived in November 1979. Fantasy and reality blurred in the story of 'Pink', a post-war baby whose father dies on the battlefield during World War Two and who flees his overly protective mother to become a rock star. 'Pink's wall is metaphorical,' explained Waters. 'But it's about the walls we all build around ourselves.'

Pink was a composite of several dissipated rock stars, including Waters and Syd Barrett. Storm and Po recognised many of *The Wall*'s characters and scenarios, from the echoes of World War Two to its absent fathers and autocratic schoolmasters. But Hipgnosis weren't invited to contribute. Waters was smarting over his missing credit in *Walk Away René*, but *The Wall* was intended to be an album, a stage show and a movie, so he had hired the artist and film-maker Gerald Scarfe to collaborate instead.

'We were totally excluded,' says Po. 'I didn't care, we had more work than we knew what to do with. But it was another rejection, which got right under Storm's skin.'

Gerald Scarfe was best known for his savage political cartoons in *Private Eye* and the *Sunday Times*. In 1974, he created animated films for Pink Floyd's stage show and an artist's impression of the group for the tour programme. Scarfe's speciality was grossly exaggerating any defining features, which he did with Waters' teeth and David Gilmour's lips.

'I was not a rock 'n' roller and nor was I a musician,' says Scarfe. 'Roger came to my house and played me these very raw tapes of *The Wall*, with him rasping over a synthesiser.' When it was over, Waters shifted uncomfortably in his chair and told Scarfe, 'I feel like I've just pulled down my pants and taken a shit in front of you.'

'I didn't realise *The Wall*'s potential, to begin with,' admits Scarfe. 'But there were things I recognised in the story. We all had bastard teachers, who visited the miseries of their own lives onto the kids, and Roger and I gradually arrived at some characters that were bizarre and memorable and bore repetition.'

Scarfe drew a stark black and white wall enveloping the gatefold's outer and inner sleeves. Inside were watercolours of Pink's mother as a blue-rinsed tartar in carpet slippers and a praying mantis-like headmaster wielding a cane. These images fitted *The Wall* as perfectly as the burning businessman on *Wish You Were Here*.

'I think Roger realised the benefits of having something fresh,' suggests Scarfe. 'But I was very naïve to the whole set-up, I wasn't aware of Storm Thorgerson.'

Scarfe's independence helped Waters realise the three stages of *The Wall*. His images drove the video for Pink Floyd's hit single, 'Another Brick in the Wall, Part 2', and returned as animations and marionettes during the live show. Pink Floyd's *The Wall* was performed in the UK, Europe and the US between February 1980 and June '81. Waters compromised his original idea of hiding completely. Instead, a 40-foot-high wall was constructed, brick by brick, during the performance and pulled down during its grand finale.

'It was a radical piece of rock 'n' roll theatre,' admits Po, 'and a logical progression from the performance art pieces we'd seen at venues like the Royal Albert Hall in the '60s.'

Director Alan Parker's *Pink Floyd – The Wall* movie followed in July 1982. Parker's creative differences with Waters and Scarfe brought the film close to collapse until Waters was forced to compromise. 'It was,' reflects David Gilmour. 'The least successful of the three ways of telling that story.'

But all three versions happened without Hipgnosis. Storm and Waters had stopped communicating and wouldn't speak to each other for another twenty-five years. 'A long time for someone I'd known since I was a boy and used to pass the ball to on our rugby team,' said Storm. 'I was upset about it for the first three or four years and then I had to get on.'

'Storm was cynical about *The Wall* and Gerald's work,' explains Po, 'and Roger stopped talking to him. But you could see there were serious rifts in the Pink Floyd camp too and the Rick Wright situation to contend with.'

Very few of the audience watching *The Wall* knew that Wright had been forced out of Pink Floyd, but re-employed as a salaried musician for the tour. His contribution to the album had been minimal but he was also browbeaten by Waters. 'Rick was not a strong person,' says Gilmour. 'Roger and I were both quite tough. I'm like a mule – I can get knocked down, but I get back up again, like in that song. Rick was thinner-skinned and he got knocked down and didn't find it so easy to get up.'

After news of his exit was made public, Wright disappeared to his villa on Lindos and sailed his boat around the Aegean for a time; like the artwork for *Wet Dream* brought to life. Meanwhile, Syd Barrett, the last musician to leave Pink Floyd before him, walked from Chelsea Cloisters to his mother's house in

Cambridge: he'd run out of money and had no other way of getting there.

'He walked home because he had no money and nobody was paying the rent on Chelsea Cloisters,' explains Rosemary Breen. 'If Roger [Syd] wanted money, he used to go to what he called "The Office", his music publishers, and they'd give him a cheque. But they weren't paying his income tax and Roger never opened brown envelopes from the tax office. The money was there, but it wasn't getting to him. He wasn't properly looked after.'

Pink Floyd hadn't seen Barrett since he'd arrived, unannounced, at Abbey Road while they were recording *Wish You Were Here*. Yet Waters was still singing about Barrett, his 'obligatory Hendrix perm' and the elastic bands 'keeping my shoes on' in 'Nobody Home' on *The Wall*.

Barrett moved into his mother Winifred's new house in St Margaret's Square, Cherry Hinton, Cambridgeshire. Two French journalists arrived soon after with a bag of Syd's laundry they'd found abandoned at Chelsea Cloisters. It was just a ruse and the subsequent conversation was published in the music magazine, *Actuel*.

One particular exchange illustrated Barrett's refusal to engage: 'Do you remember Duggie [Fields]?' they asked. 'Eh, yes . . . I never saw him again,' Barrett replied. 'All of your friends say hello.' 'Ah . . . thanks. That's nice . . .'

The pair also interviewed Storm, who told them Barrett was predisposed towards mental health issues before he took LSD and was deeply affected by his father's death. Storm also compared Barrett's rejection by Maharaj Charan Singh to 'another father figure turning his back on him'. Meanwhile, the writers cornered a testy-sounding David Gilmour in a London nightclub: 'Syd Barrett? I don't have time to talk about him,' Gilmour told them. 'It's not romantic, it's a sad story. Now it's over.'

This renewed interest in Barrett was partly due to a new generation discovering his music through second-hand copies of *The Piper at the Gates of Dawn* and the re-released *Relics*. Many of these admirers bought into the fantasy of the doomed poet who'd deliberately turned his back on fame and money.

It was horribly at odds with reality, though. After several violent episodes at home, Barrett was admitted to a local mental health facility, Fulbourn Hospital. 'We tried to look after him within the family,' says Rosemary. 'But it wasn't easy. He was not well at all.' Barrett drifted in and out of institutions for most of the 1980s.

Storm had another lost soul to take care of and there were parallels with Syd Barrett. His Cambridge friend, John 'Ponji' Robinson, had taken LSD as part of his weekly therapy sessions in the '60s. He'd renounced the drug and travelled to the Dera ashram to meet the Master. But becoming Satsangi hadn't delivered the enlightenment Ponji hoped for and he'd struggled to find a life and a career.

'He was invariably broke,' said Storm. 'Often kipping for the night, often getting fed, seeking company, but never sponging, travelling incessantly on the London Underground . . .'

When he felt mentally strong, Ponji worked for Hipgnosis and babysat Bill. 'Ponji was Storm's amiable, intelligent friend,' remembers Rob Brimson. 'He did odd jobs but often felt compelled to stand in one particular place for long periods. It could be a bus stop, where he wouldn't draw attention to himself, or in the studio, where we'd work around him, but with the exact spot varying through the day.'

Then one day neither Ponji nor Storm arrived at the studio. David Gilmour had broken the news to Storm that their friend had thrown himself under a train at a London Underground station. Two witnesses later revealed that Ponji's last words were,

'I refuse to be a coward for the rest of my life,' as he ran down the platform.

★

Andrew Ellis was nineteen years old and a student at the London College of Printing when he began working part-time at number six. 'I had the book, *Walk Away René*,' he says. 'I was writing my thesis on record sleeves and Storm and Po agreed to be interviewed. While I was talking to them, they started interviewing me. Storm said, "Do you do graphics?" I said, "Yes." They said, "Great, you're hired," and I started the next day.'

After attending lectures, Ellis would cycle from the LCP to Denmark Street, where he learned not only how to use a Hasselblad and light a set, but also performed the bizarre tasks one could only be asked to do at Hipgnosis. 'Peter Christopherson took me under his wing,' he explains. 'Peter was very much the grit in the oyster between Storm and Po. On one of my first jobs, he asked if I had a strong stomach and if I could develop some film for him. I'll never forget watching this image materialise – a teenage boy, naked, kneeling on the floor, with his guts spilling out over his hands like he'd been eviscerated. It was sheep's guts, but that image has never left my mind.'

One afternoon, Ellis saw Po in conversation with an unusually tall visitor. 'This guy must have been 6 foot 5, at least. He needed some film developing, so I took it to the darkroom. I'd expected something dubious, but the photograph just showed him standing next to a pile of builder's sand, up to his shoulder.' Ellis later asked Po why his friend wanted such a picture. 'And Po said, "It's not builder's sand, it's cocaine." I said, "*What?* But it's up to his fucking shoulder!"'

One of Ellis's days might be spent sitting cross-legged on the floor with Genesis P-Orridge, transcribing lyrics; the next, babysitting Po and Gabi's new daughter Sophie or collecting Bill from school. On one of his first Friday afternoons, Ellis was told his 'bonus' was waiting for him on the picture enlarger. To his surprise, he found the flat surface strafed with lines of cocaine.

'It was amazing how they treated me, as a nineteen-year-old. It was a complete education in this dysfunctional family of maverick photographers, designers, illustrators and re-touchers. I met their families, I went to their houses, they didn't treat me the way others would treat an assistant.'

Ellis's first sleeve was Peter Gabriel's untitled third album, nicknamed 'Melt' and released in May 1980. The idea of Gabriel's face as a dissolving wax effigy came to Storm in a dream: 'Peter quipped that he didn't mind being in my dreams as long as I wasn't in his and he gamely went along with this facial distortion.'

Storm had discovered the work of an American photographer, Les Krims, who created art by doctoring Polaroid images during the developing process. 'So we sat Peter Gabriel on the staircase at Denmark Street and were all taking Polaroids,' Ellis recalls, 'and then getting Biros and pencils and manipulating the emulsion underneath to change the shape of his face.'

Soon, Gabriel grabbed a handful of Polaroids and started defacing them, too. 'We were as happy as a group of toddlers playing in the sand,' he recalled.

The album showed a black and white version of a manipulated Polaroid, with one half of Gabriel's forehead and cheek melting down to his neck. It was a record sleeve as painted by Francis Bacon and suited Gabriel's unconventional approach to his music. He'd banished cymbals from the record, written a song inspired by the murdered anti-apartheid activist Bantu Stephen Biko and another, 'Lead a Normal Life', about mental illness.

Gabriel's American label, Atlantic, refused to release the album. 'Ahmet Ertegun, the head of the company, said to me, "Who is this Biko? Why does anyone in America care about this guy?" That was his honest reaction,' recalls Gabriel. 'When he heard "Lead a Normal Life", Ahmet started asking people, "Is Peter mental?" I think the assumption was, you couldn't write about something like that unless you had the experience of it.'

Geffen Records picked up the option and released the album in the States. It was a modest hit there but reached number one in Britain, where Gabriel's distorted features appeared in record-shop displays and on the side of buses: 'Of all the things Hipgnosis have done for me, these images are the best,' said Gabriel at the time. Yet the two parties went their separate ways afterwards. 'Peter decided he didn't want to work with us any more,' explained Storm, 'and his record company wanted him to have his picture on the cover without us messing it up beforehand.'

'My manager at the time, Gail Colson, said to me, "You need to stop doing these arty-farty covers, Peter, and show the world who you are,"' says Gabriel. Though it wasn't until 1986's *So* that his un-doctored image appeared on the cover. *So*, designed by Peter Saville, went on to sell over 5 million copies in the US alone.

'Melt' was Hipgnosis's greatest hit of 1980, but their subtly subversive art was evident on other releases from this time. The sweetly smiling group pictured on Throbbing Gristle's *20 Jazz Funk Greats* belied the darkness inside. Elsewhere, three immaculately styled models wearing veils appeared on the Alan Parsons Project's *Eve*. It looked like a conventional glamour shot, but a closer inspection revealed fake warts and cold sores under the veils. It was almost like an art prank at the expense of the group and its record company.

Storm dipped into the 'rainy day' drawer, too. When fresh-faced heavy rockers Def Leppard signed with AC/DC's producer and a US management team, they asked Hipgnosis to design their next album, *High 'n' Dry*. The central cover image of a man diving into an empty swimming pool had been lying in the planning chest since 1970, when it was considered for *Atom Heart Mother*.

Both the artists and Hipgnosis repeated themselves, too. Colin Elgie revisited his illustration for Wishbone Ash's 1973 live album, *Live Dates*, on *Live Dates, Vol. 2*. Rob Brimson shot a dressing-room scene for the inside gatefold. A set was built at Denmark Street and included a mirror, a half-eaten sandwich, a bottle of Jack Daniel's and other detritus associated with a touring rock 'n' roll group. On a whim, Brimson wrote his new studio's phone number on the wall: 'I just wanted to see if anyone would call it,' he says, 'and I took calls from around the world, from fans expecting to win a prize.'

Brimson had joined an artists' collective, which included George Hardie, who'd purchased three disused industrial buildings in London's Charterhouse Square: 'They needed one more partner to take on a sub-basement and they asked Hipgnosis,' he says. 'Peter Christopherson went along to check it out, came back and just said, "Bad vibes." So they didn't go ahead with it.'

Brimson phoned George Hardie to arrange a visit: 'It was filthy, a virtual black hole, but I loved it. I had no job and no proper income, but my grandmother had died and left me enough to buy the property. So I moved into the studio, started doing it up and lost track of things at Hipgnosis.

'One day, Storm's assistant phoned up and asked if I would do a cover shoot – a schoolboy playing the cello. I asked, "How much?" And he replied, "Forty quid." But once I'd hired a cello and bought the film, it wouldn't be worth it. I worked with Storm and Po again later, but that was the last time Hipgnosis offered me a commission.'

'I don't remember much about 1980,' claims Po. 'Only that I worked like a lunatic and made a lot of money, but I could be up for three days at a time, hardly sleeping.' Among his more memorable jobs that year, though, was 10cc's *Look Hear?* Like *Wings Greatest* and *In Through the Out Door*, it was one of Hipgnosis's last great music-business heists.

Storm was annoyed when Graham Gouldman and Eric Stewart asked him for 'something different' on *Look Hear?* 'If they wanted something different, why not ask someone different?' he reasoned. '"Dear Picasso, can you paint me a Matisse?" . . .'

Storm proposed a bold typographical statement instead of a traditional image. "Are You Safe", "Are You Right", "Are You Wrong" and "Are You Afraid" were all considered. But Storm chose "Are You Normal" as it referenced R. D. Laing's theory about two versions of one's self: the sane and the mad self. 'And which one is normal?' argued Storm.

George Hardie reproduced the statement in bold type and deliberately without punctuation. 10cc liked the idea but were concerned the graphics would fight with the album's title. They also wanted an image on the sleeve, somewhere. Storm's sideways thinking led him to a picture of a sheep on a psychiatrist's couch on a beach. In his mind, the sheep represented normality; the psychiatrist's couch was a symbol of madness and he interpreted the sea as a metaphor for the great unconscious.

'That cover was a mystery to me then and is still a mystery,' admits Graham Gouldman. 'What is it supposed to be? I don't know, but let it be.'

Hipgnosis wanted a beach with perfect sand and rolling waves and were adamant they wouldn't find this in Britain. 10cc's record label was aghast, but the group agreed to Po making a 7,000-mile trip to Hawaii's Sunset Beach. 'The explanation never registers in my mind,' insists Gouldman. 'Storm wanted to take a photo in Hawaii, the record company wanted him to go to Bournemouth. It was the artist in Storm and I always understood that.'

Finding the tools for the job proved more challenging. 'We discovered they didn't have any sheep on the main island of Hawaii,' explains Po. 'But I called the Department of Agriculture in Honolulu, who told me there was one sheep in an experimental farming community at the local university.'

Po was in Miami at the time. The lack of sheep concerned him, so he shot an alternative image as a backup. Staying with the theme of normality, he arranged a casting session and rented a fully furnished house for a day. 'I wanted a traditional nuclear family, with a mother, a father and two children,' he explains, 'standing outside their house, showing all their worldly possessions.'

Po's chosen family were photographed in front of a white-roofed bungalow, with a station wagon in the driveway and furniture, lamps, paintings and items of crockery laid out before them. It was a snapshot of middle-class Florida life in 1980 but was never used.

Hipgnosis had found a suitable Hawaiian location: Sunset Beach, a surfers' paradise on the North Shore of Oahu. But they also needed a psychiatrist's couch of the kind first used by Sigmund Freud in the nineteenth century. Unfortunately, the classic Victorian Chesterfield chaise longue, with its distinctive rolled back, never caught on in Hawaii. A theatrical props company in Honolulu were shown a sketch and tasked with creating a replica for £300.

The build took five days, during which Po and Gabi Schneider sunbathed, swam in the Pacific and watched the surfers on Sunset Beach. As each new breaker crashed onto the shore Po wondered how their cover star would cope in this strange environment.

Hawaii's only ewe arrived on set, groomed and shampooed, and accompanied by a sheep wrangler and his dog. The sand was a perfect gold, the sky a flawless blue, but the sea was turbulent and the chaise longue kept being swept away. After several failed attempts, the sheep was soon leaping off the couch and being steered back to shore by Gabi and the production scout. Po eventually abandoned the shoot, returned the beast to the university farm and sought professional advice.

'It was not my intention to cause any cruelty to the animal,' he stresses. 'But we were advised to have the sheep tranquilised with a shot of Valium.' The shoot resumed the next morning after a visit to the vet. Hipgnosis's cover star re-appeared, now as docile and compliant as if she'd swallowed a Mandrax at the Giant's Causeway in 1972. The ewe settled on the chaise longue, ignoring the waves crashing behind her and staring down the lens. Hipgnosis finally had their cover shot: 'But if you look closely,' says Po. 'You can see the absolute hatred in her eyes.'

There were now two ideas fighting for space on one sleeve, though. 10cc liked the sheep and Storm wanted the graphics. They reached a compromise. The sheep appeared on the American pressing of *Look Hear?* but only as a tiny image on the British sleeve. 'Storm and I fought over that,' says Po. 'I'd gone all the way to Hawaii for a photograph that ended up not much bigger than a postage stamp.'

Hipgnosis's graphics also presided over the cover, rendering the LP's title almost obsolete. '*Look Hear?* became known as "Are You Normal",' admitted Storm. 'which probably confused everybody, including 10cc.'

The cost of the Hawaii and Florida family shoots were charged to the band via Mercury Records in the UK and totalled around £5,000, the equivalent of £22,000 in today's money. 10cc never saw the pictures from Florida but paid for them anyway.

Graham Gouldman remains remarkably Zen about it all. 'The problem with that album is not the cover but the album itself,' he insists. 'It's just not our best work. *Deceptive Bends* was good, even though Kev and Lol had left by then, but we never had another hit after "Dreadlock Holiday". It was 1980 now and things were going downhill, to put it bluntly.'

Animals featured elsewhere in Hipgnosis's art that year. The crocodile confronting a woman wearing crocodile shoes on Brand X's *Do They Hurt?* was rented from a taxidermist. The dog on the Scorpions' *Animal Magnetism* was alive but straight from Storm's twisted imagination.

Animal Magnetism made anyone browsing in their local Our Price Records stop and stare. The sleeve showed one of Hipgnosis's assistants photographed from behind, a hand tucked into his back trouser pocket and the other holding a can of Heineken. A young woman knelt submissively in front of him, gazing upwards, while a Doberman Pinscher's head hovered alongside the male's crotch.

On the back cover, the dog's head was further forward, suggesting oral sex was taking place. 'Great dog,' said Storm, when asked about the sleeve in 2002. 'The idea was that the woman was about to commit an act of gross indecency but the dog was more curious about it than she was.'

Shooting *Animal Magnetism* was a bleak experience for its female cover model, Lana Topham. Growing up in Victoria, British Columbia, Lana visited her local bookshop to browse its sole copy of *Walk Away René*. 'I couldn't afford to buy it,' she says. 'But I thought what a dream it would be to work at Hipgnosis.'

After graduating, Lana signed up with a model agency and moved to London. She attended a casting session at Denmark Street and was hired by Peter Christopherson for a shoot the following day. Lana was told she'd be photographed on the lawn of a castle or a country manor, but her agency neglected to ask what she'd be required to do.

The next morning, Lana arrived at the studio, was taken to the first-floor darkroom and instructed to do her hair and make-up. 'That was typical in those days, although I thought an album cover warranted a make-up artist,' she says. 'The weather was bad and I was told to wait. So I waited and I waited in that room all day, realising this wasn't going to be the majestic, surreal photo shoot I'd hoped for, and my make-up sank into my skin and my enthusiasm faded.

'I don't remember what time it was, except it was dark outside when I suddenly heard a commotion coming from the main office. I was brought out into the front area. There was a lot of shouting and pointing from this man called Storm and I remember thinking, "What an appropriate name." He was simply awful and everyone ran round in circles, attempting to appease him.'

Storm demanded the stools and wastepaper bins were shunted aside to make room for the model. But he barely acknowledged Lana, only to say he didn't like the shirt she was wearing: 'So he had one of the assistants take his off and give it to me – the shirt he'd been wearing all day.'

Lana was instructed to kneel on the floor and look up at another male assistant standing over her. 'He had clearly been roped into this scenario,' she explains. There was something grubby and exploitative about what then ensued, with Lana posed to look as if she was about to perform oral sex: 'This was a design on the fly, a cover made in a hurry. But being an innocent twenty-year-old and having a sheltered upbringing, I didn't think what the image might be insinuating.'

Then, without any warning, a Doberman Pinscher was led, panting, into the studio. 'Luckily for them, I wasn't afraid of dogs,' says Lana. 'But all the while Storm was shouting about this and that, and now decided the dog's mouth should be opened wide, right up against my face.' The animal wouldn't cooperate, so Storm sent another assistant out into Soho to buy bread pudding, chunks of which were tossed at the dog, encouraging him to open his jaws closer to Lana's face.

Animal Magnetism was released a month later. As with *Lovedrive*, Storm insisted the image was supposed to be shocking and humorous, but its crudity overshadowed any wit or nuance and led to further accusations of sexism.

Lana Topham was paid £150 plus £30 overtime for the job. 'It was confusing,' she admits. 'An older friend, a staunch feminist, was furious with me and asked how I could have agreed to do that cover. I placated myself with the image on the back, where the Doberman goes for the guy, not the girl. I believe there was an *NME* article where Storm made note of this, insinuating it was a bit of a joke on the band.'

There was something unpleasant in the air. A few months later came UFO's *The Wild, The Willing and the Innocent*. It included the song 'Profession of Violence', inspired by a best-selling biography of the criminal Kray twins, which, in turn, inspired the cover. Hipgnosis's blurred torture scene involved a blowtorch and a naked woman shown clinging to a ladder. There wasn't any implied wit or nuance here; just female nudity and sadism.

'Hipgnosis tailed off towards the end,' admits Phil Mogg. 'You can't keep up that level of producing good stuff forever, and nor could we.'

Art later imitated life with the release of the spoof documentary, *This Is Spinal Tap*. It told the story of a fictional rock group, possibly a composite of several Hipgnosis clients, trying to steer a course through a challenging new decade.

In one scene, *Spinal Tap*'s American A&R rep, 'Bobbi Flekman', tells band manager 'Ian Faith', a bluff, well-spoken Brit, why the artwork for their new album, *Smell the Glove*, has been rejected. 'You put a greased naked woman on all fours with a dog collar round her neck and a leash,' she explains, 'and a man's arm extended out up to *here*, holding onto the leash, and pushing a black glove in her face to sniff it . . . You don't find that offensive? You don't find that sexist?'

'This is 1982, Bobbi, come on!' retorts Faith.

'That's right,' Bobbi replies. 'It's 1982! Get out of the '60s. We don't have this mentality any more.'

Animal Magnetism was rumoured to have inspired *Smell the Glove*, but there were other even crasser heavy-metal sleeves to choose from at the time. Despite its critics, it became the Scorpions' first uncensored LP sleeve since 1975.

The relationship didn't end well. The title track of the group's next album, *Blackout*, featured the sound of breaking glass. 'So we wanted an image of somebody diving through glass,' explains Po. 'We did it the way they do in the movies, but must have gone through fifty panes and still kept missing the moment the model smashed through.'

Hipgnosis then spent several days gluing minuscule strands of nylon to suspended shards, through which Paul Maxon was photographed pretending to jump. 'It didn't work at all and now seems utterly ridiculous, but I liked it,' insists Po. 'It was a living sculpture, something you might see in the Tate Modern. But we showed it to the Scorpions and they hated it.'

Instead, the group commissioned an illustration of guitarist Rudolf Schenker with forks bandaged to his eyes. Storm loathed the drawing so much he was compelled to write to the Scorpions' manager. 'It was a wonderful letter,' recalls Po. 'It said, "I know your band hates our cover idea and I know you paid a lot of money for it, but I believe in it and what you've got there now is an absolute crock of shit."'

The rejection pained Storm more than Po, though, who was busy shooting ad campaigns for Volvo in Sweden and Mazda in Paris. 'Looking back now, it was anything to get away from the music business and concentrate on a different style,' he admits. 'I'd say, "Hey, Storm, we made twenty grand today and here's five for you." He liked the money, but had no interest in cultivating that side of the business.'

The work wasn't creatively challenging, some of the shoots weren't even used, but the money compensated for rock 'n' roll groups walking away or saying no. Like Miles Copeland's latest clients, the Police, who were about to become the biggest pop group in the world. Copeland requested a sleeve for their next single, 'De Do Do Do, De Da Da Da' – a plum job for Hipgnosis, who'd been ignored by most of the post-punk bands.

Storm thought the title suggested the sounds an infant makes and borrowed Libby January and her husband Tibor's baby boy, Jody. Storm and two assistants were styled as gangsters, with Storm holding the baby to suggest a fraternal initiation ceremony or possible danger. It was inconsistent with the song's nursery-rhyme lyrics and the Police's lead singer, Sting, dismissed the picture as 'too menacing'. Storm then recreated 'De Do Do Do, De Da Da Da' in a headache-inducing combination of red letters on a green background. He flew to Seattle, where the Police were recording, to make his pitch, only to discover Sting was partially colour blind.

'The fact is our style didn't suit every artist,' admits Po. 'We'd been submitting ideas to Queen for years, and then I was invited to the drummer Roger Taylor's house to meet Freddie Mercury to discuss their *Greatest Hits* album.'

Hipgnosis suggested birds and table tennis balls flying over eyes and mouths. Mercury gave them all a gladiatorial thumbs down. 'Freddie wasn't having any of it. Queen had that sensual, sexual image, with the famous Mick Rock photograph on *Queen II*, and then the poster with the naked girls on the bicycles . . . That wasn't Hipgnosis. We weren't right for Queen.'

Greatest Hits was released with royal photographer Lord Snowdon's stately band portrait on the cover. Instead, Roger Taylor recruited Hipgnosis to illustrate his solo album, *Fun in Space*, with an alien reading an extra-terrestrial gossip magazine.

Freddie Mercury's sexuality was an open secret in the business but never openly addressed in interviews. Sexual prejudice remained an issue, as Hipgnosis discovered when they were asked to work with Foreigner that year. The Anglo-American group had cleaned up in the US, with three albums of booming power ballads and rugged hard rock. However, their most recent LP, *Head Games*, had been condemned for showing a distressed-looking teenage girl wiping her phone number off a men's bathroom wall.

Po met guitarist Mick Jones at New York's Electric Lady Studios, where the band were making their next album, *Silent Partners*. Over lunch at the Russian Tea Room on West 57th Street, the pair discussed spies, covert surveillance and the Cold War. Storm and Peter Christopherson turned this conversation into an image of binoculars hovering in mid-air and observing an androgynous-looking sleeping youth. Foreigner agreed to the concept and paid handsomely for the shoot.

'Then the band and their record company rejected it as being "too gay, too homosexual,"' divulges Po. 'They wanted us to change the boy for a teenage girl. Storm said, "Tell them to fuck off, we're not doing that," because the image would have lost its ambiguity.

'What you have to remember, though, is homosexuality had only been legal in the UK since the mid-'60s. Record companies had these macho rock 'n' roll bands and wouldn't risk anything which might portray them as being anything but heterosexual. Peter Christopherson was gay so we were conscious of not taking bullshit. But we'd had the same problem with Yes on *Going for the One*, except Yes supported us and Foreigner didn't.'

There was something typically contrary, though, about Storm's refusal to bow to this pressure, after Lana Topham's shabby treatment and the grubbiness of *Animal Magnetism*. Foreigner's *Silent Partners* was subsequently re-titled *4* and released in a drab grey sleeve showing the number four on a film's countdown leader – 'Boring,' declares Po, 'dull and miserable as fuck.'

★

Led Zeppelin ended unexpectedly in the early hours of 25 September 1980. After a day's rehearsal for their forthcoming US tour, the group returned to Jimmy Page's new property, the Old Mill House, in Windsor. John Bonham had been drinking steadily since lunchtime and had to be helped to bed.

Zeppelin's roadies placed him on his side and bolstered by pillows, but Bonham rolled over in the night and suffocated in his own vomit. A blood test later revealed he'd consumed the equivalent of forty single shots of vodka. The coroner listed the cause of death as 'accidental suicide'.

Peter Grant had always protected Led Zeppelin: from record companies, critics, artists and sometimes each other. But he hadn't been able to protect Bonham. No matter how often Grant was told there was nothing he could have done, he carried the guilt and regret with him for the rest of his life. 'It was a tragedy,' said Grant. 'For me, the beginning of a period of blackness.'

In the year leading up to Bonham's death, some around the band had been scheming to remove him as their manager. Grant's drug use and poor business decisions made him vulnerable, but there was something of Shakespeare's Julius Caesar about the betrayal. At the centre of the plot was Stevens Weiss's fixer, Herb Atkin, a nefarious former CIA-operative-turned-private detective. Atkin wanted a piece of Weiss's cash cow and was preying on Grant's cocaine paranoia. To isolate Grant, he had to remove Richard Cole, though.

In a murky sleight of hand, Atkin sent Cole to Rome to attend a business meeting on what he was told was Zeppelin's behalf. It never happened. The police arrived at Cole's hotel suite and went straight to the bathroom, where they found thirty-two grams of cocaine stashed under the sink. Weiss hired Mafia don John Gotti's lawyer, who advised Cole to plead guilty so he could serve a shorter sentence. Cole spent six months in prison, where he weaned himself off heroin and learned of Bonham's death from a fellow inmate: 'But when they first told me one of the band had died, I presumed it was Jimmy,' he admitted.

Led Zeppelin announced their split soon after but that didn't stop Weiss and Ahmet Ertegun from hoping they'd reconsider, or several high-profile drummers offering their services. 'Money is a huge corrupter, especially in the rock 'n' roll business,' says Po. 'It was an unbelievable mess of a time.'

One event from this time illustrated Grant's frame of mind. Po was asked to photograph Warren Grant's fourteenth birthday present being delivered to Horselunges Manor. He arrived at the manor to find the family, their friends and various Swan Song gofers and envoys gathered on the lawn. Grant loved a grand gesture and had arranged for the gift, a Suzuki trials bike, to be flown in by helicopter.

The chopper hovered into view, dipping over the Sussex countryside, with the motorcycle suspended on a chain from the undercarriage. Po started taking photographs just as the chain snapped and the bike plummeted into a field. There was a collective gasp from the party-goers and Grant's face darkened.

The helicopter landed on the lawn and Grant, flanked by Richard Cole and Clive Coulson, marched the terrified-looking pilot into the house. In an unintentionally comic moment, Grant ordered Cole to 'remove the distributor cap . . . or something' to stop the chopper from taking off again.

Po followed them all into the study: 'Warren was sent to his room and Peter told me to keep taking photos as evidence.' Grant instructed the pilot to call his boss at the charter company and arrange for £5,000 in cash to be delivered as compensation. Neither he nor the helicopter would be allowed to leave until then. A teenage boy's birthday party had suddenly turned into a kidnapping.

The pilot nervously made the call from another room, returned and told Grant his company would pay the money tomorrow but needed the helicopter now. Grant's eyes narrowed, he walked up to the pilot so he was just inches from his face: 'And said, "What's it like to be called a fucking liar?"' says Po.

Grant was so paranoid he was surreptitiously taping all his telephone calls. The recording was played back and the helicopter company boss was heard saying, 'Tell him whatever he wants to hear and get the fuck out of there.' Eventually, £5,000 in cash was delivered to Horselunges. By then, the pilot had been held to ransom for several hours.

It was disturbing behaviour, but Grant was bringing the hard lessons of the road into civilian life. He was a band manager without a band to manage. Grant was depressed, rarely picked up the phone to any of the surviving Zeppelin members, and never visited the Swan Song office. Like Caesar, his empire was crumbling.

Hipgnosis would work on one more Led Zeppelin project. John Bonham's death hadn't negated the fact Grant had agreed to renew their contract with Atlantic Records. The company expected a new album and *Coda* was assembled from outtakes spanning 1970–79: 'It was a difficult album to approach,' admits Jimmy Page. 'But it was a contractual album – we had to do it.'

Andrew Ellis's job was to prepare the rough layouts for *Coda*. 'It had been a long week and Po was on my case, "Have you finished? Hurry up, I need to show Jimmy,"' Ellis remembers. 'Eventually, the roughs were done, I handed them to Po, who took two steps towards the door, and then said, "You're coming with me." I was tired, it was late, and I didn't want to go, but Po said, "I need you for protection." I said, "What do you mean, protection?" He said, "Never mind, just get in the car . . ."'

The pair made the hour's journey west to the Old Mill House. Page had acquired the distinguished riverside property from actor Michael Caine two years earlier. Po pressed the buzzer and a pair of black gates swung open to reveal Led Zeppelin's grinning guitarist.

'Right,' Page chirruped. 'What do you want to drink?'

'I said, "White," Po said, "Red." So Jimmy beetled off and came back with a bottle of each and then led us into the dining room.' Ellis cast his eye over its distinctive décor. 'There was a round table with high-backed chairs covered in runes and designs, and this hideous orange carpet that was very 1970s,' he recalls. 'Jimmy saw me looking and said, "Yeah, now you've got to be careful with this table . . . it used to belong to Aleister Crowley." I was very un-starstruck. This was business and our job was to convince Jimmy we had a good design, but I did start to feel a bit uncomfortable.'

Page pored over the roughs, examining every detail as if he was back behind the mixing desk at Musicland Studios. Suddenly, he announced, 'Right, have you got a pen and paper to take notes?' 'I didn't, as I hadn't known I was coming until an hour ago,' says Ellis. Page disappeared and returned with a sheet of paper, before rummaging in his trouser pocket and extracting a warm pen. 'Jimmy said, "Do you know what this is? It's a fountain pen with a proper nib that also belonged to Aleister Crowley so don't break it."'

Ellis took notes as the evening became even stranger. 'Neither Po nor I were taking drugs but I think there was some drug taking going on,' he suggests. 'Jimmy kept going into the kitchen and coming out and then going back in again. Po eventually followed him there, came out and said to me, very quickly and conspiratorially, "If he offers you dinner, say no."'

Seconds later, Page re-emerged. 'Right,' he said, excitedly. 'Who wants roast beef?'

It was one o'clock in the morning, they politely declined and Po drove them both home instead. The young intern's presence had given him the protection he needed and an excuse to leave. 'Years later, I looked back in my diary,' says Ellis, 'and I'd written, "Went to Jimmy's house at seven o'clock, got home at 3 a.m."' I discovered later that was the house John Bonham died in – I just think Jimmy was a bit lonely rattling around in that big old place on his own.'

Coda's artwork was a collaborative effort. Ellis had previously taken an art foundation course in Manchester, where he'd met Peter Saville and Malcolm Garrett. 'Storm and Po were good photographers but appalling typographers,' he says. 'I told them they needed people who understood type and introduced them to Peter and Malcolm, and Neville Brody, who'd just designed a new magazine called *The Face*. This was the new guard coming in.'

Brody designed several Hipgnosis projects, including Pink Floyd's compilation, *A Collection of Great Dance Songs*, and Hipgnosis's final book, *The Goodbye Look: The Photodesigns of Hipgnosis*. After being evicted from his studio on Tottenham Court Road, Malcolm Garrett's company, Assorted IMaGes, took the space upstairs at number six. Garrett's recent work for Simple Minds and Duran Duran was as definitive as Storm and Po's for Pink Floyd and Led Zeppelin. Hipgnosis asked him to design Coda and his clean lines gave Zeppelin a new aesthetic – just too little, too late.

It was Andrew Ellis, though, who pushed *Coda*'s artwork over the finish line. Ellis collaged the pictures in the gatefold and oversaw the back cover, showing a photograph of water irrigation systems displayed to resemble Zeppelin's nine LPs.

It was a Friday evening when he delivered the final artwork to Po's house in Spencer Road. 'But I'd forgotten to re-touch the picture on the back,' he admits. 'I went cold, I thought, "Shit," because I knew the courier was on his way. I'd witnessed Po's red mist before, where he'd suddenly snap and lose his temper. "What the *fuck* are you doing?" he shouted. "I told you . . ." It was quite terrifying.'

Years later, Ellis saw the Brit gangster film, *Lock, Stock and Two Smoking Barrels*, and a scene where 'Barry the Baptist', played by real-life bareknuckle fighter Lenny McLean, threatens a pair of hopeless thieves: 'He says, "If you don't wanna be counting the fucking fingers you haven't got . . ." and it reminded me of Po and that evening.'

Ellis diffused the situation by promising to find someone to fix the picture: 'Anything to get away from the torrent of abuse,' he admits. I drove back to Denmark Street in my little Mini, but I couldn't find a re-toucher at that time of night and there were no mobile phones anyway. In the end, I got a Chinagraph pencil, made the correction and very gently smoothed it out with my thumb. I thought, "That's not too bad," and drove back to Spencer Road.'

Back in Wandsworth, Po scrutinised the photograph. '"Good," he said, finally. "Who did you use?" It was during the long silence which followed that he said, "You did it, didn't you?" I nodded sheepishly, waiting for the red mist to descend again and he just winked and said, "Great, well done."'

Hipgnosis's ethos was that anything was possible with a little talent, charm and fearlessness. As time went on, though, Ellis became acutely aware of how Storm's abruptness and working methods impacted on them all. 'Storm was brilliant and very funny and there was a lot of laughter,' he says. 'But he also made everybody cry. He made me cry, he made my girlfriend cry. How did he do that? She had no relationship with him. But I've seen clients cry, I've seen book publishers cry, tears of frustration . . .'

Despite this, Ellis found Hignosis's familial atmosphere and artistic freedom hard to give up. 'I tried to escape and took a job at a major record company,' he says. 'I lasted three months and was fired for not fitting in. I wonder why. I made a tearful journey back to Denmark Street, hoping Storm, Po and Peter would offer me some solace. Not only did they sit and listen, but they also said, "Welcome home . . . Now go and make us a cup of tea and clean the darkroom."'

★

In Peter Christopherson's compartmentalised parallel life, Throbbing Gristle broke up in 1981. The ex-members continued to operate on the fringes of art and music, with Christopherson's Hipgnosis work bankrolling his future ventures. For a time, he joined Genesis P-Orridge's new group, the cult-like, quasi-religious Psychic TV. Christopherson's film for their song 'Terminus' included a fake but grimly realistic scene of self-immolation.

Once again, it highlighted Hipgnosis's artistic differences. While Peter was filming a naked man setting himself alight in an abandoned factory, Storm was art directing ballroom dancers in a field in Dungeness for Pink Floyd's *A Collection of Great Dance Songs*. Meanwhile, Po was in Frank Sinatra's former suite at Las Vegas's Caesar's Palace Hotel, shooting showgirls for Bad Company's *Rough Diamonds*.

There was an air of finality about these projects, though. During a promotional shoot with Bad Company, Po found the atmosphere between the band members so strained, he took drastic action. He divided up a copy of the *Evening Standard* newspaper, told them to look as if they were reading, then set the pages on fire: 'Anything to lighten the mood and shake them up,' he says.

Other artists were simply moving on. Almost every year since 1973, Hipgnosis had been asked by Paul McCartney to work on his latest record. Perhaps it was a sign of the changing times, but even a Beatle wasn't exempt from Hipgnosis's recycled ideas. The picture sleeve for McCartney's recent single, 'Getting Closer', showed a man walking a lobster on a lead along the pavement; an image 10cc had rejected months earlier.

Nevertheless, in 1982, Hipgnosis received their annual summons, and Po arrived at the McCartneys' London townhouse in Cavendish Avenue. To the consternation of their straitlaced neighbours, the family had introduced animals from their farm in Kintyre into the back garden.

Ducks, dogs, cats and a cockerel roamed freely among the overgrown weeds. A glass meditation dome, containing a bed gifted to Paul by Alice Cooper, had become a vegetable patch and a run for the children's rabbits. While Linda made tea, Paul opened the French windows into the garden: 'And a sheep was standing there, looking at me,' says Po. 'In the middle of St John's Wood.'

McCartney also had an extensive collection of art. 'Every picture you ever saw in a schoolbook,' reveals Po. 'Paul sat down at the piano while I was showing him ideas and I noticed a René Magritte, just lying there on top. We each had a cup of tea and Paul plonked his cup down on top of the painting. I said, "Er, Paul . . . it's a *Magritte*, man." He said, "Ah, René won't mind," and carried on playing.'

Peter Christopherson had slipped Po an image he wanted to show McCartney. It was a prime example of Sleazy's subversive humour: 'Paul's new album was called *Tug of War* and Peter had created a beautiful photograph, reminiscent of a Gustav Klimt painting, showing a topless young man with a rope around his neck. I said, "Peter, Paul McCartney is not going to go for that." But Storm and I agreed he should see it.'

Death was hardly a theme McCartney was keen to explore less than two years after John Lennon's murder. 'But to be fair, Paul looked at it,' says Po. 'He said, "That's a very interesting idea, beautifully done, but just not for me."' Perhaps inevitably, the McCartneys had their own idea: asking Hipgnosis to merge a photograph of Paul taken by Linda with a painting by the artist Brian Clarke.

As he was leaving the house, Po kissed Linda on both cheeks. 'I'd always found her a charming person and super friendly,' he says. But it was the wrong move at the wrong time. 'Paul said, "What about me then?", grabbed my face and kissed me full on the lips. It wasn't jealousy, just a gentle reminder not to get too close, too familiar.' What Po didn't know then was that *Tug of War* would be Hipgnosis's final Paul McCartney sleeve.

Technology was moving faster than Hipgnosis or any of their musicians. Andrew Ellis remembers Peter Christopherson returning from New York with a new-fangled device called a Sony Walkman. 'It was an incredible machine,' he says. 'It wasn't much bigger than the cassette and you could plug headphones in and walk around the streets listening to your own soundtrack – we thought it was amazing.' Ellis's reaction had been the same as Marcus Bradbury's when Christopherson showed him a miniature computerised football game and told him it was 'the future'. Everybody 'Oooh'd' and 'Aaaah'd' and went back to their Letrasets.

In October 1982, Billy Joel's *52nd Street* became the first commercially available album released on compact disc, in Japan. The CD was a new format, created by the electronic giants, Sony and Philips. The disc was slim, streamlined, barely 5 inches in diameter and could contain up to eighty minutes of digital music. It was introduced to Europe the following March, as the superior-sounding replacement for the vinyl LP. The music was read by a laser, so there was no interference from a rumbling turntable or fluff on the needle. The manufacturers even claimed, erroneously, that it was shatter-proof.

The Beatles' producer George Martin showed Paul McCartney his first compact disc at Abbey Road Studios. 'George said, "This will change the world,"' recalled McCartney. 'He told us it was indestructible, that you couldn't smash it. "Look!" he said, hitting it against the desk. And – whack! – it broke in half.'

The compact disc wasn't going away, though, and its existence threatened Hipgnosis. An LP sleeve was 12.375 inches square; a CD case was 4.724 inches. Hipgnosis were used to their art being shrunk to fit on eight-track cartridges and cassettes, but these formats were secondary to vinyl. The LP was still king, a situation Po didn't believe was going to change.

'I wasn't taking much notice, because Hipgnosis was still doing well,' he admits. 'I was off shooting ads around the world, I had the place in Miami, the big house on Wandsworth Common with Gabi and Sophie . . . I was living the good life, wasn't I? I'd also hadn't been paying much attention to the grievances of my partners or their wishes. Especially when they complained about wanting to move on.'

Then the bell rang one morning at Spencer Road. Po opened the door to find Peter and Storm outside. 'Storm was holding a big bunch of flowers. I said, "It's not my birthday, what's going on?"' recalls Po. 'Storm marched into the hall, handed me the flowers, and came right out with it – "We want to stop Hipgnosis, we want to stop doing album covers and we want to make films instead. Are you with us?"'

Po sat there, stunned, as his partners outlined their reasons for this decision. It was part managerial coup and part intervention. 'Storm used the word "blinkered" about me,' he admits. 'Peter was ahead of the curve with new technology, so he knew all about CDs and realised album covers were coming to an end. I didn't, of course, I'd been blindly carrying on.'

Storm and Po had launched Greenback Films with Nigel Gordon in 1976. They'd already made promos for David Gilmour and 10cc and had filmed the inaugural Monsters of Rock Festival at Castle Donington, the precursor of the modern era's Download Festival. But Greenback was always a sideline to Hipgnosis. Storm and Peter now wanted to channel their energies into the film company and move into the pop video market.

America's new television cable network, MTV, streamed music videos 24/7 into millions of homes. Storm had always been a frustrated film-maker and didn't want to be left behind. The Australian director Russell Mulcahy's promo for the Buggles' 'Video Killed the Radio Star' was the first video shown on MTV and he'd since shot promos for Hipgnosis artists 10cc, XTC and Paul McCartney, and, notably, the new romantic pop group, Duran Duran. Mulcahy filmed his glamorous charges riding elephants in Sri Lanka and zooming around the coast of Antigua on a yacht. This was the 1980s equivalent of Pink Floyd paying for Storm and Po to photograph a burning man on a Californian film lot and a diver in Mono Lake.

'Record companies were spending on extravagant films, not pieces of album art,' explains Po. 'This was how they were promoting music now. Storm made it very clear, he thought we were working in a dying business and wanted to make music videos instead. I didn't want to hear this. I was resistant to the idea but Storm was so persuasive that within a couple of hours he'd talked me round – Storm and Peter could see what I couldn't.'

All three agreed to take time off and pursue their own projects. Then, if everyone was willing, they'd reconvene and work together again. 'We were quietly putting Hipgnosis to bed,' says Po. 'It was the strangest feeling. A relief and a loss. Storm and I had been joined at the hip for fifteen years. What happens next?'

Chapter 11

'Working for Barry Gibb was cosmic punishment . . .'

From a jacuzzi in Kidderminster with Robert Plant to a Florida beachside hotel with a senior Bee Gee: How Hipgnosis became multi-million-dollar film-makers, before breaking the bank – and each other.

'Oh yes . . . the Bee Gees thing.'

– David Gilmour

The two mechanical eyes with their emerald green irises wobbled above the stage of the San Antonio Convention Center. It was August 1982 and Hipgnosis's clients, the hard-rock group Rainbow, were touring a stage set based on their new album, *Straight Between the Eyes*. It was a literal translation and 5,000

313

Texans cheered as the huge, unblinking optics beamed rays of light across the auditorium.

Po was on his sabbatical from Hipgnosis and producing Rainbow's live show and a performance video from San Antonio. Before too long, though, his eyes resembled the band's stage set: 'I took vast amounts of cocaine that year,' he says. 'It was becoming a problem.'

Meanwhile, *The Goodbye Look: The Photodesigns of Hipgnosis* signed off without explicitly saying Hipgnosis were over. 'Hasta la vista,' wrote Storm in an introduction printed in a small typeface so readers were encouraged to look at the pictures instead. Inside, photographers and record shop managers commented on Hipgnosis's past work. Some were disparaging: 'Hated it! Looked amateurish,' said Keith Johnson, the manager of HMV Records, London, discussing Roger Taylor's *Fun in Space*.

The book also included mini-biographies for the three principals. Peter: 'Still the youngest partner, even after all the years . . .' Po: 'Still living life to the full and becoming larger on all fronts as a result . . .' Storm: 'Still lives alone with his son, Bill, aged ten, still keen on tennis, acupuncture and the deeper significance of life, huh.'

Like members of a rock group promoting solo projects, Storm and Po mentioned their new companies, STD (Storm Thorgerson Designs) and APP (Aubrey Powell Productions) and Peter's involvement with Psychic TV. Hipgnosis's final collaboration, *Music Spoken Here*, by the Mahavishnu Orchestra's John McLaughlin, snuck out at the end of 1982. Over lunch in his adopted hometown of Paris, the guitarist told Storm and Po he felt out of step with modern music, so they photographed him holding a square peg over a round hole.

Besides Rainbow, Po worked on Paul McCartney's *Tug of War* campaign and shot billboard ads for cigarette companies that year. He also sailed his boat, drove his latest muscle car and hung out with his dubious friends. After one too many late nights and early mornings, blasting Boston's 'More Than a Feeling' out of the house on Golden Beach, Po finally hit the buffers.

'I was out of my mind and ended up in hospital in Sarasota with cocaine poisoning,' he admits. 'My central nervous system was shot. Coke is an insidious drug and it had become a real issue for me. I'd had enough of that whole Miami scene, it was a dirty business. I eventually sold the house and went into therapy back in England. We had the film company, I was excited about making music videos and I didn't want to throw this opportunity away.'

Record collections the world over contained LPs purchased solely because of their covers. In 1981, CBS Records conducted a survey and claimed that 20 per cent of album sales were affected, either way, by the artwork. However, the potential audience for Greenback's work was bigger than Hipgnosis's. By 1983, 25.4 million households were subscribed to MTV. 'Storm had studied to be a film-maker,' says Po, 'so this is what we were meant to be doing.'

Greenback moved into a space at Pink Floyd's studio, Britannia Row. The partners' roles were clearly defined: they wrote scripts together, but Storm directed, Po produced and took care of the money and Peter Christopherson was the lighting cameraman. Nigel Gordon was still involved as a freelance producer/director and former Hipgnosis assistant, Anthony Taylor, as a line producer to hire crew and allocate budgets.

Storm, Po and Peter each invested £6,000 in a twenty-minute showreel, featuring Nicholas Ball, star of the TV detective series *Hazell*. Ball played another sleuth, 'trying to find out who Hipgnosis were and what we do,' explains Po, and was shown strolling around Soho, looking pensive, and thumbing through a copy of *Walk Away René* in an abandoned office.

'Storm, being a clever dick, thought that if we made an interesting film, potential film clients would become engrossed by it,' he says. 'Which they did, eventually.' Po pitched Greenback to many of the same managers and record companies they'd worked with as Hipgnosis: 'This was the problem, because I was going in there, saying, "Hey, we do films now," and everybody said, "No, you do album covers and, by the way, we have one that needs doing," and I had to say no. It was tough.'

Greenback struggled to find work, so their respective companies plugged the gaps. Peter worked on Psychic TV's new album, *Dreams Less Sweet*, which included a version of Charles Manson's 'Always Is Always'. Po went to California's Death Valley to photograph Wrangler jeans for Saatchi & Saatchi and bought a plot of land in Formentera on which to build a new house. Meanwhile, STD put a photograph of a naked woman operating a telephone exchange on the cover of UFO's *Making Contact*, an image Phil Mogg now compares to the nude organist in *Monty Python's Flying Circus*.

It was Muff Winwood, the Island Records veteran and now an A&R executive at CBS, who gave Greenback their first commission. Winwood had signed north London soul singer Paul Young and needed a promo for his cover of Marvin Gaye's 'Wherever I Lay My Hat (That's My Home)'. Young's manager, Ged Doherty, liked Greenback's showreel, but also knew they'd come cheap.

There wasn't the budget for Duran Duran's yachts and elephants, so Storm directed Young as the song's serial Casanova drifting around hotel rooms and a public telephone box before one of his wronged lovers pulls a gun on him. 'Storm was in his element,' suggests Po. 'He was brilliant as a director. That first film was a narrative and narratives were big in those days.'

'Wherever I Lay My Hat . . .' spent three weeks at number one in June 1983, and Greenback were hired to work on Young's next two singles, 'Come Back and Stay' and 'Love of the Common People'. 'Suddenly, we were in business,' says Po, 'and one job led to another.'

Greenback also played Cupid when Storm asked Andrew Ellis to screen test a model for 'Come Back and Stay'. 'Storm asked me because I was nearer Paul's age,' he says. 'I chose a girl I liked called Stacey from a model catalogue. Stacey did a screen test on the day of the shoot and I took her to meet Paul. I immediately saw this look between them and thought, "Er, okay, I'll leave you two alone." Paul later married her.'

MTV's booming popularity also presented new opportunities for Hipgnosis's older clients. Having their late-thirtysomething faces beamed into 25 million homes meant competing with the youthful likes of Duran Duran or Culture Club, but a gripping video could divert the attention from encroaching wrinkles or problematic hairlines.

Yes had re-grouped and needed a promo for their comeback single. Anthropomorphism was all the rage since Michael Jackson transformed into a werewolf in 'Thriller'. Greenback created a surreal narrative for Yes's 'Owner of a Lonely Heart', involving a kidnapping, a secret laboratory, shape-shifting and guitar solos illustrated with sparks flying from an angle grinder. Just as Storm banished artists from their sleeves, Yes appeared sparingly in the film, but the song became a US number one and re-launched their career.

Robert Plant's second solo album, *The Principle of Moments*, was released in July 1983. Plant had fired Peter Grant by letter the previous year after he'd stopped answering his phone calls: 'I have the utmost respect for you,' he wrote. 'I will always remember the good times . . .' Plant had cut his hair, while his new music contained fewer guitar riffs and more of the modish TR-808 drum machine.

The artwork was an Hipgnosis production in all but name. Richard Evans created the LP cover's wavy logo by doodling on a steamed-up kitchen window: 'I drew the logo and designed the whole cover in two days,' Evans recalls. 'Then Storm unravelled it all on a Friday and kept me there until seven o'clock at night before deciding what I'd done in the first place was best.'

Evans's squiggle, designed while he was boiling a kettle, was later splashed across the merchandise for Plant's comeback US tour. Meanwhile, Greenback pitched to make the video for his new single, a nouveau pop-blues titled 'Big Log'. 'Phil Carson from Atlantic Records was managing Robert now,' explains Po. 'Robert asked me to meet him and Phil at a hotel just outside Kidderminster, where we were going to have a sauna and a jacuzzi together.

'So we're sat there, steam everywhere, and I began reading a script – "Imagine if you will . . ." Of course, they both cracked up laughing and Robert said, "Aubrey, all you and Storm want to do is spend my money and have fun." And I said, "Er . . . yes." Atlantic knew they had a good song, but they had to have a film on MTV to make it a hit. Next thing, Storm, Peter and I are on a plane to LA with Robert and having a wonderful time for ten days.'

'Big Log' was filmed on location at the Glass Pool Inn in Las Vegas, California's Calico Ghost Town and the Amargosa Opera House in Death Valley Junction. Its non-linear narrative and familiar motifs, including a broken-down car and a desolate highway, suggested an Hipgnosis artwork brought to life. The song became a US top-ten hit and re-cast Led Zeppelin's former Viking as a modern pop star in espadrilles and stonewashed denim.

Plant drove the message home on his next single, 'In the Mood', where Storm shipped in a street dance troupe to body pop in front of the singer and his band. Plant's '80s makeover extended beyond the music and was engendered by STD's artwork and Greenback's videos. It amused him, but baffled some of his fanbase.

'As frontmen in '60s rock bands go, I've really fucked up terribly and quite regularly, but I love every one of the things I've been taken to task for,' insists Plant. 'I can't apologise. It pissed a lot of people off, but it was bold.'

There would be no MTV comeback for Pink Floyd yet. *The Final Cut*, Roger Waters' anguished study of global consumerism and the futility of war, would be his last work with the band. Waters clashed with David Gilmour during its recording and the guitarist was unhappy about using material discarded from *The Wall*.

'Roger and I argued about political points, though not from a radically different point of view,' says Gilmour. 'I wouldn't have dreamed of putting my oar in about the concept and the lyrics, but I just didn't think some of the music was up to it.'

Waters hired his then brother-in-law, photographer Willie Christie, to shoot the LP cover and direct a video for the single, 'Not Now John'. The song replaced the phrase 'fuck all that' with 'stuff all that' for radio and MTV airplay. But Pink Floyd were entirely absent from the film, something Greenback had yet to manage with any of their artists.

Waters's first solo album, *The Pros and Cons of Hitch Hiking*, arrived a year later in March 1984, with Gerald Scarfe's graphics and Alex Henderson's photo of glamour model Linzi Drew on the cover. Columbia Records later obscured Drew's bare bottom to avoid offending US record retailers.

Waters began touring the album soon after, with Eric Clapton playing guitar. The British promoter Harvey Goldsmith approached the Canadian Film Finance Board to invest in a live video from Toronto. Greenback were hired to film test footage at a date in Detroit.

During the interval, an executive from the company marched into the green room at the Joe Louis Arena and announced that they didn't think the show was terribly good and that they wouldn't be investing. 'They said this in front of everyone, including Roger,' recalled Nigel Gordon. 'We came home with our tails between our legs, having spent six grand on flights and hotels on the company's American Express card.'

Gordon asked Waters if he'd reimburse them. 'Roger said, "No, I'm not paying you anything. Take that as a lesson in life." That's exactly what he said. "Fuck you," I thought, but I didn't say it and we eventually got the money back from Harvey. I suppose Roger felt rejected by the Canadians and decided to take it out on us.'

Storm resumed his working relationship with David Gilmour on the guitarist's solo album, *About Face*, in the same year: 'I was frustrated with the whole Pink Floyd thing falling down and just wanted to go out and have another bash,' says Gilmour.

STD designed the artwork and Greenback made promos for the singles, 'Blue Light' and 'All Lovers Are Deranged'. Storm filled them with dry ice, dancing skinheads and Mary Poppins-style chimney sweeps. He even coaxed his reticent subject into throwing some guitar-hero shapes. It was an awkward transition for Gilmour, who barely moved onstage with Pink Floyd. Storm struggled too: 'It was difficult for someone of my inclination to show pictures of bands performing and singing, just as it was showing them on an album cover.'

As the songs became hits, the budgets increased and Storm indulged more of his pet obsessions: flamenco and ballroom dancers, hotel corridors, telephones, clocks, flying paint and distressed-looking women gazing longingly out of windows or running across the courtyards of Spanish-style colonnades.

He also hired his friends as extras. David Gale was shown tapping a typewriter in 'Owner of a Lonely Heart' and Matthew Scurfield (last seen on the big screen as 'Otto the Nazi' in *Raiders of the Lost Ark*) performed a backflip and was pushed downstairs by a jealous Paul Young in 'Come Back and Stay'.

'I used to escape a lot of the shit other people got with Storm, by dint of growing up with him,' suggests Gale. 'He knew he couldn't pull the wool over my eyes as we'd known each other since we were fourteen. I could enjoy Storm, because I didn't have any dogs in the fight.'

Hipgnosis had designed posters for Gale's theatre company, Lumiere & Son, and Storm had watched many of their productions. 'As a critic, Storm was exceptionally astute,' said Gale, 'and seemed to cut to the flaws in a piece of work almost effortlessly.'

He sometimes struggled, though, to suppress his film director instincts: 'He'd often come to see me in the theatre,' says Matthew Scurfield. 'But he still wanted to be the centre of attention.'

Years later, Scurfield was playing the Duke of Exeter in *Henry V* at the Globe Theatre. 'It was a matinee performance and someone fainted in the audience,' he recalls. 'Storm couldn't stop himself taking control – "Right! Hello! Someone has just fainted!" – in the middle of a big number. The theatre was packed and Storm took full advantage and became the director then – "Okay! Don't worry, everyone! We will sort this out!" I was on stage, thinking, "Storm, please just calm down."'

Greenback's client list grew, but they faced fierce competition. In retrospect, the top spot belonged to their rivals, whose work still appears near the end of every TV programme, promising the best pop videos of the 1980s.

In '84, Russell Mulcahy out-Stormed Storm Thorgerson with his promo for Duran Duran's hit, 'Wild Boys'. It had it all: flame-throwing acrobats, bare flesh, a whiff of S&M and lead singer Simon Le Bon strapped to a futuristic ducking stool.

Meanwhile, director David Mallet spliced Queen into footage from Fritz Lang's pre-war sci-fi drama *Metropolis* for 'Radio Ga Ga' and threw in a faux-military rally for good measure. His follow-up, 'I Want to Break Free', had Queen dressed in drag for a *Coronation Street* pastiche. Both songs were top-five hits and their videos became ingrained in popular culture.

Closer to home, Godley & Creme had temporarily halted their musical career and also become video film-makers. The duo's Cold War spoof for Frankie Goes to Hollywood's number-one hit, 'Two Tribes', featured a wrestling bout between a Ronald Reagan and a Konstantin Chernenko lookalike and ended with Planet Earth blowing up – even Storm hadn't thought that big.

'I never thought Storm and Po were as accomplished at music videos as they were at design,' offers Kevin Godley. 'Somehow, Lol and I were more connected to the spirit of music video than they were. They were established designers becoming film-makers and, for me, it didn't quite hit the spot.'

It didn't matter. 'The money was there,' insists Po, 'and within three years Greenback Films were turning millions of dollars a year.' That year's brilliant, melancholy hit, Don Henley's 'The Boys of Summer', epitomised the era. Henley's line about seeing 'a Deadhead sticker on a Cadillac' spoke for every lapsed hippy who'd wound up with an American Express card and a Porsche in 1984: 'I used to listen to that song all the time, driving around in my car,' says Po.

Despite Storm's reluctance to put the artist in the film, Greenback made several videos for MCA's shiny new pop star Nik Kershaw, all featuring the singer. 'I don't remember a queue of people lining up to direct my videos,' says Kershaw. 'Nobody knew who I was, but I knew Storm had designed *The Dark Side of the Moon*, and I liked his showreel, which included "Owner of a Lonely Heart".'

The first video, 'Wouldn't It Be Good', had Kershaw dashing around an abandoned building opposite Buckingham Palace, wearing a suit onto which moving images were pasted, using a precursor of today's Green Screen effect: 'Storm was a scary character with a short temper, and the volume would go up if things weren't going well. But he was an absolute sweetheart to me.'

'Wouldn't It Be Good' received heavy MTV airplay and became a UK top-five hit. Storm later went to Spain to shoot 'Don Quixote' and cast Kershaw as Sancho Panza with an imperial mullet.

'Some was shot in Spain and some of it in Fulham,' cautions Kershaw. 'Meanwhile, Duran Duran went to Sri Lanka and Wham! went to Ibiza for "Club Tropicana" . . . But I just said yes to all of it. Years later, when I didn't receive any royalties for thirty years I wondered why we'd spent fifty grand on some of these videos.'

Some of the symbolism of 'Don Quixote' zoomed over the heads of Kershaw's *Smash Hits*-reading audience, but the director was having fun. Storm also hired Emo to chase the singer down a hotel corridor in 'Wide Boy' and play Batman's the Riddler in 'The Riddle'.

Emo was nominally employed as an odd job man on David Gilmour's Oxfordshire estate, but had some brief acting experience and made a cameo appearance in *Pink Floyd: The Wall*. 'Helen Mirren got me an interview for the movie *Stardust*,' Emo recalls. 'David Gilmour taught me some guitar chords, but Dave Edmunds got the part instead. I think half the time, Storm just liked having me around for the sake of it.'

Emo had also been initiated by the Master in India. But for Storm, art came before religion. 'I was a vegetarian now,' explains Emo, 'so I told Storm I wanted nothing to do with live animals, because of the vows I'd taken with Sant Mat. But Storm still had me playing a mad chicken farmer and tossing chickens around in some video.

'Peter Christopherson was the first person to pay me Equity rates, though. I couldn't be doing a day's filming from seven in the morning until ten at night for a fiver any more. That was Storm's way and I had to stand up to him.'

During one shoot, Emo was shocked to discover Christopherson had an intimate piercing. It was still a niche practice in 1984, but several members of Psychic TV had been pierced by the Liverpudlian body-art pioneer Mr Sebastian: 'Peter had a ring through the head of his cock,' marvels Emo. 'I'd never seen such a thing before.'

'A large cock ring, sometimes two,' confirms Po. 'Which occasionally caused embarrassment when going through airport body scanners.' Some years later, Po and Peter were shooting a video in Iceland for 'Another You, Another Me', by ABBA's protégés, the Swedish duo, Gemini: 'We were filming underground in a hot springs cave, lit by candles, very dark and very warm, so the crew were naked. Peter was the last to climb down the metal ladder into the water. Suddenly, we heard "Clank, clank, clank", as his rings hit the rungs and echoed around the cave. We laughed ourselves silly, but Peter also saw the funny side.'

Christopherson's clandestine life came in useful during a shoot for ex-Rainbow keyboard player Tony Carey's 'A Fine, Fine Day': 'We were in New York and Storm was shooting all night and into the next morning and disregarding the budget,' remembers Po. 'It was snowing heavily, way below freezing, and he started behaving strangely, almost as if he was drunk.'

An American producer on set spotted the warning signs for hypothermia. A doctor was called and Storm was rushed back to his hotel: 'Peter suggested we go to a club for half an hour to warm up, as we still had more scenes to shoot. I didn't have a clue where he'd take us at that time of the morning.'

It was the Mineshaft, a gay BDSM club in Washington Street: 'Peter knew the doorman and the barman, and we all piled down there and stood around, surrounded by guys in leather hats and vests. Peter said, "You know when I'm in New York, Po, and you ask where I am . . . well, it's usually here."

'There were many wonderful humorous moments with Peter and some darker ones,' he adds. 'Our lives were so different, but Peter was never embarrassed by his sexual proclivities. He bought this big house in Chiswick in the late '70s, and I remember going round there once and seeing handcuffs on the radiator. Everything was distressed and the whole atmosphere reminded me of 10 Rillington Place. But Peter loved all that.'

As with Hipgnosis's macho rock groups, he enjoyed smuggling clues to his sexuality into mainstream pop videos, like a kinky Trojan horse. Robert Plant's side project, the Honeydrippers, scored a hit in the summer of 1984 with 'Sea of Love'. In one scene, the video cut from an al fresco party and a crooning Plant to a choir of topless young lads in the ocean.

Christopherson quit Psychic TV after *Dreams Less Sweet*: 'That dark side of Sleazy's interests were indulged much more with them than they were with TG,' suggests Cosey Fanni Tutti. 'Psychic TV was a cult, but he got out within a year. He didn't like some of the things that went on and that's why he left.'

Nevertheless, Christopherson explored his darker interests with his next group Coil, channelling their shared fascination with Crowley, paganism and sexual deviance into the work. Peter's dual life was thrown into sharp relief when he asked Andrew Ellis to photograph him and his partner, fellow Coil member, Geff Rushton (aka 'John Balance'), naked.

'The pair of them were rolling around, covered in Fuller's earth,' says Ellis, who stared at the brown clay-like substance smeared across their bodies. 'I said, "Why are you doing this? What is this all about?" And Peter gave me that cheeky little smile of his and said, "So it looks like we've been rolling around in shit." Oh, okay . . . but of course . . .'

Storm's edict of 'the art comes first, the money second' applied to Greenback as it had to Hipgnosis and his over-spending on 'A Fine, Fine Day' wasn't an isolated incident. Greenback signed a deal with the newly formed PolyGram Films to create music-related movies. Most music videos at the time cost between £100,000 and £150,000; PolyGram were offering up to £2 million.

Greenback's first project for the company was 'Incident at Channel Q', in which a video jockey (played by *Dynasty's* Al Corley) barricades himself in the studio after a dispute with his bosses and broadcasts non-stop videos by the Scorpions, Kiss and Bon Jovi. The film capitalised on the boom in hair-metal, but broke the budget.

'Our line producer, Anthony Taylor, budgeted for 200 extras at $50 each for a long night shoot in Miami,' recalls Po. 'Then Storm ordered another 300. Storm had a habit of ordering things on any film behind mine and Anthony's back, and then Greenback had to pay for them. After a row with me and Peter, Storm sacrificed his fee, but expected us to turn over our fees as well to pay the bills. Peter and I refused. But the film lost us a lot of money. It was the first serious sign of Storm getting out of control financially.'

Andrew Ellis spent a year working with Greenback. As with Hipgnosis, his junior status was rarely considered: 'Po used to take me to the Zanzibar Club in Covent Garden and the Groucho in Soho,' he says. 'When I founded my own design consultancy, would I have taken my assistant to a club or had that sort of relationship with my staff? Probably not. It was that Hipgnosis family thing again.'

Ellis experienced another baptism of fire, working with Yumi Matsutoya, a platinum-selling artist described by Po as 'the Beyoncé of Japan'. Hipgnosis had designed several artworks for Yumi and Greenback picked up the baton with 1984's long-form video album, *Train of Thought*.

PolyGram gave Greenback £1.5. million to shoot the film in the UK, Italy and Morocco. 'Yumi wanted something different from the Japanese aesthetic,' recalls Ellis. 'I went to Morocco and Po was there initially, but then told me he had another job to go to and I was in charge. I was twenty-one years old and he threw me in the deep end with a Japanese superstar, a fourteen-man crew and two Land Rovers.'

Before he left, Po handed Ellis a document written in Arabic. 'He said, "If you're ever stopped by the police or the security services, show them this letter and everything will be fine." I still have the document and, to this day, I don't know what it says or even who it's from. Knowing Po, it could have been from the President of Morocco or whoever.'

This delegation of duty demonstrated the ease with which Storm and Po pushed their employees outside their comfort zones. Richard Evans had previously flown to Japan to art direct an LP cover shoot for Yumi: 'I remember Po giving me an evening's lesson on how to light a photo shoot,' he says. 'I knew nothing about photography and was winging it completely, but was quite experienced by the time I came back.'

Regrettably, Rob Brimson's experience on the film was less rewarding. The Japanese conglomerate, Fujifilm, were supplying the filmstock for *Train of Thought* and hired Brimson as a stills photographer in Venice: 'The idea being I would shoot this Japanese megastar in an exotic location for Fuji,' he explains.

Despite contacting the Italian consulate to confirm what documents he required, Brimson's equipment was impounded by customs: 'I'd been told I didn't need carnets, only the receipts to prove I'd bought the gear in England and not on the Italian black market, but this wasn't the case. When I told Po, he was understandably pissed off, because this meant having to pay cash to the value of the equipment, just to get it released.'

Calls were made and Po suggested an alternative plan. 'Po had a contact in Venice, his Mr Fixit, shall we say, who owned a speedboat and did a bit of running down to the Yugoslavian coast,' divulges Brimson. 'This guy had a brother who worked in the customs office. Po told me to meet Mr Fixit and he'd take me to the office, where I was to ask for, let's call him "Luigi", and to give him this – and he handed me a bag stuffed with money. I realised then that I was way out of my depth.'

Brimson knew his highly paid job for Fuji wouldn't happen without cameras and reluctantly went along with the plan. 'Po's Mr Fixit was straight out of central casting,' he recalls. 'Good-looking, tanned and, I discovered later, packing a gun. He also had a speedboat, was completely reckless and knew all the short-cuts around the back of Venice.'

To deter people from using these routes, concrete speed bumps were installed just below the waterline. However, Mr Fixit's boat had a propeller tucked behind the hull, allowing it to skim over the barriers once it had gathered enough speed: 'So we're bouncing down these alleys, with me clutching a bag of money, about to bribe a customs officer and feeling absolutely terrified.'

Once they'd reached the canal-side office, Brimson asked for 'Luigi', but was told he wasn't working today: 'I couldn't get out of there fast enough,' he admits. 'I had to tell Po I still didn't have the cameras and he agreed we'd have to get them back the legitimate way. But his attitude was, "Okay, we tried it the cheap way, we gave it a go with this Yugoslav drug runner and you nearly risked going to jail, *but . . .*' So Po paid up, we picked up the cameras and he received the money back again when we checked out.'

'They were fun times,' says Po. 'We had a new lease of life. But there were a lot of drugs around. I was off them at that time, but Storm and Peter were hammering the cocaine late at night. Storm's concentration faltered and he would sit around the set chatting away nineteen to the dozen and not working. It drove me crazy.'

Brimson experienced the problem first-hand: 'They wouldn't let me onto the set as they were on such a tight deadline,' he explains. 'Greenback had made lots of individual pop videos, but they'd never made two or three on the bounce before and in a foreign location with foreign staff. No one slept, Storm was on cocaine and absolutely speeding.

'I had a Japanese interpreter, two guys from Fuji, two more from the Japanese advertising agency, all on my back, saying, "What's going on? Why isn't he shooting? What did we pay all this money for?" Storm refused to let me take a single frame. I eventually snuck my camera and tripod into one of the locations. I tried to be discreet, but Storm said I was in his sightline and went mad. He actually threw me off set. It was awful.'

The situation was only resolved when Fuji threatened to pull the film stock. 'But the pictures I took at the end of the shoot were disappointing,' says Brimson. 'Storm was in full film director mode – just manic. Po sorted me out earlier, but he didn't step in and help here. I thought, "I can't work for these people anymore," and I never did again. Which was such a shame.'

Andrew Ellis also left Greenback Films after twelve months: 'I just didn't enjoy it,' he says. 'We'd have these frenetic three weeks of work and then nothing for ages. I was still freelance, so I needed to fill the gaps. Eventually, I said to Storm, "Look, I'm going back to design, the film industry is not for me. I want to do record sleeves."'

Ellis had worked with Storm Thorgerson Designs on artwork for David Gilmour, Rainbow, UFO and the Alan Parsons Project. 'Storm was so incredibly moral,' he says. 'I remember doing a sleeve and I'd ordered the typesetting and when it came back, I didn't like it. I told Storm, and he said, "Well, you ordered it, but if you think it should be better, we'll re-do it." I said, "Yeah, but that means we're going to have to pay for it twice," and he said, "No, *you* are" – and I did. I paid for it out of my wages and it was better.

'I'd learned so much about the technicalities of photography, lighting, I'd even learned film directing, producing and editing,' Ellis explains. 'But I also learned about engaging with people and hustling for work.'

Ellis shot the sleeve for 10cc's *Windows in the Jungle* in New York. 'We'd also worked for Random House, the book publishers, so I went and knocked on their door and was commissioned to do more covers. This was what I learned from Po – deliver a piece of artwork to a record company, then knock on all the product managers' doors and come out with five more jobs.'

Over time, though, Ellis realised the company wasn't working: 'Although it was called "Storm Thorgerson Designs", Storm Thorgerson wasn't doing much designing. He was busy doing Greenback. I told Storm I wanted to change the name of the company and he was out. This didn't go down too well, but there wasn't much he could do about it. There was no argument or discussion.'

STD became Icon, with Ellis joined by another former Hipgnosis assistant, Colin Chambers, and, later, Richard Evans. The company created artworks for Robert Plant, Deep Purple, Nik Kershaw and China Crisis. But Ellis also designed logos for Katharine Hamnett's new clothing range. His bold typographical statements took their cue from 10cc's *Look Hear?* One slogan, 'Choose Life', was modelled by pop stars including Wham! and became one of the defining images of the 1980s.

Ellis was highly ambitious and often confused by his mentor's attitude: 'Storm's relationship with money was non-existent,' he says. 'He never seemed to have any ambition to be wealthy or even to move house. He was in that flat forever, whereas Po seemed to be moving every three years. Storm used to take me aside sometimes and say, "Bloody Po, jetting off to Miami all the time . . ." But Storm was precious about design, the craft and the imagery, and I admired him for that. But then, of course, there was that whole experience with Barry Gibb . . .'

★

By the mid-1980s, sibling harmony trio the Bee Gees' career had been seesawing up and down for over twenty years. After making a career comeback with 1977's *Saturday Night Fever*, the

Bee Gees made music together and apart, but with lead vocalist Barry Gibb forging ahead of his brothers, Robin and Maurice.

Barry Gibb signed a multi-million-dollar solo deal with MCA in 1983, and spent nine months recording *Now Voyager* at Miami's Criteria and Hollywood's Ocean Way Studios. He duetted with Olivia Newton-John and used some of the top-drawer session players heard on works by Joni Mitchell and Steely Dan. The album was released in September 1984, with Alex Henderson's photograph of the star on its cover. Sadly, Barry's pearly white smile belied what Po now recalls as 'three months of unbearable hell'.

Po had negotiated a $2 million deal with PolyGram to make a film for *Now Voyager*: 'Storm said, "Well done, Po, go and buy yourself a new Porsche as a gift from the company." I declined as that wasn't the way to run a business . . . and I already had a Porsche.'

Greenback's hour-long movie would have a narrative linking each of the songs; a grand undertaking, but these were still the golden years for pop video. Gibb was certainly enthusiastic about the project: 'It's time somebody made more than a video promo film,' he said in 1984. 'I think any artist should apply himself to doing something a bit more, for want of a better word, *pioneeristic*.'

David Gale co-wrote a script which began with a rock star, played by Gibb, crashing his car into a canal. He emerges from the water and finds himself in a Victorian swimming baths, in the company of a wise old sage, the Trickster, played by veteran Shakespearean actor, Sir Michael Hordern. The Trickster then guides him through various adventures, represented by the songs, on his quest for greater enlightenment: 'The idea was that there was more to life than being a debauched rock star,' explains Po.

However, Gibb also had to play a Vietnam War veteran, an astronaut and an American Southern gentleman; challenging work for a singer who'd never acted before. 'Sir Michael was wonderful,' recalls Po. 'He said, "Part of my responsibility, dear boy, will be to train this man to become an actor . . ." He was so patient with Barry, who accepted his guidance and wanted to learn from the master.'

'I'd written the script and was honoured to become Barry Gibb's dialogue coach,' adds David Gale. 'He had no acting experience and started to panic. Barry was staying in a hotel in Manchester and every morning, I would knock on the door and his minder would answer, and Barry's wife, an ex-Miss Edinburgh, would welcome me in. Then I'd sit there with Barry in his bathrobe and go through the script together. Meanwhile, Storm was creating havoc.'

'I foolishly kept Storm and Barry apart, because I felt they wouldn't get on,' admits Po. 'The chemistry wasn't right. A $2 million budget was the equivalent of $10 million today and I couldn't risk that.'

After filming some scenes in Manchester, the production moved to the Don CeSar Hotel, a bright pink beachside affair, in St Petersburg, Florida. Soon after their first meeting, Storm challenged Gibb to a game of tennis. Both men were excellent players, but Storm often used humorous quips to distract his opponents. During a previous match against Vitas Gerulaitis, he'd dropped his shorts to try to put the American pro off his serve. The act was more shocking as Storm never wore under-wear, though Gerulaitis beat him anyway.

Gibb was spared the same treatment, but Storm's aggressive play and witty asides paid off. 'Storm thrashed Barry, which you just don't do,' says Richard Evans, who was working as a stills photographer on set. 'If it's the first day before the shoot, you let the client win. Of course, Storm wasn't going to do that. Then the next thing Storm says to him is, "Right, Barry, you're going to have to shave that beard off . . .'"

'Storm, quite rightly, told Barry, "If you are an actor, and you want to play a part, you can't be Barry Gibb, so the beard has to go,"' explains Po. 'But Barry wanted to keep the beard and the flowing locks because that was his image. He was *the* Bee Gee, and he didn't want to change.'

The artist and the director were soon locked in a Mexican stand-off, with neither willing to concede. Po asked PolyGram's executive producer, Michael Kuhn, to intervene, while he delivered the final cut of *Train of Thought* to Yumi Matsutoya in Tokyo. In the meantime, the waiting actors and crew sunned themselves on St Pete Beach and enjoyed the local nightlife.

'We were all thinking, "This is great,"' admits Evans. 'We're in Florida, the sun's shining, someone was sent out to get the Charlie and we were all having fun. Meanwhile, Storm and Barry aren't talking to each other.'

Po presumed the issue would be resolved but when he arrived back in Florida, Anthony Taylor told him that Gibb still wouldn't shave and they'd had to postpone the shoot by a day. 'Time was money and I now had to defend Storm and the script,' says Po. 'But PolyGram had to defend their artist, so I was caught in the middle. Storm kept threatening to leave and Barry was saying the same.' Events took an even more dramatic turn when two emergency doctors were summoned to the Don CeSar: 'Because Barry thought he was having a breakdown and Storm thought he was having a heart attack.'

The arrival of medical personnel was the cue for Po and Gibb's manager to finally reach a compromise. It was agreed that Barry would cut his hair and his beard would eventually be shaved down for the film's final scenes, but he would remain hirsute during his sequences with Sir Michael Hordern. Unhappy about the compromise, Storm wanted Greenback to pull out of the project: 'But we took a vote between the three of us and I was outvoted,' he admitted. 'We made the video, but it was very trying. Working for Barry Gibb was cosmic punishment.'

Now Voyager's opening scene was the last to be filmed, in the fenlands surrounding King's Lynn in Norfolk. It was a chilling reminder of Hipgnosis's difficult relationship with water. Gibb's Mercedes, driven by a stuntman, was shown crashing through a set of railings into a canal. The car had been frontloaded to make it dive nose-first into the water, enabling the stuntman, Ken Shepherd, to open the door and escape. Instead, the vehicle flipped upside down and sank into the mud, trapping Shepherd in the driver's seat. A team of divers broke in and dragged him out. The stuntman gave the crew a feeble thumbs-up as he was stretchered into a waiting ambulance: 'Did you get the shot?' he asked. *All this*, they must have been thinking, *for a music video*.

Now Voyager struggled to reach the US top seventy. Its burnished funk-pop didn't match the Bee Gees' hits and even Sir Michael Hordern's rich thespian tones couldn't salvage the narrative. The beard was another issue: 'The facial hair continuity is completely deranged,' recalls David Gale, 'sprouting and receding over Barry's chin at random moments throughout.'

By the end of the project, the relationship between Storm and his partners was also close to breaking point. 'We'd gone over the $2 million budget and I'd had to beg PolyGram for more money,' says Po. Greenback still had another film to make before everything collapsed.

The American R&B vocalist Peabo Bryson had been recording since the '70s but had recently overhauled his sound and image. Bryson had just made a new album, *Take No Prisoners*, produced by soul royalty Arif Mardin, and needed a gold-standard video for the title track.

America's hottest new TV show was *Miami Vice*, a glitzy crime drama with cops 'Sonny' Crockett and 'Rico' Tubbs, tooling around in top-of-the-range Ferraris and pastel-coloured suits. The show resembled one long pop video. 'So it made sense that Peabo Bryson's video should be a spoof of *Miami Vice* and filmed in Miami,' explains Po.

Storm's frustrated film-director fantasy took over and he crammed 'Take No Prisoners (In the Game of Love)' with explosions, car chases, gunfights, speedboats, pastel-coloured suits and, true to form, a distressed-looking woman running across the courtyard of a Spanish-style colonnade.

'There was also a flying boat,' adds Po. 'Being a film director went to Storm's head in all the wrong ways. It's like being a rock star and it can happen easily. It was ten o'clock at night and we were supposed to wrap. Four o'clock in the morning, we were still going and we'd gone ten grand over budget. Peter Christopherson and I were looking at each other in disbelief. The next night, the same thing happened again and then *again* after that – Storm couldn't control himself.'

'I was besotted with lofty ambition,' admitted Storm, years later, 'and instead of exploring the limitations of video, I kept wanting to make a film.' But the gunfights and flying boat couldn't re-launch Bryson's career, and 'Take No Prisoners' was only a modest hit.

Greenback flew home, physically, spiritually and financially drained. Then came the phone call from their bank. 'We were a successful company and we should have been wealthy men,' insists Po. 'Instead, we were about £100,000 in the hole and the bank were calling it in.'

★

Hipgnosis's spending had once been the talk of record company boardrooms and recording studios. Tales of burning stuntmen, flying pigs, helicopter flights to the Swiss Alps and trips to the Sahara Desert were all part of the myth. Once, during a cover shoot for the British singer-songwriter John Miles, Hipgnosis's catering bill was so excessive senior management at Decca demanded an enquiry.

In 1985, though, Greenback Films were saddled with an enormous debt and there wasn't a Pink Floyd or Led Zeppelin to pick up the tab. 'Storm, Peter and I had a meeting and each hired solicitors,' says Po. 'All three of those solicitors told us the same thing: "You all have to put in around £33,000 each to get the bank off your back." We all agreed to do this. Peter said he was going to re-mortgage his house and Storm said he'd probably borrow the money from David Gilmour.'

Perhaps inevitably, Po already had the money, in cash. A date was arranged with the bank manager, but Po suggested they meet the day before at Spencer Road, with Anthony Taylor as referee: 'Storm and Peter arrived, and I told them I had my share of the money and asked what was happening with theirs. Peter looked a bit sheepish and said, "I don't think I can extend my mortgage any further, I'm not sure, but I might ask my parents for the money."

'I then said, "What about you, Storm?" "I don't know, man . . . I haven't asked Dave Gilmour yet," he replied. I was furious. We had a meeting with the bank the following morning and they were going to call in the debt and take away our company, and these two had done nothing about it.'

As arranged, Po arrived at the bank with his solicitor, Howard Jones from Sheridan's, and a briefcase containing approximately £33,000. The irony of the situation, considering he'd defrauded a bank almost twenty years earlier, was not lost on him.

'We waited and waited, but there was no sign of the other two,' says Po. 'Eventually, the bank manager asked me where my partners were. I told him I didn't know and Howard suggested I resign from the partnership there and then. The people we owed were banks and corporations. I said I wanted no part of it and I walked away.'

In doing so, Po walked away from both Greenback Films and its £100,000 debt. 'Our accountant and our solicitors also gave us all the same advice: "Forget the bank, start another company and carry on." But Storm, in his confusion about money, wouldn't have it. He flipped out. He said, "How can you do this to me?" I said, "You're uncontrollable, Storm. We fucked it."'

Despite Po's resignation, Storm refused to follow suit. 'It was a tragedy,' says Po. 'From that day forward, Storm and I didn't speak to each other for twelve years.'

Chapter 12

'He'd shout at somebody and then go and play tennis . . .'

In the words of 10cc: 'Art for art's sake;
money for God's sake.'

'Storm was a man who'd never take "yes" for an answer.'

— Nick Mason

So what am I going to do now? he thought. It was early summer 1985 and Aubrey 'Po' Powell found himself standing outside a West End bank, holding a briefcase containing approximately £33,000. He'd left his house that morning intending to give it to a bank manager. Instead, he took the money home and bought a plane ticket to Bolivia.

'I needed to clear my head,' he says. 'So I went to Coroico in the Andes, stayed there for a month and then toured around

South America. I came back in September and hadn't a clue what I was going to do. I'd lost my partners, the company had gone belly up and I was out of work.'

Then the telephone rang. The rock supergroup Asia were the fluffier-haired offspring of Yes, Emerson Lake & Palmer and King Crimson. Their 1982 debut had gone platinum within three months, like punk never happened. Asia wanted Greenback to make a video for their new single, 'Go': 'They didn't know Storm and I had split,' admits Po. 'I said yes anyway, but now I needed a director.'

In another of those serendipitous Hipgnosis moments, Peter Christopherson reappeared unexpectedly. Greenback Films had limped along for several months after Storm cut a deal with the bank and Peter borrowed a large sum of money but they lacked a steadying hand or any financial restraint.

The company folded before the end of the year, but Storm refused to walk away from the debt: 'Storm's admirable ethics required him to pay people back and get himself out of it,' explains David Gilmour. 'But I do remember his disgruntlement and me saying, "Hey, there is a law, you go bankrupt and you start again." But he didn't want that bankruptcy staining him forever. It didn't mean he paid back all of what he owed. He negotiated a deal and paid people back a tenth of it or whatever . . . He certainly pushed some deals to get them to sign him off.'

Gilmour had other pressing matters to consider besides his friend's finances. In December 1985, Roger Waters informed EMI and CBS Records that he was no longer a member of Pink Floyd. Waters and Gilmour's creatively brilliant but combative partnership had followed the same career arc as Storm and Po's.

Gilmour had joined Pink Floyd shortly before his friends started Hipgnosis but he and Waters were thrown together by circumstance rather than friendship, while Hipgnosis's original partners had been like brothers. After their divorce, Waters and Gilmour settled on a mutual stony silence and years of simmering resentment. So, too, did Storm and Po. Except now Storm's estrangement from Po extended to Peter Christopherson: 'Peter left him and Storm couldn't forgive that,' says Po. 'So Peter showed up at my door, needing work and wanting to become a director, and I had a film to make and needed a director.'

Halfway through shooting Asia's 'Go', a piece of sci-fi hokum featuring a female model in a bikini and space helmet, Po took a call from Phil Carson, who was now managing Jimmy Page and Paul Rodgers' new group, the Firm: 'Phil said, "I have £600,000 to make three videos. Can you do it?" "Yes, of course."'

Po and his team created three films for the Firm's second album, *Mean Business*. But video wasn't a comfortable medium for everyone involved: 'In the '80s you were being shown what you were supposed to think when you heard the records,' grumbles Jimmy Page.

APP now included a third partner, producer Fiz Oliver: 'My background was documentaries,' says Fiz. 'After the Firm, Po offered me a job but I wanted a share of the company. Po had 51 per cent and Peter and I shared 49. Po wanted to be more involved in the business and he had all the connections so Peter progressed up the ladder to become the director, Po hustled and I did the other work.'

Where one old Hipgnosis client went, another followed. Soon everyone was in Zagora, in the Sahara Desert, with Robert Plant. It was like a Hipgnosis reunion: APP were making a video for Plant's new single, 'Heaven Knows', and Richard Evans was there, overseeing the cover shoot for his album, *Now and Zen*. Unlike Jimmy Page, Plant continued to embrace the new medium: swishing his hair, striding purposefully through the dunes and channelling his inner Bedouin.

It wasn't all old clients, either. APP shot two films in Bolivia and Peru for the post-punk group The The and brought the same spirit of adventure to the work as Hipgnosis had to *Wish You Were Here*. The films included hallucinogenics, tribal rituals and frontman Matt Johnson strapped to a boat – in the Peruvian city of Iquitos, where Werner Herzog had filmed some of his epic drama, *Fitzcarraldo*.

'Somehow I found the guy who'd been the fixer on *Fitzcarraldo*, which was who we needed to film there,' recalls Fiz. 'There were no mobile phones, so I had to meet him outside a post office in Iquitos with a huge bag of money.'

Just as before at Hipgnosis, advertising agencies started wooing the company: 'Account managers were seeing narrative films on MTV and asking around for directors,' says Po. 'Peter Christofferson had a genius head on his shoulders and the work started pouring in.'

Between pop videos, APP were soon making TV adverts with actress Jane Seymour for Max Factor and shooting Nissan car commercials in Sweden. 'Peter was still recording with Coil,' says Po, 'and his knowledge of working in music studios became an asset. He'd often compose jingles for the commercial spots we filmed.'

'The videos and adverts funded Peter's music and lifestyle,' points out Fiz. 'The music came first for Peter. The work Po brought into the company was not necessarily what he wanted to do, but this was the era of big corporate sponsorship and money. It wasn't always challenging artistically.'

In 1987, the Holmes Knight Ritchie agency hired APP to shoot three commercials for the Bristol & West building society, starring Joan Collins, currently a TV superstar as 'Alexis Colby' in the US soap, *Dynasty*. 'The agency reportedly paid Joan £1,000,000 and expected total dedication,' divulges Po. 'For Joan, it was a bit of a laugh and an excuse to be in England all summer, plus she had no illusions and regarded it as money for old rope.'

Joan's off/on relationship with property developer 'Bungalow' Bill Wiggins was rich tabloid fodder that year. 'The "bungalow" nickname was given to Bill as there wasn't much on top, it was all down below,' says Po. 'Being around them on a good day was just the best as Bill could be very funny.' But the couple had a spectacular falling-out three weeks into the shoot. One day, filming was meant to begin at Ascot Racetrack at 6 a.m. with a huge cast of extras. Joan was due on set at nine, but an hour later, she'd still not arrived.

'The agency were screaming at me to do something – call the lawyers, read her the riot act, claim a breach of contract. Then an electrician sidled up and asked if I'd seen a copy of today's *Sun* newspaper. The headline inside read something like "Bonking Bill dumps Joanie over wig" – and I knew we were in trouble. A call finally came through that Joan was on her way and in the meantime, I sent runners to Windsor to buy every copy of *The Sun* they could find.'

A limousine pulled up outside the dressing room trailer and Joan emerged, wearing a large hat, dark glasses and a pink candlewick bathrobe. She bolted up the steps with Monique, her make-up artist, following behind.

'Thirty minutes later, after repeated attempts to speak with Joan, Monique ushered me into the gloom,' says Po. A despondent Joan was sat with her head in her hands and a lustrous black wig in a supermarket shopping bag beside her. 'Joan asked if I'd seen the papers and did everyone know. I answered yes and the whole crew were fully supportive and how dare Bill be such a cad . . . Joan asked if we could give her twenty minutes.'

Meanwhile, Po and his team rounded up the extras and film crew and positioned them outside the trailer, each holding a copy of *The Sun*: 'Four handsome young men in tuxedos stood by the steps and when Joan walked out, looking like a million dollars, the cast and crew waved their newspapers, gave her three cheers and the boys led her off to where we had a tray waiting with a bottle of Champagne. Joan was a pussy cat for the rest of the day.'

A photograph from the shoot captured a resplendent Joan, flanked by Po, Peter and Fiz. It was hard to imagine that the gently smiling director in the smart suit and tie had just recorded a new album with Coil containing the song 'The First Five Minutes After Violent Death'.

★

While Po was shooting adverts with Joan Collins, Storm was making pop videos and paying off Greenback's debts. One of his former cover models also came back into his life. Lana Topham, last seen kneeling beside a Doberman Pinscher on the Scorpions' *Animal Magnetism*, was now working for EMI's film wing, Picture Music International.

When Lana first heard that PMI were planning to employ Storm Thorgerson, she advised them not to. 'Naturally, my warnings went unheeded, and a short time later, I transitioned into working in production on many of Storm's videos,' she recalls. 'Storm pushed everyone to their limits but, equally, I learned so much.'

Lana worked with Storm on two videos for Scottish rockers Big Country. *Look Away* involved a night shoot in a forest and ran into overtime for three days straight. On the drive back to London, she woke with a start to see the driver asleep at the wheel and their car veering into the path of an oncoming lorry: 'My scream woke the driver up with seconds to spare. The next day I marched into the office, explained how four of us had nearly died and something had to be done about working to these extremes. At that point, I decided not to work with Storm any more.'

Lana's words would come back to haunt her. Meanwhile, Storm's video for Big Country's 1986 hit 'One Great Thing', which he'd filled with dancers, cheerleaders, beekeepers and coal miners, was later adapted by Tennent's lager for an award-winning TV ad campaign.

Not that he cared. Storm still struggled with making adverts of any kind. 'I really can't maintain what they call "product focus",' Storm wrote later. 'The idea that I need to admire and believe in a product, in a can of beer, for instance, is beyond me.'

The call to work with Pink Floyd again couldn't come soon enough. In 1986, David Gilmour and Nick Mason revived the brand, re-hired Rick Wright and started recording a new album, *A Momentary Lapse of Reason*. It was a lengthy, arduous process, hindered by Roger Waters, who was appalled to discover 'the muffins', as he called them, were carrying on without him.

Waters began legal proceedings to prevent the others using the name; threatened to sue promoters if they booked a Floyd tour and almost issued an injunction to freeze his ex-bandmates' bank accounts. Gilmour and Mason fronted some of their own money for the first few dates, with Mason offering his cherished 1962 Ferrari 250 GTO as collateral.

Ultimately, Waters' threats couldn't halt the album or the tour, but the barrage of legal correspondence and lawyers' phone calls sapped their time and energy. In February 1987, Floyd decamped from London to Los Angeles to finish the album: 'It was fantastic,' says Gilmour, 'because office hours are not in sync and the lawyers couldn't call in the middle of recording, unless they were calling in the middle of the night.'

New companies were also invited to pitch for the album's artwork. 'Steve O'Rourke and Nick Mason wanted to get other people in,' remembers Gilmour. 'We were in Los Angeles and Storm was a long way away in England. We met these people and I thought, "No way, these ideas do not fit the ethos, this stuff is shit." So I said, "Can't we just go back with Storm?" Steve and Nick weren't keen because Storm was quite a lot of aggro to deal with.'

'There may have been a pressure from Steve about not doing things the old way and bringing in new people instead,' suggests Mason. 'Steve and Storm had a fractious relationship, because Storm's job was to be as difficult as possible and Steve's was to try not to pay him anything.'

'I think once one feels one is in safe hands, it seems like a good idea to stick with them,' says Gilmour. 'The other two came round to my way of thinking. Storm flew out and we went from there.'

Storm's starting point for the artwork was the lyric 'the vision of an empty bed' in the song 'Yet Another Movie'. 'I'd drawn an empty bed with bedside tables, with empty picture frames and the bed had been slept in,' explains Gilmour. 'It was obviously a thing about absence. Storm looked at the picture and said, "Yes, okay . . . but how about 500 beds?" If I am completely honest, I think I gulped a bit.'

By 1987, the Wild West days of the music business were passing into folklore. There was something wonderfully cavalier and old-fashioned then about Storm asking to shoot 500 beds on a beach for an LP sleeve. Pink Floyd without Roger Waters were an unknown quantity, but they backed him anyway: 'Through most of our career, we tried to avoid cutting corners and thought that if the art is right, the rest of it will take care of itself,' offers Gilmour.

'I wanted a long line of beds, stretching across the landscape as far as the eye could see,' Storm explained. 'Real beds in a real place. I thought it would be so insane, it would qualify as a momentary lapse of reason.'

Storm's first choice of location was one of Hipgnosis's old haunts, Death Valley, but wrought-iron Victorian hospital beds weren't available in California. Storm was specific about his requirements and an enterprising location manager sourced the beds from a British government department.

After much deliberation, Storm chose Saunton Sands in north Devon for the flatness of its beach. Exactly how many beds were used varies with each telling of the story. Storm asked for 1,000, but at least 100 were left in the trucks.

Each bed was freshly painted, made up with sheets, blankets and pillows and spaced out on the sand, curving off into the distance. Other songs were also represented in the tableaux, with a microlite overhead to illustrate 'Learning to Fly' and five Alsatians in the sand for 'The Dogs of War' – although Storm could never recall the significance of the French maid on the back cover.

Robert Dowling, who'd shot the ear underwater for *Meddle*, was re-hired to photograph the cover. Meanwhile, a helicopter crew circled above, ready to shoot the event for a film to be shown during the forthcoming tour. Storm's art was again part of Pink Floyd's live show.

Then, with every bed, dog and French maid in position, it began to rain: 'That terribly English rain that turns everything grey and misty and limits visibility to about 50 feet,' said Storm. The shoot was abandoned, the beds were collected and Steve O'Rourke was confronted with the bill for a wasted day.

'Steve said, "Did you get the shot?"' recalled Storm. '"No." "*Why*?" "I couldn't see the beds." "So!"'

Storm and his team returned a fortnight later and did it all over again. A lifeguard helped them gauge where to position the beds so the tide could come in and out without causing them to move or, worse, be washed away. Dowling and two other photographers shot as quickly as they could, before Mother Nature intervened. The shoot began at 5 a.m. and finished at 10 p.m. and Pink Floyd picked up the bill, again.

Even before the creation of Photoshop, it would have been possible to duplicate the beds in the studio. But Hipgnosis had always shot for real and Storm wasn't going to change his ways now. Robert Dowling claimed some beds on the horizon were 'drawn in', but, ultimately, this was an LP sleeve created without computer trickery.

A Momentary Lapse of Reason reached number three in the UK and US in September 1987, demonstrating that Pink Floyd was stronger than the sum of its parts. This was some compensation, then, for the album's expensive cover. Storm later revealed that it had cost almost £50,000; a staggering amount considering cassette sales had superseded vinyl, meaning for many, the cover picture measured less than five by three inches. The compact disc would soon overtake cassette sales, offering a marginally larger canvas, but still tiny compared to vinyl.

Storm's involvement was beneficial in another way, though. He was a link to Floyd's illustrious past at a time when they wanted to prove they could function without Roger Waters. The A Momentary Lapse of Reason tour ran for almost a year until

August 1988. Storm joined them on the road, as his films for 'Learning to Fly' and 'On the Run' were being screened during the show.

When it was over, he went to Tuscany for a holiday with friends and met the woman that would become his wife. Barbie Antonis was part of the same group of acquaintances. 'I was having a post-divorce, one-week break from my children,' says Barbie. 'I clicked immediately with Storm. I was lucky to have found him and he was lucky to have found me.'

Barbie was living in Cambridge, singing in a blues band and soon training to become a psychoanalyst: 'Storm and I had a huge amount in common. We both liked rock 'n' roll and the blues, we went to concerts together and also had the same huge set of art books.

'Storm was a huge romantic,' she insists, 'a tender, romantic bloke with a very big brain. But we still had some really impressive arguments, marathon arguments, because he was such a strong character and so am I.'

Storm's timekeeping frustrated Barbie as much as it did others in his life: 'If we went to dinner with friends, we were nearly always late because we had to do something else first. But he'd never arrive to see me or our friends without a bunch of flowers. He loved flowers, I don't think I ever knew anyone who appreciated colour as much as Storm did.

'Storm could be tough on his colleagues and bossy as shit and drive people crazy. I knew he wasn't squeaky clean, but he wasn't as fearless as people thought. He would get anxious if a deadline to submit was coming up, or a piece was going to the printers, and we would have to talk this through.'

There was something else which Barbie believes made him even more anxious. Early on in their relationship, the couple went into London's West End, where Storm showed her Number 6 Denmark Street and took her on a tour of Soho.

'I thought, "Wow, what is the amazing world I've just entered?"' she recalls. 'We were walking along the pavement near this Polish restaurant and suddenly he was gone – vanished into thin air. I looked and Storm was crouched down, hiding. He said, "Shhh", as if we were in mortal danger. I froze for a few seconds and then he finally stood up again. I said, "What is going on?" He said, "I just saw Po on the other side of the road." I said, "What? You're a grown man." He said, "I am tough, I can argue, but I cannot fight, not physically." I think he was terrified of Po.'

'Storm and I had some huge arguments,' stresses Po. 'But they were never physical and I don't believe he was terrified of me.'

★

At some point in the early 1990s, Po realised his time in the world of corporate advertising was over when a stranger walked into his office and punched him out. One of APP's runners had made the company's receptionist pregnant and her father wanted revenge: 'As if it were somehow my fault as her employer,' says Po. 'It was the last straw.'

APP had continued to make pop videos but also landed high-paying jobs from the likes of Saatchi & Saatchi and Pan American Airlines. Sometimes the two worlds collided, when corporate brands struck deals with rock stars, and the company shot TV ads for Coca-Cola starring Robert Plant and Miller Lite featuring the Who and actor Randy Quaid.

Po had acquired a five-storey office building on Ledbury Road with an editing suite in Notting Hill and recruited several other creative directors. Over time, there were echoes of his earlier life in Miami. He'd split with Gabi Schneider, married his Japanese girlfriend, Bino Honda, brought another house and a sailboat and refurbished his finca in Formentera.

'I became a ghastly show-off,' he admits. 'I had compromised the ethos at Hipgnosis of "the art comes first, the money later". It was all late lunches and all-night binges and courting some of the most unethical people around.'

The advertising world was now competing with rock 'n' roll, and antics on foreign shoots sometimes resembled life on the road with Led Zeppelin: 'I once found my crew waiting in line in a hotel corridor scoring coke off an agency director and I had to bail out a creative director in New York after a rowdy night which involved all the plants in a hotel going missing and a stash of cocaine.'

There was growing dissent, too, among Peter and Fiz. When APP made the Paul McCartney documentary, *From Rio to Liverpool*, Po and his creative director stayed in the same hotel as McCartney, while Fiz and Peter were billeted with the crew: 'There was a division,' says Fiz, 'Peter and I said, "Look, we are the motherfuckers making you the money, Po."'

'Those two thought I was earning too much and they'd had enough of me being the playboy,' admits Po. 'But I was the one who got most of the work in. The financial recession of 1990 dealt us another blow. The glory days were over. Major clients realised they had been wrung out to dry by the agencies and now every bill and receipt was being carefully scrutinised.

'The real issue for me, though, was I was forty-five years old and realised I was probably halfway through my life. I had this beautiful sailing boat and I'd always wanted to do a long trip. The company was still sufficiently solvent, so I decided to go away.'

Po issued strict instructions not to be contacted, sailed his boat, *Ceres Two*, to the Mediterranean and stayed there for several months: 'I had never been so free and had time to contemplate who I was and what I wanted to do. Bino became pregnant with our daughter, May, and I felt happy, healthy and calm for the first time in years.'

His peaceful frame of mind didn't last after he returned to work: 'We staggered on with APP for a while,' he says. 'I found myself being the headmaster, the bringer of work, the psychiatrist . . . as well as having to deal with Peter Christopherson and his scandals.'

Po's attitude towards Peter's parallel life hadn't changed since the '70s. 'I still didn't care as long as it didn't affect the work,' he says. 'Out of financial desperation, though, I agreed to shoot nine TV spots with McDonald's, featuring the mascot, Ronald McDonald, and with Peter directing. This was scraping the barrel and something I would never have considered unless under pressure.

'Everybody turned up on set first thing in the morning, except for Peter. McDonald's were a corporate brand and particular about who they worked with, and there was no sign of my director. Peter eventually arrived more than an hour late, as he'd been up most of the night with friends. He told me later that when he was waiting at the bus stop he realised he still had some actual shit in his ear from the night before and had to go home and have a shower.'

Like Joan Collins, Ronald McDonald, the clown mascot in the orange wig, was blissfully unaware of his director's scatological interests. Although Peter's alternative lifestyle couldn't remain a secret forever.

Psychic TV had evolved into Thee Temple Ov Psychic Youth, an artistic collective with a keen interest in the occult and magick. Genesis P-Orridge and his family were in Nepal when their house in Brighton was raided by the obscene publications squad. Two decades worth of books, art, films and tapes were seized. Among them was a video which the police believed showed a forced ritualistic abortion. The footage was fake, but newspaper stories about 'bloody satanic rituals' were followed by a TV documentary claiming TOPY were black magic practitioners with links to paedophilia.

Peter had long since left Psychic TV to work with Coil, but the two groups shared musicians and ideas. 'The police raided Genesis P-Orridge and Peter was concerned he was going to be next,' explains Po. 'I knew he was hardcore in his private life, but I knew that any film was fake because he was good at doing that stuff. But then he turned up at the office in Ledbury Road with what looked like foetuses in jars, and hid them there. This really pissed me off. I didn't want to be associated with it. I loved Peter in Hipgnosis, but to see this person get darker and darker . . .'

'Peter and I eventually left Po for various reasons,' says Fiz. 'I couldn't stand one of his directors, who ended up costing the company a lot of money. I loved the way Peter worked and he and I both had similar political ideas. We wanted to do something more challenging.'

The pair went on to make films for pop artists Marc Almond and Erasure, and new alternative rock acts, including Rage Against the Machine and Nine Inch Nails. TG and Coil were an influence on some of these musicians and Peter struck up a close working relationship with Nine Inch Nails' frontman, Trent Reznor.

Reznor's live-in studio in LA was at 10050 Cielo Drive, where the Manson Family cult had embarked on their notorious killing spree. Peter directed a film for NIN's *Broken* EP, deliberately shot to resemble a snuff movie, with scenes of blood, torture, decapitation and a penis being sliced off with a razor.

'Obviously it was never going to be shown on MTV,' under-states Fiz. 'But Trent released a few copies and the videos got copied, so it looked even grainier, and people started to read things into it that weren't there. Peter was very clever at that.

'I always went along with Peter's notions, because I knew him as a loving human being,' she stresses. 'But I also knew he was into S&M and his gay sexuality was extreme. My atti-tude was: that's up to you, each individual can do what the hell they like as long as it's consensual. I worked with him on that basis, though it wasn't something I ever wanted to be involved in.'

Fiz later resumed working with Po; Peter never did. 'From the day he left, I saw him only twice more and neither time was comfortable for either of us,' says Po. 'After eighteen years, first at Hipgnosis and then directing at APP, we parted ways, never to work together again.'

Po walked away from the company soon after his partners abandoned him. He'd also received another of his serendipitous telephone calls. 'Paul McCartney wanted me to be his creative director,' he says. 'I remained with Paul for the next few years, and then I started directing films and making documentaries. But I'd still not heard a word from Storm. It was inevitable, I guess, but I missed his wit and his intelligence. Despite all we'd been through, I missed him.'

★

The designer Peter Curzon's earliest memory of Storm Thorg-erson was thinking how appropriate his name was. 'He was like a whirlwind,' Curzon recalls. 'He'd walk into the studio, shout at somebody, and then go off and play tennis.'

It was 1987 and Curzon was sharing a studio with the graphic designer and artist Keith Breeden: 'Storm asked Keith to design a sleeve for the Cult's single, "Love Removal Machine". I didn't really know who he was because I'd grown up with punk.'

Five years later, they were working together. Storm and Barbie had bought a house in West Hampstead and Storm now had a studio at Hillfield Mansions. Curzon refused to work there full-time 'because it was an absolute dump', but he eventually became a partner in a new company, StormStudios: 'I'd come from a stylistic pop background, with logos and portraits of the bands,' he says, 'so it was a totally different way of working for me.'

Storm was also unlike anyone he'd worked with before. 'A car journey with Storm was always a white-knuckle ride. He had this mint-green metallic BMW and he drove like his brain worked – tearing around the streets with people rushing out the way.

'He also made you do things you wouldn't choose to do,' says Curzon. 'For one of my first shoots, he sent me off to Marks & Spencer to buy women's lingerie. When I came back, Nick Mason's daughter, Chloe, who was working as his assistant, had already bought some. He'd done it just to get me out of my comfort zone.'

In winter 1993, Pink Floyd commissioned Storm to create the artwork for their new album, *The Division Bell.* The theme of communication ran through many of the songs. David Gilmour's soon-to-be wife, journalist and author Polly Samson, contributed many lyrics, including those in 'High Hopes', a song which flashed back to Cambridge in the early '60s.

'Polly and I had not been together that long,' Gilmour recalls. 'I'd written the music to "High Hopes" and was going to write the lyrics, and she asked me, "What's this about?" I said, "Uh . . . I don't know." Polly jogged my memory and it still reminds me of those early days by the River Cam with Storm and all those people.'

Despite new computer technology, Storm was committed to doing everything for real and proposed two sculptured heads facing each other, with their mouths open, as if talking. Keith Breeden drew the sketches from which two sets were created: metal heads for the vinyl LP and CD and stone versions for the cassette. Each one was 7 metres high and weighed half a ton.

Storm soon surrounded himself with other gifted designers, illustrators, prop-makers and photographers who could tolerate his idiosyncrasies. Among them were Tony May and Rupert Truman, who were tasked with shooting the heads in a field in Cambridge. In a further nod to Storm's past, the statues were positioned so that Ely Cathedral was visible in the gap between their mouths.

Tony May later recalled a meeting at Hillfield Mansions, where Storm luxuriated in a bubble bath, while he himself sat on the lavatory seat, listening. Rupert Truman had a harsher experience while photographing a sleeve for cowboy-booted rockers Thunder: 'Storm called me a cunt for not bringing two Hasselblads,' he sighs. 'He gave me such a hard time and yet I came back for more.'

May and Truman spent two weeks in January 1994 trying to take the picture for *The Division Bell*. They parked their Land Rover in the field and waited. The weather was poor and the heads were covered in camouflage netting, to stop the press or sightseers taking pictures: 'We stayed with these darned things for a fortnight,' says Truman. 'Living in a caravan and with a Little Chef nearby.'

Pink Floyd had only decided on the album title after EMI imposed a deadline. This meant the sleeve was rushed and

Storm delayed it even further. Steve O'Rourke told Storm that if they could finish the artwork the next day, he'd pay for a seat on Concorde for Peter Curzon to deliver it to Sony in LA. 'Storm said, "No, no, no, it's not ready,"' recalls Curzon. 'Damn! A few days later when it was ready, Floyd paid for me and my wife to fly to LA, but cattle class.'

The Division Bell was released in March 1994 and reached number one in the UK and the US. 'I consider this one of the best things I've ever done,' said Storm. 'Majestic, elegant and monolithic.' Meanwhile, David Gilmour told interviewers he thought it sounded more like 'a genuine Pink Floyd album' than anything since *Wish You Were Here*.

While StormStudios were designing the cover, PMI's Lana Topham was meeting with Steve O'Rourke's PA. O'Rourke wanted Lana to oversee seven concert screen films for Pink Floyd's upcoming tour. When Lana discovered Storm would be directing, she refused the job: 'I said, "I will not collaborate with Storm, he's a nightmare," and I left.'

After hearing this, O'Rourke was convinced she was the right person for the job and Storm also insisted on Lana being involved. 'I only agreed, after setting certain parameters,' she says. 'If I found him being mean to anyone, he was to apologise immediately. He was well-behaved and too busy to cause trouble. However cantankerous Storm was, there was still something forgivable and likeable about him.

'Storm and Steve had a precarious relationship, though. So I became the middle person, relaying Storm's wants and needs so they didn't have to communicate.'

'I suffered at the hands of Steve O'Rourke's virulent and bombastic nature,' Storm once told me. 'Unfortunately, the bullishness that was useful against record companies, agents or anyone that might abuse the Floyd wasn't so useful when turned on those nearest and dearest.'

'Steve had enormous respect for Storm,' insists David Gilmour, 'but there were arguments about what exactly Storm's role was. Is he a fifth member of the band or is he just being paid to do the artwork? Difficult questions. But at the time it was Steve's job to basically set him right so we didn't have to.'

The Division Bell extolled the virtues of communication, but Storm and Po still weren't speaking. By 1998, their silence had lasted the best part of twelve years. Then the publishers Dorling Kindersley began casting around for authors to compile the book, *One Hundred Best Album Covers*, and Richard Evans recommended Storm and Po.

'I had a call from the editor,' says Po. 'She asked me what the chances were of Storm and I working together and I said they were slim. But they offered us a deal. We both had our own careers, but there was still unresolved business. I'd also heard through the Floyd grapevine that people thought it a shame we didn't talk any more.'

'I have no memory of saying anything,' cautions Gilmour. 'But Po rose from the ashes differently from Storm and I don't think Storm could quite forgive him, though I'm not entirely sure what there was to forgive.'

It was Po who made the first move: 'I told Storm there was a book deal and we should at least meet up. Storm was quite cool at first, but we met in the pub and within five minutes it was like we were back at Hipgnosis – the same language, the same in-jokes. We decided on the spot we would do the book.'

One Hundred Best Album Covers corralled almost forty years' worth of Storm and Po's favourite LP art, including their own, with assistance from Richard Evans and Peter Curzon. 'It was an absolute pleasure,' recalls Po, 'because we were doing a job that was about other people's work.'

The publishers were delighted and booked the duo on an American press tour. This included a trip to a TV studio in LA, where they'd be interviewed live over three hours by thirty different stations, coast to coast. A couple of hours into the broadcast, both had grown weary of hearing the same questions and giving the same answers. Po bristled when a TV host in Louisiana asked him 'What kind of name is "Aubrey"?' and Storm joined in with the gag. Tempers started to fray.

'There was a thirty-minute break between a couple of spots,' recalls Po, 'and Storm suddenly turned to me and said, "If you tell that fucking story about *Houses of the Holy* again . . . I can't stand hearing it, and it's not right." I said, "What the fuck are you talking about?" So we ended up having a stand-up row, with Storm threatening to walk.

'The producer was freaking out, as we were due back on air. Ten seconds and counting, we both sat down and did the next interview as if nothing had happened. I didn't tell the story, but Storm left anyway and caught a flight back to England on his own.'

Storm and Po stopped speaking, again. 'Our rift was exactly like being in a band,' admits Po. 'Ridiculous, I know.'

Eventually, Po made another call. 'I said, "This is stupid, isn't it, Storm?" And Storm said, "Okay, Povis . . ." We knew we'd never work together like before, but at least we started talking again.'

★

By the end of the twentieth century, StormStudios had found new clients and re-connected with many of Storm's old ones. His pet obsessions reappeared, just on a smaller canvas and with higher production values. He stuck a flashing LED light in the spine of Pink Floyd's live album, *Pulse*; photographed a naked man cowering from a giant pair of eyes for Irish pop-rockers the Cranberries and shot a trio of elegant swimmers underwater for the alternative rock band, Catherine Wheel.

Storm still struggled with rejection, though. Those who incurred his disapproval included *Tubular Bells* composer Mike Oldfield (for trying to claim ownership of a test photo), Kiss ('They hired me and fired me') and the Scorpions again: 'They rejected my idea and chose a humongous pile of crap.' Storm was even annoyed when the nouveau power trio Muse picked an existing design for their *Absolution* album, instead of commissioning something new.

The illustrator and designer Dan Abbott first encountered Storm during one such rejection. Abbott was working for the agency, Stylorouge, and designing modern psychedelic rockers Kula Shaker's new album, *Peasants, Pigs & Astronauts*.

'Somehow, Storm got the idea he was designing the album instead,' says Abbott. 'We were all at a cinema in Piccadilly for the premiere of *Fear and Loathing In Las Vegas* and Storm cornered Kula Shaker's singer, Crispian Mills, in the loo. Crispian later described how Storm almost had him up against the wall and was ranting at him – "Why aren't I doing this cover, dear?" He said he was scary, but camp with it.'

In 2001, Abbott found himself irresistibly drawn into Storm's orbit: 'Storm was like a vortex, and that studio was like the black hole of Belsize Park,' he says. 'I knew Sam Brooks, who ran Storm's website, before he stormed out. There was an illustrator there, Finlay Cowan, who'd also stormed out, and after he left, Sam asked if I wanted to try a day's work.'

Abbott's impression of the studio was much like Richard Evans's at Denmark Street in 1973. 'I'd expected a huge attic with skylights and white drawing boards. Not some mad old grandma's flat that hadn't been tidied for two decades. There were phone bills and Post-it notes everywhere, and taxi receipts pinned to the wall. Storm didn't even talk to me for the first four hours. But I'm tolerant and tend to stick around when other people storm out.'

'All Storm was interested in was the image,' explains Rupert Truman. 'He had the ability to shut off from everybody's emotions and that allowed him to push through, no matter what. He pushed himself so hard and couldn't understand why other people fell by the wayside.'

Storm's behaviour crossed language barriers, too. Lana Topham joined him on a shoot in the Amazon rainforest, for Gentlemen Without Weapons, a band whose album, *Transmissions*, comprised entirely of sampled natural sounds: 'Within a short time the Karaja tribe in Brazil had dubbed him "Tempestade", meaning thunderstorm,' says Lana. 'They laughed at his moods while mumbling the word.'

For Pink Floyd's 2001 compilation, *Echoes*, Dan Abbott appeared as a cover model, holding a briefcase, but Storm pushed Rupert Truman to breaking point. 'We set up the shoot near Grantchester Meadows,' he recalls. 'I came back early from a holiday in the south of France to do the job and Storm gave me hell. I just thought, "I've had enough." I started walking up the hill to catch a train and Storm begged me to stay. That changed our relationship, because he needed people to stand up to him.

'There were lots of shortening of holidays or trips with significant others,' concurs Abbott. 'Storm would say, "Why can't you go a day later?" or "Do you like holidays more than art?" It was like a conjuring trick — "Don't look there, look here". He could have been a great salesman if he'd cared about such things.'

There was the issue of money, too. Abbott remembers Storm having as many as twenty different accounts, all with the same bank: 'The cheque books had different names, like "Roger" or "Pink Floyd 1987". He'd write cheques for £100 from one, £50 from another . . . and you'd just hope they all went through.'

'He had a lousy sense of money,' admits Barbie. 'I couldn't tell you the origins of that, even though I'm a shrink. I knew the body of work he'd been involved with and one day I said to him, "Where is the money?" Not "Why aren't you rich?" Just "Where is the commensurate payment for all this?" Storm said, "One day the Floyd will pay me adequately."'

In the late 1990s, Storm sold the copyright for Hipgnosis's artwork to Pink Floyd for approximately £10,000, and without Po's knowledge: 'When I found out, I was absolutely incandescent,' he says.

Storm later requested a further sum (believed to be around £1 million), which he thought he was owed for his contribution to Pink Floyd's sales. The band refused. 'He asked us for 15 per cent of the gross receipts for *The Dark Side of the Moon*,' recalls Roger Waters. 'Somebody had told him 15 per cent of its sales were due to the cover. I thought to myself, "Well, if they are, we should be paying them to George Hardie, not you."'

By now, though, Hipgnosis's work had become part of the wider culture. Their original audience had grown up and were writing books, movies and television shows. The first evidence was heard in the 1989 film comedy, *Bill & Ted's Excellent Adventure*. '470 BC,' intoned Keanu Reeves, playing teenage rocker Theodore 'Ted' Logan, 'a time when much of the world looked like the cover of the Led Zeppelin album, *Houses of the Holy*.' The sleeve never appeared, but the film-makers knew their audience were in on the joke.

Ideas drawn up on scraps of paper at 6 Denmark Street had become like the McDonald's Golden Arches, the Nike tick or the Mona Lisa of the rock 'n' roll age and were now being repurposed on box sets and remastered versions of old albums.

The Dark Side of the Moon had sold in excess of 50 million copies worldwide, but the cover art's value was impossible to define. 'It doesn't matter how artistic we thought we were, we were being paid to come up with an idea to go on a piece of cardboard,' says Po. 'Is it fine art? Is it commercial art? This is the dichotomy. Storm considered himself a fine artist. I did in some respects, but it was still a job and we were paid for that job.'

In 2003, Storm and event organiser and curator Paula Stainton were hired to create the 'Pink Floyd Interstellar' exhibition at the Cité de La Musique in Paris. Paula had previously worked for Nick Mason and was familiar with Storm's work ethic and exacting standards.

The exhibition was scheduled to open in October, just nine months after Pink Floyd signed the contracts. It was a major undertaking to unearth almost four decades' worth of inflatable pigs, arcane musical instruments and artwork in such a short time. 'It was intense,' says Paula. 'Storm was charming, cantankerous and brilliant, and everyone had to keep up with him. But museums don't understand music.'

The exhibition's original plans included a rectangular space, meaning visitors had to enter and leave by the same door. Storm sent back a proposal entitled 'A Momentary Lack of Exit' and demanded a triangular space. 'It was the thirtieth anniversary of *Dark Side*, so three was the number,' explains Paula. 'The thirtieth anniversary in the third year of the third millennium of a record with a three-sided icon. So, in Storm's mind, there should be three axioms for the exhibition.'

France closed down for most of the summer, during which Storm married Barbie and the couple honeymooned in the Seychelles. He later recalled sitting on the beach drawing triangles in the sand and thinking about how he was going to illustrate the thirtieth-anniversary edition.

A month before opening day, the Cité de La Musique had only just started installing the exhibits. 'We fought big battles,' admits Paula, 'and there were daily showdowns with the museum over everything.'

On the day of the opening, Storm discovered key dates from Pink Floyd's history had been positioned incorrectly in a walk-through tunnel. He demanded the dates be removed, but the designers refused. 'There was a stand-up argument and Storm started physically removing them. I stood between Storm and the head of the museum because I thought there might be fisticuffs. Storm's blood pressure must have been getting higher and higher and he'd been running on caffeine for days.'

The dates were finally removed and then repainted in the correct order. An hour before the opening, Paula left to get changed, returned to the space and realised Storm was missing: 'Someone told me he was in the office. I went up there and he was sitting down, Barbie was holding his hand and they were waiting for an ambulance.'

'I arrived a quarter of an hour into Storm having a stroke,' says Barbie. 'I could hear people shouting my name and asking where I was. Storm was sitting collapsed in a chair. I took one look at him and it was obvious what was happening.'

Storm was rushed to hospital and Paula phoned Steve O'Rourke, who was stuck in traffic with a group of record company executives. 'I don't know if Storm was having a row with

Steve when it happened,' she says. 'If he was, it would have been on the phone as Steve was late arriving.'

'There was so much tension at that exhibition, how does one ever know?' offers Barbie. 'I don't think drinking however many neat espressos a day helped, I don't think having arguments five times a day with Steve O'Rourke helped. Storm was not in a good state.'

News of his condition reached the studio in London. 'Paula phoned us,' recalls Peter Curzon. 'We were doing a cover shoot for the Offspring and it was a picture of a Roman bust with an exploding head. Can you believe it? Just at the point Storm was having his stroke.'

'I stayed in Paris for a week,' says Paula, 'and came home when I realised Storm was going to survive, although I wasn't allowed to see him.' Three weeks passed and then she received a shocking phone call: Steve O'Rourke had suffered a stroke and died at his home in Miami. The awful coincidence wasn't lost on anyone: 'Everything changed in Pink Floyd after that.'

★

Storm spent a week in a Parisian hospital before being flown home and transferred to the Royal Free in Hampstead. 'Before long, we were being summoned to his bedside,' says Dan Abbott. 'His brain was still swollen and he wasn't sure what time of year it was, but he was still trying to design things.'

Storm had lost mobility on his left side and faced a long road ahead and years of therapy. Pink Floyd and Roger Waters rallied around so the house could be adapted to his needs. 'They couldn't have been more generous, all of them,' stresses Barbie.

'If they hadn't helped us financially, I don't know what we would have done.'

Storm's body was lagging behind his brain, but he soon started working again. 'I didn't think he should stop working,' says Barbie. 'But I did feel conflicted about it. But for Storm, working was synonymous with being alive. If he was alive, he could work.'

'His energy was remarkable,' recalls David Gale. 'He was being wheeled everywhere and being lifted in and out of cars. But he was still the same noisy bastard as ever. Storm seemed to regard his stroke as a source of great sorrow and anger, annoyance and inconvenience.'

'I ended up driving Storm all over the place and we had some increasingly tender moments,' says Rupert Truman. 'He had a sense of being superhuman before the stroke, but now he needed other people. It was also a pleasure being in his company when we weren't shooting and meeting his friends. Storm had some lovely, intelligent people in his circle.'

Storm's HQ now extended to Black & Blue, the café restaurant below the studio. As he had lost the use of his left arm, the waiting staff would cut up his food for him; if an able-bodied customer snuck into the disabled lavatory, he'd rap on the door with his walking cane. Several of the café's waitresses and patrons appeared as extras in photo shoots.

'One customer got roped in because Storm wanted someone with big ears,' recalls Abbott. 'It was the same with the people in his local hairdressers – "Ask 'em if they want a hundred quid for a day's work, dear . . ."'

Ancient wounds still hadn't healed, though. In July 2005, Pink Floyd and Roger Waters briefly put their differences aside and performed together at Live 8, a charity concert in London's

Hyde Park. Storm attended the show and spotted the now 'Sir' Paul McCartney backstage.

'Paul walked past Storm and did a rather aggressive thumbs-up gesture at him, as if to say, "I'm not your friend, but I'm looking at you,"' recalls Barbie. 'Half an hour later, he walked back again and Storm, who was in his wheelchair, held out his stick as if to say, "And I'm not your friend either."'

In contrast, Storm's younger clients, Muse, the Mars Volta and Biffy Clyro, were often drawn to his idiosyncrasies: 'Young bands liked him because he was always putting the record companies down,' explains Curzon. 'They loved that he was a rock 'n' roll personality and didn't give a shit. They saw him as an artist, as one of them.'

These artists also knew his work, because they'd grown up around those album covers. 'Storm had a funny relationship with Hipgnosis,' suggests Abbott. 'I was nerdy about that stuff – "Hey, I never knew you did that 10cc sleeve." But he'd be dismissive – "Why do you care? Looks amateur to me." But just before the stroke he started getting interested again, thinking about doing more books and selling more prints.'

In 2008, Storm and Po co-authored *For the Love of Vinyl: The Album Art of Hipgnosis*. 'Storm and Po were different but similar,' says Abbott, who worked on the book with the rest of StormStudios. 'Both were very articulate when angry, although Storm used to get high-pitched and abrasive. I didn't meet Po until about 2007 and I was expecting Count Dracula, and certainly someone taller. I blurted out, "I thought you'd be taller," and luckily Po found it funny.'

Po's humour abandoned him, though, when it came to Storm and the money. It was still an issue and it was getting worse. Led Zeppelin had acquired the rights to Hipgnosis's artwork for a six-figure sum in October 2007. 'I'm not going to tell you how much we paid,' says Jimmy Page, 'but it was a sizeable amount, because we wanted to own everything.'

The timing was right, as Zeppelin were about to perform a reunion concert at London's O2 Arena with John Bonham's son, Jason, playing drums. Boxes of prints, transparencies and sketches related to *Houses of the Holy* and the rest were delivered to the band's accountant, ready to be plundered for the next round of archival releases. Then, sometime later, Page visited a Led Zeppelin collector's apartment in New York and saw dozens of alternative outtakes from *Presence*.

'I must admit, they looked bloody good,' he says. 'I asked this guy where he'd got them from and he told me he'd bought them recently from Storm Thorgerson. When I told him that they weren't his to sell, he asked me not to give Storm a bad time about it because he knew he wasn't well.' At a meeting with the other group members, Robert Plant insisted they didn't act against Storm and the matter was dropped. But Page wouldn't forget.

'By then I'd already discovered Storm was selling loads of Hipgnosis's work to collectors,' continues Po. 'People were wandering into the studio – "Can I have this?" "Yes, five hundred quid, please." After Jimmy found out about the stuff in New York, it came out about all the other things Storm had been selling to various people.

'I was in another world by then. I had a film company, so I hadn't thought about record covers for a while, until I found out what was going on. I asked Storm how we were going to resolve this, because by my estimation he owed me something like £180,000. He said, "I am sorry, Po, I just didn't think . . ." A few days later he turned up with one of his guys and a whole bunch of Hipgnosis artworks – "Here, these are yours in lieu of payment." Rather than fall out with him again, I put them in a lock-up and tried to move on.'

Then Po discovered a third party was using the 'Hipgnosis' name. Music manager Merck Mercuriadis had represented such high-profile clients as Guns N' Roses and Beyoncé. Mercuriadis was a Hipgnosis fan, collected their work and had now acquired the name.

'My favourite Floyd albums growing up were *Wish You Were Here* and *Animals*,' says Mercuriadis. 'For the better part of two years, I didn't go to sleep at night without listening to Led Zeppelin's "Achilles Last Stand". So, when I went into the music business at sixteen, seventeen years old, all I was interested in was finding Storm Thorgerson.'

Mercuriadis was introduced to Storm while working for Iron Maiden's management company, Sanctuary Music, and managing the alternative-rock group Catherine Wheel. 'Storm had the most amazing way of doing things,' he recalls. 'Storm and his team would present you with these ideas on big boards and then leave cards showing the images for you to choose the one you wanted. You'd pick an image, he would make a model of it and come back and show you. Everyone would say how wonderful it was and then Storm would say you couldn't have it, show you something else and say, "*This* is the one you need to have."

'He did it every time – "I'm the expert, I know better than you do, you've got to trust me, this one will stand the test of time." Inevitably, there would be three weeks of, "Fuck that guy, we are never talking to Storm again . . ." But, of course, he was always right.'

Over time, Mercuriadis began unofficially managing Storm. 'It was an unspoken thing, done on a handshake, I never took any money,' he says. 'But Storm needed somebody who could communicate in a way that was more political and had some understanding of other people's feelings. We became very close. I named my son "Storm" and Storm put my kids on the cover of Catherine Wheel's *Wishville* album.'

When Mercuriadis left Sanctuary to form his own management company, Storm asked him what he was going to call his new venture: 'He caught me off guard and I said, rather facetiously, "I'd like to call it Hipgnosis, but I know the name is taken."'

A few weeks later, Mercuriadis received a letter from Storm, granting him permission to use 'Hipgnosis': 'Storm said, "The name has done nothing for years and I want you to have it." Typically, Storm had also designed logos for the company, with price tags attached to each one. That was his way of getting me to pay for it.'

Hipgnosis Songs Fund, the music-management and investment company, launched with a logo showing what most people presumed was an upside-down elephant. 'Of course, Storm told me I was wrong,' says Mercuriadis, 'and explained it was an elephant being blown away by how good the music is.'

'I'd registered Hipgnosis as a limited company, though,' explains Po. 'The first thing I knew about this was when I saw someone using "Hipgnosis" on Instagram and it had nothing to do with us. I said to Storm, "You can't really give the name away, it belongs to me," and he said, "Oh, but it's done . . ."'

What muddied the waters further was that Storm had been diagnosed with stomach cancer, an especially cruel blow after surviving the stroke. Naturally, he kept working and the stories were legion: how he flew to San Francisco to present twenty-five cover ideas to 'The Joker' songwriter Steve Miller, who was so overwhelmed he didn't know which to choose; how he'd fallen asleep after a long day's shoot in Lanzarote with a wad of banknotes in his hand, trying to pay a restaurant bill; how he'd commissioned a giant sculpture of a head out of suitcases for a cover by an obscure artist few had heard of.

'He would do work for bands that couldn't afford to pay him,' says Barbie. 'But because he liked the song or the people or the idea.'

'It was funny how Storm's morality could chop and change,' offers Po. 'But I'd stopped trying to figure him out. We used to meet regularly for lunch and I knew he wasn't going to make old bones, so I wasn't going to make his life a misery about the money any more. We were both too old now.'

There were frequent reminders of their mortality. Syd Barrett and Rick Wright had already passed away and Peter Christopherson was just fifty-five when he suffered a heart attack and died on 25 November 2010. Peter had left film-making to concentrate on music and had been living in Thailand for the past five years. 'I asked him if he wanted to be involved in an Hipgnosis exhibition once,' says Po. 'But he wanted nothing to do with it. He was not interested at all.'

'Peter didn't even tell me he'd stopped making music videos,' says Fiz Oliver. 'He just started going back and forth to Thailand and was never available for work. In the end, I gave up. I stayed with Peter in Thailand later and he was great fun but completely outrageous. He was into the spiritual, ceremonial side of the lifestyle, but there were stories of him hiring an entire club for the night and all the boys in it.'

Po was interviewed for a BBC obituary and compared Peter to the French surrealist Antonin Artaud. Storm didn't speak about their former partner, despite the fact he was now collaborating on a documentary with the American film-maker, Roddy Bogawa. *Taken by Storm: The Art of Storm Thorgerson* was released in 2011 and showed Storm in the studio, having acupuncture and pondering his life and work, with sage comments from Po, several famous musicians and his StormStudios associates.

At the same time as Bogawa's film, Storm was rounding up his old friends for a documentary he was directing about Syd Barrett. It would also give him an excuse to say goodbye to them all. Storm was taken ill after Christmas 2012, in South Africa. He'd recently completed another round of chemotherapy and his immune system was depleted. He returned to London several weeks later than planned and went back to work – until he couldn't work any more, but carried on anyway.

'He just wanted to get things done,' says Peter Curzon. 'A few days before the end he was still trying to sign fortieth-anniversary prints of *The Dark Side of the Moon* and getting me to hold them because he didn't have the strength himself.'

There was a procession of visitors to the house and it was usually a musician, an old Cambridge friend or a colleague from the studio. Peter Gabriel sent Storm a DVD of *This Is Spinal Tap* as a reminder of the good old bad old days.

'I saw him twice before the end,' says Po. 'I showed him the proofs of my new book, *Hipgnosis Portraits*, and he was lying on the bed exhausted, but still being Storm – "Povis, why did you put the picture there? No, no, no, the colours are all wrong." Stuff like that. I humoured him because I knew it wouldn't be long.'

The next time Po visited was with their mutual friend, John Whiteley, who'd worked on *A Saucerful of Secrets*. Bill Thorgerson helped his father sit on the edge of the bed, where Storm put his arms around Po and John. 'Suddenly he burst out with "I don't want to die,"' says Po. 'We all cried and told him we loved him. It was a sad afternoon and I drove away thinking about all the great work we had done together and how meeting him had changed my life.'

★

Storm died peacefully at 3 p.m. on Thursday, 18 April 2013. 'The next morning, I turned on Radio 4, as I did every morning, and it was the first item on the news,' says Barbie. 'I remember thinking, "No, you can't make this public, this is private." And then I thought, "No, it's not, his work was everywhere in popular culture, and in a good way."'

'I remember getting the call to say he'd gone and suddenly there was this mad storm,' recalls Jill Furmanovsky. 'I watched it from the window and it had come and gone in fifteen minutes. I remember thinking, "Oh, Storm would have loved that."'

Hipgnosis's cultural impact work was revealed in the days after Storm's death. *The Guardian*'s illustrator, Martin Rowson, repurposed *The Dark Side of the Moon*'s prism for a political cartoon. Meanwhile, Peter Brookes, his opposite at *The Times*, parodied the burning businessman from *Wish You Were Here*. These images were so ingrained in the collective conscience that they could now be used to skewer prime ministers and rival politicians.

David Gilmour sang 'Wish You Were Here' at Storm's funeral service, held in North London's Lauderdale House. Po and David Gale were among those who delivered eulogies. Roger Waters was rehearsing in São Paulo, so Andrew 'Willa' Rawlinson read a message on his behalf. Nobody shied away from mentioning Storm's lateness or irascibility.

'Storm was not only profoundly intellectual, he was also profoundly late,' wrote Waters, 'not trying to make a joke under present circumstances but . . .'

'Storm was the rudest person I have ever met,' said David Gale, 'but actually very loveable, despite being very rude.' Gale's eulogy recounted Storm's stand-off with Barry Gibb and the time he was summoned to LA to direct Bill Cosby's Christmas TV special but rubbished the script and was fired. It also mentioned how Storm was 'never especially self-conscious about bodily functions' and 'how he lifted our spirits, while insulting us'.

Storm was buried in Highgate Cemetery. To this day, fans still leave notes reading 'Shine On . . .' and 'Wish You Were Here . . .' beside his grave.

A month after the funeral, Po was invited to a summit with Pink Floyd's management: 'Storm had talked to David and Nick about me carrying on as Pink Floyd's creative director in his absence. But I had my own company and wasn't sure I wanted to do that.'

Po had a new life now. He'd married interior designer Diana Sieff and was living in London and Oxfordshire. But he was still dealing with creative individuals who didn't get along and was about to shoot Monty Python's reunion shows at London's O2. David Gilmour and Nick Mason needed someone to mediate with Roger Waters on a forthcoming Pink Floyd exhibition: 'And I was the only person who could speak to all three of them.'

Po took the job and was immediately tasked with conjuring up artwork for 2014's *The Endless River*, a collection of reworked outtakes from *The Division Bell*. Further Floyd box sets and anniversary editions would appear on the schedule and Po was soon commissioning artwork again. 'It was strange at first,' he admits, 'as I could hear Storm in my ear for the first year and I sometimes still do.'

Unlike in the '70s, Po preferred to delegate. 'I would rather somebody else with superior technical knowledge, point and shoot exactly what I want to see,' he says. 'It's not so different from Hipgnosis, though. The difference is accuracy, high quality and the ability to adjust colour, shape and sharpness at the touch of a button. God bless the modern world.'

'Storm used to call himself "The Art Department,"' says Gilmour. 'That's not Po, it's different. But I like to have members of, if not my genetic family, but my *family* being part of this.'

In 2017, Hipgnosis's work was featured in *Their Mortal Remains: The Pink Floyd Exhibition* at London's Victoria and Albert Museum. Po, Paula Stainton and their team created the largest exhibition on one subject ever staged at the V&A. But it was also a ground-breaking music exhibition against which all others would be measured, with handwritten lyrics, Syd Barrett's letters, a replica of Battersea Power Station and a 3D holographic prism on display: 'I only wish Storm had been there to see it,' says Po.

Even after Storm's death, the pair's relationship mirrored that of Waters and Gilmour or Page and Plant. They were artists unavoidably bound to each other by the creative work they did together as young people. The fine art versus commercial art question could never be answered, though.

For millions of consumers, album artwork was an image the size of a postage stamp on Apple Music or Spotify. Hipgnosis's images, though, lived on in second-hand record shops, on T-shirts, mouse mats and coffee mugs, but also in galleries and museums. 'Not everything can be a Picasso,' cautions Po. But their greatest work never aged and was now co-opted and used in the unlikeliest of places.

The *Dark Side* prism appeared in the cartoon comedy *The Simpsons* and on a flag flown by Syrian freedom fighters and Bulgarian anti-European Union protestors. It even accompanied

NASA astronaut Piers Sellers during his time on the Space Shuttle 'Discovery' in 2016. Sellers played a CD of the album while orbiting planet earth. It was as if the prism belonged to everybody now.

Barely a week went by without a journalist or podcaster telling Po, 'Hey, Hipgnosis designed my record collection.' Meanwhile, those who'd appeared on the sleeves had stories to tell their children or grandchildren. There they were: with long hair, *any* hair, wearing clothes from another century, or as naked as the day they were born and crawling over what looked like the surface of Mars. 'It's a strange feeling,' said one, 'to be wandering around a boot fair on a Sunday morning and suddenly see a picture of your bottom on a record sleeve.'

In May 2014, Jimmy Page visited Dubai. Wilting in the shimmering heat, the guitarist gazed into the distance at the 75-storey Cayan Tower, with its distinctive 90-degree spiral. 'I thought, "My God, that's the object from *Presence*,"' says Page. 'It was so hot and surreal over there, I thought I was hallucinating. But, no, there it was, it had the same twist in it as the black object, the same strange energy . . .'

Storm would have loved the comparison and the idea that his art had inspired the tallest building in the world. Life in Hipgnosis had been an adventure, filled with the grandest of schemes and dreams. But even Storm Thorgerson couldn't have dreamed that.

Acknowledgements

Us and Them would not have been possible without with the support, trust and boundless patience of Aubrey Powell. Thanks also to Pete Selby, Melissa Bond and all at Nine Eight Books, Lora Findlay and my agent Matthew Hamilton (the Hamilton Agency).

This book draws on several interviews with Storm Thorgerson, conducted between 2006 and 2012, and new interviews with Aubrey Powell. Special thanks to everybody else who spoke to me about Hipgnosis: Dan Abbott, Barbie Antonis, Bruce Atkins, Howard Bartrop, Sandie Blickem (née Sandra Juby), Marcus Bradbury, Rob Brimson, Gai Caron (Gabrielle Harris), Lindsay Corner, Peter Curzon, Andrew Ellis, Richard Evans, Jill Furmanovsky, David Gale, David Gilmour, Kevin Godley, Graham Gouldman, Alex Henderson, Nik Kershaw, Richard Manning, Nick Mason, Merck Mercuriadis, Phil Mogg, Iain 'Emo' Moore, Humphrey Ocean, Fiz Oliver, Jimmy Page, Gala Pinion, Andy Powell, Matthew Scurfield, Paula Stainton, Lana Topham, Rupert Truman, Cosey Fanni Tutti, Roger Waters, Denis Waugh.

Plus past interviews and contributions from: Roddy Bogawa, Rosemary Breen, Richard Cole, Duggie Fields, Peter Gabriel, Jenny Lesmoir-Gordon, Nigel Lesmoir-Gordon, Stuart Harris, Peter Jenner, Evelyn 'Iggy' Joyce, Susan Kingsford, Paul McCartney, Jonathan Meades, Robert Plant, Andrew 'Willa' Rawlinson, Mick Rock, Scott Rowley, Gerald Scarfe, Anthony Stern, Rick Wakeman, Peter Watts (for the Theo Botschuijver quotes, taken from the book *Up in Smoke*), Marc Wolff and back issues of *Classic Rock*, *Creative Review*, *The Guardian*, *The Independent*, *Mojo*, *Q*, *Prog*, *Rolling Stone*, *The Times* and *Uncut*. Additional thanks to my friends at *Mojo* and *Classic Rock*, all at Raindog Films, my wonderful family (including Matthew Blake for transcribing interviews – 'Remember, son, what happens in Vegas, stays in Vegas . . .') and the Crown & Sceptre, CR2.

Select Bibliography

Blake, Mark. *Pigs Might Fly: The Inside Story of Pink Floyd*, Aurum Press, 2007, 2013, 2017

Blake, Mark. *Bring It On Home: Peter Grant, Led Zeppelin & Beyond, The Story of Rock's Greatest Manager*, Constable, 2018

Croall, Jonathan. *Neill of Summerhill: The Permanent Rebel*, Law Book Co of Australasia, 1984

Curzon, Peter and Thorgerson, Storm. *The Raging Storm, The Album Graphics of StormStudios*, De Milo and StormStudios, 2011

Doyle, Tom. *Man on the Run: Paul McCartney in the 1970s*, Ballantyne, 2014.

Evans, Richard. *The Art of the Album Cover*, Compendium, 2010

Furmanovksy, Jill. *Moment*, Paper Tiger, 1995

Green, Jonathan. *Days in the Life: Voices from the English Underground 1961–1971*, Random House, 1998

Harris, John. *The Dark Side of the Moon: The Making of the Pink Floyd Masterpiece*, Fourth Estate, 2005

Hipgnosis and George Hardie. *Walk Away René: The Work of Hipgnosis*, Paper Tiger, 1978

Levin, Bernard. *The Pendulum Years: Britain in the Sixties*, Icon Books, 2003

Lucas, Hussein. *After Summerhill: What Happened to the Pupils of Britain's Most Radical School?*, Pomegranate Books, 2011

Maclean, Ingrid. *Behind Open Doors: The Life & Times of Nigel Lesmoir-Gordon*, Resonancebookworks.com, 2018

Mason, Nick. *Inside Out: A Personal History of Pink Floyd*, Weidenfeld & Nicolson, 2004

Matlock, Glen. *I Was a Teenage Sex Pistol*, Reynolds & Hearn, 2006

Miles, Barry. *London Calling: A Countercultural History of London Since 1945*, Atlantic Books, 2010

Newton, Liam. *10cc, The Worst Band in the World*, Rocket 88, 2020

P-Orridge, Genesis and Mohr, Tim. *Non-Binary: A Memoir*, Abrams Press, 2021

Palacios, Julian. *Lost in the Woods: Syd Barrett & The Pink Floyd*, Boxtree, 1998

Pink Floyd: Their Mortal Remains, V&A Publishing, 2017

Powell, Aubrey. *Classic Album Covers of the 1970s*, Collins & Brown, 2012

Powell, Aubrey. *Vinyl. Album. Cover. Art: The Complete Hipgnosis Catalogue*, Thames & Hudson, 2017

Powell, Aubrey. *Through the Prism: Untold Rock Stories from the Hipgnosis Archive*, Thames & Hudson, 2022

Powell, Aubrey. *Hipgnosis Portraits*, Thames & Hudson, 2022

Pryor, William. *The Survival of the Coolest*, Clear Press, 2003

Scarfe, Gerald. *Long Drawn Out Trip*, Little, Brown, 2019

Scurfield, Matthew. *I Could Be Anyone*, Monticello, 2008

Sedgwick, Nick. *In the Pink (Not a Hunting Memoir)*, Nick Sedgwick, 2004

Spitz, Bob. *Led Zeppelin: The Biography*, Penguin, 2021

Thorgerson, Storm. *The Goodbye Look: The Photodesigns of Hipgnosis*, Vermilion, 1982

Thorgerson, Storm. *Classic Album Covers of the 60s*, Paper Tiger, 1989

Thorgerson, Storm. The *Eye of the Storm: The Album Graphics of Storm Thorgerson*, Sanctuary, 1999

Thorgerson, Storm. *Mind over Matter: The Images of Pink Floyd*, Sanctuary, 2000

Thorgerson, Storm. *Taken by Storm: The Album Art of Storm Thorgerson*, Omnibus Press, 2007

Thorgerson, Storm. *The Gathering Storm: A Quartet in Several Parts*, Insight Editions, 2015

Thorgerson, Storm and Powell, Aubrey. *One Hundred Best Album Covers*, Dorling Kindersley, 1999

Thorgerson, Storm and Powell, Aubrey. *For the Love of Vinyl*, Picturebox, 2008

Tutti, Cosey Fanni. *Art Sex Music*, Faber & Faber, 2017

Watts, Peter. *Up in Smoke: The Failed Dreams of Battersea Power Station*, Paradise Road, 2015

Willis, Tim. *Madcap: The Half-Life of Syd Barrett, Pink Floyd's Lost Genius*, Short Books, 2002

Credits